The Newly Independent States of Eurasia
Handbook of Former
Soviet Republics

The Newly Independent States of Eurasia
Handbook of Former
Soviet Republics

by

Stephen K. Batalden
and
Sandra L. Batalden

Foreword by
Sergei A. Arutiunov

ORYX
1993

The rare Arabian Oryx is believed to have inspired the myth of the unicorn. This desert antelope became virtually extinct in the early 1960s. At that time several groups of international conservationists arranged to have 9 animals sent to the Phoenix Zoo to be the nucleus of a captive breeding herd. Today the Oryx population is over 800, and nearly 400 have been returned to reserves in the Middle East.

Copyright © 1993 by The Oryx Press
4041 North Central at Indian School Road
Phoenix, Arizona 85012-3397

Published simultaneously in Canada

Printed and Bound in the United States of America

∞ The paper used in this publication meets the minimum requirements of American National Standard for Information Science—Permanence of Paper for Printed Library Materials, ANSI Z39.48,1984.

Maps in text prepared by Lisa Harner

Library of Congress Cataloging-in-Publication Data
Batalden, Stephen K.
    The newly independent states of Eurasia : handbook of former
Soviet republics / by Stephen K. Batalden and Sandra L. Batalden.
        p. cm.
    Includes bibliographical references and index.
    ISBN 0-89774-763-1
    1. Former Soviet republics—Handbooks, manuals, etc.
I. Batalden, Sandra L.   II. Title
DK17.B34 1993   93-26307
947.086—dc20   CIP

To Peder and Karl

CONTENTS

LIST OF MAPS

FOREWORD

Many voices in the late 1960s and early 1970s had begun to predict the imminent and unavoidable collapse of the Soviet empire. Soviet dissidents, some open and outspoken, others silent and hidden, were sure this collapse would come quite soon. Still, it caught most people in the West—and not only in the West— surprisingly unprepared.

How well I recall those compelling "Moscow kitchen sessions" of the 1970s and early 1980s, when we discussed within a close circle of friends and colleagues possible scenarios for such a collapse. Our projections concerning the basic events and their sequence proved amazingly accurate, but we were utterly wrong on the timing. We predicted a "Gorbachev"—one of our generation born in the early 1930s—would become general secretary of the Communist Party around 1992. (Gorbachev himself was little known in the 1970s, and unforeseen as the one likely to pull the trigger leading to collapse.) In such a scenario, conflicts would develop in the late 1990s—we thought a crisis in the Farghona Valley in Central Asia would precede the Karabakh conflict in Transcaucasia. The secession of the Baltic republics would be followed by the break-up of the entire Kremlin axis in the early 2000s.

In fact, all this happened at least ten years earlier than anticipated, even by those inside the system who were better informed about the latent volcanic activity present in Soviet society. Our Western colleagues, meanwhile, seemed to think that the stagnation of the Soviet imperial system would simply continue for an indeterminate period of time.

Soviet anthropologists by the late 1950s and early 1960s already had recognized the growing interethnic tensions in their society. These tensions, while well known to specialists, were never allowed to be published openly. Our "top-secret" classified reports submitted to the Communist Party Central Committee after each season's fieldwork were received grudg-

ingly. We were often told from the top that we overexaggerated the miserable conditions of the minorities of the far north, and so on. It was astonishing to what extent wishful thinking had become the basic *modus operandi* among the Party's top brass during the Brezhnev era (1964–82).

Perhaps only Iurii Andropov (Communist Party General Secretary, 1982–84) really knew and understood the true scale of the threat to the Soviet establishment. His reign was too short, however, and his methods, oriented toward police repression, could not alter the actual course of events. Nevertheless, Andropov appears to have been very instrumental—perhaps unwillingly and unknowingly—in the education of Mikhail Gorbachev, instructing him in dealing with arch-conservative Brezhnevites.

One of the hallmarks of official Communist ideology was the notion of a new historic "*Soviet* people." According to such ideology, all nations of the USSR would tend toward "mutual rapprochement" and eventual merger. Professional anthropologists in the Soviet Union never took seriously this wishful thinking. It was unacceptable, however, to emphasize openly the differences between the constituent nations of the USSR—differences that in Central Asia, for example, seem actually to have been created deliberately by the Soviet regime to supplant the initial, rather undifferentiated ethnic situation. These ethnic differences, the development of which was powerfully triggered by official "nation building" *(natsionalnoe stroitelstvo)* of the 1920s and 1930s, continued to grow. There had been, of course, a short period in the 1920s of "proletarian internationalism," a movement quite naturally proletarian since those who possessed nothing had little to quarrel about. Eventually, after World War II, the standard of living improved, especially during the years of Nikita Khrushchev (Communist Party General Secretary, 1953–64). But this improvement occurred with a very different tempo in each region—rapidly in Georgia, Armenia, and the Baltic republics, and very slowly in Central Asia. In fact, this differentiation yielded not a "mutual rapprochement" of Soviet nations but, on the contrary, a process of mutual alienation and separation.

Soviet statistics and popular literature, based upon the same wishful thinking, tended to exaggerate the level of literacy among the peoples of the far north and of Central Asia. Official propaganda grossly overstated the proficiency and use of Russian as a second language. And, it fabricated the demise of religious practices and the spread of atheism. I must confess that the authentic preservation, despite terrible persecution, of shamanistic and animistic, "pagan" traditions not only among people of Siberia, but also in the middle Volga basin, was never fully understood even by those anthropologists who, facing incredible difficulties, tried to study such phenoma professionally. Similarly, they failed to comprehend the practical functioning of the norms of *adat* (customary law) and *sharia* (Islamic law) among peoples of Central Asia and the Caucasus.

Thus, it is not surprising that for most people outside the USSR the Soviet Union was basically "Russia." The cultural and social differences between the constituent nations of that Union seemed to be obsolete, irrelevant, and largely nonexistent. Clearly that misperception yielded serious shortcomings in Western understanding and public opinion.

Today, more than ever, people in America and Europe need to overcome such misperceptions. Increasingly they need to deal not with some loose "Soviet Russia," or Moscow, but directly with Ukrainians, Georgians, Uzbeks, and Kyrgyz—also perhaps very soon with Tatars, Iakuts, Tuvinians, and Chechens. In such a context, this important, insightful work of the Bataldens, filled with accurate, useful, and up-to-date information, will prove particularly valuable.

Sergei A. Arutiunov, July 1993
Chair, Department of Caucasian Studies, Institute
of Ethnology and Anthropology (Moscow)
Corresponding Member, Russian Academy of
Sciences

PREFACE

Until its collapse in 1991, the Soviet Union was a world superpower incorporating within its borders the great landmass of Europe and Asia—modern Eurasia. Conditioned to view the Soviet state as a unified great power, many people have found it difficult to comprehend the rapid dissolution of this once mighty empire. Yet, the former Soviet republics, responding to events in Eastern Europe and the abortive August 1991 *coup d'état* in Moscow, have established their independence. In asserting their sovereignty, the newly independent states of Eurasia became the successors to the once powerful Union of Soviet Socialist Republics (USSR).

For specialists, policy makers, and citizens alike, the dissolution of the Soviet Union into independent states now calls for far greater study of regional and ethnic diversity in Eurasia. In the era of the Cold War, regional and international events tended to be interpreted within the framework of a simple bipolar view of the world—there was the Soviet Union along with its allies, and there was "the West." Even as the breakup of the Soviet Union has undermined such fixed Cold War assumptions, it has also forced us to reconsider the lands and peoples of the former USSR. In this rethinking, the newly independent states of Eurasia must be seen for their own historical, geopolitical, economic, and environmental significance, quite apart from their identification with the former Soviet Union. This book seeks to help in such rethinking by addressing the regional and ethnic diversity of the Eurasian states, while also examining elements of continuity that inevitably link these independent states with their Soviet past. Using historical narrative, geographical description, and basic statistical data, this handbook provides a systematic introduction to the newly independent states of Eurasia.

HISTORICAL FRAMEWORK

Two basic assumptions have guided the preparation of this handbook. The first, often obscured by Cold War rhetoric, is that despite centuries of tsarist and Soviet imperial domination the subject non-Russian nations have not only managed to endure, but they have also developed their own unique histories and cultures worthy of public understanding. Shortly after the attempted 1991 Moscow coup, one historian compared the Soviet Union to the surface of a timeworn linoleum floor. Aged and unserviceable, the floor came to reveal through its wornout areas the original set of wooden floorboards. Upon examining the floor, it was seen that the old wooden floorboards predated by centuries the relatively recent linoleum or Russian veneer. (See Edward L. Keenan, "Rethinking the U.S.S.R., Now That It's Over," *The New York Times* [September 8, 1991], E3.) Russian (including Muscovite, Imperial, and Soviet) rule over its Eurasian empire dates from the fifteenth century, with most areas added between the sixteenth and nineteenth centuries. Yet the peoples who came to be drawn into that empire have their own rich histories that existed for centuries before Russian rule. Thus, the first assumption of this handbook is that the histories and cultures of these non-Russian, as well as Russian, peoples of the former Soviet Union are important in their own right. One of the central tasks of this volume is to introduce the history of these diverse peoples. This handbook proposes, then, to uncover the wooden floorboards.

The second assumption behind this handbook may appear on the surface to be in conflict with the first. For this volume assumes the defining and ongoing significance of Soviet rule for Eurasia. Politically, many of the new states continue to operate with the legacy of Communist Party rule. Many former Communist Party leaders now serve as state presidents, such as Leonid Kravchuk of Ukraine and Nursultan Nazarbaev of Kazakhstan. Although they have abandoned their Party affiliations, the reality is that beneath the rule of these leaders Communist Party-appointed officialdom or "nomenklatura" has remained remarkably secure at virtually all levels of the new state bureaucracies. In much of Central Asia and Trauscaucasia, as well as in other European republics, the continuity in political leadership has been accompanied by a retreat from democratization. Aided by security police who have rarely been demobilized, many of the newly independent states have sought to limit the influence of informal political groups.

Although the development of regional and republican independence in economic life has progressed fairly rapidly, many former Soviet republics remain more or less within the so-called ruble zone, a Eurasian area in which commerce continues to function with the Russian ruble as common currency. In this regard, the newly independent states have had to confront the Soviet legacy of centralized planning. As with the cotton monoculture described in the Uzbekistan chapter, Soviet economic planning centralized the processing of regional and republican production in Moscow, using a transport system that linked outlying republics to Moscow like spokes on a wheel. Despite the development of private business and freer markets, this Soviet economic legacy continues to be felt.

Among other areas of continuity in Soviet and post-Soviet Eurasian life perhaps the most serious are those involving environmental or ecological problems. Simply put, environmental disasters such as the Chernobyl nuclear explosion near the Ukrainian-Belarusian border and the drying up of the Aral Sea in Central Asia have also been a legacy of the Soviet period. The magnitude of these problems, however, defies a solution at the level of any single independent state, for, like the health problems they have in turn generated, these larger ecological crises require regional, interstate cooperation. (See Murray Feshbach, *Ecocide in the USSR*, Basic Books, 1992.)

Ironically, the dissolution of the Soviet Union has tended to undermine the kinds of interrepublican solutions needed to address major health and environmental problems. In the case of the vanishing Aral Sea, any long-term solution requires cooperation between the states where the richest water resources are located (Kyrgyzstan and Tajikistan) and the states drawing most heavily upon those water resources (Uzbekistan, Turkmenistan, and Kazakhstan). Under the administration of the first and only Soviet Minister of the Environment (Nikolai N. Vorontsov, a research biologist sensitive to ecological problems) both short- and long-term plans were developed for solving interrepublican environmental issues such as that of the Aral Sea. Those plans have now been shelved and await the unlikely prospect of interstate cooperation without central planning and authority. Thus, to be fair, the Soviet Union also offered mechanisms, however undemocratic, for resolving interrepublican (and interethnic) conflict.

The legacy of Soviet rule is also reflected in the structure of this volume. We have consciously used the former union republics of the Soviet Union, now the newly independent states of Eurasia, for the basic chapter structure of the handbook. In using these old Soviet republican divisions, the volume recognizes the importance of borders that were often set arbitrarily during the 1920s at the onset of Soviet rule. The point, of course, is that these internal Soviet borders often reflected lines of genuine national and cultural division, and, therefore, they cannot be so readily discarded as was the Soviet authority that brought them into being. Occasionally, as in Central Asia, Soviet political decisions on republican borders came to reward certain national and regional "winners," at the expense of other, often minority, interests. Such Soviet decision-making, although now subject to reexamination, has determined the course of political and national leadership. The result is that questions of sovereignty and independence continue, in the main, to be raised within borders established as union republics in the early Soviet years. The calamitous civil war that began in Yugoslavia in 1991 has demonstrated for political leaders of Eurasia the potential horrors that can be unleashed when revisionists seek to challenge established republican borders. It is just such border challenges that make the territorial conflicts noted in the chapters on Transcaucasia so dangerous and intractable.

ARRANGEMENT

The chapters of this book correspond to 12 of the former 15 Soviet union republics. The three Baltic republics—Lithuania, Latvia, and Estonia—have been excluded from the volume. These three Baltic republics secured their full independence in August 1991, four months before the formal dissolution of the Soviet Union. There are several reasons for not including the Baltic states. Each has a legacy of independence in the interwar period before Soviet occupation under secret terms of the Nazi-Soviet Pact of 1939. Despite heavy Russian migration into Latvia and Estonia after World War II, the Baltic republics remained significantly apart from the rest of Soviet society. The history of the Baltic region, even after imposition of Russian imperial rule in the eighteenth century, drew upon traditional ties to a dominant German culture and did not become an integral part of wider Russian, Eurasian patterns. Since 1991, the Baltic states have also moved decisively outside the ruble zone. Finally, the Baltic states are among the few former Soviet republics not to have joined the informal Commonwealth of Independent States (CIS), a loose confederation established in late December 1991 to coordinate interrepublican policies in the wake of the fall of the Soviet Union.

The 12 chapters of this handbook reflect the initial membership of the CIS (except for Georgia, which was never a member). The Russian Federation, much larger in size and population than the others, has been divided into two subchapters—one on western or European Russia, the other on eastern or Asiatic Russia, including Siberia and the Far East. This division conforms to the natural east-west divide cut by the Ural Mountain range. Each chapter is preceded by a map that locates autonomous regions within republics and identifies important rivers, cities, and physical features. For purposes of clarity all of the chapters have been grouped into four major parts, one for the Russian Federation; one for the European republics of Belarus, Moldova, and Ukraine; one for Transcaucasia; and one for Central Asia. Bibliographical suggestions accompany the introductions at the opening of each new section of the handbook.

Because the handbook is also intended to serve as a general reference work, each chapter opens with a readily accessible statistical profile highlighting major demographic, ethnographic, economic, and physical data pertaining to the republic. Unless otherwise noted, the statistical data have been drawn from the 1989 Soviet census and related government documentation published in the former Soviet Union or abroad. Because of the very substantial population migrations that have been occurring in and between the former Soviet republics, the 1989 census data is not as reliable as might be desired. In the case of Central Asian republics, for example, the 1989 statistics will not reflect the very substantial outward migration of Slavs (Russians, Ukrainians, and Belarusians) from the area. Nevertheless, the statistical data provide a point of departure for the narrative section of each chapter.

Following the statistical profile is a comprehensive, analytical discussion of each republic. This narrative is divided into two major sections. The first section—a history and description of the republic—includes subsections devoted to topography, the origins of the dominant ethnic group(s) of the republic, and the history of the territory, including its incorporation into the Russian Empire and its recent Soviet experience. Alongside the republic's political history, there is a description of major self-governed, or autonomous, regions within each republic. Twentieth-century Communist Party leadership is identified, as are the circumstances leading to declarations of sovereignty in the recent period.

The second section of each chapter narrative is devoted to an examination of the contemporary issues facing each newly independent state. This section on current affairs builds on the prior narrative, but is structured in such a way as to allow readers to move directly to discussion of contemporary issues should that be the reason for consulting the handbook. The contemporary issues section includes a variety of topics, such as political and ethnic conflict, economic restructuring, environmental/ecological affairs, and cultural/intellectual developments.

As recently as five years ago, the reading public was largely unaware of the power of internal forces at work in such disparate parts of the former Soviet world as Kazakhstan, Uzbekistan, Belarus, and Georgia. Today, formal embassies are housed in these independent states, and the peoples of these lands command attention as much for their own rich history as for the products they now wish to introduce on the world market. This handbook builds upon Western scholarship regarding the ethnography and history of Russian and non-Russian peoples of the former Soviet Union. It provides basic reference information regarding the lands and peoples of Eurasia.

SPELLINGS

In identifying place names, we have tried to include the most recent changes (e.g., St. Petersburg, not Leningrad; Nizhnii Novgorod, not Gorky). Occasionally we have provided the old name in parentheses. Many of the cities of the non-Russian republics now bear a spelling different from that used during the Soviet period. Such spelling changes often reflect abandonment of Russian place names in non-Russian areas. We have tried to incorporate these spelling changes for all non-Russian names, using the transliteration employed by the *National Geographic* map ("Russia and the Newly Independent Nations of the Former Soviet Union,"

1993). In some cases the more familiar Russian transliteration is offered in parentheses. For Russian place names, we have followed a modified Library of Congress transliteration system, with the exception of cities commonly known by Anglicized spellings (such as Moscow).

ACKNOWLEDGEMENTS

It is a pleasure to acknowledge the help of others in the preparation of this handbook. Two graduate assistants contributed significantly to the work—Jonathan Haring in working on the statistical profile sections as well as substantial parts of the Armenia and Azerbaijan chapters; Dylan Zoller in her work on Siberia and the bibliographic entries. The maps have been prepared with the able assistance of Lisa Harner. We are grateful to Eleni Bužarovska and Eugene Clay for their reading of the text, and to Sean Tape for his professional editorial counsel.

Sandra L. Batalden
Stephen K. Batalden
Tempe, Arizona
August 1993

The Newly Independent States of Eurasia
Handbook of Former
Soviet Republics

PART ONE

THE RUSSIAN FEDERATION

INTRODUCTION

The Russian Federation, formerly the Russian Soviet Federated Socialist Republic (RSFSR) of the Union of Soviet Socialist Republics (USSR), is today the world's largest country. Even after declaring its own sovereignty and separating from the other 14 union republics with which it was previously joined, the Russian Federation remains almost twice the size of the United States. The new Russia continues to be a country of rich natural resources and great ethnic diversity. Originally the home of the Great Russians, a people who dwelt in the wintry and forested lands around Moscow, Russia now encompasses a landmass covering more than six and a half million square miles, or approximately three-fourths of the old Soviet Union. Russia's immense territory was accumulated over many centuries, first by a series of autocratic, often despotic, tsars, and later by Communist Party rulers. It continues to be the home of dozens of distinct ethnic groups that speak non-Russian languages and observe varied cultural traditions. The territory comprising the Russian Federation falls naturally into two major topographical regions that are divided by the Ural Mountains: the lands of western or European Russia; and the lands of eastern or Asiatic Russia, most of the latter constituting Siberia. Part One has been subdivided to reflect this geographic division of Russsia.

YELTSIN VS. GORBACHEV: TOWARD AN INDEPENDENT RUSSIAN FEDERATION

According to the traditional Soviet exercise of power, political leaders of the 15 union republics were to be unfailingly loyal to the directives of the Moscow center. There was opportunity for flexibility on certain local issues, but republican leadership did not routinely challenge the central institutions of the Communist Party of the Soviet Union. Nevertheless, in the person of the maverick populist and Communist Party leader, Boris Yeltsin, a remarkably independent executive authority came to be associated with the unprecedented drive in 1990–91 for the autonomy of the Russian Republic (RSFSR) *within* the wider Soviet Union.

Boris Yeltsin's political ascendancy came to be linked with the Russian Republic following his conflict with the reforming Soviet President Mikhail Gorbachev. After having risen from his post as head of the Communist Party of Sverdlovsk (Ekaterinburg) to head the Moscow Party organization, Boris Yeltsin was summarily dismissed from the Moscow post in November 1987. As an outspoken advocate of more rapid economic reform and democratization, and as an opponent of political cronyism, Yeltsin had by the end of 1987 established a reputation as a popular politician. In his ongoing policy disputes with Gorbachev, Yeltsin tied his own political fortunes to two strategies—winning electoral support and, somewhat later, gaining autonomy and eventual independence for the Russian Republic.

Yeltsin's personal popularity came to be measured in a series of stunning electoral triumphs, first in the March 1989 elections to the Soviet parliament, the All-Union Congress of People's Deputies. An effective campaigner, Yeltsin won a 90 percent electoral majority. Later, on the republican level, Yeltsin added to his 1989 victory by being elected a deputy to the Russian Congress of People's Deputies in March 1990. His majority was more than 80 percent. Yeltsin followed these electoral successes by seeking the office of president of the Russian Soviet Republic. This new republican presidency, established by Gorbachev, was to be chosen by ballot of the deputies of the Russian Republic's Congress of People's Deputies. In the May 1990 balloting, Yeltsin secured 535 votes, barely more than the 50 percent needed for election. In winning the office, moreover, Yeltsin scored a major electoral triumph over Gorbachev's own hand-picked candidate, Aleksandr Vlasov, who received 467 votes. Adding yet further to his public mandate, Yeltsin called for popular election of the Russian president, ran for the office, and won a landslide election to the Russian presidency in June 1991.

What Yeltsin had accomplished in little more than three years was to focus public debate upon the slow pace and relative ineffectiveness of Gorbachev's domestic reforms, while at the same time using republican offices as the springboard for his own political ascendancy. In mid-1991, Yeltsin was in the unchallenged position of being the only popularly elected president of a Soviet republic still called the Russian Soviet Federated Socialist Republic (RSFSR).

Along the way, however, Yeltsin had built considerable momentum for Russian republican autonomy. In a landmark measure approved by 544 members of the Russian Congress of People's Deputies in June 1990, the Russian Republic asserted its right to veto any federal Soviet law affecting Russian territory. While the constitutional standing of such a measure was dubious, the clear message was that of support for Yeltsin's political drive toward Russian republican sovereignty. Symbolic of Yeltsin's commitment to republican, as opposed to all-union or Soviet, institutions was his resignation from the Communist Party in July 1990.

By distancing himself from Soviet Communist Party organizations, Russian President Boris Yeltsin was in a unique position to bring his own leadership and that of Russian parliamentary institutions to bear against the attempted August 1991 *coup d'état*. Rallying popular support in Moscow against the coup, and ultimately securing support from the military as well, Yeltsin effectively led the drive to overthrow those who had staged the August events. The coup plotters, perhaps reflecting their conservative, old-style Soviet ways, had arranged to place Soviet President Gorbachev under house arrest, but they had failed to muzzle the ascendant republican leadership in Moscow. The Russian Republic's own formal declaration of independence from the Soviet Union followed immediately on 24 August 1991, along with its name change, effectively becoming the "Russian Federation" (Rossiiskaia Federatsiia).

HOW RUSSIA IS RULED

There is irony in considering "how Russia is ruled," for the phrase, coined by the late Merle Fainsod in his important study of the exercise of Soviet power, came to mean for the twentieth century the rule of *Soviet* Communist Party and government elites. Today, "how Russia is ruled" must refer to the exercise of power in a Russian Federation in which even the term used for "Russian"

(Rossiiskaia) has the politically sensitive ring of a multi-ethnic state, not a homogeneous state of ethnic Russians.

The government of the Russian Federation, like that of the United States, is composed of three branches—the executive, legislative, and judicial. Executive leadership is exercised by a president and a cabinet of ministers, headed by a prime minister. Under Boris Yeltsin's presidency, this has been an activist presidency, despite the fact that the legislative branch has had the power to approve or reject presidential appointments to the offices of prime minister, as well as the ministers of defense, security, and foreign affairs. Presidentially initiated reforms have also faced occasional legislative challenge.

The most powerful legislative branch of the government is the Russian Congress of People's Deputies, a unicameral (one chamber) legislative body that normally meets twice a year. Elected to a four-year term in republican-wide elections in March 1990, prior to the collapse of the Soviet Union, this Russian Congress of 1,033 deputies is composed of a mixture of well-established former Communist bureaucrats, managers of state enterprises, and deputies elected on more reformist slates. Among the deputies are a number of non-Russian leaders representing regional, ethnic homelands within the Russian Federation. From within the Russian Congress of People's Deputies, one quarter (256 members) are elected to the Russian Supreme Soviet (a standing legislature commonly called the Russian Parliament).

By the end of 1992, an increasingly assertive Russian Congress, coupled with a Supreme Soviet broadly empowered to disburse money, had collided with the activist presidency of Boris Yeltsin. That collision led to a public referendum on the Russian presidency and on the legislature in April 1993. The same impasse ultimately led to Yeltsin's executive order of 21 September 1993 disbanding the Russian Parliament and calling for December elections. (See "September 1993 Showdown.") The conflict also prompted Russian President Yeltsin to speed preparation of a new Russian constitution.

The issue of the Russian constitution stands at the center of the highest judicial authority in the Russian Federation, the Constitutional Court. Established in 1991, the independent Constitutional Court was intended to be an important arbiter of the constitution and of the legality of legislative and executive action. Authorized to have 15 members (only 13 were serving in the spring of 1993), the Court is headed by its Chief Justice Valerii Zorkin. Zorkin and the Constitutional Court have undertaken highly controversial rulings overturning the constitutionality of both presidential and legislative actions. The Court's actions in 1993 have tended to align it more directly in support of the Russian Parliament, and in conflict with the Russian presidency. Nevertheless, in one of its most controversial decisions, the Court ruled on the eve of the April 1993 popular referendum that the Congress had inappropriately set as the standard for passage a majority of all eligible voters, rather than the simple majority of all votes cast. While the Constitutional Court has been criticized for what some see as its partisan support for the Russian Congress in its conflict with Russian President Yeltsin, the reality is that all determinations regarding the legality of legislative and executive action are clouded by the nature of the old Soviet constitutional documents still in formal operation.

FRAMING A NEW RUSSIAN CONSTITUTION

With renewed support from the April 1993 popular referendum, President Yeltsin has sought to limit the authority of the Russian Congress by speeding work on a new post-Soviet Russian constitution. In June 1993, a constitutional conference was held to approve a draft constitutional document. Reflecting Yeltsin's own wishes, the conference approved the draft (still not a public document as of this writing), which calls for a presidential republic with a two-chamber parliament and restraints on all three branches of government. The implementation of any such constitution awaits its formal adoption, a matter very much complicated by the impasse between the Russian president and the leadership of the Russian Parliament.

No doubt the most divisive issue confronting the framers of the new constitution is that of the autonomy to be assigned to those 21 internally independent ethnic republics and other autonomous regions, districts, and cities found within the Russian Federation. Sensitive to the heightened demands and potentially secessionist impulses of some of these autonomous national homelands, as for example in Tatarstan and Checheniia, the constitutional framers have accorded these republics a formal measure of independence in the new constitution. In reaction to this, other traditionally Russian ethnic areas within the Federation sought to secure the same rights by suddenly declaring themselves republican units, such as the "Republic of the Urals" in Ekaterinburg, the "East Siberian Republic" in Irkutsk, or the "Maritime Repub-

lic" in Vladivostok. Clearly, the most fateful problem facing Russia's constitutional architects is how to maintain the integrity of the Russian Federation, while recognizing the claims of independence on the part of the more assertive autonomous regions. The irony in this balancing act is that these autonomous ethnic republics, as in the case of the newly independent republics of former Soviet Central Asia, were the product of a nationalities policy devised by Joseph Stalin to give the appearance, though rarely the reality, of support for ethnic identity and national self-determination.

SEPTEMBER 1993 SHOWDOWN

In the absence of an effective post-Soviet constitution, the impasse between executive, parliamentary, and court authority came to a head on 21 September 1993 when Russian President Boris Yeltsin by executive decree disbanded parliament and called for new elections. Parliament responded by impeaching President Yeltsin and appointing its own claimant to the presidential office, Aleksandr Rutskoi. Yeltsin's decree, which met with support from Western powers, was defended as a means of overcoming the crippling impasse between legislative and executive authority. For now, the question of how Russia is to be ruled continues to be the subject of destablizing controversy, even as an embittered electorate becomes increasingly cynical.

BIBLIOGRAPHY

Bobrick, Benson. *East of the Sun: The Epic Conquest and Tragic History of Siberia.* New York: Poseidon Presss, 1992.

Bradshaw, Michael J., ed. *The Soviet Union: A New Regional Geography?* London: Belhaven Press, 1991.

Cambridge Encyclopedia of Russia and the Soviet Union. Cambridge, England: Cambridge University Press, 1982.

Chan, Adrian. *Teaching About the Soviet Successor States: A Teacher's Guide and Resource for History and Social Science.* Stanford: American Association for the Advancement of Slavic Studies, 1993.

Collins, David Norman. *Siberia and the Soviet Far East.* Oxford, England: Clio Press, 1991.

Conquest, Robert, ed. *The Last Empire: Nationality and the Soviet Future.* Stanford: Hoover Institution Press, 1986.

Current Digest of the Post-Soviet Press. Columbus, Ohio: Current Digest of the Post-Soviet Press. Published weekly since 1949.

Dewdney, J. C. *USSR in Maps.* New York: Holmes & Meier Publishers, Inc., 1982.

Diuk, Nadia and Adrian Karatnycky. *The Hidden Nations: The People Challenge the Soviet Union.* New York: William Morrow and Company, Inc., 1990.

Ellis, Jane. *The Russian Orthodox Church: A Contemporary History.* Bloomington: Indiana University Press, 1986.

Fainsod, Merle. *How Russia is Ruled.* Cambridge: Harvard University Press, 1953. (See also the edition revised by Jerry F. Hough, *How the Soviet Union is Governed.* Cambridge: Harvard University Press, 1979.)

Feshbach, Murray and Alfred Friendly, Jr. *Ecocide in the USSR: Health and Nature under Siege.* New York: Basic Books, 1992.

Forsyth, James. *A History of the Peoples of Siberia: Russia's North Asian Colony, 1581–1990.* Cambridge, England: Cambridge University Press, 1992.

Hajda, Lubomyr and Mark Beissinger, eds. *The Nationalities Factor in Soviet Politics and Society.* Boulder: Westview Press, 1990.

Horak, Stephan M., ed. *Guide to the Study of the Soviet Nationalities: Non-Russian Peoples of the USSR.* Littleton, CO: Libraries Unlimited, Inc., 1982.

Horak, Stephen M. *Russia, the USSR, and Eastern Europe: A Bibliographic Guide to English Language Publications, 1981–85.* Littleton, CO: Libraries Unlimited, 1987.

Hosking, Geoffrey. *The Awakening of the Soviet Union.* Cambridge, MA: Harvard University Press, 1990.

Lydolph, Paul E. *Geography of the USSR.* 5th ed. Elkhart, WI: Misty Valley Publishing, 1990.

Katz, Zev, ed. *Handbook of Major Soviet Nationalities.* New York: The Free Press, 1975.

Mandelstam Balzer, Margerie, ed. *Shamanism: Soviet Studies of Traditional Religion in Siberia and Central Asia.* New York: Armonk, 1990.

Marks, Steven G. *Road to Power: The Trans-Siberian Railroad and the Colonization of Asian Russia, 1850–1917.* Ithaca, NY: Cornell University Press, 1991.

Miller-Gulland, Robin with Nikolai Dejevsky. *Atlas of Russia and the Soviet Union.* Oxford, England: Phaidon, 1989.

Modern Encyclopedia of Russian and Soviet History. Gulf Breeze, FL: Academic International Press, 1975–1990. 53 vols.

Nahaylo, Bohdan and Victor Swoboda. *Soviet Disunion: A History of the Nationalities Problem in the USSR.* New York: The Free Press, 1990.

RFE/RL [Radio Free Europe/Radio Liberty] *Research Report.* Munich: Board of Foreign Broadcasting. *RFE/RL Research Report* was formerly published under the title, *Report on the USSR* (1989–91), and prior to 1989 under the title, *Radio Liberty Research Bulletin Weekly.*

Riasanovsky, Nicholas V. *A History of Russia.* 5th ed. New York: Oxford University Press, 1993.

Rorlich, Azade-Ayse. *The Volga Tatars: A Profile in National Resilience.* Stanford, CA: Hoover Institution Press, 1986.

Shabad, Theodore. *Geography of the USSR: A Regional Survey.* New York: Columbia University Press, 1951.

Smith Graham, ed. *The Nationalities Question in the Soviet Union.* New York: Longman, 1991.

Solzhenitsyn, Aleksandr. *The Gulag Archipelago.* 3 vols. New York: Harper & Row, 1976.

Stewart, John Massey, ed. *The Soviet Environment: Problems, Policies, and Politics.* Cambridge, England: Cambridge University Press, 1992.

Thompson, Anthony, ed. *Russia/U.S.S.R.: A Selective Annotated Bibliography of Books in English.* Santa Barbara: Clio Press, 1979.

Vaillant, Janet and John Richards. *From Russia to USSR and Beyond: A Narrative and Documentary History.* New York: Longman, distributed by Addison Wesley, 1993.

Vakhtin, Nikolai B. *Native Peoples of the Russian Far North.* London: Minority Rights Group, 1992.

Wixman, Ronald. *The Peoples of the USSR: An Ethnographic Handbook.* Armond, NY: M. E. Sharpe, 1984.

Wood, Alan and R. A. French, eds. *The Development of Siberia: People and Resources.* London: MacMillan, in association with the School of Slavonic and East European Studies, University of London, 1989.

Wood, Alan, ed. *The History of Siberia: From Russian Conquest to Revolution.* London: Routledge, 1991.

Russian Federation

Bering Sea

Pacific Ocean

Sea of Okhotsk

Sea of Japan

JAPAN

N. KOREA

S. KOREA

CHINA

MONGOLIA

Lake Baikal

RUSSIAN FEDERATION

Arctic Ocean

KAZAKHSTAN

KYRGYZSTAN

TAJIKISTAN

PAKISTAN

AFGHANISTAN

UZBEKISTAN

TURKMENISTAN

IRAN

Caspian Sea

GEORGIA

ARMENIA

AZERBAIJAN

Black Sea

UKRAINE

BELARUS

POLAND

LITHUANIA

LATVIA

ESTONIA

★ Moscow

FINLAND

SWEDEN

Baltic Sea

| National Boundary |
| ★ Capital City |

750 Miles

750 Kilometers

0

STATISTICAL PROFILE

Demography

Population: 147,022,000
Ethnic population:

Russian	119,866,000	81.5%
Tatar	5,522,000	3.8%
Ukrainian	4,363,000	3.0%
Chuvash	1,774,000	1.2%
Bashkort	1,345,000	0.9%
Belarusian	1,206,000	0.8%
Mordvinian	1,073,000	0.7%
Chechen	899,000	0.6%
German	842,000	0.6%
Udmurt	715,000	0.5%
Mari	644,000	0.4%
Kazakh	636,000	0.4%
Avar	544,000	0.4%
Jewish	537,000	0.4%
Armenian	532,000	0.4%
Buriat	417,000	0.3%
Ossetian	402,000	0.3%
Kabard	386,000	0.3%
Iakut	380,000	0.3%
Dargin	353,000	0.2%
Komi	336,000	0.2%
Azerbaijani	336,000	0.2%
Kumyk	277,000	0.2%
Lezghin	257,000	0.2%
Ingush	215,000	0.1%
Tuvinian	206,000	0.1%
Moldovan	173,000	0.1%
Kalmyk	166,000	0.1%
Gypsy	153,000	0.1%
Karachai	150,000	0.1%
Komi-Permiak	147,000	0.1%
Karelian	125,000	0.1%
Adygei	123,000	0.1%
Korean	107,000	0.1%
Lak	106,000	0.1%
Polish	95,000	0.1%
Other	1,614,000	1.1%

Historic religious traditions:

Christianity	88.8%
Islam	7.3%

Population by age:

Age	Total	Males	Females
0–4	8.1%	4.1%	4.0%
5–9	7.4%	3.7%	3.7%
10–14	7.1%	3.6%	3.5%
15–19	6.4%	3.2%	3.2%
20–24	7.4%	3.7%	3.7%
25–29	9.1%	4.7%	4.4%
30–34	8.6%	4.3%	4.3%
35–39	7.6%	3.8%	3.8%
40–44	3.9%	1.9%	2.0%
45–49	7.5%	3.5%	4.0%
50–54	5.7%	2.6%	3.1%
55–59	6.5%	2.9%	3.6%
60–64	4.9%	1.7%	3.2%
65–69	2.8%	0.9%	1.9%
70–	7.0%	1.7%	5.3%

Male/Female ratio: 46.3% male/53.7% female
Rural/Urban population: 26.1% rural/73.9% urban
Growth over time, 1979–91: 8.0%
Population density: 22.3 persons/sq mi

Politics/Government

Date of sovereignty declaration: 11 June 1990
Date of independence declaration: 24 August 1991
Major urban centers and populations:

Moscow	8,967,000
St. Petersburg	5,020,000
Nizhnii Novgorod (Gorky)	1,438,000
Novosibirsk	1,436,000
Ekaterinburg (Sverdlovsk)	1,367,000
Samara (Kuibyshev)	1,257,000
Omsk	1,148,000
Cheliabinsk	1,143,000
Kazan	1,094,000
Perm	1,091,000
Ufa	1,083,000
Rostov na Donu	1,020,000
Volgograd (Stalingrad)	999,000
Krasnoiarsk	912,000

Saratov	905,000
Voronezh	887,000
Vladivostok	648,000
Izhevsk	635,000
Iaroslavl	633,000
Togliatti	630,000
Irkutsk	626,000
Simbirsk (Ulianovsk)	625,000
Krasnodar	620,000
Barnaul	602,000
Khabarovsk	601,000
Novokuznetsk	600,000
Orenburg	547,000
Penza	543,000
Tula	540,000
Kemerovo	520,000
Riazan	515,000
Astrakhan	509,000
Tomsk	502,000
Naberezhnye Chelny	501,000

Autonomous republics:	**[Capital]**
Republic of Adygeia	Maikop
Republic of Altai	Gorno Altaisk
Republic of Bashkortostan	Ufa
Republic of Buriatiia	Ulan-Ude
Republic of Checheniia	Groznyi
Republic of Chuvashiia	Cheboksary
Republic of Dagestan	Makhachkala
Republic of Ingush	Nazran
Republic of Kabardino-Balkariia	Nalchik
Republic of Kalmykiia	Elista
Karachai-Cherkess Republic	Cherkessk
Republic of Kareliia	Petrozavodsk
Republic of Khakassiia	Abakan
Republic of Komi	Syktyvkar
Republic of Marii-El	Yoshkar Ola
Republic of Mordviniia	Saransk
Republic of North Ossetiia	Vladikavkaz (Ordzhonidze)
Sakha (Iakut) Republic	Iakutsk
Republic of Tatarstan	Kazan
Republic of Tuva	Kyzyl
Republic of Udmurtiia	Izhevsk

Education

Level of education for persons over 15:

completed higher level education	11.3%
completed secondary education	48.3%
incomplete secondary education	21.0%

Number of higher education institutions: 514
(2,824,500 students)

Major institutions of higher education and enrollment:

Moscow

Polytechnic Institute	43,000
Timiriazev Academy of Agriculture	31,000
Commercial Institute	30,000
Lomonosov State University	28,000
Civil Engineering Institute	20,500
Institute of Railway Engineers	16,500
Bauman State Technical Institute	15,000
Russian State Medical University	7,500
Lumumba People's Friendship University	6,700
State Financial Academy	3,000
State Institute of International Relations	3,000
Architectural Institute	2,000
State Institute of Cinematography	1,550
Tchaikovsky State Music Conservatory	865

St. Petersburg

State University	21,035
Technical University	16,000
University of Economics and Finance	12,000
Electrical Engineering Institute	10,000
Civil Engineering Institute	10,000
Forestry Academy	9,000
State Agrarian University	7,000
Repin Institute of Painting, Sculpture and Architecture	1,370
State Institute of Theatre, Music and Cinematography	1,160
Rimskii-Korsakov State Music Conservatory	1,000
Russian Orthodox Theological Academy and Seminary	800

Barnaul

Altai State University	5,257
Altai State Agricultural University	4,000

Cheboksary

Chuvash State University	11,000

Cheliabinsk

State Technical University	15,000
State University	3,200

Ekaterinburg

Law Institute	8,500
Institute of National Economy	6,700
Urals State University	7,000
Urals Forestry Technical Institute	6,350
Mining Institute	6,000
Institute of Architecture and Arts	1,212
State Theatrical Institute	350

Groznyi

Checheno State University	5,600

Iakutsk

State University	7,500

Iaroslavl

State University	3,590

Ioshkar Ola

Mari University	3,400

Major institutions of higher education and enrollment: *(continued)*

Irkutsk

Polytechnic Institute	16,000
State University	7,000
Agricultural Institute	4,800

Ivanovo

State University	5,000

Izhevsk

Udmurt State University	7,235

Kaliningrad

Technical Institute for the Fishing Industry and Economy	7,110
State University	6,000

Kazan

State University	7,470
Civil Engineering Institute	4,500
State Music Conservatory	614

Kemerovo

State University	6,500

Krasnodar

Kuban State University	9,800

Makhachkala

Dagestan State University	8,000

Nalchik

Kabardino-Balkar State University	9,000

Nizhnii Novgorod

N. I. Lobachevskii State University	9,500
Glinka State Music Conservatory	700

Novosibirsk

Institute of Electrical Engineering	11,900
Institute of National Economy	4,800
State University	3,700

Omsk

Polytechnic Institute	8,000
State University	3,634

Petrozavodsk

State University	6,101

Rostov na Donu

State University	9,600
Institute of National Economy	6,000
Don Agricultural Institute	4,500
Music Pedagogical Institute	527

Saransk

Mordvinian State University	16,000

Saratov

Chernyshevskii State University	10,000
Institute of Economics	4,000

Syktyvkar

Syktyvkar State Univerity	3,000

Tiumen

State University	6,000
State Medical Institute	2,500

Tomsk

Polytechnic Institute	17,000
State University	9,000
Civil Engineering Institute	5,423

Ulan-Ude

Buriat Agricultural Institute	5,000

Vladikavkaz (Ordzhonikidze)

North Ossetian State University	7,000
North Caucasian Institute of Ore Mining and Metallurgy	5,000

Vladivostok

Far Eastern State University	10,000
Far Eastern Polytechnic Institute	8,500
Far Eastern Institute of Trade	2,760

Voronezh

State University	12,500

Socioeconomic Indicators

Birthrate: 13.4/1,000
Infant mortality: 17.4/1,000 live births
Average life expectancy: 69.3 (males, 63.9; females, 74.4)
Average family size: 3.2
Hospital beds per 10,000 persons: 137.5
Production of electrical energy: 7,284 kwh/person
Length of rail lines: 54,052 mi
Length of highways: 545,042 mi

Physical/Territorial/Geopolitical Features

Area: 6,592,812 sq mi (76.2% of USSR total)
Land use:

Cultivated	8%
Pasture	4%

Highest elevation: Mt. Elbrus (18,510 ft)
Principal products: potatoes, sugarbeets, grain, flax, tobacco, dairy cattle, sheep, swine; energy production, machinery, petroleum, natural gas, textiles, chemicals, cement, metallurgy, coal, gold, tin, copper, iron, mica, lead, manganese, diamonds, rocksalt, asbestos, graphite, aluminum, uranium, timber, motor vehicles
Per capita GNP (1991): $3,220.

Sources

Narodnoe khoziaistvo SSSR v 1990g. (Moscow, 1991); Matthew J. Sagers, "News Notes. Iron and Steel," *Soviet Geography* 30 (May 1989): 397-434; Lee Schwartz, "USSR Nationality Redistribution by Republic, 1979-1989: From Published Results of the 1989 All-Union Census," *Soviet Geography* 32 (April 1991): 209-48; *World of Learning*, 43rd ed. (London: Europa Publications Limited, 1993); "Russia. . ." (National Geographic Society Map, March 1993).

EUROPEAN RUSSIA

History and Description

Topography

Despite the Eurasian character of Russian civilization, the center of Russian cultural and political life has always been in Europe. European Russia, the eastern half of the European continent, is bordered on the north by the Arctic Ocean, more precisely by three seas of the Arctic—the Kara, the Barents, and the White. At its northwesternmost corner, the Russian boundary touches Norway and then traces southward along the Finnish-Russian frontier to the Gulf of Finland at the extreme eastern edge of the Baltic Sea. The Russian border continues southward from the Baltic along the frontiers of the newly independent states of Estonia, Latvia, Belarus, and Ukraine, all former republics of the Soviet Union. Southeast of Ukraine, Russian lands encompass the eastern shoreline of the Sea of Azov and the Black Sea. Approaching Transcaucasia, European Russia includes the northern slopes of the Caucasus Mountains. The Caucasus range provides a formidable natural barrier between Russia and the former Soviet republics of Georgia and Azerbaijan to the south. From the Caucasian boundary with Azerbaijan, Russian lands extend north along the western shore of the Caspian Sea as far as the territory of the newly independent state of Kazakhstan, another former Soviet republic. The Kazakh-Russian boundary then follows a crooked path from the Caspian Sea up toward the Ural Mountains. The Urals, as they stretch northward to the Arctic Ocean, constitute the geographical dividing line between European Russia to the west and Asia to the east.

European Russia is essentially a lowland area dominated by the East European Plain, occasionally referred to as the Russian Plain. Nowhere on this plain does the altitude reach any significant height, although the vast territory is distinguished by a number of upland regions.

The most important of these is the somewhat raised area beginning near the Belarusian-Russian border. Known as the Valdai Hills, this area gives rise to such important Russian rivers as the Volga, the Dnieper, and the Western Dvina. Aside from a series of uplands separating river valleys in the southern part of the East European Plain, Russian lands increase in altitude only as they approach the country's mountainous borders in the south and east.

One additional piece of territory making up the Russian Federation is Kaliningrad, located along the Baltic Sea between Poland and Lithuania. Separated geographically from the rest of Russia, Kaliningrad (formerly part of East Prussia) is primarily an agricultural area similar in size to Connecticut. Its capital is a naval port with fishing and shipbuilding industries.

The lands of European Russia are made up of seven basic vegetation and soil zones running in more-or-less horizontal bands across the width of the country. In the far north, the arctic tundra prevails, a landscape in which extremes of cold yield an inhospitable soil type known as permafrost, although moss, lichen, and berries can be found there. (See Siberia chapter, page 25, for a more complete description of arctic tundra.) South of the tundra lies the vast coniferous forest zone, the taiga. A landscape most often thought of as "Russian," the taiga's extensive pine and birch forests at one time covered almost all historic Russian lands. A transitional zone of mixed forest called the wooded steppe leads to the famous black earth (*chernozem*) area that supports much of European Russia's agricultural output. This zone, composed of rich dark soil, is the true steppe, the lands of which were once thickly covered by grasses but are now almost entirely under cultivation. The progressively drier climate of the south eventually turns to the semi-desert north of the Caspian Sea. A true desert zone may be found

European Russia

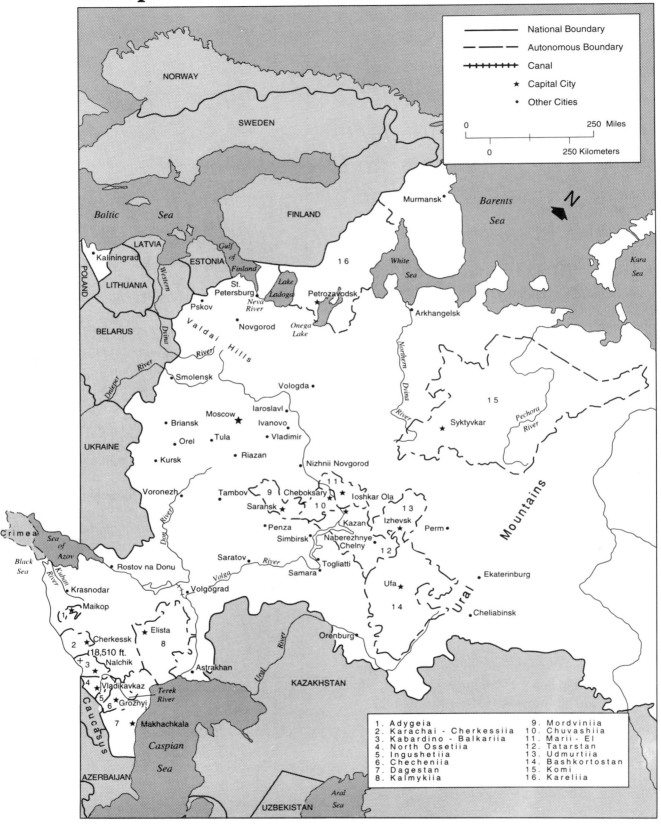

Legend
- National Boundary
- --- Autonomous Boundary
- +++ Canal
- ★ Capital City
- • Other Cities

0 ——— 250 Miles
0 ——— 250 Kilometers

NORWAY
SWEDEN
FINLAND
Murmansk
Barents Sea
Baltic Sea
LATVIA
Kaliningrad
ESTONIA
Gulf of Finland
LITHUANIA
POLAND
St. Petersburg
Neva River
Pskov
BELARUS
Valdai Hills
Western
Dvina
Dvina River
Dnieper River
Smolensk
Lake Ladoga
Petrozavodsk
16
White Sea
Onega Lake
Novgorod
Arkhangelsk
Northern Dvina River
Vologda
15
Syktyvkar
Pechora River
Kara Sea
Iaroslavl
Moscow
Ivanovo
Briansk
Orel
Tula
Vladimir
Kursk
Riazan
Nizhnii Novgorod
Voronezh
Tambov
9
Cheboksary
11
Ioshkar Ola
13
Izhevsk
Perm
UKRAINE
Don River
Saransk
10
Kazan
12
Penza
Simbirsk
Naberezhnye Chelny
Ural Mountains
Crimea
Sea of Azov
Black Sea
Saratov
Volga River
Samara
Togliatti
Ekaterinburg
Kuban River
Rostov na Donu
Ufa
14
Cheliabinsk
Krasnodar
Volgograd
Maikop
1
Elista
8
Orenburg
Ural River
2
Cherkessk
18,510 ft.
3
Nalchik
Astrakhan
KAZAKHSTAN
4
Vladikavkaz
Terek River
5
Grozhyi
Caucasus
6
7
Makhachkala
Caspian Sea
AZERBAIJAN
Aral Sea
UZBEKISTAN

1. Adygeia	9. Mordviniia
2. Karachai - Cherkessiia	10. Chuvashiia
3. Kabardino - Balkariia	11. Marii - El
4. North Ossetiia	12. Tatarstan
5. Ingushetiia	13. Udmurtiia
6. Checheniia	14. Bashkortostan
7. Dagestan	15. Komi
8. Kalmykiia	16. Kareliia

farther south in Central Asian lands located beyond the borders of European Russia. Finally, a mountainous zone exists along the northern slopes of the Caucasus in the south.

Rivers. The river systems of European Russia have long been essential to the economic and political development of the Russian state. The early availability of short portages between rivers led to the construction of canals, and eventually to a network of water passages that linked the lowland areas of historic Russia from the northern waters of the Baltic and Arctic seas to the shores of the Caspian and Black seas far to the south. The Volga River, celebrated in Russian music and literature, may be the most well-known waterway in this network, but because the Volga empties into the landlocked Caspian Sea its importance would be diminished without the canals that link it to internationally accessible waterways. Other major Russian rivers draining into the somewhat salty Caspian, the world's largest inland sea, are the Ural and the Terek rivers. In the south of Russia, the Don and Kuban rivers feed into the Sea of Azov and thence into the Black Sea. In northern European Russia, the Neva and the Western Dvina rivers empty into the Baltic Sea, while the Northern Dvina and the Pechora rivers drain into the Arctic. In northwestern Russia, especially in formerly glaciated areas, there are many freshwater lakes, the largest being Lake Ladoga near St. Petersburg, and Onega Lake to the northeast of Ladoga.

Climate. The climate of European Russian is clearly continental and, therefore, subject to extremes of heat and cold. Although located far from any oceans, the vast and very open stretches of the East European Plain do receive a limited flow of warm air from the Atlantic via the Baltic Sea, serving to balance the frigid polar air masses that also visit the area. Rainfall averages appear greatest in the more westerly parts of European Russia, gradually decreasing to the east and south.

Cities. Although it has become a land of large cities, two metropolitan areas overshadow all other urban centers in European Russia. Moscow (approximately nine million residents) and St. Petersburg (over five million) dwarf all of the country's remaining cities. Many other urban centers of European Russia reflect historic administrative and economic regions. Associated with the industrialized area around Moscow are the nearby cities of Iaroslavl, Ivanovo, Vladimir, Tula, Smolensk, and Briansk. To the south of this area, the central black earth region accommodates the large cities of Orel, Tambov, Voronezh, and Kursk. European Russia's northern cities of Murmansk, Vologda, and Arkhangelsk, and its historic centers of Novgorod, St. Petersburg, and Pskov have all become industrialized in the modern period. Nizhnii Novgorod (Gorky), Kazan, Saratov, Samara (Kuibyshev), Volgograd, and Astrakhan are some of the large cities along the Volga. The metropolitan center of Rostov na Donu (Rostov on the Don) in the south rests on the Don River, while Ekaterinburg (Sverdlovsk) and Cheliabinsk are mining centers located in the Urals. Although the Volga cities are among the oldest of historic Russia, the large industrial cities on the Don and in the Urals now approximate in size these early river centers.

Agriculture. Agricultural activity is not ideally suited to the lands of European Russia. The fact that much of its landmass is located at a very northerly latitude (north of the Canada-United States border) and that this area is also subject to severe extremes of climate has resulted in just a small percentage of the land being truly arable. Much of European Russia is covered by forests and swamps. The area most suitable for planting lies between the inhospitable cold of the north and the arid heat of the south. The best arable land is found in the Volga region, the northern part of the Caucasus, and the area to the west of the Urals.

The highest yielding grain crops of European Russia are wheat, barley, oats, and rye. These are supplemented by potatoes and traditional vegetable crops such as beets, cabbage, peas, carrots, onions, cucumbers, and tomatoes. Fruits that do well are apples, pears, and plums. In the last two decades Russians have been sowing much of their arable land with fodder crops to support livestock raising. The planting of such feed crops has led to shortages of wheat. After years of being a wheat exporter, Russia has in the past 25 years become dependent on other countries for its most staple food product.

Autonomous Regions

On the edges of European Russia many so-called autonomous regions were long ago established as national homelands for peoples whose ethnic and religious backgrounds differed from those of the dominant Russian population. The Soviet authorities created most of these autonomous regions in the 1920s to provide a territorial base for specific nationalities within the confines of the larger Russian republic. Administratively, each autonomous region was designated either as a republic, *oblast*, or *okrug*. Autonomous Soviet republics ranked directly beneath union republics, their autonomous standing due

Russia's Republics: Population in Absolute Figures and Share of Titular Nationality and Russians in Percentages

Adygeia	**432,000**	**Kareliia**	**790,000**
Adygei	22.1	Karelians	10.0
Russians	68.0	Russians	73.6
Altai	**191,000**	**Khakassiia**	**567,000**
Altai	31.0	Khakass	11.1
Russians	60.4	Russians	79.5
Bashkortostan	**3,943,000**	**Komi**	**1,251,000**
Bashkort	21.9	Komi	23.3
Russians	39.3	Russians	57.7
Tatars	28.4	**Marii-El**	**749,000**
Buriatiia	**1,038,000**	Mari	43.3
Buriats	24.0	Russians	47.5
Russians	69.9	**Mordviniia**	**964,000**
Checheno-Ingushetiia	**1,270,000**	Mordvins	32.5
Chechen	57.8	Russians	60.8
Ingush	12.9	**North Ossetiia**	**632,000**
Russians	23.1	Ossetians	53.0
Chuvashiia	**1,338,000**	Russians	29.9
Chuvash	67.8	**Sakha (Iakutiia)**	**1,094,000**
Russians	26.7	Iakuts	33.4
Dagestan	**1,802,000**	Russians	50.3
Dagestanis	80.2	**Tatarstan**	**3,642,000**
Russians	9.2	Tatars	48.5
Kabardino-Balkariia	**754,000**	Russians	43.3
Kabard	48.2	**Tuva**	**309,000**
Balkars	9.4	Tuvinian	64.3
Russians	31.9	Russians	32.0
Kalmykiia	**323,000**	**Udmurtiia**	**1,606,000**
Kalmyks	45.4	Udmurts	30.9
Russians	37.7	Russians	58.9
Karachai-Cherkessiia	**415,000**		
Karachai	31.2		
Cherkess	9.7		
Russians	42.4		

NOTE: There are no separate data for Checheniia and Ingushetiia, since Checheno-Ingushetiia was officially separated into two republics only in 1992.

Source: RFE/RL Research Report, vol. 2, no. 20 (14 May 1993), p. 38.

to the fact that their nationality group was not considered sufficiently powerful or large enough to merit full union republic status. Autonomous oblasts were set aside for relatively small nationality groups that lived in remote areas. Autonomous okrugs were designated for yet smaller nationalities and were often located on large tracts of undeveloped land inhabited by relatively few people. Amidst the breakup of the Soviet Union, however, virtually all of these autonomous regions have declared independence, often accompanying such declarations with a change of name to reflect their new status. These declarations of independence should not be confused with the declarations made by the former union republics, which have achieved full status as independent states.

Because of recent legislation regarding the status of these autonomous regions, European Russia is now home to 16 formerly autonomous republics and three autonomous okrugs. Responding to the declarations of sovereignty proclaimed by most of these autonomous republics, the sixth session of the Congress of People's Deputies of the Russian Federation adopted in April 1992 a constitutional amendment deleting the word "autonomous" before the word "republic." Thus, what had been an "autonomous republic" in the RSFSR became simply a "republic" within the newly independent Russian Federation. The Congress went on to adopt status changes for four of the five autonomous oblasts, raising them also to the level of republics. No change was made in the status of the autonomous national okrugs.

These formerly autonomous regions of European Russia tend to be located on the outskirts of the lands considered as historic Russia. (See map on p. 12.) In the northwest, for example, between Finland and the White Sea, lies the Republic of Kareliia. The Karelians are an Eastern Orthodox, Finnic-speaking people. Farther north, along the shore of the Barents Sea, live the Nenets, a Samoyed-speaking group that follows a combination of Eastern Orthodox and shamanist religious practices. To the south of the Nenets are the Republic of Komi and the Udmurt Republic, both ethnically Finnic regions. Far to the east of Moscow lie two other regions of ethnically Finnic population—the Republic of Marii-El (Mari), whose people practice shamanism with admixtures of Islam and Eastern Orthodoxy; and the Republic of Mordviniia, inhabited by a traditionally Orthodox population. Adjoining Mordviniia and Marii-El is the Chuvash Republic, home to a Turkic-speaking people that adopted Eastern Orthodox Christianity in the modern period.

Farther to the east and south, between the Volga River and the Ural mountains, there are regions inhabited by primarily Turkic populations, traditionally Muslim in their culture. The Republic of Tatarstan, centered in Kazan, is the homeland of the predominantly Sunni Muslim Volga Tatars. Adjacent to Tatarstan is the Republic of Bashkortostan (Bashkiriia), traditional homeland of the Turkic, Sunni Muslim Bashkorts. Farther to the south, the Republic of Kalmykiia is populated by descendants of the Mongols who traditionally followed Buddhist religious practices.

Yet farther south, along the northern slopes of the Caucasus Mountains, the plethora of local ethnic groups resulted in the establishment of seven autonomous regions, some of them originally representing more than one ethnic group per administrative unit. The Kabardino-Balkar Republic is named for the Sunni Muslim Kabard people who speak a Circassian tongue. The Republic of North Ossetiia that borders modern Georgia (see the chapter on Georgia, page 108) is inhabited primarily by Ossetians whose language is related to modern Iranian. Many of the North Ossetians converted to Eastern Orthodoxy in the modern period. Also in the Caucasus, the Chechen Republic (formerly part of the Chechen-Ingush Autonomous Oblast, subsequently the Chechen-Ingush Republic) has been recognized since mid-1992 as a separate republic. The Chechen people are traditionally Sunni Muslims who speak a Caucasian language. The Ingush of the newly separate Ingush Republic also speak a Caucasian-based language, but a different dialect. They are also Sunni Muslims.

Inhabiting a nearby area adjacent to the Caspian Sea are the Dagestani people of the Republic of Dagestan, an indigenous Sunni Muslim group that speaks yet another Caucasian language. The Chechen, Ingush, and Dagestani people are among the dozen or more separate north Caucasian nationalities, each of which speaks a distinct language within the family of Caucasian languages. In addition to these indigenous Caucasian nationals, the region is also home to the Republic of Adygeia and the Republic of Karachai-Cherkess. The Adygei, representing an ethnic group formed by the unification of as many as ten Circassian tribes, are Sunni Muslim. The peoples of Karachai-Cherkess are divided between the Karachai, who speak a Turkic language, and the Cherkess, whose speech derives from the Circassian branch of the Caucasian language family. Both Karachai and Cherkess are Sunni Muslim by religious tradition.

Although the removal of the word autonomous before the title of republic now reflects the greater measure of sovereignty assumed by many of the formerly autonomous regions, the Russian government considers these republics and okrugs integral parts of the Russian Federation. In many places, such as the capital city of Tatarstan (Kazan), for example, there continues to be a large ethnic Russian population in the urban centers of these "republics within a republic." Indeed, the majority population of these ethnic republics is sometimes Russian, leaving the titular nationality in the minority.

Defining Russia's Past

Statist View. The Great Russians or, simply, Russians are the largest of the East Slavic nations. They became the dominant nationality within the Muscovite, Imperial, and Soviet Russian empires. As Russia expanded territorially, it imposed its own institutions, language, and culture upon the multinational landscape of Eurasia. Because of the sheer power of this Russian imperium, it is tempting to define Russia's past exclusively in terms of the political and legal changes that marked each stage of its empire. According to this view, the Great Russians were the inheritors of the early Kievan

Rus grand princedom, a state that united Eastern Slavic tribes from the ninth to the thirteenth centuries. When that Kievan political structure was destroyed by the Mongol invasions of the Golden Horde in the mid-thirteenth century, new centers of Eastern Slavic, Russian civilization arose on the Volga river tributaries of the north. One such settlement, the city of Moscow, became by the fifteenth century an independent center of power. In defeating the Mongols in the fifteenth and sixteenth centuries, the tsars of Muscovy (the Muscovite Empire based in Moscow) established an independent Russian state that eventually stretched from Poland (the Polish-Lithuanian Commonwealth) in the west all the way to the Pacific Ocean in the east.

According to this "statist" view, political, legal, and institutional changes once again transformed the Muscovite state in the seventeenth and eighteenth centuries, first during the crisis of succession known as the "Time of Troubles" (1598–1613), and then definitively during the reforms of the Romanov tsar, Peter the Great (1682–1725). The result of Peter's reforms was the creation of an early modern bureaucratic state that came to be known as the Russian Empire (*Vserossiiskaia Imperiia*, literally the "All-Russian Empire"). Until the fall of the Romanov dynasty and the collapse of that state in the Revolutions of 1917, the Russian Empire maintained effective bureaucratic and military control over its expanding territories.

While the earliest Soviet constitution of 1918 proclaimed the new revolutionary state to be federalist, this federalism was not clarified until December 1922 when the four republics under Bolshevik control—Russia, Ukraine, Belorussia, and Transcaucasia—united to form the "Union of Soviet Socialist Republics." Throughout the 1920s, the identity of the constituent republics of the USSR continued to change. Thus, in 1922, when the Red Army took Vladivostok, the Far Eastern Republic was dissolved and it became a part of the Russian Soviet Federated Socialist Republic (RSFSR). Not until 1924 were the five Central Asian republics established. The integration of outlying republics into the new Soviet empire awaited in each case the successful advance of the Red Army, a key force engineering Bolshevik triumphs in the aftermath of the Revolutions of 1917.

As in the case of earlier political and institutional transformations from Kievan Rus to the twentieth century, statist historians can find in the Bolshevik Revolution and the ensuing Civil War yet another new stage in Russian history in which political, institutional, and military forces have continued to determine the course of Russia's past.

Marxist View. Marxist historians, on the other hand, see the political evolution of Russia as secondary to fundamental, underlying economic forces. In such a view, the defining feature of Russian history has been the "feudal" nature of agrarian economic relations that prevailed for virtually a millennium, from the ninth to the nineteenth centuries. According to the Marxist perspective, this feudalism existed in Russia at least until the emancipation of Russian serfs in 1861. (Vladimir Lenin, the Russian revolutionary leader, considered Russia to be a feudal, agrarian state even into the twentieth century.) Until the 1980s, Soviet historians rigidly divided Russian history into three periods—a period of feudalism (ninth century to 1861), a period of capitalism (1861–1917), and a period of socialism (1917–). Such periodization was also reflected in the structural organization of academic departments of history in the Soviet Union. Underlying this definition of Russia's past was the assumption that the most important cause of change in Russian history was economic conflict. Such conflict, in this view, determined the control and organization of economic production.

Intellectual and Cultural View. Others have defined Russia's past in terms of major intellectual and cultural changes shaping the world view of the Russian people and their leaders. Accordingly, for some the most significant event in early Russian history was the baptism of Kievan Grand Prince Vladimir into Byzantine-rite, Eastern Orthodox Christianity in 988 A.D. The Christianization of pagan Russia became, in this view, a defining process in Russian culture. By the sixteenth century, however, Russian religious life was no longer controlled by the ecclesiastical institutions of Byzantium. Russia's independent authority in the Eastern Orthodox world was recognized by the creation of the office of the autocephalous (self-ruled) Moscow Patriarchate (1588). The subsequent religious schism of the seventeenth century and the subordination of church to state in the administration of Peter the Great paved the way, in this view, for Russia's secularization. For writers such as Aleksandr Solzhenitsyn, official Soviet atheism was but a culmination of this process of secularization or "perversion" of Russia's earlier "moral foundation":

> For a thousand years Russia lived with an authoritarian order—and at the beginning of the twentieth century both the physical and spiritual health of her people were still intact.

. . . that authoritarian order possessed a strong moral foundation . . . not the ideology of universal violence, but Christian Orthodoxy, the ancient, seven-centuries-old Orthodoxy of Sergei Radonezhsky and Nil Sorsky, before it was battered by Patriarch Nikon and bureaucratized by Peter the Great. . . . Once this moral principle was perverted and weakened, the authoritarian order, despite the apparent external successes of the state, gradually went into a decline and eventually perished. (Aleksandr Solzhenitsyn, *Letter to the Soviet Leaders*, trans. by Hilary Sternberg, New York, 1974, p. 52)

By whatever means one defines Russia's past—be it in terms of state power, economic production, cultural inheritance, or some other organizing principle—the twentieth century has surely been its most revolutionary and fateful epoch. From the turbulent events of the 1917 Revolutions and subsequent Civil War to the agricultural collectivization, industrialization, and purges of the 1930s, the Soviet experiment brought lofty utopian goals to the modernization of Russian society, but at an unprecedented price in human suffering. As many as one million free-holding peasants (*kulaks*), not counting their families, were either killed in the process of collectivization or were sent to labor camps in the expanding gulag of Soviet Asia. (See Siberian chapter, page 32, for a more complete description of the gulag.) In the forced industrialization of the country, dramatic increases in production were accomplished in heavy industry, but the very people who were forced to work harder were confronted with shortages of basic consumer goods and widespread rationing. The great purge (arrests followed by imprisonment or execution) of the 1930s further filled the labor camps of the gulag, as the Communist Party began to consume its own. Reaching a crescendo of violence in the period after 1936, the purge affected all Party and government offices, including the army. The purges also fell heavily upon the Russian technical and academic intelligentsia.

Stalin. Behind both the collectivization and industrialization policies, as well as the purges, stood the figure of Joseph Stalin (1879–1953). Born and raised in the Georgian town of Gori as Josef Dzhugashvili, he later joined the Russian Social Democratic Worker's Party, aligning himself with its Bolshevik wing after 1903. Assuming the name of Stalin, he rose within Party ranks until, after the Bolshevik Revolution, he assumed a position of Party leadership by taking the post of commissar for national minorities. In 1922, Stalin secured for himself the post of Communist Party general secretary. Using his leadership in Party affairs, Stalin gradually eliminated potential rivals as he built an increasingly loyal Party machine. By 1928, the onset of the first "five-year plan" for industrialization, Stalin was in complete personal control of Party and governmental affairs—a control he would maintain until his death in 1953.

World War II. Of all the tragedies of Stalinism, none was more fateful than the losses sustained in World War II. The Soviet Union initially sought to avoid confrontation with German armies by signing the Nazi-Soviet Pact of 1939—an agreement that divided Eastern Europe between German and Soviet spheres. While the Soviet Union was able to use the pact to secure additional territorial gains at the expense of Polish and Baltic lands, Stalin was left unprepared militarily for Germany's invasion of Russia in June 1941. The Red Army suffered catastrophic losses in the early months of fighting. Countless civilians also perished under the most dire circumstances. They died in the fighting itself or in German camps or from starvation (as in the beseiged city of Leningrad, now St. Petersburg). In the case of Jews, Gypsies, Communists, and certain other groups, the Germans pursued forcible exterminations, or mass killings.

The Red Army eventually held against the invading German forces at the prolonged Battle of Stalingrad, and the subsequent rout of the German Army in 1943–44 served as the turning point in World War II. Appealing for patriotic support, even making concessions to the Russian Orthodox church, Stalin in the end managed to preserve the Soviet regime, but the cost in human life was unprecedented. As many as 27 million people died in the Soviet Union, at least half of them civilians. (See Nicholas Riasanovsky, *A History of Russia*, fifth ed., New York, 1993, p. 528. Riasanovsky has altered his assessment of war losses from 20 to 27 million in the fifth edition of his standard text, a reflection of new demographic evidence.) In effect, World War II yielded a biological revolution in the Soviet Union, for an entire generation of males was lost in the war effort. Meanwhile, information about World War II continued to appear in the Soviet media well into the 1980s as a propaganda device seeking to use the defeat of fascism as justification for Soviet rule.

Post-Stalin Era. Stalin's death in 1953, while it did not prove the final end of Stalinism, nevertheless opened up prospects for liberalization under the reformist leadership of Party General Secretary Nikita Khrushchev. Khrushchev's 1956 speech to the Twentieth Congress of the Communist Party publicly exposed the evils of Stalinism and the purges. While Khrushchev's liberalization measures did not extend to religious communities, several of which suffered even worse persecution in the

Khrushchev era than they had in the aftermath of World War II, the "thaw" could be felt in other areas of Russian culture where censorship in literature and the arts was relaxed.

In 1964, Nikita Khrushchev was relieved of his position in both the Communist Party and the government, and his post as general secretary of the Party was assumed by Leonid Brezhnev. While Brezhnev's leadership came to be associated with a period of detente with the West in the 1970s, the formal relaxation of tensions between the Cold War superpowers was matched by a strengthening of Soviet military power. The costs of such a military build-up eventually came to be felt in economic dislocations and shortages that had become increasingly difficult to hide from consumers by the time of Brezhnev's death in 1982. Within three years, following the brief tenure of Communist Party leaders Iurii Andropov and Konstantin Chernenko, Party authorities were prepared to turn to a vigorous new leader, the future architect of

perestroika (restructuring), Mikhail Sergeevich Gorbachev.

From his earliest 1985 measures directed against alcoholism and lost worker productivity, Gorbachev presented a new and much more vigorous style of Russian leadership. His goal was to restructure social, political, and economic life in such a way as to modernize the flagging Soviet economy. In spite of his focus upon domestic restructuring, however, he was forced to deal with one international crisis after another—including the Chernobyl nuclear power plant disaster of 1986, the withdrawal of Soviet military forces from Afghanistan, and the dismemberment in 1989 of the once solid Soviet bloc in Eastern Europe. Gorbachev found that he was ultimately unable to maintain the commanding political authority of the Communist Party in the reform process. The radical transformation of Russian life that ensued has yet to play itself out.

Contemporary Issues

Political Transformation and the Limits of Democratization

Communist Party General Secretary Mikhail Gorbachev already appeared to be struggling in 1990–91 to maintain a middle ground between the forces of political democratization, on the one hand, and the entrenched conservative forces of the Party and its *nomenklatura* (Party-appointed bureaucratic apparatus), on the other. That struggle, if indeed Gorbachev genuinely sought to command a middle ground, was rendered impossible by the dramatic and abortive Moscow coup attempt of August 1991. During the coup, the very figures that Gorbachev had appointed to high-level ministerial positions effectively sought to topple him from power, while secretly keeping him under house arrest in the Crimea.

The failure of the August 1991 coup demonstrated the degree to which political power had, in the six short years of Gorbachev's tenure, shifted away from the Communist Party and into the hands of an elected Russian Parliament headed by an elected Russian president. In the crucial showdown between the coup plotters

and the new Russian President Boris Yeltsin, the armed forces refused to back the coup. By the time Gorbachev was released and returned to Moscow, his authority was already crippled. His effort to secure a union treaty that would maintain the unity of the Soviet republics was definitively undermined. By the end of August, most Soviet republics, including the Russian Federation, had declared their independence. In December 1991, the Soviet Union ceased to exist. The Communist Party was also outlawed (a measure partially reversed by the courts in 1992). Gorbachev was out of power, and the Soviet parliament was effectively supplanted in Russia by its republican counterpart, the Russian Congress of Peoples' Deputies. A new Commonwealth of Independent States (CIS) was launched in December 1991 by the republics of Russia, Ukraine, and Belarus, and the CIS ultimately included all the former Soviet republics except the three Baltic states and Georgia. Azerbaijan, however, withdrew its membership in the fall of 1992; Moldova in 1993. Nevertheless, the politics of republican sovereignty, not those of an interrepublican Commonwealth, came to dominate most policy making in the post-Soviet era.

While the prospects for political restructuring and democratization may have looked bright in the aftermath of August 1991, the politics of the Russian Federation have become mired in a conflict that has pitted the reform-minded president, Boris Yeltsin, against a willful Russian Parliament and an increasingly intransigent Russian bureaucracy. Yeltsin, former Communist Party leader from Sverdlovsk, had broken with both Gorbachev and the Soviet Parliament in 1990, decisively casting his political fate with "Democratic Russia," a coalition seeking democratic reform in the Russian Republic. In June 1991, Yeltsin won an overwhelming public mandate and became the very first popularly elected Russian president. With a corps of bright young academic advisors, Yeltsin overshadowed what was in the beginning a deferential Russian Parliament. In November 1991, the Parliament even granted Yeltsin special powers to undertake radical economic reform in Russia. A series of far-reaching measures, including sweeping price deregulation, ensued in January 1992. The personal authority of Boris Yeltsin, reinforced by support from the Democratic Russia movement that had brought him to power in 1990, seemed destined to sustain the momentum for political and economic reform.

By the end of 1992, however, especially at the seventh session of the Russian Congress of People's Deputies in December, the process of political and economic reform had come under significant challenge from a Parliament that had ultimate supreme authority and sought to limit President Yeltsin's power. Yeltsin loyalists could claim with some justification that the Russian Parliament had been elected in 1990 when Communist Party influence still affected the outcome of elections. In this view, the Parliament's conservative brake on reform was a reflection of its ties to old politics and the apparatus of the Party-appointed nomenklatura. In fact, former Communist and right-wing nationalist deputies—a coalition that was far stronger in Parliament than in the public at large—did lead the opposition to an evermore dispirited Yeltsin alliance. Responding to these challenges to his executive power, Boris Yeltsin sought to reach beyond the Russian Parliament by seeking a direct mandate from the people. To do this he scheduled a popular referendum for April 1993. That referendum specifically asked the electorate to pass judgment on his presidency and the Russian Parliament. The April referendum effectively reasserted presidential leadership, while demonstrating widespread popular opposition to the machinations of Parliament. In the absence of a new post-Soviet constitution, however, the office of the Russian presidency remained the subject of controversy.

The weakened position of Yeltsin was not, however, the simple result of this defiant Parliament. The Russian Congress of People's Deputies was also responding to wider public uneasiness over the pace and impact of economic reform. In particular, the "shock therapy" of price deregulation and tightened money supply posed a threat to large state-subsidized heavy industries, with consequent public concern over rising unemployment. By mid-1992, an industrial lobby had organized itself into a "Civic Union," and this union declared its opposition not only to radical economic reform, but more generally to Yeltsin's political leadership. In a symbolic victory over the Yeltsin reform agenda, the Russian Parliament in December 1992, led by its chair Ruslan Khasbulatov from the Chechen Republic, secured the right to approve or reject four key presidential cabinet appointments. The subsequent parliamentary rejection of Egor Gaidar, Yeltsin's architect of radical economic reform, and his replacement by the Civic Union favorite Viktor Chernomyrdin signaled how powerful the Russian Parliament had become.

Amidst the conflicts of Russian political life, there are some developments launched by the Yeltsin government that have garnered considerable support in the provinces. Among these, the most significant may be Yeltsin's decision to delegate to regional leaders most local appointments as well as much major economic decision making. The result has been the rise of significant regional leadership, for example in the city of Nizhnii Novgorod (Gorky) where the local provincial governor Boris Nemtsov developed a reputation for effective political reform. This decentralization of political and economic life has served to ingratiate the Yeltsin government with several of the Russian Federation's formerly autonomous republics, which continue to press for greater independence. It has also served to undermine the position of those conservative elements in the Russian Parliament who would like to reimpose Moscow-based central planning over the outlying provinces.

The political transformation of modern Russia has not come without dissension. The basic conflict between executive and legislative power, despite the occasional mediation of constitutional court authorities, has yet to be resolved. In the absence of a new and effective constitution, this conflict shows little sign of early resolution. As political strife deepens, there has also arisen an increased acrimony between forces loyal to President Yeltsin and those in opposition to him. For many Russians struggling to keep up with rampant inflation, the political impasse in Moscow breeds only further cynicism.

Economic Restructuring and Privatization

If 1991 marked the major turning point in Russia's political transformation—including the presidential elections, the August coup, and the collapse of the Soviet Union—then 1992 marked the most dramatic restructuring of the Russian economy. Effective January 1992, broad measures eliminating price controls, except on basic energy and food commodities, were introduced throughout the Russian economy. Not only did this set off a wave of price increases in the Russian Federation, but the ripple effects of this deregulation impacted virtually every republic of the former Soviet Union, forcing accommodation throughout the "ruble zone" of newly independent Eurasian republics. The elimination of price controls was intended to establish real market prices for Russian goods.

This "shock therapy," a term used to describe similar radical economic reforms launched in Eastern Europe, particularly Poland, included a tight monetary policy and carefully monitored wage increases designed to avoid excessive inflationary pressure. While some of the inspiration for the reforms may have come from Western economic consultants, the Russian architect of these radical economic measures was President Boris Yeltsin's closest economic advisor, Egor Gaidar.

Accompanying price deregulation and monetary controls was a plan for the privatization (*privatizatsiia*) of some state property and industrial assets. In 1992, for example, it became possible for individuals to "privatize" their state-owned apartments. In the high-demand urban markets of Moscow and St. Petersburg, however, brokers emerged on the scene offering financial inducements and more spacious apartment units outside the city core to cramped inner-city communal apartment dwellers. The incentive for such brokers was that office space in prime areas, such as central Moscow, had skyrocketed in value to as much as $1,000 per square meter. (See "In Moscow, Privatization Brings Real Estate Boom," *New York Times*, 28 February 1993.) The conversion of crudely divided communal apartment units into spacious offices and multiroom apartments constitutes one of the many curious post-Soviet reversals in which once elegant prerevolutionary, nineteenth-century buildings are now being restored in what might be called the "regentrification"

(upgrading to previous elite standards) of prime Moscow and St. Petersburg property. Obviously, those Russian cities less accessible to international investment and foreign commerce have not experienced the scale of property privatization and gentrification under way in Moscow and St. Petersburg.

Privatization has also affected the service sector and some manufacturing. Although the difference between state-owned and private enterprises is often blurred, three types of nonstate enterprises have emerged—joint stock companies, cooperatives, and small private enterprises. Privatization at the outset proceeded very slowly. By late 1992, only about 5 percent of industrial, small trade, and service establishments had been privatized. (See Erik Whitlock, "New Russian Government to Continue Economic Reform?" *RFE/RL Research Report*, 15 January 1993, pp. 23-24.) Equally slow has been the implementation of a system of vouchers, by which every Russian citizen has been granted a certificate worth 10,000 rubles ($35 at the official exchange rate when first issued in October 1992—a figure in excess of one month's average wages) for the purchase of government assets being offered for privatization. Not until the vouchers had been distributed did the auctioning of state enterprises begin to gather steam in late 1992 and early 1993. In late 1992, the presence of vouchers on the market without adequate opportunities for investment not only added to inflationary pressures, but also led many Russians to sell off their vouchers for cash. (See Steven Erlanger, "Russia's Big Sell-Off of Companies Gains Speed," *New York Times*, 25 February 1993.)

Three major problems confront economic restructuring and privatization in contemporary Russia. First, production figures for the Russian economy plummeted in 1992. In some industrial sectors real production declines reached over 20 percent. Much of this loss of productivity reflected the lack of market demand for goods produced in the traditional state-run military and heavy industry sectors. Nevertheless, continued declines in production can only mean serious unemployment and/or continued inflationary pressure upon the government in the form of monetary subsidies for outmoded industries. In effect, the dramatic drop in production figures points to the dilemma of market-oriented restructuring. Either, as shock therapists would argue, the restructuring should be implemented with greater firmness, or, as the directors of large state enterprises argue, the restructuring should not be allowed to undermine previously productive enterprises before new productive sectors have been established.

Second, the Russian Parliament's deposing of Egor Gaidar as chief economic advisor and his replacement by Prime Minister Viktor Chernomyrdin have introduced uncertainty regarding the long-term economic policy goals of the Russian government. Both foreign investment and domestic markets suffer from economic policies that are wildly fluctuating. This uncertainty can also affect the process of privatization, inasmuch as many privatizing enterprises are faced with substantial indebtedness and need to know what government policies will be with respect to price regulation, credit guarantees, debt forgiveness, etc. To date, there seems to be substantial continuity between the Chernomyrdin and Gaidar policies, but a relaxation in monetary policy threatens to trigger hyperinflation (already at 20 percent per month at the end of 1992), thus undermining the restructuring process.

Third, although the Russian Federation has ample natural resources and a remarkably well-trained, literate work force, the process of economic restructuring requires far greater international investment. Such investment is needed not only for the success of restructuring, but also for continued political stability. Despite Russia's membership in the International Monetary Fund and the stated willingness of creditor nations to assist the Russian economy, there are limits to international credit, especially at a time of slow growth in the domestic economies of the European Community, Japan, the United States, and Canada.

Problems of Cold War Demobilization

Added to the problems of economic restructuring has been the drain upon the economy of a costly military defense budget geared to old Cold War realities. At the time of its collapse at the end of 1991, the Soviet Union continued to field the world's largest armed forces, with over four million in uniform. (The United States by comparison had a combined military force of approximately two million.) While over half a million Soviet troops had been stationed in Eastern Europe under Warsaw Pact auspices, the gradual return of those units following the 1989 revolutions (some forces remained in the Baltic lands even in 1993) added untold financial and housing burdens to the Russian economy. Finally, and most significantly, the Russian state along with three of its partners in the Commonwealth of Independent States (Kazakhstan, Ukraine, and Belarus) continue through

1993 to maintain large nuclear weapons bases, the decommissioning of which under international agreements required yet further spending. In short, the legacy of the Cold War will continue well into the forseeable future to drain an already overtaxed Russian state budget.

Perhaps the most complicated problem facing the military was to clarify the command structure of the armed forces. Following the August 1991 coup attempt, Russian President Boris Yeltsin secured the appointment of a new Soviet defense minister, Evgenii Shaposhnikov. Upon the demise of the Soviet Union in December 1991, the Soviet defense ministry effectively came to be identified as the headquarters of the central military command of the Commonwealth of Independent States. Yet there remained the clear problem that even though the Soviet Union had split up into sovereign republics, the military command structure still reflected unified Soviet organizational patterns. The new civilian political realities were simply not reflected in the military command structure. For a time in early 1992, the only way in which this awkward situation could be overcome was through the personal intermediation of Russian president Yeltsin and CIS armed forces head Shaposhnikov.

Nuclear Weapons. Three problems forced a further clarification of civil-military relations in Russia. The first of these was the obvious need to develop a post-Soviet policy on nuclear weapons. In the initial talks between CIS leaders in late 1991, the decision was taken that all nuclear weapons not on Russian soil should either be transferred to the Russian Federation or destroyed. In the meantime, the CIS military command structure remained nominally in control of the various republican nuclear arsenals. There followed in 1992 a transfer of all tactical nuclear weapons to Russia from the other republics with nuclear weapons, Ukraine, Belarus, and Kazakhstan. When the issue of the larger, strategic nuclear arsenals was reopened in mid-1992, Ukraine and Kazakhstan pulled back from their initial position to destroy or transfer these arsenals to Russia. Russia and Kazakhstan would ultimately conclude a bilateral agreement on the matter of the strategic nuclear weapons. The sticking point, however, became the increasing independence of Ukraine on this matter. Arguing that it needed security guarantees in return for transferring the weapons and noting the need for Western financial aid to assist in destroying the weapons, Ukraine held out for financial and security agreements in exchange for cooperation. Despite successful last minute efforts made by the outgoing U.S. administration of George Bush to secure an agreement on mutual United States-Russian nuclear warhead reductions, the continued presence of strategic nuclear weapons in four of the new Eurasian states remains in 1993 a source of concern both in the CIS and in the West.

Independent Armed Forces. The second major issue to confront the CIS military command was the establishment of independent republican armed forces in several of the new post-Soviet states. Again, Ukrainian initiatives forced this issue. Over half a million former Soviet troops were still being housed on Ukrainian soil. From the perspective of Ukrainian sovereignty, there was a need to clarify the lines of authority between the Ukrainian civilian government and these CIS troops. In early January 1992, Ukraine announced that all forces on Ukrainian soil would henceforth be directly under the authority of the Ukrainian defense minister. This announcement was followed by measures calling for an oath of allegiance to Ukraine by all those former Soviet troops intending to continue their military service in Ukraine. Although there were some desertions and some who sought reassignment, over half of the forces in Ukraine took this oath of allegiance by the end of January 1992. (On the question of the Black Sea Fleet, see the chapter on Ukraine, page 74.)

Meanwhile, Moldova and Azerbaijan also moved to create their own national armies. In the end, the Russian decision in May 1992 to establish its own independent Russian army ended any hope that the CIS military forces would be able to maintain a unified command structure throughout the territories of the former Soviet Union. Russian civil-military relations still need to be sorted out, as does the relationship between CIS forces and the new Russian military command structure. It is increasingly clear, however, that Russia, like Ukraine, has its own military policy and its own military command drawn from former Soviet and CIS forces.

Troops Outside Russian Federation. The third major military issue confronting Russia was how to deploy those troops that continued to be stationed outside the borders of the Russian Federation. President Yeltsin faced increasing pressure from Russian nationalists to wait with the full evacuation of Russian forces from the Baltic countries until the rights of minority Russian nationals living in the region were guaranteed. Some of the Russian forces from the Baltic were also evacuating to Kaliningrad (former Prussian Koenigsberg), the small slice of heavily fortified Russian territory south and west of Lithuania. In Moldova, Russian forces appeared to have been drawn into support for the Trans-Dniester Russian republic that broke with the Moldovan government in 1992. Having intended to send Russian troops into Checheniia, Yeltsin, under local pressure, settled for the more modest deployment of troops in North Ossetiia, ostensibly for the purpose of quelling local rebellions against the Ossetiians in the Caucasus. Finally, in Central Asia, particularly in the volatile Republic of Tajikistan, Russian forces are being employed by the old power structure in a way that maintains the arrangement in place during the Soviet period. President Yeltsin has indicated that these ongoing deployments of Russian troops are meant simply to quell interethnic fighting, and that the deployment is subject to bilateral interrepublican agreements. At the same time, Yeltsin must still contend with military and Russian nationalist leaders who cling to the fading hope that Russian/CIS forces will be able to secure some military reintegration of the Commonwealth of Independent States.

KGB. Not all the problems confronting Russian Cold War demobilization are confined to the fate of the former Red Army. There is no institution more symbolic of the Cold War than the vaunted KGB (Komitet gosudarstvennoi bezopasnosti/Committee of State Security). As one commentator put it, "Where has the KGB gone?" (Victor Yasmann, *RFE/RL Research Report*, 8 January 1993, pp. 17–20). A search for the KGB in contemporary Russia reveals both significant changes and some continuity in this former Cold War security agency.

To begin with, the name of the agency has changed. Although Russian citizens still refer to the "KGB," the legal successor to the KGB in Russia is the new Ministry of Security. Officially the size of the agency has remained about the same—the ministry reported in September 1992 that it had 135,000 officers, a slight drop from its pre-August 1991 officer-level figures. The law on security passed by the Russian Supreme Soviet in March 1992 has also extended to other agencies the right to gather intelligence. These other agencies include the Foreign Intelligence Service, the armed forces, and the Ministry of Internal Affairs. The relationship between former Soviet KGB offices and KGB personnel in other republics remains unclear. The need for intelligence in other republics continues, especially in connection with problems of political instability, and former KGB officers working in such republics may well have been retained because of their training. Yet, the nature of the links between the intelligence personnel of Russia and the other newly independent republics is rarely examined in the public media.

What has been openly discussed is the expansion of intelligence gathering capability to include agencies and tasks previously not part of the KGB. Political leaders in Russia have been remarkably candid about the new tasks that they envision for the intelligence community. Egor Gaidar, as acting prime minister, authorized creation of a Commission for Combating Corruption and for Financial Control, a government effort to use intelligence officers to identify schemes involving illegal foreign trade and commerce, as well as other forms of corruption. While the old KGB played an occasional role in anticorruption campaigns, such efforts invariably focused upon the widespread official corruption amongst Soviet government and Party personnel.

There is the sense that while maintaining the old components of internal and foreign security forces, the new Russian Federation is involved in a modest effort to redirect the focus of intelligence gathering. Such a focus is reflected in the pronouncements of Evgenii Primakov, director of the Russian Foreign Intelligence Service, who has called for collaboration with Western intelligence agencies in attacking problems of nuclear proliferation, international terrorism, and drug trafficking.

On the other hand, despite the sensational articles published in Russian newspapers and the revelations offered from KGB archives, the details of most former KGB operations have remained secret, as have the estimates of the number of paid informers in Russia, a figure assumed to be somewhere in the millions. KGB records documenting abuses in the gathering of Soviet domestic intelligence have also been largely inaccessible. It appears as though new assignments have been delegated to the Ministry of Security and other intelligence agencies without any systematic effort to root out the intelligence abuses of the Soviet period. The KGB was powerless to halt the collapse of the Soviet Union, and it is no doubt also incapable of directing the course of Russian domestic politics in the present. Nevertheless, the failure to undertake major reform in the intelligence field, much less to limit the influence of the old KGB officers, suggests the degree of difficulty encountered in Cold War demobilization.

The Recovery of Ethnic and Religious Identity in Russia

One of the reasons Russian political leaders are anxious to maintain up-to-date domestic intelligence is that ethnic tensions *within* the Russian Federation potentially threaten the very existence of the Federation itself. As noted in the discussion of "autonomous regions," the Russian Federation is a multinational state incorporating the historic homelands of several dozen non-Russian peoples. (Some of these are discussed in the chapter on "Siberia and the Far East.") While the dismemberment of the Soviet Union into its former constituent republics yielded newly independent nation-states on the borders of the Russian Federation, there still remain within the Federation many national groups that seek greater independence from Russia. Conversely, Russian nationals have also begun to cultivate a sense of their own religious and ethnic identity.

The case of the Republic of Tatarstan, one of the former autonomous republics within the Soviet Union, is instructive. Tatarstan is situated on the northern Volga. Its capital, Kazan, is a city of mixed Russian and Volga Tatar population. The Volga Tatars, Islamic by religious tradition, speak a Turkic language. In 1992, the local Volga Tatar leadership confronted Russian authorities with a significant threat to the unity of the Russian Federation. The threat came in the form of a March referendum asking people of the Tatar Republic, be they Russian or Tatar, whether they wanted Tatarstan to be "a sovereign state and a subject of international law whose relations with the Russian Federation and other republics and states are based on equal treaties." (See Steven Erlanger, "Tatar Area in Russia Votes on Sovereignty Today," *New York Times*, 21 March 1992.) In the voting, 61.4 percent of the voters of the former Tatar Autonomous Republic of the Soviet Union approved the referendum on sovereignty. Despite the fact that the chair of the Tatar Supreme Soviet, Farid Mukhamadshin, assured Russian leaders that the referendum did not imply any intention on the part of Tatarstan to secede from the Russian Federation, the message was clear. The Volga Tatars, as with other groups in European Russia, Siberia, and the Far East, wish to be treated as sovereign units within a confederated Russian republic.

The political situation in Tatarstan, as in other national homelands within the Russian Federation, is also very complicated. Into 1993, the prevailing leadership in

Tatarstan is made up of old Communist Party figures who have, on the issue of national sovereignty, sought to retain their power by making common cause with Tatar nationalists. Tatarstan President Shamiev is just such a figure. Thus, the real issue leading to the Tatar referendum was not political democratization, but a subtle jockeying for power among Tatar politicians. In the end, the vote confirmed Tatarstan's sovereignty, but Tatarstan remains a turbulent part of the Russian Federation, and may not continue to pay taxes in the federated system.

President Yeltsin's unwillingness to use force to stop the Tatarstan referendum reflected a new caution on his part. He had earlier threatened to send Russian forces into the Chechen-Ingush Republic in the Caucasus to stop the secessionist claims of General Dudaev, a former Soviet air force general who declared the Chechen Republic independent in late 1991. Recognizing that it could be counterproductive to appear as the outside imperial warlord, Yeltsin was far more conciliatory in 1992 toward the ethnic and regional republics of the Russian Federation. To date, while most sovereign republics within the Russian Federation have continued to pay taxes, the potential challenge to Russian leadership in these regions is unmistakable.

Seeking to maintain some normality in Russian relations with the other republics of the Russian Federation, Yeltsin in late March 1992 proceeded to sign a federal treaty with these subunits of the Federation. He sought to put the Tatarstan voting behind him as he noted in the signing of the treaty that "there is a particularly strong understanding that only together will we be able to overcome our difficulties and turn our common homeland of Russia into a free, democratic and prosperous state" (Erlanger, "Most Pieces of Russia Agree to Coalesce, For Now," *New York Times*, 1 April 1992). Interestingly, the Tatarstan, Chechen, and Ingush Republics were only observers at the signing ceremony, but eighty governmental leaders of autonomous republics, oblasts, and other regions agreed to the terms of the compact. Unexpectedly, even the leader of the Bashkir Republic (Bashkortostan) signed onto the pact. The treaty offers greater political and economic independence to the autonomous regions, especially over their considerable natural resources. For now, President Yeltsin's cautious approach to Russian relations with non-Russian homelands of the Federation has served to maintain an uneasy alliance between center and periphery. The ultimate test of this relationship will be seen in whether the government of the Russian Federation can establish effective new constitutional guidelines providing for the autonomy, as well as integration, of autonomous ethnic regions within a common state.

For Russian nationalists, concessions to the non-Russians of the Federation beg the equally urgent question of Russian national identity within the new Russian Federation. The rediscovery of Russian national and religious identity, while it has been made possible by a greater measure of openness or *glasnost*, has not come without a certain measure of pain. The Russian Orthodox church has emerged as a key institution in the reawakening of this national and religious consciousness. The Orthodox church, however, has also suffered from the perception that during the Soviet years it preserved itself by making excessive compromises with state authority. (See Stephen Batalden, ed., *Seeking God: The Recovery of Religious Identity in Russia, Ukraine, and Georgia*, DeKalb, 1993.) The result has been a challenge to Russian Orthodoxy, not only from emigre-based Orthodox groups, but from Protestant sectarian interests, and even from right-wing Russian nationalists who have a more radical, often anti-Semitic, agenda. Surely one of the most significant debates occurring within Russia today is the internal debate over the future of the Russian nation and Russian national identity.

The danger for the Russian Federation is that in seeking to appease independently minded non-Russian ethnic regions it will generate a more powerful Russian reaction. At the June 1993 constitutional conference there were signs of just such a reaction. For European Russia, as for all of the Russian Federation, the politics of nationalism remains the most fateful issue for political leadership.

SIBERIA AND THE FAR EAST

History and Description

Topography

Siberia is the great land mass stretching east from the Ural Mountains and European Russia all the way to the Pacific Ocean—a distance of approximately three-thousand miles. Larger than the entire United States, this vast northern territory comprises essentially the Asian part of the former Russian and Soviet empires. It is bordered by Kazakhstan, China, Mongolia, and North Korea on the south and by the icy waters of the Arctic Ocean in the north. The term "Siberia" (in Russian, *Sibir*) comes from the Tatar Khanate of Sibir. Before Russian conquest in the sixteenth century, the Tatars of Sibir controlled much of the Ob River valley in Western Siberia. Although scholars have not always agreed on how to divide Siberian lands into economic, political, ethnographic, and administrative units, three general regions corresponding to economic zones are most often employed. These regions are called Western Siberia, Eastern Siberia, and the Far East.

Western Siberia. Western Siberia extends from the edge of the Urals to an area just west of the Enisei River. The basic geographic feature of this region is the immense flat plain called the Western Siberian Lowland. This great plain includes in the north much tundra, a treeless type of landscape prevalent within the Arctic Circle. Tundra features low vegetation, lichens, mosses and stunted shrubs. In most of the tundra region, permafrost conditions exist. The moisture below the ground's surface becomes permanently frozen, leaving just a thin layer of soil remaining on top. Thickness of permafrost varies from a depth of more than three-thousand feet along the shores of the Arctic Ocean to a depth of three feet along the southern boundary of the permafrost region. Farther south the permafrost zone evolves into small frozen patches.

Spring floods are common in the Western Siberian Lowland, due in part to overflowing rivers that thaw in their upper courses to the south before reaching the still frozen northern points where they empty into the Arctic. Because of poor drainage in this region, large areas of marsh and bog prevail as well as many shallow lakes. About half of Western Siberia is swamp; indeed, the world's largest swamp, the Vasiugan Swamp, is found here between the Ob and Irtysh rivers.

Interspersed with the marshes and bogs is the taiga, a type of land characterized by a wealth of coniferous forests. Fir, spruce, cedar, larch, and pine cover the taiga, providing vast lumber resources and accommodating an abundance of animal life such as brown bear, elk, and small furbearing animals. In all, Siberia possesses the world's largest coniferous forest, a resource of enormous ecological significance in an age of global warming. Toward the southern border with Kazakhstan and Mongolia, the Siberian terrain becomes drier and better suited to agriculture. The taiga gives way to an area of deciduous forest, a land of wooded steppes conducive to the growth of aspen and birch. Continuing south the landscape gradually changes to open steppe, a distinctly flat almost treeless panorama in which grasses predominate. A rich black earth is found here, its grassy matlike covering revealing underneath a fertile loamy soil prized by Russian peasants who colonized the area in earlier centuries.

The major rivers of Western Siberia all flow northward and empty into the Arctic Ocean. Rising in the mountainous border regions shared with China and Mongolia, the Ob River and its main tributary, the Irtysh, cut through the steppe and continue across the taiga and tundra before exiting into the frigid Arctic Ocean. The rivers of the Western Siberia region became major trans-

Siberia and the Far East

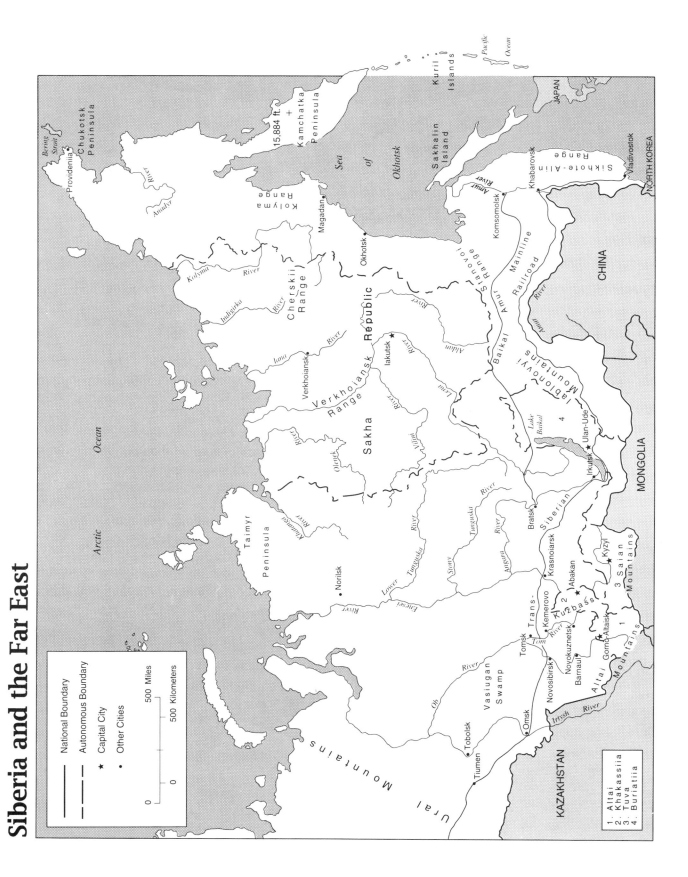

Legend:
- National Boundary
- Autonomous Boundary
- ★ Capital City
- • Other Cities

500 Miles

500 Kilometers

1. Altai
2. Khakassiia
3. Tuva
4. Buriatiia

portation routes during Russian colonization, linking the lumber and fur-trading industries to urban markets.

On Western Siberia's southern frontier, the Altai Mountain range provides a natural barrier to China. Mount Belukha, on the Kazakh border, is the highest point in this range at 14,783 feet. Two subsidiary ranges extend to the northwest around the heavily industrialized Kuznetsk Basin (Kuzbass).

The Western Siberian region is noted for winters that last as long as seven or eight months even in the more southerly zones. Temperatures range from minus 22° F. in the north, to minus 5° F. in the south. The summers are moderate, occasionally quite warm, with temperatures not usually exceeding 55° F. in the north and 68° F. in the south.

Most farming in Western Siberia takes place in the southern black earth regions shared with northern Kazakhstan. The Virgin Lands program established there in the 1950s successfully increased agricultural output for some years. (See Kazakhstan chapter, page 129.) Dry farming of spring wheat and corn, plus acreage for fodder and pasturage, provide the most common usage of arable land. A greater resource in Western Siberia is the coniferous forest that provides valuable timber and wood products.

By far the greatest wealth of Western Siberia is the rich oil, gas, and coal reserves found in many parts of the region. Coal has long been mined in the Kuznetsk Basin in the area of the Tom River. Oil was found beginning in the 1950s in several parts of Tiumen oblast (particularly in the great Vasiugan Swamp). Natural gas has more recently been discovered in the far north near the mouth of the Ob River and adjacent areas of the Arctic hinterland.

The Trans-Siberian Railroad (5,800 miles) provides the major means of transportation in Western Siberia with many secondary spurs augmenting the main line. Although river routes supplement the rail link, pipelines have been used extensively to transport oil and gas. Air transport continues to be vital for travel to more remote areas, such as the Arctic coast.

Eastern Siberia. Eastern Siberia extends from the Enisei River to the western frontier of the autonomous Sakha Republic (formerly the Iakut ASSR). This region of Siberia comprises primarily an elevated area called the Central Siberian Upland, augmented by numerous highland regions. Eastern Siberia, like Western Siberia, exhibits a pattern of climate, soil, and vegetation zones that begin with tundra in the frozen north and gradually change to taiga in the mountainous south. The zone of permafrost in this region descends to the northern border of Mongolia. The taiga zone here is extremely dense because of good drainage.

The Saian Mountain system, located west of Lake Baikal along the border with Mongolia, features peaks more than 11,000 feet high. The Iablonovy Range to the east of Baikal serves to divide rivers flowing to the Arctic from those flowing to the Pacific. Lesser mountain ranges are found to the west and northeast of Lake Baikal. In the far north, mountains on the Taimyr Peninsula along the Arctic Ocean fall within the tundra zone.

The major East Siberian river system, draining into the Arctic Ocean, is made up of the Enisei and its three main tributaries: the Angara, the Stony Tunguska, and the Lower Tunguska. These rivers provide Siberia with an immense potential for hydroelectric energy. The Angara River is the only outlet for Lake Baikal, the world's largest and deepest fresh water lake—approximately 400-miles long, 30-miles wide, and 4,250 feet deep. More than three hundred rivers flow into Lake Baikal.

Although little farming is done in Eastern Siberia, some spring wheat is planted in the southern regions. Grazing pastures for cattle, sheep, and goats are extensive and in the north reindeer herding is common. The greatest natural wealth of Eastern Siberia may be considered the heavily wooded lands that constitute more than one third of Russia's forest reserve. The conservation of these forested lands, along with those of Western Siberia, is vitally important to the world's ecological balance. Poorly planned forestry practices during the Soviet period polluted the waters of formerly pristine Lake Baikal with the wastes of wood-product factories.

Other natural resources abound in the Eastern Siberian region, most prominently coal. Coal deposits are found in many parts of Siberia and abundant reserves are assured far into the future. Gold, copper, and iron ore fields are also widespread.

The Far East. The Far East region is clearly the largest economic and administrative unit within the Russian Federation. Encompassing more than a quarter of Russian territory, this region extends from the area watered by the Lena River and its tributaries east to the Pacific Ocean, and from the Arctic Ocean south to the Russo-Chinese border. Including the Sakha Republic, the Kamchatka Peninsula, the Chukotsk Peninsula, the coast along the Sea of Okhotsk, and Sakhalin Island, the predominant landscape of the Far East is mountainous.

Most of the mountain ranges in the Far East are low in altitude, although they have an alpine appearance because of the northerly latitudes in which they are located. The Stanovoi Range in the southern reaches of the Sakha Republic divides the rivers of the area between those flowing to the Arctic and those extending to the Pacific. To the southeast of the Stanovoi lie smaller ranges. Parallel to the coast is the heavily timbered Sikhote-Alin Range. Across the water, the mountainous island of Sakhalin shows much volcanic activity. North of the Stanovoi Range, steep and rugged mountains cling to the coastline of the Sea of Okhotsk. Still farther north, highland areas have spread out in such a fashion that the entire remainder of the region is basically mountainous. The Verkhoiansk Range east of the valley of the Lena River leads to the Cherskii Range, where the heights are covered with tundra vegetation. From the Chukotsk Peninsula to the Kolyma Range farther south, the mountainous terrain extends onto the volcanic Kamchatka Peninsula. Of the more than one hundred volcanos found on Kamchatka, twenty or more are currently active, the highest being Mt. Kliuchevskaia (15,884 feet). Trailing off the southern tip of Kamchatka are the Kurils, a chain of islands formed by the tips of volcanic mountains.

The river systems of the Far East region are vitally important both as sources of hydroelectric power and as means of transport. Much has been done to take advantage of the short navigation periods of these Siberian rivers before they freeze during the winter months. Two major river systems drain the lands of the Far East. The Amur, second longest river in the Russian Federation, flows toward the Pacific from the region east of Lake Baikal (the Trans-Baikal). The Lena and its tribuaries, the Aldan and the Viliui, third longest river system in Russia, lie within the interior of the Far East region and flow toward the Arctic. The Olenek, Kolyma, Indigirka, and Iana rivers also empty into the Arctic. With the exception of the Amur, spring thaws in the headwater areas of these rivers bring widespread flooding to the more northerly river deltas that remain frozen much later in the year. One other river in the Far East, the Anadyr on the Chukotsk Peninsula, flows into the Bering Sea.

The climate of the Far East is similar to that of the rest of Siberia and generally exhibits the same arctic to subarctic temperature range. In fact, some of the lowest winter temperatures in the world have been noted in northern interior valleys of the Far East, specifically in the Iana river valley at Verkhoiansk where a minus 90° F.

was once recorded. Although these record low temperatures occur in the interior regions, winter along the Arctic and Pacific coasts can be even harsher because constant strong wind makes for a phenomenal windchill factor. Winter lasts from eleven months in the Chukotka area, six to eight months in the Amur basin, and seven to eight months on Sakhalin Island. Summers are short in the Far East, with a frost-free season of only forty-five days in some places. Local topographical conditions and solar radiation cause a marked rise in temperature in May, such that spring passes so quickly it is scarcely recognizable. On the coastal regions of the southeast, the climate is damp and foggy with frequent rain.

The northern zone of the Far East region, like the rest of Siberia, consists of tundra, and most of the soil lies on perennially frozen ground with poor drainage. South of this zone lies forest tundra, which gradually gives way to coniferous taiga. The taiga belt is relatively large, extending through twenty or more latitudes.

Agriculture has played a minor role in the economy of the Far East. Most of the arable land is used for grazing; crops are limited primarily to grains, soybeans, and sugar beets. Forestry products from the southern part of the region and Sakhalin Island are proving increasingly valuable. Reindeer herding is a common occupation for those who still live on the land. The Far East has also become the most important region in Russia for production of fish and fish products, especially along the Amur River and in the Sea of Okhotsk. Furs, once the primary focus of early Russian settlement, still constitute a limited economic resource for the region.

Important natural resources in the Far East region are the largely unexploited reserves of coal, iron ore, oil, and natural gas. Even more significant, however, are rich gold and diamond mines (the latter in the Sakha Republic), valuable sources of foreign currency. The region also holds tin, tungsten, mica, lead, and zinc.

The Trans-Siberian Railroad, built in the 1890s, continues to provide the region's major transportation system. Although the supplementary BAM (Baikal-Amur Mainline) north of the Trans-Siberian, was opened in 1984, it was built at considerable cost in labor and natural resources and has been plagued with problems. River and air transport complement the rail system.

Ethnic and Historical Background

Although Russians make up by far the largest percentage of the population (95 percent) in Siberia and the

Far East, dozens of smaller ethnic groups reside within the boundaries of this territory. In very few of the regions or autonomous units, however, do the indigenous peoples make up a majority of the population. The highest percentages of non-Russian population are in the Tuva Republic where 64.3 percent of the people are Tuvinian, and in the Sakha Republic where 33.4 percent of the people are Iakut or Sakha. One way of categorizing these non-Russian ethnic groups is on the basis of the language they speak. Four major language groups have been identified amongst Siberian inhabitants: 1) Paleo-Asiatic; 2) Uralic; 3) Altaic; 4) Indo-European.

Paleo-Asiatic languages are spoken by the indigenous population of Siberia. Their languages do not appear to be a part of any major language family. Called in Russian the "peoples of the north," these traditionally nomadic tribes hunted, fished, and gathered for a living. Those who bred reindeer followed their herds from place to place. The seminomadic tribes changed their residence twice a year, whereas the sedentary tribes lived in more permanent villages or towns.

Amongst the traditional reindeer-herding peoples who speak a Paleo-Asiatic language are the Chukchi (numbering approximately 14,000), the Koriak (8,000), the Eskimos (1,500), and the Iukagirs (800). These tribes all live in the Arctic region from the Kolyma River to the Bering Strait and from the Anadyr River as far south as the central portion of the Kamchatka Peninsula. Other tribal peoples in the Paleo-Asiatic category are the Itelmen (1,300) on Kamchatka, the Nivkh (4,400) of Sakhalin Island, and the Lower Amur people, formerly called Giliak.

Uralic languages are spoken by the Samoyedic peoples (Nenets, Selkup, and Nganasan) and the Ugrian peoples (Khant and Mansi). The Nenets (29,000) live in the Arctic tundra region east of the Ob river valley. The Selkup (3,500) live east of the Nenets near Tomsk; they were formerly known as the Ostiak-Samoyed. The Nganasan (860), whose name means "people," live in the tundra on the Taimyr Peninsula. The Khanti (21,000), in the Ob and Irtysh river valleys, are an Ugrian speaking tribe, as are the semi-nomadic Mansi (7,500), in the Tiumen oblast.

The Altaic-speaking tribes employ either a Tungusic, Turkic, or Mongolic language. The six main Tungusic tribes are 1) the nomadic Orok (1,200) on Sakhalin Island, some of whom were resettled on Hokkaido (Japan) alongside 1,500 Ainu after World War II; 2) the nomadic Evenk (27,500), formerly called Tungus, living along the Enisei River; 3) the nomadic Even (12,500) east of the Lena River along the Arctic coast as far as the Sea of Okhotsk and down into the Kamchatka Peninsula; 4) the Negidal; 5) the Nanai; and 6) the Udegei—the latter three being semi-sendentary hunters and fishers.

The most populous Turkic-speaking people of Siberia are the Sakha (328,000), who under the Soviet system had their own autonomous republic (Iakut ASSR), the capital of which is Iakutsk on the Lena River. The Sakha literary language is written in Cyrillic; their religion is syncretic Eastern Orthodox with overtones of shamanism. The reindeer-breeding Dolgan (5,000), who live in the tundra south of the Khatanga River, are also Turkic speaking.

Other Turkic-speaking tribes in the region are the Siberian Tatars living north of Kazakhstan on the southern edge of Western Siberia. Among these tribes are the Shor, the Khakass, the Altai of the Altai-Saian mountain region, the Tuvinian near the Mongolian border, and various groups of Kazakh nomads. The combined population of these primarily nomadic tribes is approximately 175,000.

A Mongolic language is spoken in Siberia by the Buriat people who live around Lake Baikal in the southern part of Eastern Siberia. They make up a large, formerly seminomadic tribe numbering approximately 353,000. The Buriats were also granted an autonomous republic (the Buriat Mongol ASSR) under the Soviet system. The Buriat literary language, earlier rendered in Old Mongolian, is now written in Cyrillic. Although subjected to secularizing pressures under Soviet rule, the Trans-Baikal Buriats maintain their religious ties with Buddhism.

One other indigenous group in Siberia is the Ket tribe living between the Ob and Enisei river valleys. They speak a unique language seemingly unrelated to any other and therefore have attracted the attention of historical linguists. Numbering less than 1,200 people, they too have followed the life of seminomadic hunters and fishers.

The Indo-European language group is represented in Siberia and the Far East by Slavs and other European people who settled in this area mainly as colonizers. Russians, Ukrainians, and Belarusians migrated eastward into Siberia as soon as it was incorporated into the Russian Empire in the latter half of the sixteenth century. German-speaking colonists arrived later in the nineteenth century. The Indo-European, particularly Russian, population dominates the urban centers of Siberia and the Far East.

Religions of Siberia and the Far East

Shamanism, an ancient form of belief dating perhaps from the Stone Age, has long been common among the indigenous peoples of Siberia. The word shaman is derived from the Tungusic word *saman* meaning "one who is excited." The Tungusic word is itself drawn from the Sanskrit *Sramana*, meaning "ascetic." Although shamanism has varied from tribe to tribe, all its manifestations feature a spirit helper or shaman who mediates between the visible and spiritual worlds. Shamans heal the sick by invoking a trance-like state; they also guide dead souls to the "other world," communicate between the living and dead, perform sacrificial rites to appease angry spirits, and carry out traditional tribal ceremonies.

With the settlement of Siberia by Europeans, the Russian Orthodox church attempted to convert native peoples to Christianity. Early imperial policy, dating from the reign of Peter the Great in the first quarter of the eighteenth century, required such conversion. The Khant and Mansi groups moved from their original homelands to avoid converting, but they could not escape for long. While ostensibly adopting Christianity, they continued to practice their shamanist religion well into the nineteenth century. The Sakha accepted Russian Orthodoxy through bribery and gifts, but they also continued to practice shamanism. Invariably the conversion process was paralleled by the retention of tribal religious practices.

In addition to Russian Orthodoxy, Buddhism spread north into Siberia from Mongolia. Buriat Mongols in the Lake Baikal region adopted the Buddhist religion in the eighteenth century and, as a result, were the only native Siberians to have a written language before 1917. Nineteenth-century Protestant missionaries from England, along with missionaries from the Russian Orthodox church, later made largely unsuccessful attempts to convert the Buriats to Christianity.

The Siberian Tatars meanwhile had adopted the religion of Islam. With the influx of Russian settlers, however, they began to lose their hunting grounds and traditional ways, eventually becoming quite impoverished. The process of intermarrying with the Christian Orthodox Russians followed, and many Tatars merged into the dominant culture.

In the 1920s, the new Soviet government banned shamanism. The drums and costumes of the shamans were confiscated and those who opposed the process were prosecuted. Soviet authorities accused the shamans of deceiving and cheating their own people in pursuit of riches. The shamans in general opposed the incursion of Slavic civilization and spoke against the development of schools, deeming them unnecessary to the traditional way of life. As the healers of native families and clans, they also felt displaced by the introduction of modern medical services. In order to defend themselves against Soviet bureaucrats, however, many shamans did learn to read and write. Buddhism was also affected by official Soviet atheism. The number of lamas in the autonomous Republic of Buriatiia declined and Buddhist monasteries were closed. Today, however, aspects of shamanism have survived alongside Russian Orthodoxy, Buddhism, and Islam.

The Russian Experience

According to the Russian Siberian chronicle literature, a Cossack mercenary, Ermak Timofeevich, led an army of several hundred Muscovite Russian loyalists against the Khanate of Sibir in the Ob River valley in 1581. By the fall of 1582, Ermak's forces defeated these Tatars and occupied the capital of Sibir (near the present-day city of Tobolsk). This campaign was the opening round in what became the ultimate Russian conquest of north Asia or Siberia. By 1605, Russians had spread as far as the Enisei, Lower and Stony Tunguska, and Angara rivers. By the 1640s they had reached the Sea of Okhotsk and the Pacific Ocean and soon established power in the Lake Baikal region also. Russia had crossed Siberia in about fifty years. The new land was treated as a single province and divided into nineteen districts ruled by a military governor.

A policy of building forts near strategic points on the river systems was implemented. Tiumen, Tobolsk, Tomsk, Iakutsk, Okhotsk, and Irkutsk were some of the first forts built at this time. These forts were generally built near native tribes in an attempt to discourage alliances between the indigenous peoples.

By the eighteenth century, Russian adventurers had begun to take an interest in Siberia for its vast wealth in furs, iron, gold, silver, and salt; traders and trappers exploited the region for profit. Russian peasants also were encouraged by the government to move to Siberia and work the land. Often accompanying or in advance of Russian settlement, Russian Orthodox missionaries were sent to convert the indigenous population to Christianity. Alongside Russian settlement came bureaucratic control, with local administrative officials maintaining order and collecting tribute from the local population. As small centers of settlement grew, bureaucratic and commercial interests expanded accordingly. During the eighteenth century, mining for copper, lead, silver, and iron ore was carried out in Western Siberia on the eastern slope of the Ural Mountains, as well as in the more southerly Altai mountain range and in the Trans-Baikal area. Despite these efforts to open up the region, Siberian natural resources in the nineteenth century remained relatively unexploited, even as the fur trade became less profitable.

The most ambitious modern effort to integrate the vast lands of Siberia with the European centers of Russian imperial power was the construction of the Trans-Siberian Railroad begun in 1891 and completed as far as Irkutsk in 1900. By the time of World War I, the Trans-Siberian track covered over 4,600 miles reaching from Moscow to Vladivostok on the Pacific. The railroad made the vast reaches of Siberia and the Far East more accessible for economic exploitation and launched major Russian and Ukrainian colonization of the region. While the rail line provided transport for Russian troops and thereby strengthened Russian military authority along its southern border, the Trans-Siberian line also led Russia to negotiate special rights of access through Manchuria, rights that ultimately brought Russia into conflict with Japanese imperial power in the Far East (the Russo-Japanese War of 1904–05).

At the end of the nineteenth century, a combination of peasant uprisings and revolutionary movements prompted the tsarist government to encourage increased colonial settlement and migration to Siberia. The consequent colonization, especially after peasants had become legally free to leave their communal holdings, reached as high as 750,000 per year by 1908. Even more dramatic, perhaps, was the fact that by 1910 Siberia had become agriculturally self-sufficient and even produced enough surplus for export. In contrast, the industrial development of Siberia during the tsarist period was minimal, and manufacturing often came to depend upon foreign investment.

In 1912, the Lena goldmine strike, basically a protest of working conditions, took place in Iakutiia. Government forces brutally crushed the revolt, but not before

further labor unrest had spread across Siberia. At the beginning of World War I, Siberians, both colonists and indigenous people, found themselves mobilized into the army.

Soviet Rule

Following the 1917 October Revolution, Irkutsk and Krasnoiarsk declared their initial loyalty to the new Bolshevik government, a loyalty that was matched in other regions of Siberia in the early months of 1918. Seeking to keep Russia in the war, however, the western allies supported the counterrevolutionary forces of the tsarist admiral Aleksandr Kolchak, a prominent leader during the Russian Civil War that followed the 1917 Revolution. Drawing upon a coalition of local citizens, Cossacks, and various anti-Bolshevik groups, Siberia soon became a center of counterrevolutionary activity. By June 1918, these forces, led by Admiral Kolchak and what came to be known as his White Army, overthrew the Bolshevik government in Siberia. In the months that followed, however, the White forces came under increasing challenge from both the Red Army and from sporadic guerilla activity. By 1921, the Bolsheviks had reestablished their power throughout most of Siberia and the Far East.

To make the administration of this large region more manageable, the new Soviet government divided Siberia into political-administrative units roughly based on the distribution of native ethnic groups. Autonomous regions were established for many of these indigenous peoples. These autonomous administrative regions varied in size and prestige all the way from the autonomous republic (not to be confused with a union republic), to the autonomous *oblast* (not to be confused with the purely administrative oblast), to the autonomous *okrug*. Although always subordinate to Moscow, autonomous republics had their own formal constitutions. Since the late 1980s, the importance of these autonomous divisions, and of the ethnic homelands they represent, has been reinforced by their own declarations of sovereignty and independence. Of the twenty-one republics now forming part of the Russian Federation, five are in Siberia—Altai, Buriatiia, Khakassiia, Sakha, and Tuva. Declarations of sovereignty have been forthcoming not only from all five of these republics, but also from several of the other formerly autonomous subdivisions.

Occasionally inspired by grandiose engineering plans, Soviet leaders have sought to exploit the rich resources of Siberia, frequently without regard to potential environmental damage. In the name of modernization and development, major efforts have been launched to explore for mineral deposits, develop local forest and related industries, and otherwise extract the natural resources of the vast Siberian territory. The first Soviet Five Year Plan (1928–32) mandated the construction of giant hydroelectric plants and a number of metallurgical plants as well. The Kuznetsk coal basin in Western Siberia was developed and iron ore deposits were discovered nearby. In the 1930s, on the lower Amur River, huge industrial complexes and power stations were built, and military installations now dot the Far East. Not all large-scale development plans have been carried through to completion. One of the more controversial plans, noted later, called for the massive diversion southward of northerly flowing Siberian rivers for the purpose of irrigating the drier fields and cotton-growing regions of Kazakhstan and Central Asia.

During World War II, industrial plants were converted to military production and to the manufacture of tanks and other products needed for the war. Factories in European Russia were moved to the Urals and to Siberia, remaining there after the war's end. Despite the difficulty of access and the fragile terrain, ambitious efforts were renewed in the postwar period to exploit Siberia's large mineral deposits, hydroelectric potential, forest preserves, and oil and natural gas resources. Dams and power plants harnessed the energy of the region's many rivers, most notably the large plant in Krasnoiarsk. Wood processing factories were built in Bratsk, diamonds were mined in Iakutiia, and agricultural machinery was produced in the Altai province. Squirrels, polar fox, ermine, and sable supplied the fur industry. Oil and natural gas were extracted and shipped via a large pipeline across the Urals to Moscow and Leningrad.

During Nikita Khrushchev's leadership in the 1950s and early 1960s, greater investment in agriculture was proposed, and the "virgin lands" of southern Siberia and northern Kazakhstan were marked for grain production. Yields reached their peak in 1956, but totals thereafter declined due to poor cultivation methods, for the farms did not rotate crops or let the land lie fallow.

Plans for a new line to supplement the Trans-Siberian Railroad were mapped in the early 1970s. The BAM (Baikal-Amur Mainline) railway line is located over five-hundred miles from Russia's southern boundary, unlike the Trans-Siberian, which runs just fifty miles above the border with China. Although track-laying for the BAM (2,250 miles) was completed in 1984 from Bratsk to Komsomolsk near the Pacific coast and traversing the permafrost region north of Lake Baikal, the line continues to face major operational problems related to the frozen soil it crosses, as well as to the seven mountain ranges through which it has had to be tunneled.

Siberia's "Special" Purpose

In addition to the explorers, traders, settlers, and others who gravitated to Siberia in ever-increasing numbers during the nineteenth and twentieth centuries, one group of "immigrants" represented, in an entirely different way, the place of Siberia in Russian history. These were the prisoners and exiled subjects who were unwilling to go along with the policies of the tsarist or Soviet systems. In the days of the tsars, Siberia was first used as a place of exile for political prisoners. This practice was continued by Stalin, under whose arbitrary leadership hundreds of thousands of people termed "anti-social" were sent to prison camps located primarily in Siberia. The gulag (a Russian acronym for "Chief Administration of Corrective Labor Camps"), written about so movingly by Soviet writers, such as Aleksandr Solzhenitsyn in *The Gulag Archipelago*, was a vast system of work camps and prisons housing the innocent victims of Soviet rule. From peasants unwilling to accept collectivization, to political rivals, to writers, religious believers, and returning Soviet prisoners of war—all were swept off to the camps, in some cases for perpetually renewable terms of imprisonment. The gulag supplied endless workers to exploit the economic riches of the tundra and taiga, many of them giving their lives in the process. According to Solzhenitsyn, between 13 and 25 million people perished in the gulag.

Organized in the 1930s and run initially by the NKVD, a precursor of the KGB, the center for one area of camps in the Far East was at Magadan on the Sea of Okhotsk. Magadan served as a transit point for prisoners sent to work in the gold mines located in the frigid climate of the Kolyma region. Another Siberian area worked by prisoners was the Taimyr Peninsula at Norilsk where thousands labored in another Arctic setting to develop Soviet mining interests.

Contemporary Issues

Modernization and the Indigenous Peoples of Siberia

As in the European settlement of the United States, the interests and way of life of indigenous, native populations have been threatened in the Russian settlement of Siberia. Whether it be the native peoples of North America or the small nations of the Siberian north, the advance of modern, industrial society has posed for the indigenous population the same difficult alternatives. These alternatives range from forced assimilation into the majority society, to uneasy accommodation at the margins of society, to conscious preservation of traditional culture. What makes these alternatives so painful for the indigenous minorities, however, is that they are posed in a context in which the majority has colonized the territory and now claims it as its own.

To frame the question in this way, however, is already to challenge those Soviet observers who have maintained that the Siberian experience has actually been very different from its American counterpart. According to this Soviet view, the Native Americans suffered near genocidal losses of population from European diseases, armed conflict with colonists, restrictions in location, and loss of herds. On the contrary, Russian nineteenth- and twentieth-century settlement did not result in native depopulation. Moreover, in those regions where natural resources such as oil or diamonds are extracted, the native population has been able to secure gainful employment. Finally, unlike their American counterparts, Russian settlers have not, according to this view, hesitated to intermarry with the local indigenous population. In the end, the argument is that the European settlement of America was associated with a pattern of violent domination and expropriation of land and resources, whereas the Russian settlement of Siberia has been humane and understanding.

The debate over modern Siberian development and its impact upon the small nations of the north may now be addressed more openly in a way hardly imaginable a decade ago before the advent of glasnost. In this debate, the basic demographic realities provide an appropriate starting point. These demographics weigh heavily against the indigenous peoples of Siberia and the Far East. Only in the small Republic of Tuva does the native population exceed that of the Russian settlers. In the Buriat Republic,

the Buriats comprise only about one-fourth of the total population. In the Sakha (Iakut) Republic, the Sakha comprise about one-third the total population. Similarly, in the Altai Republic, the Altai comprise no more than one-third of the population. In other regions of the more sparsely populated north, as for example among the Evenk, Nenets, Khant, Mansi, and Chukchi, the native population comprises a much smaller fraction of the total, rarely more than 10 percent. Given the high concentration of Slavic population in the larger urban centers, Siberia has now become a land where indigenous people operate as minorities within a dominant Russian culture.

While the successive Russian and Soviet governments have regarded their efforts as beneficial to the small nations of the north, the fact is that these regimes fundamentally sought to alter the basic nomadic patterns of the northern reindeer herders, fishers, and hunters. In the tsarist period, "ownership" of reindeer herds passed from the indigenous people to the more wealthy Russian adventurers and merchants. In the Stalinist and post-World War II periods, forced collectivization and consolidation of settlements effectively took the marketing of hunted game out of the hands of local people and placed it in the hands of Party bureaucrats. The results have been devastating to those northern peoples who have lived for centuries by reindeer herding, fishing, and hunting. There have been dire predictions that unless management of the once lucrative reindeer herding is returned to the native tribes, reindeer herds will be overkilled and lost, and the hunting and grazing skills of the next generation will pass away. Estimates have been made that no more than 180,000 Paleo-Asiatic indigenous peoples still inhabit northern Siberia (less than the Native American population of Arizona alone).

Alongside its threat to traditional nomadic hunting, herding, and fishing patterns, the state has also been intrusive with respect to the family life and religious patterns of local northern peoples. Committed to mass literacy, the Soviet state in the 1920s established central bases in the Siberian north for the introduction of formal schooling, literacy, and civilization. These cultural bases (also called "Red Tents") became the locations for boarding schools that drew young native children away from their families, trained them in Russian language and culture, and established the authority of Soviet institutions. As a result of these boarding schools, according to critics, young native students were unable to be trained in basic family customs, including survival skills necessary for traditional life in the north. The study of native languages was also largely abandoned by young people who attended the boarding schools.

As noted earlier, Soviet authorities also sought, without complete success, to eliminate the shamans from local village life. This intrusion into local beliefs and practices was not coupled with any provision for alternative health care or social services. The consequent disruptions of local family patterns have, in the view of some, led to the widespread abuse of alcohol now afflicting many Siberian northern peoples. Prior to Russian settlement in Siberia, the small nations of the north had never tasted alcohol. (On these and other observations regarding the breakdown of local indigenous culture, see several northern writers quoted internally in Kathleen Mihalisko, "Discontent in Taiga and Tundra," *Radio Liberty Research*, 7 July 1988.) It has been estimated that, since World War II, the life expectancy for indigenous northern peoples of Siberia has dropped by more than 10 years (45 for men, 55 for women).

Mounting fears over the fate of the Paleo-Asiatic peoples of Siberia and the Far East led the former Soviet State Commission for Arctic Affairs (formed in 1988) to broach the idea of establishing "zones of restricted economic activity," clearly a euphemism for something similar to the American "reservation." A frequently quoted Evenk writer, Alitet Nemtushkin, who has aired publicly his ecological concerns over both oil and gas exploration and the plans for yet further hydroelectric power stations, has added his strong support to the proposal for Siberian "reservations" (quoted in Kathleen Mihalisko, "North American-Style Native Reservations in the Soviet North?" *Report on the USSR*, 21 July 1989). From the point of view of some of these northern peoples who seek to recover a sense of their own nomadic traditions, the establishment of reservations—however negative the term may be considered in North America—can even be viewed as a positive force for arresting the physical, cultural, and ecological threats to the small northern nations of Siberia.

Although these smaller nations are peculiarly vulnerable to modern industrialization, a related set of concerns in the more southerly Republic of Tuva led to public demonstrations and violence directed against the Russian population. The Tuvinians, a Turkic-speaking Buddhist

people numbering more than 200,000 constitute approximately two-thirds of the population of the Tuva Republic. (Russians comprise approximately one-third of the population of Tuva.) The large post-World War II Slavic migration into Tuva was benefited by an industrialization policy that did little to assist the underemployed and more rural Tuvinians. Riots erupted in 1990, triggered by a dance-floor conflict between Tuvinian and Slavic youth. The violence spread in May 1990 to Kyzyl, the capital of Tuva, where a young person was murdered for failing to answer a question in Tuvinian. Leaflets calling for a Slavic exodus from Tuva led to widespread Russian uneasiness and substantial departures. Eventually troops from the Soviet Ministry of Internal Affairs were called in to Tuva, a sign of how seriously this attack upon Russians and other Slavs was taken in Moscow. Subsequent declarations of Tuvinian sovereignty have only confirmed the potentially explosive interethnic friction between Slavs and the indigenous populations, particularly in more southerly regions of greater Siberia.

Not unlike the Republic of Tuva, the Republic of Sakha (formerly Iakutiia) has also been the scene of independence movements directed against Russian political and economic authority. The leadership of the Sakha Republic has used such movements effectively to challenge the Russian Federation's monopoly on marketing the republic's diamond reserves. In 1992 an agreement was reached whereby a jointly held Russian/Sakha stockholding company would control all diamond production and sales. According to this agreement, the Sakha Republic would keep 20 percent of the diamonds it produces, as well as 45 percent of all hard currency earnings derived from foreign diamond sales. There remain unreconciled Sakha nationals who decry the diamond mining and its impact upon traditional Sakha pastoral ways of life. Others, including the republic's old-style political leadership, see the new Russian-Sakha profit-sharing arrangements as a significant improvement on earlier Russian-Iakut relations, especially the prospect of sharing in the estimated $1.4 billion annual diamond sales exported through the DeBeers South African diamond monopoly. For now, the Sakha diamond case, unlike the problems in Tuva, suggests that the Russian Federation can perhaps continue to win local support by sharing the monopoly mineral rights it formerly controlled. Whether such concessions will guarantee lasting Russian ties with a Siberian native population rediscovering its own ethnic and shamanist religious traditions remains to be seen.

From the indigenous Arctic peoples to the sovereign republics of Sakha and Tuva, the tension between Russian industrialization and natural resource exploitation, on the one hand, and traditional non-Russian rural, nomadic cultures, on the other, has become one of the greatest forces for conflict in contemporary Siberia.

Ecological Compromises in Modern Siberia

A second major dilemma faces those who would seek to exploit the rich natural resources of Siberia—namely, the long-term ecological well-being of Siberia and the Far East can too readily be damaged by bad planning and short-term thinking. The signs of such damage are today strewn across the land, with yet further dangers to the fragile Siberian environment clearly in the offing.

As a resource-rich frontier region, Siberia now provides an inordinate share of the Russian Federation's overall natural wealth. More than 60 percent of Russian mining production takes place in Siberia; more than 50 percent of its fuel production; nearly 40 percent of its production of nonferrous metals; and more than one-third of its timber, wood, and paper-product production. Yet, less than 25 percent of the Russian Federation's population lives in Siberia and the Far East. Such exploitation of Siberian natural resources, including the current drive for foreign investment to access and market Siberian oil, natural gas, and timber, has become an absolutely essential part of the overall Russian economy. Yet, this exploitation has come with a great price, so much so that the ecological future of Siberia and the Far East now hangs in the balance.

No area exemplifies the issue of ecological compromise in Siberia as strongly as the use and misuse of water resources. The northward-flowing rivers of Western and Eastern Siberia provide an abundant source of water for the region. In their effort to harness these water resources, however, Soviet engineers have put at risk large parts of northern Siberia. A case in point has been the construction of large dams and hydroelectric power projects now dotting the Siberian landscape. By limiting the normal northward flow of river waters, these projects have in some instances affected the salinity of river deltas, in turn affecting the grazing habits and local herding of reindeer and other Arctic game animals.

More complicated has been the secondary impact of the hydroelectric stations. Launched early in the Soviet era, these power plants provided electrical capacity be- yond the needs of the sparsely populated Siberian tundra and taiga. In a classic case of "cart before the horse," the hydroelectric plants then became the occasion for transferring heavy industry to use the available power resources. Movement of industry into this cold, fragile Siberian climate involved further migration of population into regions with limited infrastructure. The movement of industry into artificially created Siberian urban communities led to fundamental environmental and health problems related to the Siberian climate. Weather extremes in winter, combined with normal industrial pollutants, have created serious temperature inversions and caustic air pollution that endanger the health of local residents. Even basic provisions for waste disposal have not always met elementary health standards. At stake in the debate over the construction of additional dams and hydroelectric power stations is the question of how much priority to give to the industrial and urban development of Siberia. This issue began to be discussed at higher policy-making levels only during the leadership of Soviet First Party Secretary Mikhail Gorbachev (1985–91).

In the debate on Siberian water, the region's fledgling environmental movement found its first tentative victory in the so-called Siberian Rivers Diversion Project. The Siberian Rivers Project, drawn up by an army of Soviet hydroelectrical engineers, sought to divert part of the flow of the Ob and Irtysh rivers southward into Kazakhstan to augment the Syr Darya and Amu Darya rivers and irrigate the Central Asian cotton fields. The appeal of this engineering plan was that it would also provide some additional water to replenish the disappearing Aral Sea. Environmental critics of the plan, however, began to note the potentially dangerous impact of the project upon the Ob-Irtysh river valley. Not only would fishing, timber rafting, and navigation be affected, but the reduced flows would potentially affect the permafrost conditions of northern Arctic regions. In the end, perhaps the most damaging evidence came from those who projected that the reduced flows into the Arctic Ocean would increase the ocean's salinity, melting parts of the polar ice cap. In short, an impressive engineering plan, one of many such grandiose ideas proposed for Siberia, ended up having potential implications of truly global proportions. The Siberian Rivers Diversion Project appears to have been shelved during the Gorbachev years, but the plan occasionally has resurfaced, fueled by land reclamation and water resource engineers who continue to hold posts in Russian governmental ministries.

Related to the use and misuse of water resources is the ongoing pollution of Lake Baikal, the world's deepest lake and, by volume, the world's largest body of fresh water. Lake Baikal, because of its unique ecosystem—it contains numerous underwater species that exist nowhere else in the world—has become a focal point of international attention from marine biologists, ecologists, and concerned environmental activists. While there is no single source of pollutants flowing into Lake Baikal, the most serious and easily identifiable culprits are the forest and wood-products industries located along streams and rivers flowing into the lake. Of these industries, the notorious Baikal Pulp and Paper Combine is the worst. Forced to make plans for conversion into a furniture manufacturing plant by 1993, the Combine continues to exist. Concern for workers disaffected by closure or conversion has held up the process, as have the conflicting signals of governmental ministries. Despite the hundreds of specialists who have focused in some way or other upon the pollution of Lake Baikal, there still seems to be no comprehensive assessment of the sources of the lake's pollution, nor any clear sense of the damages inflicted. (See Zeev Wolfson, "Anarchy Mirrored in Lake Baikal," *Report on the USSR*, 26 May 1989.)

Related to the Baikal issue, forestry remains one of the most environmentally sensitive issues confronting Siberia. Possessing the largest coniferous forest in the world, an invaluable resource offsetting potential global warming, Siberia now must respond to contending interests covetous of these resources. On the one hand, these forest reserves hold great potential for revenue. International lumbering companies are already well represented in Russia and along with local combines are seeking to utilize the forests for commercial gain. The Russian Federation and the local Siberian economies desperately need this revenue from the forest industry. At the same time, in the present chaotic state of the Russian economy there is virtually no way of establishing what the real value of these forest reserves is. While international corporations may seek to exploit this chaos to secure undervalued forest products, the fear persists that widescale deforestation could compromise global environmental interests.

An indication of how unprepared Siberia is for the debate between environmental and economic interests can be seen in the region's forest fire policies. Outfitted with the largest aerial fire-fighting force in the world, Russian forest rangers confront a bewildering conflict over policy—or absence of policy—that reflects the fundamental dilemma over how best to evaluate the Siberian forest reserves. In principle, the Russian aerial firefighters are committed to putting out all fires, but in practice the control of fire over such a vast region is impossible.

Although the problem of establishing market value is not so great in the area of mining and oil drilling, associated environmental and occupational problems are just as troubling. Western and Eastern Siberia account for more than 70 percent of all oil drilled, more than 85 percent of all natural gas extracted, and more than 60 percent of all coal mined in the Russian Federation. Yet, environmental safeguards are woefully lacking. In Western Siberia alone it is estimated that "one million tons of oil are spilled annually onto the territory of Tiumen and Tomsk oblasts" (Mihalisko, "North American-Style Reservations"). The strip mining of coal in the Siberian Kuzbass has left large swaths of territory denuded and unfit for habitation.

For workers in these industries, the effort to extract natural resources at minimal cost has yielded a shocking set of working conditions that violate elementary safety standards. Responding to these conditions and to the absence of consumer goods and basic infrastructure in the western Siberian mining towns of the Kuzbass, local coal miners in July 1989 struck the Sheviakov mine. They presented a list of 42 demands. These included safety concerns, provisions for longer vacations, ultimatums for more and better consumer goods (e.g., a demand for eighty grams of soap each month for each worker), further demands for better infrastructure (one mining community complained about having running water only two hours a day), and even political appeals for the independence of their mine and for local leadership on environmental issues. Not only did the strike extend to adjacent mining towns of the Kuzbass, affecting some 150,000 workers and enormous productive capacities, it also spread to the Ukrainian Donets coal mining region. Although the Soviet authorities ultimately sought to resolve the strike by providing higher salaries and seeking to guarantee access to consumer goods, the long-term problems remain in Siberian society. One of the ironies in the former Soviet Union, with its ideological commitment to the advancement of the proletariat, was the exploitative mining practices undertaken at the expense of workers.

The environmental crises and the grievances of local workers affect not only the indigenous native population of Siberia, but also Siberian-born Russians who now consider Siberia their homeland. The talented Russian writer Valentin Rasputin has become a champion of Lake Baikal and has written widely on Siberian environmental concerns. Out of a common commitment to the environment there is the potential for alliance between indigenous peoples of Siberia and the far more numerous Slavic settlers. The long-term problem of coordinating economic development with respect for the fragile environment remains as much a dilemma for Russian Siberia as for Siberia's original native peoples.

Siberia and Its Neighbors

Siberia borders Kazakhstan, Mongolia, North Korea, and China to the south; Japan on the Pacific; and Alaska in the far northeast. The southern borders, while not without occasional incident, have been relatively quiet. Nevertheless, the border with China at the Amur River has long been a sore point in Russian-Chinese relations, the Chinese believing that the "unequal" treaties ending World War II violated their interests. In the case of the Russian-Mongolian border, modern Trans-Baikal Buriat traditions are rooted in a Mongolic language and Buddhist religious practice, thus making for natural ties between the Buriat Republic and Mongolia. Travel between the two republics is now possible in the more open atmosphere operating in both regions.

The most troublesome current diplomatic relationship confronting the region of Siberia and the Far East is that between Russia and Japan. Although both Soviet leader Mikhail Gorbachev and Russian President Boris Yeltsin traveled to Japan in the 1990s, the normalization of Russian-Japanese relations has foundered on the basic issue of the Kuril Islands. The Kuril Islands lie south of the Kamchatka Peninsula and north of the main Japanese islands.

The recent history of the Russian-Japanese dispute over these islands dates to World War II. At the Yalta conference, the Soviet Union was promised possession of the Kuril Islands in return for entering the Pacific war against Japan. Japan has never accepted the loss of the Kuril chain, particularly the four southernmost islands that are referred to in Japan as the "Northern Territories."

Despite the longstanding reluctance of the Soviet Union to reconsider any of the post-World War II peace terms, the assumption to power of Mikhail Gorbachev in the 1980s brought a fresh desire to relax tensions in Asia. For a time it appeared as though the Soviet authorities might wish to arrange a negotiated settlement regarding some of the southernmost islands in return for Japanese diplomatic support and foreign investment in the development of Siberian natural resources. The subsequent cancellation by Boris Yeltsin of his second visit to Japan and the Russian nationalist reaction against any concessions on the Kuril Islands seem, for the time being, to have closed the opportunity for renegotiation of the conflict. For Japan, which has taken a consistently hard-line position insisting on full sovereignty over all four of the southern Kurils, satisfactory resolution of the contending claims remains a prerequisite for full normalization of relations with the Russian Federation.

For the far northeastern peninsula of Chukotka, the most dramatic development in neighborly relations has been the opening of direct flights between the regional center of Provideniia and Alaska. Initially started for the purpose of allowing relatives on either side of the Bering Strait to visit each other—something that had been impossible since the 1930s—flights can now be chartered between Chukotka and Nome, among other Alaskan cities. Regularly scheduled airline passenger service between major ports of call in Alaska and the Russian Far East is now possible.

Renewed travel opportunities between the Far East and Alaska, as well as the Pacific Northwest, point to the potential for expanded American, as well as Japanese, trade with resource-rich Siberia. Such travel is also a mark of the dramatic relaxation of East-West tensions that has occurred in the region. Still heavily fortified by military installations, the Russian Far East is nevertheless open to international trade and commerce in an atmosphere unrecognizable a mere decade ago when Soviet forces shot down a Korean passenger airliner that had strayed into Soviet air space.

Part Two

Belarus, Moldova, and Ukraine

INTRODUCTION

While the Russian Federation is clearly the largest and most heavily populated successor state to the Soviet Union, there are, in addition to the Baltic republics, three other newly independent European states of the former USSR—Belarus, Moldova, and Ukarine. Belarus and Ukraine take their names from the two Eastern Slavic peoples who inhabit these republics—Belarusians and Ukrainians. Moldova, which borders the Balkan state of Romania, takes its name from the Moldovan (or Moldavian) people whose Romance language is virtually indistinguishable from that of modern Romanian.

These European republics were first incorporated into the Russian Empire over the course of a two-hundred year period from the early seventeenth to the nineteenth centuries. While parts of Ukraine were incorporated into the Muscovite Empire in the sixteenth century, the lands of the Black Sea coastal areas and those lands west of the Dnieper River were annexed from the Crimean Khanate and the Polish-Lithuanian Commonwealth in the eighteenth century. Full incorporation of Ukraine into the Russian Empire awaited institutional changes of the later eighteenth and early nineteenth centuries.

Belarus was annexed by the Russian Empire during the partitions of Poland in the last third of the eighteenth century. Moldova, known as Bessarabia at that time, was then part of the Ottoman Empire. The annexation of Bessarabia first brought the lands of Moldova into the Russian Empire in 1812. Following World War I, parts of western Ukraine and Belarus again became a part of Polish territory, and Moldova rejoined Romania. The present borders of these three European republics were established by the Soviet Union at the end of World War II, with the exception of the Crimean Peninsula, which was transferred from the Russian to the Ukrainian Soviet Republic in 1954.

Although the Belarusian, Ukrainian, and Moldovan nations have placed their own cultural stamp upon their newly independent states, there continues to be a large Russian minority in each of these three republics. Moreover, the lands west of the Dnieper River constituted the traditional center of Jewish settlement during the centuries of the Polish-Lithuanian Commonwealth. Following Russian incorporation of the area, Jewish settlement was restricted to these lands, which came to be called the "Pale of Settlement."

Heavily industrialized during the Soviet era, each of these republics has subsequently experienced environmental and health crises in the modern period. Along with other parts of Eastern Europe and the Baltic region, these European republics experienced the worst of the impact of the Chernobyl nuclear reactor explosion in 1986. The Chernobyl plant is situated near the Ukrainian-Belarusian border.

Two of the most troubling border disputes confronting the former Soviet republics have broken out in this region. In the case of Ukraine, the status of the Crimean Peninsula remains a source of conflict between the Russian Federation and Ukraine, as does the disposition of the Black Sea naval fleet. With respect to Moldova, a dissenting Russian minority has sought to claim sovereignty over the slice of land north and east of the Dniester River, calling the region the "Trans-Dniester Republic." This trans-Dniester border dispute, yet to be resolved, has brought open fighting and violence to a region just five-hundred miles from the center of Europe.

Bibliography

Batalden, Stephen K., ed. *Seeking God: The Recovery of Religious Identity in Russia, Ukraine, and Georgia.* DeKalb: Northern Illinois University Press, 1993.

Bociurkiw, Bohdan. *Ukrainian Churches under Soviet Rule: Two Case Studies.* Cambridge, MA: Harvard Ukrainian Research Institute, 1984.

Bruchis, Michael. *Nations, Nationalities, People: A Study of the Nationalities Policy of the Communist Party in Soviet Moldavia.* Boulder, CO: East European Monographs, distributed by Columbia University Press, 1984.

Conquest, Robert. *The Harvest of Sorrow: Soviet Collectivization and the Terror-Famine.* New York: Oxford University Press, 1986.

———.*Man-Made Famine in Ukraine.* Edmonton, Alberta: University of Toronto Press, 1986.

Dima, Nicholas. *From Moldavia to Moldova: The Soviet-Romanian Territorial Dispute.* Boulder, CO: East European Monographs, distributed by Columbia University Press, 1991.

Dolot, Mirom. *Execution by Hunger: The Hidden Holocaust.* New York: W. W. Norton, 1985.

Gross, Jan Tomasz. *Revolution from Abroad: The Soviet Conquest of Poland's Western Ukraine and Western Belorussia.* Princeton, NJ: Princeton University Press, 1988.

Horak, Stephan M., ed. *Guide to the Study of the Soviet Nationalities: Non-Russian Peoples of the USSR.* Littleton, CO: Libraries Unlimited, Inc., 1982.

Hosking, Geoffrey, ed. *Church, Nation and State in Russia and Ukraine.* Basingstoke, England: Macmillan, 1991.

Hrushevsky, Michael. *A History of Ukraine.* New Haven, CT: Yale University Press, 1941.

Jewsbury, George F. *The Russian Annexation of Bessarabia, 1774–1828: A Study of Imperial Expansion.* Boulder, CO: East European Quarterly, distributed by Columbia University Press, 1976.

Judge, Edward, H. *Easter in Kishinev: Anatomy of a Pogrom.* New York: New York University Press, 1992.

Kipel, Vitaut and Zora, eds. *Byelorussian Statehood: Reader and Bibliography.* New York: Byelorussian Institute of Arts and Sciences, 1988.

Kohut, Zenon E. *Russian Centralism and Ukrainian Autonomy: Imperial Absorption of the Hetmanate, 1760s–1830s.* Cambridge, MA: Harvard Ukrainian Research Institute, 1988.

Levin, Nora. *The Jews in the Soviet Union Since 1917: Paradox of Survival.* 2 vols. New York: New York University Press, 1988.

Marples, David R. *Chernobyl and Nuclear Power in the USSR.* New York: St. Martin's Press, 1986.

———. *Ukraine Under Perestroika: Ecology, Economics and the Workers' Revolt.* London: Macmillan, in association with the Radio Free Europe/Radio Liberty Research Institute, 1991.

RFE/RL Research Report, 1992–. This publication of Radio Free Europe/Radio Liberty was formerly titled *Radio Liberty Research Bulletin* (through 1988) and *Report on the USSR* (1989–1991). Weekly

Rudnytsky, Ivan L. *Essays in Modern Ukrainian History.* Edmonton: Canadian Institute of Ukrainian Studies, 1987.

———., ed. *Rethinking Ukrainian History.* Edmonton: Canadian Institute of Ukrainian Studies, 1981.

Solchanyk, Roman, ed. *Ukraine: From Chernobyl' to Sovereignty. A Collection of Interviews.* London: Macmillan in association with the RFE/RL Research Institute, 1992.

———.Solchanyk, Roman, ed. *Ukraine Under Perestroika: Politics, Religion and the National Question.* London: Macmillan, in association with the Radio Free Europe/Radio Liberty Research Institute, 1991.

Ukraine: A Concise Encyclopedia. 2 vols. Prepared by the Shevchenko Scientific Society. Toronto: Toronto University Press, 1963–71.

Vakar, Nicholas P. *Belorussia: The Making of a Nation, A Case Study.* Cambridge, MA: Harvard University Press, 1956.

Wexler, Paul N. *Purism and Language: A Study in Modern Ukrainian and Belorussian Nationalism, 1840–1967.* Bloomington, IN: Indiana University Press, 1974.

Wilkinson, William. *An Account of the Principalities of Wallachia and Moldavia.* New York: Arno Press, 1971.

Wixman, Ronald. *The Peoples of the USSR: An Ethnographic Handbook.* Armond, NY: M. E. Sharpe, 1984.

Belarus, Moldova, and Ukraine

BELARUS

Statistical Profile

Demography

Population: 10,152,000
Ethnic population:

Belarusian	7,905,000	77.9%
Russian	1,342,000	13.2%
Polish	418,000	4.1%
Ukrainian	291,000	2.9%
Jewish	112,000	1.1%
Other	84,000	0.8%

Historical religious tradition:

Christianity	98.1%

Population by age:

Age	Total	Males	Females
0–4	8.4%	4.3%	4.1%
5–9	7.8%	4.0%	3.8%
10–14	7.3%	3.7%	3.6%
15–19	7.5%	3.7%	3.8%
20–24	8.1%	4.1%	4.0%
25–29	8.7%	4.4%	4.3%
30–34	7.6%	3.8%	3.8%
35–39	6.8%	3.4%	3.4%
40–44	4.2%	2.0%	2.2%
45–49	6.6%	3.1%	3.5%
50–54	6.2%	2.8%	3.4%
55–59	6.3%	2.8%	3.5%
60–64	5.0%	1.8%	3.2%
65–69	2.7%	0.9%	1.8%
70–	6.8%	1.9%	4.9%

Male/Female ratio: 46.7% male/53.3% female
Rural/Urban population: 32.9% rural/67.1% urban
Growth over time, 1979–91: 7.3%
Population density: 128.0 persons/sq mi

Politics/Government

Date of independence declaration: 26 August 1991
Major urban centers and populations:

Minsk (Mensk)	1,612,000
Homyel (Gomel)	500,000
Mahilyow (Mogilev)	356,000
Vitsyebsk (Vitebsk)	350,000
Hrodna (Grodno)	270,000
Brest	258,000
Babruysk (Bobruisk)	223,000
Baranavichy (Baranovichi)	159,000
Barysaw (Borisov)	144,000
Orsha	123,000
Pinsk	119,000
Mazyr (Mozyr)	101,000

Autonomous areas: none

Education

Level of education for persons over 15:

completed higher level education	10.8%
completed secondary education	49.4%
incomplete secondary education	16.8%

Number of higher education institutions: 33 (188,600 students)
Major institutions of higher education and enrollment:

Minsk:

Polytechnic Institute	22,500
State University	18,700
Technological Institute	5,000
State Pedagogical Institute of Foreign Languages	3,000
State Conservatory	855

Brest:

Polytechnic Institute	1,900

Homyel:

State University	7,000

Hrodna:

State University	6,200
Agricultural Institute	3,000

Mahilyow:

Mechanical Engineering Institute	4,000

Vitsyebsk:

Technological Institute of Light Industry	3,500

Socioeconomic Indicators

> **Birthrate:** 13.9/1,000
> **Infant mortality:** 11.9/1,000 live births
> **Average life expectancy:** 71.3 (males, 66.4; females, 75.9)
> **Average family size:** 3.2
> **Hospital beds per 10,000 persons:** 132.3
> **Production of electrical energy:** 3,850 kwh/person
> **Length of rail lines:** 3,453 mi
> **Length of highways:** 60,884 mi

Physical/Territorial/Geopolitical Features

> **Area:** 80,134 sq mi (.9% of USSR total)

Land use:

Cultivated	29%
Pasture	9%

Highest elevation: 1,122 ft. (Mt. Dzerzhin)
Rainfall: 24 inches/year
Temperature: average in winter 24° F in the southwest, 18° F in the northeast; lowest temperature: -42° F. Average in summer 63° F in the north, 66° F in the south; highest temperature: 99° F.
Principal products: grain, flax, sugar beets, potatoes, dairy cattle, swine; agricultural machinery, motor vehicles, chemicals, textiles, food processing, forestry, peat
Per capita GNP (1991): $3,110.

Sources

"Belorusskaia sovetskaia sotsialisticheskaia respublika," *Bol'shaia sovetskaia entsiklopediia* (Moskow, 1977); *Narodnoe khoziaistvo SSSR v 1990g.* (Moscow, 1991); *Naselenie SSSR* (1989); Matthew J. Sagers, "News Notes. Iron and Steel," *Soviet Geography* 30 (May 1989): 397-434; Lee Schwartz, "USSR Nationality Redistribution by Republic, 1979-1989: From Published Results of the 1989 All-Union Census," *Soviet Geography* 32 (April 1991): 209-48; and *World of Learning,* 43rd ed. (London: Europa Publications Limited, 1993); "Russia. . . " (National Geographic Society Map, March 1993).

History and Description

Topography

Belarus, frequently referred to in English as "White Russia" (a translation of the Russian, Belorussiia), occupies a forested and lake-filled region in the northern part of Eastern Europe. Adjacent to the Baltic republics of Lithuania and Latvia along its northwest boundary, Belarus is bordered on the east by Russia, on the south by Ukraine, and on the west by Poland. Belarus is a small country (80,154 square miles) comparable in size to the state of Kansas. Its capital is Minsk.

The lands of Belarus make up part of the great East European Plain. Belarus is basically a lowland area divided by an upland ridge of hills running from the southwest to the northeast. In the northwestern part of the country, where rivers flow toward the Baltic Sea, a region of numerous lakes and a remnant of the primeval forest exist. In the southeastern part of Belarus, where rivers flow toward the Black Sea, the vast Pripet Marsh and its many crisscrossing waterways spread across the landscape.

Rivers. The rivers of Belarus have, from earliest times, served as vital transportation links in a region generally unsuitable for travel by road. The exception to such river travel is the ancient highway along the upland ridge of hills that constitutes the main Warsaw-Minsk-Moscow trade route. This highway also served invading powers and was one of the strategic routes the Germans used to approach Moscow in 1941.

Major rivers in the southeastern part of Belarus are the Dnieper, flowing south before entering Ukraine on the way to the Black Sea, and the Pripet, flowing east through the southern part of Belarus to join the Dnieper just below Chernobyl. In the northwestern part of Belarus, the Western Dvina River flows north to the Gulf of Riga; the Neman (Nyoman) flows northwestward to the area of Kaliningrad; and the Western Bug flows west to join the Vistula above Warsaw. The latter three rivers do not have sharply defined beds. They tend to be slow and to overflow often into adjacent marshy areas.

Belarus

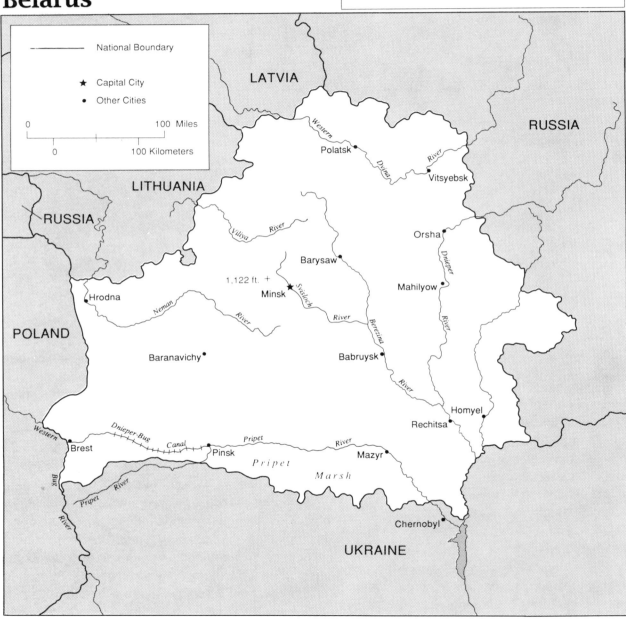

Legend:
- National Boundary
- ★ Capital City
- • Other Cities

0 — 100 Miles
0 — 100 Kilometers

LATVIA

RUSSIA

LITHUANIA

RUSSIA

Polatsk

Western *Dvina* River

Vitsyebsk

Orsha

Viliya River

Barysaw

Mahilyow

Hrodna

1,122 ft. +

Minsk

Svisloch

Dnieper River

Neman

River

Berezina

POLAND

Baranavichy

Babruysk

River

Homyel

Rechitsa

Western

Dnieper-Bug

Canal

Pripet

River

Brest

Pinsk

Pripet

Mazyr

Bug

Pripet *River*

Marsh

River

Chernobyl

UKRAINE

The Pripet River and the lowland region through which it flows, the Pripet Marsh, represent the type of landform remaining after glacial ice deposits had receded. A land of bogs, marshes, and swamps, the area has poor soil but much good pine forest. When sufficiently drained, however, the waterlogged soil yields a rich earth suitable for cultivation. Drainage projects, consequently, have often been attempted.

Climate. The cool and damp climate of Belarus marks a shift between the coastal weather patterns of the Baltic republics to the north and the continental extremities of Russian lands to the east. Temperatures tend to stay in the mid-sixties during the moderate summer season when much of the annual average 24 inches of rain falls. Winters are short with many thaws.

Low temperatures and frequent cloudiness combined with the generally poor soil have not made agricultural development a priority in Belarus. Nevertheless, the raising of beef, dairy, swine, and poultry for domestic and foreign consumption, as well as the growing of flax, grains, potatoes, and orchard crops, constitute a significant portion of the Belarus economy. The forests of Belarus, a cross between the predominantly pine taiga of Russia and the deciduous woodlands of Europe, provide substantial timber resources. Lumbering and wood products, especially paper, plywood, furniture, and prefabricated housing, furnish much revenue.

Natural Resources and Industry. Until the twentieth century, Belarus was thought to be quite lacking in natural resources. In recent years, however, oil has been discovered in the southeastern part of the country at the town of Rechitsa. In nearby Mazyr, an oil refinery has been built to complement the refinery already existing in the north at Polatsk, site of a major oil pipeline between Latvian ports and Russia's Volga-Ural oil fields.

The major mineral resource of Belarus is its vast store of peat, found throughout the country and used for centuries as the primary local energy source. Potash and reserves of various mineral salts have also been exploited. In addition, such building materials as quartz, limestone, clay, sand, and gravel are abundant in Belarus.

The industrialization of the Belarus economy under the Soviet system was well supported financially and now provides a base for future development. Factories producing tractors, motorcycles, and trucks; metal-processing works that support auxiliary manufacturing; and plants turning out plastic and other synthetic products, especially fabrics, constitute much of the industrial activity in Belarus. Pianos, musical instruments, radios, and electronic equipment are also produced.

Cities. The largest city in Belarus is its capital, Minsk (Mensk). Founded in the year 1067, it has suffered many invasions and endured control by foreign rulers. Almost totally destroyed in World War II, it has since been rebuilt and symbolizes for the Belarusians their survival as a people. Located in the very middle of Belarus, Minsk is both the cultural and commercial center of the country. Other Belarusian cities of historic importance are Polatsk, site of an eleventh-century cathedral; Brest (Brest-Litovsk), where the February 1918 peace treaty was signed, removing Russia from further participation in the First World War; Vitsyebsk (Vitebsk), native region of the artist Marc Chagall; and Hrodna, a heart of Jewish life during the nineteenth and early twentieth centuries. During that time Belarus made up a part of the so-called Pale of Settlement, the territory west of the Dnieper River wherein the tsars sought to confine Jewish settlement. Jews constituted a majority or near majority of the population in most cities located within the Pale, but they were also settled in substantial numbers in the surrounding rural areas.

Ethnic Background and Historical Development

The origin of the term Belarus, or White Rus, is uncertain, and many theories have been put forward to explain its usage. For example, the attribute "white" could relate to white clothing commonly worn in Belarus. It could refer, as in Turkic sources, to the pale coloration of Western tribes. It could reflect local geographical terminology in which the syllable "bel" is included in the names of rivers and towns. It could also refer to a god from early Slavic mythology. It could derive from a Tatar term for people free from taxation. Or "bel" could refer to the "sovereignty" of this early Slavic people. The term was first used in historical documents dating from the fourteenth century, but its meaning has since been altered and its precise etymology remains a mystery.

Belarusians are ethnic Slavs and their language, written in Cyrillic, is closely related to Ukrainian and Russian. Belarusian belongs to the East Slavic branch of the Slavic language family. It is possible that Belarusians are descended from early Slavic tribes—in particular the Krivichi—that migrated to the area between the Pripet and Dnieper rivers in approximately the sixth century

A.D. The relationship between these migrant Belarusians and the early east Baltic tribes already inhabiting the region remains a matter of dispute.

Russian Conquest and Rule

By the ninth century, an East Slav Polock principality on the Western Dvina River was known to the early Kievan Rus state. This principality, located on a major Baltic-Mediterranean trading route, eventually became one of the cities making up the medieval Kievan state, and thus lay within the realm of Eastern Orthodox Christendom. By the fourteenth century, however, Belarusian lands had fallen under the domination of the neighboring Lithuanian Empire. Two-hundred years later, after the subsequent establishment of the Polish-Lithuanian Commonwealth in 1569, a part of the Belarusian population converted to Roman Catholicism. Others maintained Eastern Orthodox practices, but were drawn into a form of ecclesiastical union with the Roman church known as the Uniate or Greek Catholic church. The partitions of Poland by Russia at the end of the eighteenth century brought the area of Belarus entirely within the Russian Empire. Subsequent Russification was accompanied in the nineteenth century by coercive efforts to reconvert Belarusian Uniates to Eastern Orthodoxy.

The substantial Jewish presence in Belarusian territory and throughout the lands of the former Polish-Lithuanian Commonwealth dates, according to most accounts, from the invitation of the Polish King Casimir in the fourteenth century. Rarely possessing their own lands, Jewish settlers in the Commonwealth came to live on leased land or, more commonly, in the small towns and cities of the region. By the nineteenth century, Jewish population constituted between one- and two-thirds of most Belarusian cities, including Minsk, Hrodna, Vitsyebsk, and Pinsk.

Belarusian territory remained under imperial Russian administration until the end of the First World War. Although the nineteenth century had seen the development of a national consciousness amongst ethnic Belarusians, the Belarusian homeland was divided by the terms of the postwar Treaty of Riga. The western part of Belarus was joined to Pilsudski's interwar Polish Republic, while eastern Belarus was established by Moscow as the Belorussian Soviet Socialist Republic. Such a division between two unfriendly powers did not, however, stem the desire of the Belarusians themselves to live together within their own unified state.

Soviet Rule

During the period between the two World Wars, as Bolshevik power was being consolidated in Moscow, Soviet Belarusians endured both the trials of forced collectivization in the 1920s and Stalin's purges during the 1930s. By 1933, hundreds of thousands of small landholdings had been reconstituted into collective farms, in spite of active resistance by local villagers. Those peasants who objected were deported, and often died.

An intensive effort was made by Soviet authorities during the late 1920s and early 1930s to eliminate signs of Belarusian nationalism. Anyone not oriented toward socialism was suspected of being a nationalist. Even those who merely affirmed the use of the Belarusian language, instead of Russian, fit the nationalist definition. In this manner, Moscow sought the destruction of Belarusian cultural identity. An early purge of Belarusian intellectuals in 1929-30 was followed by further periodic purges, including the Great Soviet Purges of 1937-38 that killed thousands of innocent victims in Soviet Belorussia and elsewhere in the Soviet Union. The recent discovery of mass graves in the Kurapaty Woods just outside Minsk has served to focus national attention upon this period of Stalinist genocide.

On 22 June 1941, Germany broke the Nazi-Soviet Pact of 1939 and Hitler's forces attacked Russia. Heading east toward Moscow, the German army passed through Belarusian territory near Minsk, over the same terrain that Napoleon had traveled many years before. While Hitler's armies met with some support from Belarusian nationals, most of this backing could be explained by the persistence of strong anti-Stalinist feelings in the region and did not reflect widespread fascist ideological fervor. The subsequent German occupation and the battles that followed devastated Belarus. The countryside was ravaged, villages were flattened, and thousands of peasants burned alive. The many Jewish communities, urban and rural, that had been divided between Polish and Soviet territory after World War I were sacked and millions were sent to concentration camps. Including its Jewish population, Belarus lost more than 25 percent of its prewar inhabitants. During the German retreat in 1944, the cities of Belarus were systematically destroyed by Hitler's direct orders. The

Red Army eventually regained control of all of Belarus, and, following the postwar exchange of territory that shifted Poland westward, most of the lands historically considered Belarusian were brought together in 1945 as the new Belorussian Soviet Socialist Republic.

The most important task faced by Stalin in the immediate postwar period was to integrate within the Soviet system the western part of Belarus that had been part of Poland during the interwar years. First, however, citizens suspected of possible collaboration with the Nazis, including even former prisoners-of-war, were sent to the gulag, that vast network of Soviet prison and labor camps dotting the Russian, and especially Siberian, landscape. (See Siberian chapter, page 32.) The Communist Party proceeded to implement a cultural policy to make Belarussia more firmly "Russian." Linguistic controls lay at the heart of this policy, and, in the attempt to bring Belarusian into sufficient conformity with Russian, Belarusian grammatical rules were changed. Belarusian words derived from Polish were eliminated, and Russian was mandated in all schoolrooms, even when Belarusian remained as the language of instruction.

After Stalin's death in 1953 and the emergence of the more liberalizing leadership of Nikita Khrushchev, these Russification policies continued to be followed in the Belorussian Soviet Republic. Under the republic's first secretary, Kirill Mazurov (1956–65), and his successor, Petr Masherov (1965–80), Belarus remained integrally tied to Moscow. Located at the western border of the Soviet Union and possessing nuclear weapons, Belorussia was considered by Soviet Party leadership to be among the most strategically significant republics. In addition, Soviet concern about possible infiltration of western ideas from the Polish Solidarity movement in the 1980s may also have played a part in the identification of the Belorussian Republic as one of the most important outposts of Soviet rule.

Contemporary Issues

Belarusian Ecocide: The Aftereffects of Chernobyl

The explosion that rocked the Chernobyl nuclear generating plant in April 1986 occurred in the Ukrainian Soviet Socialist Republic, less than fifteen miles south of the Belarusian border. Carried aloft by southeasterly winds, the radioactive cloud and debris from the Chernobyl explosion passed to the north and west immediately over much of Belarus, leaving large parts of the countryside contaminated. Today, Belarus suffers more from the aftereffects of the Chernobyl disaster than any other region of the former Soviet Union, including Ukraine.

More than 2,000,000 people, including 800,000 children, live in contaminated areas. Approximately one-third of the Republic of Belarus has experienced significant radioisotope contamination. In measuring contamination levels, scientists typically use as a baseline the unit of the kilobecquerel. One kilobecquerel per square meter (kBq/m^2) is the residual radiation level found on the earth's surface from above-ground nuclear weapons testing. In southern Belarus there is today an area of about 1,000 square kilometers (386 square miles) where the surface contamination is more than 1,480 kBq/m^2. In that most heavily contaminated region, more than 10,000 people were still living as of 1990 in some 70 villages. In another larger area of 3,000 square kilometers (over 1,000 square miles), only slightly less contaminated (555 to 1,480 kBq/m^2), there remained in 1990 approximately 100,000 people in over 300 villages. According to the estimates of the International Atomic Energy Agency, another 1,200,000 people are living today on lands where the contamination level is between 184 and 555 kBq/m^2—an unsafe level, but one that is not, strictly speaking, uninhabitable. Four and a half years after the disaster, in 1990, approximately 150,000 Belarusians still awaited evacuation from lands judged so contaminated as to be uninhabitable.

The magnitude of the Chernobyl disaster has left Belarus powerless to address the crisis alone. Indeed, one of the great fears of the newly independent nation is that, having separated itself from the old Soviet Union, it will not be able to call upon outside international sources of support to assist in the cleaning up of the health and environmental aftereffects of Chernobyl. When, in May 1991, the International Atomic Energy Agency issued a report downplaying the existence of any serious international health problems, the Ukrainian and Belarusian foreign ministers quickly sought to challenge the findings, noting that their local and regional health problems had not been taken into consideration. For Belarus, in particular, there is an urgent need to maintain an international focus upon the aftereffects of Chernobyl in order to secure needed humanitarian aid.

In the meantime, the Chernobyl crisis has revealed the unusually complicated and conservative politics of the former Belorussian Soviet Socialist Republic (BSSR) and its newly independent successor state, the Republic of Belarus. Responding to popular pressure, the newly elected BSSR Supreme Soviet formed in the spring of 1990 a Chernobyl investigatory commission charged with examining the actions of local republican officials immediately after the explosion in 1986. The commission heard testimony revealing that local BSSR leadership, including then Communist Party First Secretary Sliunkov, as well as the security apparatus, knew of the dangers to the local population as early as 29 April 1986, three days after the incident. Yet, in formal meetings held at the time, the decision was taken not to ask for outside international help and not to cancel May Day celebrations for fear of alarming the public. When the head of the investigatory commission released a preliminary report in June 1991, pointing the finger at high officials and agencies in the Belorussian Soviet government, the elected Belorussian Supreme Soviet astonished everyone by abolishing its own investigatory commission.

In short, the conservative, Party-dominated Supreme Soviet—the very institution that continues to preside over the newly independent Republic of Belarus—sought to control information about the Chernobyl events well into 1991. Perhaps not unpredictably, much of that same conservative Belorussian Communist Party leadership supported the abortive Moscow coup in August 1991 and discredited themselves in the process.

Political Change in Belarus

For Belarus, as for several other former Soviet republics, 1991 became the pivotal year for political change. In conservative Belarus, the year began inauspiciously in March with the Union-wide Soviet referendum on whether or not to preserve the status quo, that is the Soviet Union itself. Of those voting in the Belorussian

Soviet Socialist Republic, 83 percent supported preservation of the Union, a margin of support even exceeding the Union-wide average of 76 percent.

Yet, despite this conservative mandate for the preservation of the Soviet Union, Belarusian workers launched a series of strikes in April 1991 that shattered the relative calm of Belarus political life. On 4 April more than 100,000 workers demonstrated in Lenin Square in Minsk calling for wage increases, worker benefits, and, most significantly, the resignation of the political leadership of the Belorussian Soviet Republic. Neither the Communist Party First Secretary Anatolii Malafeyeu nor the chairman of the Belorussian Supreme Soviet Mikalai Dzemyantsei supported the calls for an emergency meeting of the Supreme Soviet. By 23 April the increasingly powerful independent workers' movement staged a highly successful one-day general strike, closing most large factories in Minsk and other Belarusian cities. By May the government was forced to concede across-the-board wage increases for Belarusian workers, even though the escalating demands of the workers for the nationalization of Communist Party property were rejected by the Supreme Soviet that remained dominated by Communist Party leadership.

In this atmosphere of uneasy truce between workers and government, the events of the abortive Moscow coup in August 1991 reopened the process of political change in Belarus. Party First Secretary Malafeyeu and most other local Party leaders openly supported the coup, a move that severely discredited the Belorussian Communist Party. Moreover, even though most of the conservative bureaucratic heads of government ministries and the Supreme Soviet had remained "safely" noncommital during the coup, Supreme Soviet Chairman Dzemyantsei was forced to resign after pointedly refusing to take sides when interviewed publicly during the coup itself.

Threatened with their own demise, the Belorussian Communist Party and the republic's Supreme Soviet united immediately after the Moscow coup in support of a formal statement of Belarusian independence. The Supreme Soviet declared the independence of the Belorussian Soviet Socialist Republic on 25 August and in September changed the official name to the "Republic of Belarus." In October, the Supreme Soviet elected a moderate political newcomer and ally of Russian President Boris Yeltsin, Stanislau Shushkevich, as its chairman. As head of the Belarus Supreme Soviet, Shushkevich remained the de facto head of state in Belarus as the republic groped toward new forms of political life in the months following the turbulent events of 1991.

Stanislau Shushkevich seems an unusual figure to be leading the new Belarus republic in its first years of independence. Born in 1934, he is the son of a recognized Belarusian poet who spent time in the Soviet gulag. The young Shushkevich was trained in nuclear physics at the Belorussian State University in Minsk. After earning the degree of doctor of science, he was later appointed to the faculty at the university in Minsk and subsequently rose to the position of corresponding member of the Belorussian Academy of Sciences. Having achieved recognition in academic circles, Shushkevich came very late to a career in politics. Although a member of the Communist Party, he did not hold political appointment until elected to the Belorussian Supreme Soviet in the March 1990 open elections. During the campaign he was supported by the Belarusian Popular Front and came to be identified as one of those seeking to expose official negligence in the aftermath of the Chernobyl disaster. Viewed as a moderate or centrist, Shushkevich was elected interim chairman of the Supreme Soviet on 25 August 1991, following the resignation of Dzemyantsei, and assumed the regular chairmanship by vote of the Supreme Soviet in October 1991. As with numerous other Communist Party leaders in republics of the former Soviet Union, Shushkevich formally abandoned his Party membership following the August 1991 abortive coup. Indicative of Shushkevich's late entry into the political arena was the fact he had never traveled outside the Soviet Union prior to 1991.

Under Shushkevich's moderate leadership, and with the Belarusian Supreme Soviet still in the hands of former Communist Party leaders, Belarus has followed a slow and uncertain path toward political democratization. Steering a calculated centrist course between the more conservative Supreme Soviet and the reformist Belarusian Popular Front (chaired by Zyanon Paznyak), Shushkevich has been able to avert a series of political crises since assuming leadership of the Supreme Soviet. Repelling opposition from a Popular Front that desires Belarus to follow a more independent course, Shushkevich has guided the new Republic of Belarus into full membership and collaboration in the post-Soviet Commonwealth of Independent States (CIS—Nezavisimoe sodruzhestvo gosudartsv). The CIS is a loose organization of all the newly independent republics of the former Soviet Union (exclusive of the Baltic states) established in December 1991 on the ashes of the old Soviet state. Initially

launched by Boris Yeltsin of Russia, Leonid Kravchuk of Ukraine, and Stanislau Shushkevich of Belarus, the CIS continues to meet periodically to coordinate interrepublic affairs, particularly in the areas of military, defense, and environmental matters.

If Shushkevich's lead in the formation of the CIS constituted a bow toward supporters of the former Union, his early support for the nationalization of Belarusian Communist Party property garnered him the momentary support of the Belarusian Popular Front. Already in December 1991, Shushkevich secured Supreme Soviet majorities for renunciation of the 1922 treaty that formally tied Belorussia to the Soviet Union, as well as for the nationalization of Communist Party property.

Since 1991, Shushkevich has been far less inclined to pursue a reformist agenda. His more conservative political posture is a reflection of the continuing strength of former Communist Party deputies in the Belarusian Supreme Soviet and a challenge to the liberal minority opposition in the Supreme Soviet, an opposition led by the Belarusian Popular Front. Conservative resistance to rapid democratization of public life is grounded in the control over key government offices and policy making still held by the nomenklatura. The nomenklatura or Communist Party-appointed bureaucratic managers continue to exercise great influence over military and security matters as well as over the press and economic policy.

Military and Security

Belarus was forced to establish its own defense ministry following the collapse of the Soviet Union in late 1991. Nevertheless, the majority of the officers within the old Soviet Belorussian Military District were Russian. As a result there was initial resistance at highest military command levels to any break with the union-wide CIS military command structure. Only approximately 20 percent of the officer corps within Belarus at the end of 1991 was Belarusian. Today, Belarus's military policies continue to be closely harmonized with those of the Russian Federation. This includes the vital strategic question of nuclear weapons installations on Belarus territory—Belarus is one of four former Soviet republics (along with Russia, Ukraine, and Kazakhstan) possessing nuclear weapons. Unlike his Ukrainian counterparts, Shushkevich has steadfastly indicated that Belarus is committed to decommissioning all its nuclear installations, while control over those nuclear installations continued into 1993 to rest in the hands of Russian/CIS military units.

More indicative of the control maintained by the old Party nomenklatura is the continued role of the KGB (Committee on State Security) in Belarus. Contrary to the situation in other former Soviet republics, the KGB in Belarus has not even changed its name, much less its personnel, its policies, or its closed archives. Appointed head of the KGB in October 1990, General Eduard Shirkousky has continued to lead the agency in 1993. Underneath Shirkousky, the KGB has maintained its Communist deputy division heads and has continued to advance an agenda tied to the old Communist leadership of the Supreme Soviet. Moreover, despite Belarus's newly independent, sovereign status, the Belarusian KGB has sought to strengthen pre-existing all-union ties with KGB security personnel in adjacent republics. Symbolic of this unreformed Belarusian security agency is the fate of the statue to Felix Dzerzhinsky, founder of the precursor of the Soviet KGB. In Moscow, a similar statue to Dzerzhinsky was torn down in 1991, and the name of the square over which it presided was changed. In Minsk, however, the Dzerzhinsky statue still stands opposite KGB headquarters, and portraits of Dzerzhinsky, a native of Belarus, continue to grace the offices of local KGB affiliates. (See Alexander Lukashuk, "Belarus's KGB: In Search of an Identity," *RFE/RL Research Report,* 27 November 1992, p. 18. Lukashuk is a writer and reformist member of the Belarus Supreme Soviet.)

Despite proposals for political control over the Belarusian KGB, no such legislation has been adopted, and there is unlikely to be any reform of the Belarus KGB before the next scheduled elections to the Supreme Soviet in 1994. In the meantime, the argument of the old KGB personnel who retain their positions is that, in the face of economic corruption and rising crime, there is renewed need for the old security apparatus—despite its close ties to the former Communist government.

Economic Reform

Finally, the continued strength of the old Party-appointed bureaucracy or nomenklatura has also served to slow the pace of economic reform in Belarus. Despite the proclaimed support for development of a market economy, Belarus leaders have been reluctant to shift the ownership of the means of production into private hands. While new laws on private property and foreign investment have been adopted, the government has sought to maintain control and authority over the reform process. Until 1993, when Belarus developed its own currency, it remained within the ruble zone, only gradually developing its own national economic policy. A 1992 project for privatizing state-owned enterprises ended up being limited to 147 plants. In the case of land reform, the popular support for private farm holdings has been partially undermined by well-connected managers of large collective and state-run farms who either serve as deputies in the Supreme Soviet or have access to conservative Supreme Soviet leadership. Meanwhile, the Belarusian press remains closely controlled by a Ministry of Information bent on exercising its own authority over publishing.

So deadlocked was the process of political reform under the heavy weight of the nomenklatura that, in mid-1992, close to a half million signatures were gathered on a petition calling for a national referendum on early parliamentary elections. The desire for early elections reflected frustration over the pace of political reform set by a Supreme Soviet elected before the politically transforming year of 1991. In the end, the petitioners were unsuccessful in dislodging the conservative political leadership, although in August 1992 a new draft constitution offered a vision of a Belarusian state ruled by law, with a division of powers, an independent court system, and a commitment to civil and human rights. The procedures for adoption of the constitution have not yet been determined and several provisions are still under debate, but the process of political democratization is underway in Belarus—slowly.

Religion, Language, and National Identity in Belarus

As in other regions of Eastern Europe, national identity has been historically linked to religious identity in Belarus. Like the Republic of Ukraine, however, Belarus confronts the reality of religious, or confessional, division. Belarus has historically been at the crossroads of Latin and Eastern Orthodox Christian confessions, while also being home to Jews and other non-Christian peoples. This religious diversity, while it could be a source of strength, also poses for the Belarusian national movement the absence of a single confessional authority, as in Poland, to reinforce national identity.

Historically, the conflicts between Roman Catholicism and Eastern Orthodoxy date to the late sixteenth and early seventeenth centuries. It was then under the Polish-

Lithuanian Commonwealth that Belarusian parishes of the eastern rite were wedded to the Roman Catholic hierarchy in a series of unions that created the Greek Catholic or Uniate church. This Eastern-rite Catholic church, which came to dominate Belarusian lands in the seventeenth and eighteenth centuries, recognized the Roman Catholic hierarchy, but retained use of the Orthodox liturgy (worship services) in the Slavonic language. The Uniate parishes also were permitted to retain married clergy. Following Russian acquisition of Belarusian lands during the partitions of Poland in the late eighteenth century, Russian clerics made sustained efforts in the nineteenth century to bring the Belarusian Uniate parishes back into the Orthodox church. In the Stalinist period, the Uniate church was formally outlawed in both the Belorussian and Ukrainian Soviet Socialist Republics.

While there has been a reawakening of the Eastern-rite Catholic or Uniate church in contemporary Belarus, the dilemma confronting the national movement is that both of the major confessions vying for the loyalty of Belarusian nationals—Roman Catholicism and Eastern Orthodoxy—draw their leadership and their language from outside Belarus. In the case of the Roman Catholic church of Belarus, its approximately two-hundred parishes today are served overwhelmingly by Polish clergy, who continue to use the Polish language in church services. To be sure, as many as a quarter of the estimated one and a half million Roman Catholics in Belarus (15 percent of total population) are, indeed, ethnic Poles living in Belarus. Nevertheless, the continued effort to polonize the Catholic church of Belarus has been a source of aggravation within the Belarusian national movement. In particular, Pope John Paul II's appointment of Monsignor Tadeusz Kondrusiewicz of Hrodna as Catholic archbishop of Belarus in 1989 reinforced the fear of Polish influence in the Belarusian Catholic church. Born of ethnic Belarusian parentage, Kondrusiewicz was nevertheless educated as a Pole and used only Polish in his Hrodna parish. Kondrusiewicz's consecration was conducted in Polish.

Responding to this concern over external domination of national religious life, the Belarusian Popular Front included specific proposals in its program of "Renewal" (Adradzhen'ne) regarding the conduct of Christian confessions in Belarus. While the Popular Front sought to eliminate registration of churches and other state interference in religious affairs, it also recommended that all denominations in Belarus have their own territorial administration within Belarus. The Renewal program also called for translation of liturgical service books and Holy Scripture into Belarusian for use in all Belarusian Christian denominations—these injunctions have not been applied to Islamic, Jewish, or other small religious minorities whose religious freedom has been explicitly recognized (Elizabeth Ambrose, "Language and Church in Belorussia," *Report on the USSR*, 9 February 1990, pp. 18–24).

These proposals were directed not only at the polonizing practices of the Roman Catholic church in Belarus, but also toward the Eastern Orthodox church administered by the Belarus Exarchate of the Russian Orthodox church. The designation of the diocese of Minsk and Belarus as an exarchate reflects the prestige of this post within the Russian church hierarchy. The Belarus Exarchate remains closely tied to the Russian Orthodox Church, a tie that is well illustrated in the person of the presiding Exarch of Minsk and Belarus, Metropolitan Filaret, an ethnic Russian and former head of the Moscow Patriarchate's Division of External Church Relations. For the Orthodox church in Belarus, there are two dilemmas in responding to the proposals from the Belarus Popular Front. First, Orthodox worship in all of the Slavic world has traditionally been conducted in Old Church Slavonic, an ecclesiastical language dating from the ninth-century Byzantine missions to the Slavs. While there were early efforts in the sixteenth century to translate Holy Scripture into a Belarusian dialect (the translations of Francis Skoryna [Fratsishek Skaryna]), the Orthodox faithful of Belarus have maintained the use of Old Church Slavonic in liturgical worship. The sudden introduction of a vernacular language into the church service might even meet with resistance by more conservative laypeople.

A second and equally compelling reason for Orthodox reluctance to introduce modern translated Belarusian texts into the liturgy has to do with the national complexion of the Orthodox church in Russia. Just as the Roman Catholic church includes thousands of Poles in its parishes, so also the Orthodox church includes a great number of ethnic Russians residing in Belarus. Not only do Russians make up more than 13 percent of the Belarusian population, but there are also a substantial number of Belarusian nationals who, over the course of the Soviet period, came to adopt Russian as their primary spoken language. Sudden introduction of Belarusian into

Orthodox church services would do little to assist those local parishes where Russian is the common spoken language of the faithful. In the meantime, both Roman Catholic and Eastern Orthodox church leaders are sponsoring translation projects. One or more new editions of the Bible in modern Belarusian will shortly be in publication.

The wider question of the Belarusian language remains at the heart of the Belarus Popular Front's national agenda. Long before the onset of a more liberal Soviet regime in the 1980s under Mikhail Gorbachev, Belarusian intellectuals argued that there was insufficient instruction in Belarusian in local schools and at higher educational institutions. One of the early victories of the Belarusian intelligentsia was the passage by the Supreme Soviet in 1989 of a law on languages, which declared Belarusian to be the state language, while recognizing continued use of Russian. The hurdle faced by those seeking to strengthen use of Belarusian in the republic is dramatized by circulation figures for the daily press. According to a recent report by a freelance Belarusian journalist, there are more than a million copies of Russian-language dailies distributed in Belarus, but only eighty-thousand copies of the one and only Belarusian daily, *Zviazda* (Alexander Lukashuk, "Belarus After Glasnost," *RFE/RL Research Report*, 2 October 1992, p. 21). The circulation figures for the weekly press are even more one-sided. Some of the press has taken to printing bilingual editions, but the disproportionately high Russian-language readership demonstrates why the Belarusian Popular Front is so concerned about cultivation of the Belarusian language. Obviously there are many Belarusian nationals raised under Soviet Russian domination who continue to operate with Russian as the preferred language of communication.

As the Republic of Belarus moves toward the adoption of its first post-Soviet constitution and seeks to project its own national identity, it confronts not only the devastation wrought by the Chernobyl disaster, but a conservative nomenklatura, divided confessional loyalties, and the long-term impact of Soviet Russification.

MOLDOVA

Statistical Profile

Demography

Population: 4,335,000

Ethnic population:

Moldovan	2,795,000	64.5%
Ukrainian	600,000	13.8%
Russian	562,000	13.0%
Gagauz	153,000	3.5%
Bulgarian	88,000	2.0%
Jewish	66,000	1.5%
Belarusian	20,000	0.5%
Other	51,000	1.2%

Historic religious traditions:

Christianity	97.3%

Population by age:

Age	Total	Males	Females
0–4	10.5%	5.4%	5.1%
5–9	9.1%	4.7%	4.4%
10–14	8.7%	4.4%	4.3%
15–19	8.6%	4.3%	4.3%
20–24	8.2%	4.2%	4.0%
25–29	7.9%	3.9%	4.0%
30–34	7.6%	3.6%	4.0%
35–39	7.1%	3.4%	3.7%
40–44	4.2%	1.9%	2.3%
45–49	6.1%	2.8%	3.3%
50–54	5.4%	2.5%	2.9%
55–59	5.1%	2.4%	2.7%
60–64	4.1%	1.6%	2.5%
65–69	2.8%	1.1%	1.7%
70–	4.6%	1.6%	3.0%

Male/Female ratio: 47.8% male/52.2% female

Rural/Urban population: 52.5% rural/47.5% urban

Growth over time, 1979–91: 10.6%

Population density: 335.6 persons/sq mi

Politics/Government

Date of independence declaration:
27 August 1991

Major urban centers and populations:

Chişinău (Kishinev)	665,000
Tiraspol	182,000
Bălţi (Bel'tsy)	159,000
Bender (Bendery)	130,000

Autonomous areas: none

Education

Level of education for persons over 15:

completed higher level education	8.7%
completed secondary education	46.4%
incomplete secondary education	20.4%

Number of higher education institutions: 9
(54,700 students)

Major institutions of higher education and enrollment:

Chişinău

Moldovan State University	11,800

Socioeconomic Indicators

Birthrate: 17.7/1,000

Infant mortality: 19.0/1,000 live births

Average life expectancy: 68.7 (males, 65.2; females, 72.0)

Average family size: 3.4

Hospital beds per 10,000 persons: 131.4

Production of electrical energy: 3,595 kwh/person

Length of rail lines: 713 mi

Length of highways: 1,240 mi

Physical/Territorial/Geopolitical Features

Area: 13,012 sq mi (.2% of USSR total)

Land use:

Cultivated	50%
Pasture	9%

Highest elevation: 1,407 ft. (Mt. Balansi)

Rainfall: 20 inches/year

Temperature: average in winter 25° F; lowest temperature: -33° F. Average in summer 67° F in the north, 72° F in the south; highest temperature: 106° F.	**Principal products:** corn, sunflowers, grapes, grain, sugar beets, cattle, swine, sheep; food processing, wine, textiles, lignite, gypsum **Per capita GNP (1991):** $2,170.

Sources

"Moldavskaia sovetskaia sotsialisticheskaia respublika," *Bol'shaia Sovetskaia Entsiklopediia* (Moscow, 1977); *Narodnoe khoziaistvo SSSR v 1990g.* (Moscow, 1991); *Naselenie SSSR* (1989); Matthew J. Sagers, "News Notes. Iron and Steel," *Soviet Geography* 30 (May 1989): 397–434; Lee Schwartz, "USSR Nationality Redistribution by Republic, 1979–1989: From Published Results of the 1989 All-Union Census," *Soviet Geography* 32 (April 1991): 209–48; and *World of Learning*, 43rd ed. (London: Europa Publications Limited, 1993); "Russia. . ." (National Geographic Society Map, March 1993).

History and Description

Topography

Moldova, a picturesque country of rolling hills and rich lowlands deeply cut by an extensive river system, lies in the southwestern corner of the European part of the former Soviet Union. Bordered on the north, east, and south by Ukraine, Moldova's western neighbor is Romania. The capital of Moldova is Chişinău (in Russian, Kishinev). Second smallest of the former Soviet republics, Moldova (13,012 square miles) is approximately half the size of West Virginia. With a population of well over four million, Moldova has the greatest population density of all the former republics.

Lying between the Prut (Pruth) River in the west and a stretch of territory along the left bank of the Dniester River in the east, Moldova is blessed with a climate conducive to agricultural success. Summers are mild and wet, winters not too harsh. Corn, wheat, sugar beets, and sunflowers are major crops, but Moldova is primarily known for the wines produced from its famous vineyards. In some years it has yielded half of the former Soviet Union's grapes. Other fruits and vegetables are also intensively farmed here, and food processing plants constitute an important part of the mainly agricultural economy, for Moldova has few natural resources.

The largest Moldovan city is Chişinău, situated on the Byk River among the Kodry Hills. It is the center of the main grape-growing region of Moldova. Bălţi (Beltsy), a regional center in the north, is a transportation cross-road. To the south are Bender (Bendery) and Tiraspol, on the west bank and the east bank, respectively, of the Dniester. Both are important commercial towns. Tiraspol served as the capital during the years between the first and second World Wars when Soviet authorities set up the autonomous republic of Moldavia there.

Ethnic Background and Historical Description

Moldovans, formerly called Bessarabians, are ethnic Romanians thought to be descended from Roman legions stationed in the ancient territory known as Dacia (similar to modern Romania). Over the course of many centuries, however, other peoples mixed with these Romanian peoples, amongst them Greeks, Slavs, and Turks. The Moldovans speak an eastern Romance language, basically a dialect of Romanian, although in writing they have most recently been using the Cyrillic alphabet rather than the Latin. The Moldovans are by tradition Eastern Orthodox Christians.

In the fourteenth century, two Balkan principalities (nation-states) were founded by the powerful Basarab family. These principalities, Wallachia and Moldavia, served as the basis of the future Romania. In the fifteenth and sixteenth centuries, the Moldovan prince Stephen the Great (1457–1504) fought many battles against the Turks of the Ottoman Empire, and he has come to be regarded

Moldova

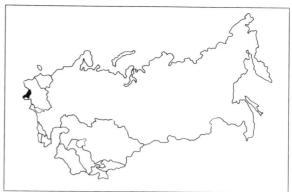

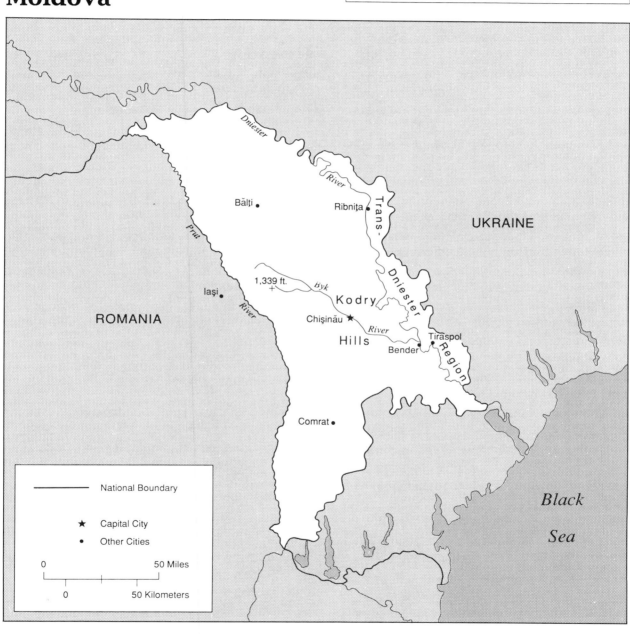

UKRAINE

Dniester

River

Bălţi

Ribniţa

Trans-

Prut

River

Iaşi

1,339 ft.

Byk

Kodry

Dniester

ROMANIA

Chişinău

River

Hills

Tiraspol

Bender

Region

Comrat

Black

Sea

National Boundary

★ Capital City

• Other Cities

0   50 Miles

0   50 Kilometers

as the father of the Moldovan nation, despite its ultimate fall to the Ottomans.

By the eighteenth century the Black Sea had become a virtual Ottoman lake. Russian military victories and conquests in southern Ukraine and Novorossiia (northern Black Sea coast), however, began to alter the power relationships in the area. Russian troops, for the third time in a forty-year period, entered Moldovan territory during the Russian-Ottoman war of 1806–12. In the concluding Treaty of Bucharest, shortly before the Napoleonic invasion of Russia, Russia secured the annexation of Bessarabia (Moldova). Thus Moldovan territory north and east of the Prut river came to be integrated into the Russian Empire in the nineteenth century. Russian Bessarabia, lying between the Prut and Dniester rivers roughly equals present-day Moldova minus its Trans-Dniester region.

After the Crimean War (1853–56), Moldovan territory west of the Prut River, along with three southern Bessarabian districts, were united with Wallachia to form the foundation for what became in 1878 the independent state of Romania. In the aftermath of the Russo-Turkish War of 1877–78, the southern Bessarabian districts were returned to the Russian Empire. As a result of World War I, however, Bessarabia was reunited with the rest of Moldova into the greater Romanian state, a union that lasted only until 1940 and Soviet reannexation.

During the interwar period, in 1924, the Soviet Union established just east of the Dniester in western Ukraine an autonomous Moldavian republic, which was attached administratively to the Ukrainian Soviet republic. Although this Moldavian republic represented but a fraction of the territory of greater Moldova, whose historic capital was Iaşi (Jassy, located west of the Prut), Romanians living east of the Dniester River were designated Moldavians by the Soviets in an attempt to influence the disposition of Romanian-held Bessarabian lands claimed by the Russians.

In 1940, at the beginning of World War II, as Romania was moving into the German orbit, the Soviet Union demanded the return of Bessarabia, and the Romanian king acceded to the Russian ultimatum. In 1941, with German military assistance, Bessarabia was temporarily recaptured by Romania only to be reconquered by Soviet troops in 1944. At the end of the war, the interwar Moldavian autonomous republic was abolished, and a new Moldavian Soviet Socialist Republic was established, including the lands of Bessarabia up to the Prut River. This Moldavian Soviet Republic lasted formally until the breakup of the Soviet Union in 1991, at which time Moldova declared itself independent.

The population of Moldova, although primarily Moldovan (64.5 percent), contains substantial minority groups, almost all of whom live in urban centers. Ukrainians are the most numerous, due in part to the frequent shifting of the Moldovan/Ukrainian border. Many Russians also live in Moldova, a reflection of the long-term Russian imperial interest in the region. During the eighteenth century and up until the Russian Revolution of 1917, Russians, Ukrainians, and Jews were encouraged by the government to resettle in the Bessarabian lands of Moldova. Smaller percentages of Turkic peoples (Gagauz), Bulgarians, and others also inhabit Moldova. In 1902, Jewish settlement in the Russian Bessarabian capital of Kishinev (Chişinău) was submitted to one of the worst of a series of pogroms, the random racist acts of violence then frequently directed against Jewish persons and property.

The origins of the Gagauz, who migrated to southern Bessarabia late in the eighteenth and early in the nineteenth centuries, are uncertain. They are thought to derive from either a Bulgarian or Turkish background. The Gagauz speak a Turkish dialect but profess Eastern Orthodoxy as their religion. At the time of their emigration they received large land grants from the tsar but under Soviet authority have known no cultural autonomy. In 1957 a Cyrillic alphabet was imposed on their language.

Soviet Leadership

Soviet policy in the postwar Moldavian Soviet Republic was devoted to integrating Moldova into the Soviet Union by promoting the cultural identification of Moldova as a nation separate and unique from Romania. Thus, relations with Romania were not only discouraged but, from 1964, when Romania raised questions over the annexation of Bessarabia, were actually forbidden. Moldovan nationalists during the 1950s and 1960s struggled against the collectivization of agriculture (see page 000 for a description of broader collectivization policy), as well as against the antireligious propaganda introduced by Soviet authorities. Following the brief tenure of Leonid Brezhnev as first secretary of the Moldavian Communist Party from 1950 to 1952, the leadership of the Moldavian Soviet Republic was given over to ethnic Moldovans, despite the continued Moscow orientation of local Communist Party decision making. In the late 1960s and 1970s, the first secretary of the Moldavian Communist Party, I. I. Bodiul, spoke publicly about the unacceptable nationalistic expressions that were of great concern to the Party. Bodiul's successor, Semen Grossu, continued the basic policy of subservience to Moscow in Moldavian Soviet leadership.

Contemporary Issues

Moldovan Politics and the Language Question

The politics of the former Moldavian Soviet Socialist Republic and the newly independent Republic of Moldova have been dominated by an attempt to reach political consensus among a multi-ethnic population. At the center of this effort has been the controversy over the Moldovan language and its status in the public life of the country.

Following Soviet occupation of Bessarabia and its reabsorption as Soviet Moldavia after World War II, the Soviet authorities declared that the Moldovan and Romanian languages were entirely separate. To bolster these claims, the Latin alphabet for Moldovan was replaced by Cyrillic, and Romanian literature was virtually banned from Soviet Moldavia. Although legally there was no official language, Russian became the effective language of the republic, and use of and instruction in Moldovan declined.

This Soviet language policy, a source of grievance for the Moldovans and a source of anti-Soviet propaganda for Romanian nationalists, came under heavy fire during the mid-1980s as Moldovan writers and intellectuals pressed for greater use of Moldovan and for admission by the Soviet government that Moldovan and Romanian were essentially the same. The reemergence of the language issue in Soviet Moldavia was partly owing to the greater openness in public discourse in an era of glasnost. The issue quickly became a major agenda item for newly formed indigenous informal groups, including the Moldovan Popular Front. The language question also inevitably came to stir the fears of non-Moldovan nationals, particularly the Slavic (Russian and Ukrainian) inhabitants of the Trans-Dniester region and the Gagauz of southern Moldova. The fears of non-Moldovan nationals lay in the assumption that, if the Moldovan language were to be recognized as official and its linkage with modern Romanian confirmed, pressure for territorial reunification with Romania would intensify.

The Soviet Moldavian Communist Party's Language Problems. Soviet Moldavia's most powerful institution, the Moldavian Communist Party, found itself particularly ill-prepared to respond to the language issue and ultimately disintegrated over the politics of ethnicity and language. The Moldavian Communist Party enjoyed special favor from the Soviet government during the Brezhnev era, a time that has since come to be known as the period of "stagnation" (*zastoi*). It is not insignificant that Leonid Brezhnev briefly served as first secretary in the Moldavian Communist Party from 1950 to 1952. Very much tied to the Brezhnev era, Semen Kuzmich Grossu, first secretary for the Moldavian Communist Party throughout the 1980s, came under mounting criticism during the more reform-minded Gorbachev years because of the legacy of corruption and inefficiency in the Moldavian Republic. Grossu's position was further weakened in the eyes of Moldovan intellectuals and writers because of the Communist Party's firm commitment to a Soviet language policy that subordinated Moldovan to Russian.

Seeking to reestablish support among ethnic Moldovans, the Moldavian Soviet Republic and the Communist Party announced in May 1987 two concessions on language policy. The first was a resolution calling for expanded use of Moldovan (then still called "Moldavian") in social life, literature, media broadcasts, and in the schools. A parallel resolution set forth policies for use of Russian, so as not to give the appearance that there had been any prior inadequacy in the use of Moldovan. In fact, there were wide areas of Moldovan life where Russian continued to be used exclusively, including some higher educational institutions.

While state and Party leaders sought to keep pace with rising public disaffection, the language issue had become by 1988 central to the platform of two significant informal political groups—the Alexe Mateevici Literary and Musical Group and the Democratic Movement in Support of Restructuring. The Mateevici Group, primarily concerned with cultural issues, was named for a Moldovan poet and Orthodox priest who agitated for Moldovan culture within the Russian Empire at the beginning of the twentieth century. The more directly political Democratic Movement laid out a comprehensive platform calling for democratic government, cultural autonomy for all ethnic groups, and privatization of industry. Both groups called for Moldovan to be the republic's official language, the return of a Latin script, and the recognition of Moldovan as identical to Romanian.

To quiet the agitation on the language issue, the Moldavian Supreme Soviet established in 1988 a "Commission on the Study of the History and Problems of the Development of the Moldavian Language." Although the Commission was largely ineffective, it did recommend in December 1988 during the height of public demonstrations over the language question that Moldovan be recognized as an official language of the republic. Semen Grossu, the Moldavian first secretary, remained opposed to such concessions but authorized the publication of the works of the popular dissident writer Ion Drutse in the Latin script. He also tentatively approved establishment of a new periodical, *Glasul,* also to be published in the Latin script.

The slow pace of reform and the government's failure to make good on its limited concessions regarding the language issue led to increasingly hostile confrontations between popular forces and the government. Failing to secure prompt publication of *Glasul,* the Chişinău Writers' Union arranged to have it printed in Riga, Latvia. Discovering that copies were circulating in Chişinău, Grossu declared the issue illegal and ordered that searches be undertaken for the galley proofs of the second issue. Despite Grossu's declaration that the informal groups were illegal, in March 1989 these groups combined to win three of the six seats in elections for the Soviet Union's Congress of People's Deputies. The defeat of three of the Communist Party candidates did little to halt Grossu's continued harassment of the informal groups.

New Language Law. When in late March 1989 the government formally proposed its new language laws, few were satisfied. The proposals called for Moldovan to be the official language of the republic, but identified Russian as the official language of interethnic communication. For Moldovans, this was taken to mean the continued subordination of Moldovan to Russian, and 25,000 Moldovans demonstrated against the laws. Meanwhile, for the Gagauz and the Slavic groups of Soviet Moldavia, the designation of Moldovan as the official language of the republic was unacceptable, and these groups launched their own demands for separation and autonomy *vis-a-vis* the Moldavian Soviet Socialist Republic. In short, the failure to resolve the language issue forthrightly and effectively was creating by mid-1989 a dangerous situation that threatened to set the ethnic communities of Soviet Moldavia against one another.

Acting as an umbrella group for the Democratic Movement, the Mateevici Group, the Moldovan Greens and others, a Moldovan Popular Front (MPF) was established in May 1989. The MPF led the largest public demonstrations to date in June 1989. As many as eighty thousand supporters ralled in Chişinău protesting the 1940 Soviet annexation of Bessarabia. The MPF further demanded that the former Bessarabian areas of northern Bukovina (north of Soviet Moldavia) and southern Bessarabia (between Soviet Moldavia and the Black Sea) be returned by Ukraine to Moldova.

By the end of August 1989, the Soviet Moldavian government offered to concede on the proposed language laws. The section making Russian the official language of interethnic communication was changed to make Russian coequal with Moldovan for such purposes. Moreover, the government conceded that the Cyrillic script would be replaced by the Latin script in printed Moldovan. While Russian workers in the Trans-Dniester region responded with strikes organized by a group calling itself Edinstvo (Unity), as many as a half-million Moldovans, many of them peasants from outlying villages, crowded into Chişinău to join an MPF rally in support of the new provisions, which became law in September 1989. The law also provided cultural concessions to other ethnic groups, including Ukrainians, Gagauz, Jews, and Bulgarians.

The issue of the Soviet occupation of Bessarabia starting in 1940 continued to spawn public demonstrations, including protests directed at the presence of troops called in from the Soviet Ministry of Internal Affairs. Amidst this increasingly bitter outpouring of public disfavor with the government, Moscow authorities removed Semen Grossu as first secretary in November 1989.

In March 1990, the first open elections were held for the republic's Supreme Soviet. Supporters of the MPF gained control of this legislative body, securing 40 percent of the seats. Adherents of other informal groups took an additional 30 percent. When the Supreme Soviet convened, Grossu's replacement as chair, Petru Luchinsky, was ousted, and Mircea Snegur, a commited reformist figure, was named to the post. Subsequently, Snegur was chosen to the newly created position of president of the republic.

New Moldovan Republic Breaks with Soviet Union

By June 1990, eighteen months before the formal end of the Soviet Union, the Moldavian Supreme Soviet declared the republic to be a sovereign state. Soviet occupation was declared to be illegal, and, in subsequent legislation, the Soviet military draft was suspended. Enforcing the 1989 Moldovan language reform, Russian place names were converted to Moldovan (Kishinev became Chişinău, for example). Staunchly opposing efforts to revive the Soviet Union through a new union treaty, Moldovan President Snegur rejected Gorbachev's entreaties. Moldovan representatives to the Congress of Peoples' Deputies in Moscow were even called back. The old Moldavian Communist Party joined with the Edinstvo group in the Trans-Dniester in opposing Moldovan sovereignty, but Soviet control continued to slip. In May 1991, the government formally changed the republic's name to the Republic of Moldova. Following the abortive *coup d'état* in Moscow in August 1991, the new Moldovan Republic moved to outlaw the Moldavian Communist Party and to eliminate its special internal role in the former Moldavian Soviet Socialist Republic. After the crisis of August passed, the Moldavian Communist Party was banned and its assets were seized.

During the August coup the Moldovan Supreme Soviet and a national assembly of informal political groups together declared the Republic of Moldova to be independent. President Snegur sought formal diplomatic recognition for the new state, he secured membership in the United Nations, and began negotiations for the removal of Soviet troops from Moldova. Simultaneously, Snegur moved to establish a new Moldovan military force.

Since the declaration of independence, Moldovan officials have faced at least three extraordinarily difficult problems. Two of these problems involve internal ethnic demands for secession or union with other countries—the Trans-Dniester Slav demand for reunion with Russia and the drive of some of the former members of the Moldovan Popular Front to secure reunion with Romania. The third problem is the very immediate one of a crumbling economy and rampant inflation.

The Trans-Dniester Issue

The Trans-Dniester region (also called Transnistria) is the narrow Moldovan corridor east of the Dniester river adjacent to the Ukrainian border. Before Soviet occupation of Bessarabia in 1940, the region formed the Moldavian ASSR (Autonomous Soviet Socialist Republic) within the Ukrainian Soviet Socialist Republic. The population was exposed to the collectivizing and Russifying efforts of the 1920s and 1930s. The area was also subjected to an influx of Russian and Ukrainian workers. By the time the Trans-Dniester was incorporated with Bessarabia as a Soviet union republic, the Moldavian SSR, it was predominantly Eastern Slavic (Russian and Ukrainian). The region's current population (ca. 600,000) is about two-thirds Slavic.

The Russians and Ukrainians in the Moldavian SSR began demanding autonomy after the Moldavian government proposed Moldovan as the republic's official language. Although Russian would continue to be an official language of interethnic communication, Trans-Dniester Slavs overwhelmingly opposed this position. The August 1989 designation of Moldovan as the republic's official language prompted strong reactions from the Trans-Dniester Slavs. Edinstvo called for strikes by Russian workers. Although the Moldovan Popular Front kept the factories in Chişinău open with volunteer anti-sabotage committees, strikes broke out in the Dniester cities of Tiraspol, Bender, and Rybniţa.

When the Moldovan Popular Front gained control of the Supreme Soviet in 1990, tensions escalated in the Trans-Dniester. Slavic deputies boycotted the Supreme Soviet. In September 1990, Slavs in the Trans-Dniester proclaimed their own Dniester Soviet Socialist Republic (Dniester SSR), electing their own Supreme Soviet. The new Dniester Republic formed a militia that clashed with Moldovan police along the Dniester as well as in Chişinău. The showdown in Chişinău left six dead, hardening the positions of all sides in the dispute. The Moldovan government refused to negotiate with the Dniester Republic.

In August 1991, the Dniester Republic, along with the old Moldavian Communist Party and Edinstvo, supported the Moscow coup attempt, continuing to do so even after the coup had failed. Nevertheless, the general collapse of the Communist Party after the failure of the Moscow coup began to put the Trans-Dniester Slavs in a more defensive position.

In March 1992, the Moldovan government declared emergency rule in the Trans-Dniester, sending in its own armed forces in fighting that left 40 people dead. The violence continued into April with Moldovan forces attacking separatist-held enclaves in Bender. In June 1992, despite assurances from Russian President Boris Yeltsin that Russian troops would withdraw from the Dniester region, the Russian army assisted Dniester separatists against Moldovan troops.

Responding to United States' and European calls for a peaceful resolution of the conflict, Moldovan President Snegur met with Yeltsin, Romanian President Ion Iliescu, and President Leonid Kravchuk of Ukraine in an attempt to end the conflict. By the end of 1992 those talks had not reached a satisfactory conclusion. Moldovan troops now control part of the Trans-Dniester as well as lands in northern Bukovina and southern Bessarabia formerly within the Ukrainian Republic. While it is unlikely that the Russians and the Ukrainians will allow the Moldovans to secure an unconditional military victory in the regions, the fact that the Romanians may be willing to come to the aid of the Moldovans makes this military showdown one of the more serious, if somewhat hidden, locations for potential wider European conflict.

Internally, the new Moldovan state has made it clear that it has no intention of seeking unification with Romania, and it has made very serious efforts to ease the tensions between the ethnic communities within the old Bessarabian heartland of Moldova. The Snegur government has appointed a number of prominent Slavs to cabinet level positions. The result has been that the Slavs of Chişinău, as elsewhere in the lands south and west of the Dniester, have begun to demonstrate a measure of loyalty to the Moldovan government. Whether, and to what extent, that support will be heard from Trans-Dniester Slavs remains uncertain.

The Gagauz and Bulgarians

In addition to the Trans-Dniester Slavs, the Gagauz and the Bulgarians came to be alienated by Moldovan language demands in the 1980s. The Turkish-speaking Gagauz and the Bulgarians both reside in the southernmost regions of Moldova.

Under Soviet rule, the Gagauz and the Bulgarians occasionally protested the absence of instruction and published literature in these languages. According to the 1979 census, however, the overwhelming majority of both Gagauz and Bulgarians claimed Russian as their first language. In concessions to the two groups, the Moldavian Soviet government in the mid-1980s granted monthly broadcasts, occasional news columns, and expanded instruction in their respective languages. In 1988, during demonstrations by Moldovans for language concessions, the government launched two journals, one in Gagauz (*Ana Sozu*) and one in Bulgarian (*Rodno Slovo*).

Nevertheless, when the Moldavian government proposed to make Moldovan the official language of the Moldavian Soviet Republic, the Gagauz decided to seek their own autonomy. Largely Russianized, and with a very small percentage of Moldovan speakers, the Gagauz were afraid that they would be forced to learn Moldovan or face discrimination. Out of this concern came the creation of the Gagauz popular political movement Khalky (The People), a cultural and debating society. After the language law was proposed in 1990, Khalky called for secession from Moldavia and the creation of a Gagauz Autonomous Soviet Socialist Republic (Gagauz ASSR). Another informal political group, Arkalyk (Cooperation), proposed the creation of a Bulgar-Gagauz ASSR within the Moldavian Soviet Socialist Republic. In July 1990, the Khalky gathered in the town of Comrat (Komrat) and proclaimed the founding of the Gagauz ASSR. In Gagauz regions, the Gagauz flag, a white wolf's head in a gold circle on a blue field, was even flown at government buildings. When the Moldavian Supreme Soviet responded by banning all Gagauz rallies, a 754-member Gagauz national congress convened in August 1990, voting unanimously to secede from the Moldavian SSSR.

The Moldovan Popular Front and its supporters in the Supreme Soviet sought to defuse the situation through concessions to the Gagauz. The Popular Front had always favored cultural autonomy for the Gagauz, and the Supreme Soviet made offers of such autonomy, also infusing financial aid into Gagauz regions and inviting Turkish performers and representatives of Turkish culture to Moldova. On the matter of secession, however, the Moldovan Supreme Soviet refused any territorial autonomy and condemned the Khalky group for generating such disruptive activity.

During the August 1991 Moscow coup, the Gagauz supported the junta and opposed Moldova's subsequent declaration of independence. When the Moldovan government banned the Communist Party and seized its assets, the Gagauz continued to support it. As a result, however, the ensuing collapse of the Moldavian Communist Party undermined the Gagauz secessionist move. The Snegur government has since been effective in reaching understandings with some of the Gagauz regional leaders.

Moldova's Agricultural Economy

The Moldavian Soviet Socialist Republic was one of the poorer European republics of the former Soviet Union. In attempting to strengthen its largely state-operated economy, the new Moldovan government confronts both the advantages and disadvantages of a largely agricultural economic base. It may well be, however, that a country dependent largely on agriculture will not face the extreme levels of unemployment feared in more industrialized areas of the former Soviet Union. Early discussions with Romanian officials indicated their interest in processing Moldovan agricultural products, but the economic problems facing both countries, including the paucity of foreign investment, have made cooperation difficult.

As elsewhere in the former Soviet Union, 1991 and 1992 were years when Moldovan industrial production dropped, while consumer prices rose dramatically with the sudden absence of government subsidies. The result was a bitter "stagflation," common to much of the former Soviet Union. As an agricultural producer with a more industrialized neighbor on its northeastern border, Moldova has faced other, unexpected incursions. In January 1992, Ukrainians flooded across the border with rubles that were devalued in Ukraine, buying everything in sight. Ukraine, like Moldova, operates with mixed currencies. Such external pressures sped the drive for an independent and less inflation-prone Moldovan currency. The result has been the introduction of the Moldovan *leu,* a currency that now circulates alongside Russian and Ukrainian currencies. The economy remains weak, however, and continued conflict with Trans-Dniester separatists adds to Moldova's burden.

Ecocide in Moldova

Moldova's environment has suffered badly from the policies of the Soviet regime. Under first secretaries Bodiul and Grossu, the republic's agriculture was "modernized," with nearly catastrophic results for the ecosystem. Excessively heavy pesticide applications polluted the soil to such a degree that over a half-million acres had to be taken out of rotation. More than 90 percent of the beneficial insect population was destroyed, and virtually no birds are left in Moldova. The full impact upon the topsoil has yet to be established.

The republic's water supply was not unaffected by this chemical experimentation. Water shortages were made worse by pesticide pollution. Drinking water is in short supply in many rural areas, and the river system shows signs of considerable pesticide contamination.

International Relations

The long-expected special fraternal ties between Romania and Moldova have yet to develop. Although Snegur during his February 1991 visit to Romania spoke often of a cultural confederation, economic cooperation has been slow to develop. The economies of both countries are still state controlled, and Moldovan trade with Romania is small. Construction of desperately needed housing in Moldova, a project launched with Romanian aid, has run aground on Romanian insistence that only Romanian labor be used. Further complicating the relationship has been the demand of the Romanian democratic opposition party for reunification with Moldova, a demand that President Iliescu and his foreign minister have so far dismissed. Iliescu's visit to Moldova in May 1992 was very low key in a deliberate effort by the Moldovan government to quell any suspicions that the Moldovans desired reunification.

One area of Moldovan-Romanian relations that has grown, owing to the Dniester conflict, is that of military sales and training. The Romanian government has supplied Moldova with military equipment—mostly obsolete armored personnel carriers—and is training the newly created Moldovan military. Romania is also training Moldovan diplomats and attempting to make the world aware of Russia's involvement in the Trans-Dniester region.

The United States has established diplomatic relations with the Republic of Moldova, as have the nations of western and central Europe. Moldova is also now a full voting member of the United Nations.

Initially warm Russian-Moldovan relations soured with the Trans-Dniester conflict. In September 1990, the day after Soviet President Mikhail Gorbachev condemned the Moldavian government, Russian President Boris Yeltsin signed a bilateral treaty between Moldavia and the Russian Socialist Federated Republic. As late as May 1992, Yeltsin promised to withdraw Russian troops from the Dniester region, but the involvement of Russian troops in support of Trans-Dniester Slavs one month later in June 1992 has now complicated the future of Moldovan-Russian relations. While there is some prospect for formal withdrawal of Russian forces from the area, such a withdrawal might well be disobeyed by married officers who have settled permanently in the region.

Recovering the Past

In the process of their determined drive for language reform, the Moldovans rediscovered their own national heritage. Long suppressed by Moscow, the place of Romania in Moldova's past became as important a facet of popular appeal as was the more obvious anti-Soviet feeling. Literature by Romanian writers circulated as Romanian-Moldovan cultural cooperation became the only aspect of anticipated Romanian-Moldovan relations to flourish.

At the same time, a distinctly Moldovan national identity has also been fostered. The Moldovan demands for northern Bukovina and southern Bessarabia aimed at re-creating such an integrated Moldovan national identity. This Moldovan, as opposed to Romanian, identity has not been repudiated by the new Moldovan government. Demonstrations in 1989 included the tricolor flag

of the brief 1917–1918 Democratic Moldavian Republic, and protesters frequently began their rallies around the statue of Stephen the Great (1457–1504), the recognized father of the Moldovan nation. In 1991, the anniversary of Stephen's death became a state holiday, and the Moldovan Orthodox Church canonized him later that year.

The surge of nationalism has also brought with it popular religiosity. Before the Soviet occupation, Bessarabia was known for its large number of churches and monasteries. Under Soviet rule, however, most of these buildings were converted to warehouses, theaters, and museums, or otherwise fell into disuse and ill-repair. There were 1,120 active churches in Bessarabia before 1940 but only 300 in 1980. In 1988 volunteers began restoring many of the ruined churches. Despite occasional opposition from the Moldavian Communist Party, the restoration effort by the end of that year had brought 62 church structures back into service. Historic preservation remains one of the most daunting tasks confronting the newly awakened Moldovan nation.

As Moldova seeks to avoid the extremes of Romanian unification on the one side and secessionist moves on the other, the test of its internal success will be its ability to energize its multi-ethnic population while offering security to its many minorities. The record of the nineteenth and early twentieth centuries, scarred by the memories of the Kishinev pogroms against the Jews, is not a particularly bright one to build upon. The far more inclusive leadership drawn together by President Snegur, however, offers modest hope for the future.

UKRAINE

Statistical Profile

Demography

Population: 51,471,000

Ethnic population:

Ukrainian	37,419,000	72.7%
Russian	11,356,000	22.1%
Jewish	486,000	0.9%
Belarusian	440,000	0.9%
Moldovan	325,000	0.6%
Bulgarian	234,000	0.5%
Polish	219,000	0.4%
Others	992,000	1.9%

Predominant religious tradition:

Christianity	97.2%

Population by age:

Age	Total	Males	Females
0–4	7.6%	3.9%	3.7%
5–9	7.2%	3.7%	3.5%
10–14	7.1%	3.6%	3.5%
15–19	7.0%	3.6%	3.4%
20–24	7.4%	3.8%	3.6%
25–29	7.8%	3.9%	3.9%
30–34	7.2%	3.5%	3.7%
35–39	6.8%	3.3%	3.5%
40–44	4.6%	2.1%	2.5%
45–49	8.0%	3.7%	4.3%
50–54	5.8%	2.7%	3.1%
55–59	6.6%	2.9%	3.7%
60–64	5.6%	2.0%	3.6%
65–69	3.3%	1.1%	2.2%
70–	8.0%	2.2%	5.8%

Male/Female ratio: 46.0% male/54.0% female

Rural/Urban population: 32.5% rural/67.5% urban

Growth over time, 1979–91: 4.4%

Population density: 222.9 persons/sq mi

Politics/Government

Date of independence declaration:
24 August 1991

Major urban centers and populations:

Kiev	2,587,000
Kharkiv	1,611,000
Dnipropetrovs'k (Ekaterinoslav)	1,179,000
Odessa	1,115,000
Donets'k	1,110,000
Zaporizhzhya	884,000
L'viv	790,000
Kryvyy Rih	713,000
Mariupol (Zhdanov)	517,000
Mykolaiv	503,000
Luhans'k (Voroshilovgrad)	497,000
Makiyivka	430,000
Vinnytsya	374,000
Sevastopol	356,000
Kherson	355,000
Simferopol	344,000
Horlivka	337,000
Poltava	315,000
Chernihiv	296,000
Zhytomyr	292,000

Autonomous area:
Crimea

Education

Level of education for persons over 15:

completed higher level education	10.4%
completed secondary education	50.6%
incomplete secondary education	18.4%

Number of higher education institutions: 149
(881,200 students)

Major institutions of higher education and enrollment:

Kiev

Polytechnic Institute	32,000
T. G. Shevchenko State University	19,883
Institute of National Economy	11,000
Technological Institute of Food Industry	8,000

Civil Engineering Institute	7,900
Technological Institute of Light Industry	6,294
Automobile and Road Construction Institute	5,500
Tchaikovsky Music Conservatory	950
State Art Institute	800
Dnipropetrovs'k	
State University	12,345
Metallurgical Institute	7,000
Institute of Chemical Technology	6,300
Donets'k	
State University	12,000
Polytechnic Institute	2,300
Kharkiv	
State University	12,000
Institute of Radio Electronics	8,000
State Agricultural University	5,603
Road Transport and Road Construction Institute	5,500
Institute of Engineering and Economics	5,000
Medical Institute	3,600
Pharmaceutical Institute	1,300
Kryvyy Rih	
Ore Mining Institute	4,500
L'viv	
Polytechnic Institute	23,000
State University	13,000
Agricultural Institute	6,500
Institute of Forestry and Wood Technology	5,500
Institute of Trade and Economics	5,000
Academy of Veterinary Medicine	4,036
State Music Conservatory	800
State Institute of Applied and Decorative Art	640
Mariupol	
Metallurgical Institute	5,600
Odessa	
State University	12,000
Institute of National Economy	7,200
Institute of Low Temperature and Power Engineering	3,500
State Music Conservatory	680

Poltava	
Civil Engineering Institute	4,250
Sevastopol	
Machine Engineering Institute	7,000
Simferpol	
State University	6,600
Uzhhorod	
State University	8,000
Zaporizhzhya	
Engineering Institute	8,000
Industrial Institute	5,000
Zhytomyr	
Agricultural Institute	3,493

Socioeconomic Indicators

Birthrate: 12.7/1,000

Infant mortality: 12.9/1,000 live births

Average life expectancy: 70.5 (males, 65.7; females, 75.0)

Average family size: 3.2

Hospital beds per 10,000 persons: 135.5

Production of electrical energy: 5,737 kwh/person

Length of rail lines: 14,136 mi

Length of highways: 169,694 mi

Physical/Territorial/Geopolitical Features

Area: 233,089 sq mi (2.7% of USSR total)

Land use:

Cultivated	55%
Pasture	8%

Highest elevation: 6,762 ft. (Mt. Goverl)

Rainfall: 26 inches/year in the northwest, 43 in the Crimea, 55 in Carpathia

Temperature: average in winter 19° F in the northeast, 37° F in the south. Average in summer 65° F in the northwest, 74° F in the southeast.

Principal products: grain, sugar beets, sunflowers, cattle, swine; metallurgy, machinery, chemicals, minerals, sugar refining, railroad cars, iron ore, coal, steel.

Per capita GNP (1991): $2,340.

Sources

Narodnoe khoziaistvo SSSR v 1990g. (Moscow, 1991); *Naselenie SSSR* (1989); Matthew J. Sagers, "News Notes. Iron and Steel," *Soviet Geography* 30 (May 1989): 397-434; Lee Schwartz, "USSR Nationality Redistribution by Republic, 1979-1989: From Published Results of the 1989 All-Union Census," *Soviet Geography* 32 (April 1991): 209-48; "Ukrainskaia sovetskaia sotsialisticheskaia respublika," *Bol'shaia Sovetskaia Entsiklopediia* (Moscow, 1977); and *World of Learning,* 43rd ed. (London: Europa Publications Limited, 1993); "Russia. . ." (National Geographic Society Map, March 1993).

History and Description

Topography

Ukraine, a country whose very name means "borderland," occupies the great plains region between Europe and Asia. This Eurasian frontier, part of the East European steppe, is situated north of the Black Sea and south and west of the vast Russian Federation. After the breakup of the USSR, and Ukraine's subsequent declaration of independence, this former Soviet republic became, except for Russia, the largest country in Europe (233,000 square miles), nearly as large as the state of Texas. Along its many miles of frontier, Ukraine shares borders with six neighboring states in addition to the Russian Federation. To the northwest lies newly independent Belarus, while on the west the boundary line touches four nations previously a part of the Soviet bloc—Poland, Slovakia, Hungary, and Romania. The newly independent Republic of Moldova lies to the southwest. The southern border of Ukraine follows the coastline of the Black Sea and the smaller Sea of Azov. The Black and Azov seas feature significant international ports by virtue of their direct water access to the Mediterranean.

The Ukrainian landscape is typically one of rolling plains, characterized by a soil composed of rich black earth. With the exception of the mountains in extreme western Ukraine and the mountains along the southern edge of the Crimean Peninsula, these Ukrainian plains follow a pattern of wooded plateaus and lowlands in the north changing to flat, treeless steppe areas in the south. Broadleaf trees and various grasses grow in this part of Ukraine. In the northern third of the country, however, where the lowland area constitutes a continuation of the Pripet Marsh in neighboring Belarus, the soil is poor. Although pine forests predominate in this region, marsh grasses flourish in the less-well-drained bog portions. The Carpathian Mountains extend into Ukraine from Slovakia. They reach their highest point in Ukraine at Mount Goverl (6,762 feet) in the vicinity of the headwaters of the Prut River.

The three main river systems of Ukraine are the Dnieper, the Southern Bug, and the upper Dniester, supplemented by important effluents and tributaries such as the Donets and the Desna. The Dnieper (Dnipro in Ukrainian), one of Europe's longest rivers (1,420 miles), has been used as a commercial waterway for centuries. It divides the country into what has historically been called right-bank (western) and left-bank (eastern) Ukraine.

Eastern Ukraine. In the heavily industrialized eastern half of Ukraine, the Donets Basin (Donbass), constitutes one of the world's richest areas of natural mineral wealth. First developed commercially in the late nineteenth century during the course of the industrialization of the Russian Empire, the heavily populated urban centers of the Donets Basin and the Dnieper Valley still contain reserves of coal, iron ore, natural gas, oil, manganese, mercury, uranium, graphite, phosphorite, kaolin, limestone, titanium, and zirconium. Steel production is of paramount importance in Donbass, and iron ore provides a vital export item to Europe and Asia. A modern petrochemical industry has grown up in the Donbass, turning out such products as nitrogen fertilizers, superphosphates, and sulfuric acid. Numerous machine manufacturing plants are also located in this part of Ukraine. To provide enough water to meet all the human, agricultural, and industrial needs of Donbass, the Dnieper has been dammed in many places, and major hydroelectric plants have been constructed.

Western Ukraine. Even though the western part of Ukraine is not as richly endowed with mineral and other natural resources as eastern Ukraine, small deposits of coal, oil, gas, sulfur, as well as potassium and magnesium salts are found west of the Dnieper. In the 1970s, Ukraine turned to the use of nuclear power with the building of the Chernobyl nuclear power generating plant north of Kiev on the outer edges of the Pripet Marsh. Furthermore, the discovery in the south of oil and gas fields in the Crimea and the Sea of Azov may yield additional sources of these precious commodities. Yet another kind of energy is to be found in the extensive peat bogs of the Pripet Marsh. The chemical industry of western Ukraine manufactures nitrogen fertilizers, plastics, synthetic fibers, and rubber products. Automotive plants and food processing activities also strengthen the region's economy. Ukraine's international ports on the Black Sea and the Sea of Azov allow for vital military and trading ventures, and the local fishing industry provides food exports.

Ukraine

LITHUANIA

BELARUS

POLAND

Pripet Marsh

Western Bug River

Galicia

L'viv

Carpathian

SLOVAKIA

Uzhhorod

HUNGARY

Dniester River

+ 6,762 feet

Mountains

Prut River

MOLDOVA

ROMANIA

Zhytomyr

Vinnytsya

Southern Bug River

Kryvyy Rih

Mykolayiv

Odessa

Kherson

Chernihiv

Chernobyl

Desna River

Kiev

Pereiaslav

Dnieper River

Poltava

Dnipropetrovs'k

Zaporizhzhya

RUSSIA

Kharkiv

Donets River

Luhans'k

Horlivka

Donets'k • Makiyivka

Donets Basin

Mariupol

Sea of Azov

RUSSIA

Crimea

Simferopol

Sevastopol

Yalta

Black Sea

National Boundary

Autonomous Boundary

★ Capital City

• Other Cities

0   200 Miles

0   200 Kilometers

Agriculture. The prosperous agricultural heartland of western Ukraine, blessed with rich black earth, a relatively mild climate, and sufficient rainfall, has traditionally grown much more than its share of farm products. Formerly referred to as the breadbasket of the Soviet Union, Ukrainian lands excel in yields of sugar beets, grains, potatoes, flax, tobacco, sunflowers, legumes, and other vegetables and fruits, including grapes. The densely populated rural areas of western Ukraine also support livestock breeding, especially swine or cattle, and associated dairying activities. Eastern Ukraine, in spite of heavy industrialization and lower rainfall, also cultivates intensively its own remaining rich farmland. Near the Sea of Azov, in the sunny Crimea, and around Odessa, where rainfall is insufficient, irrigation has helped improve yields, and vineyards have become crucial to the wine industry. The success of irrigation has likewise led to the introduction of rice and cotton along the northern Black Sea coast.

Cities. Ukraine has 50 urban areas with more than 100,000 inhabitants. The largest of these areas is the historic city of Kiev (Kyiv in Ukrainian), located on the high right bank of the Dnieper near its confluence with the Desna. Kiev, a picturesque city of wide boulevards lined with beautiful chestnut trees, offers magnificent views of both the Dnieper and the countryside beyond. The center of East Slavic civilization between the ninth and the thirteenth centuries, Kiev was the cultural and political capital of the grand princely state known as Kievan Rus. After adopting Christianity from Byzantium at the end of the tenth century (Grand Prince Vladimir [Volodymyr] was baptized in 988), Kievan Rus drew upon the religious and cultural inheritance of Byzantium. The multidomed Cathedral of St. Sophia (1037), the Monastery of the Caves (Kievo-Pecherskaia Lavra, 1051) on the hillside above the river, and the statue of St. Vladimir looking down on the Dnieper all call to mind the early conversion of Kievan Rus to Byzantine, Eastern-rite Christianity. Kiev is also the long-established seat of the Ukrainian Academy of Sciences and of the "red" Kievan State University (so called for its brightly painted red exterior) founded in 1834. Modern Kiev, having expanded to the east or left bank of the Dnieper to accommodate a population of more than two and a half million residents, has become a center for manufacturing of computers and electronics, clothing production, and food processing industries. It is today the capital of the independent Republic of Ukraine.

Other important large cities in western and southern Ukraine include Lviv, a medieval university town founded in 1241 and previously part of both the Austro-Hungarian Empire and the Polish-Lithuanian Commonwealth; Odessa, an international port on the Black Sea as well as a resort and spa; Mykolayiv (Nikolaev), a shipbuilding center on the estuary of the Southern Bug; and Kherson at the mouth of the Dnieper. In the Crimean Peninsula, which was transferred administratively from the Russian to the Ukrainian Soviet Republic in 1954, the city of Sevastopol is a strategic naval port. The Crimean resort city of Yalta was the site of World War II meetings between Churchill, Roosevelt, and Stalin in February 1945, at which time controversial territorial divisions for postwar Europe were secretly worked out by the Allied powers.

It is in the heavily industrialized Donbass region of eastern Ukraine, however, that most of the country's largest urban centers are to be found. These include such cities as Dnipropetrovs'k and Donets'k with populations of more than one million, and Zaporizhzhya and Kryvyy Rih with populations approaching one million. Ukraine's second largest city, numbering more than 1.6 million, is Kharkiv, just north of the Donbass. Founded by Ukrainian Cossacks in 1650, Kharkiv became in the nineteenth century an important transport and railroad junction. Later, between 1922 and 1934, it served as the capital of Soviet Ukraine. Modern Kharkiv is a center of the machine construction industry, producing agricultural and transport vehicles. Poltava, site of Peter the Great's defeat of Sweden in 1709, is located less than a hundred miles southwest of Kharkiv. The modern city of Poltava, near the battle site, is a regional agricultural processing center.

Ethnic Background

Ukrainians belong to the group of Slavic peoples known as the Eastern Slavs. This group also includes the Russians, Belarusians, and Rusyns (Carpatho-Russians). Before 1917, Ukrainians were referred to within the Muscovite and Russian empires as the Little Russians (Malorossian'e), a term that is now obsolete. This term dates from early Byzantine references to the territorial location of this people. Although Ukrainians are traditionally Eastern Orthodox by religion, there exists in western Ukraine a substantial population of Uniates or Greek Catholics—those who continue to follow Orthodox liturgical practices but are administratively within the ecclesiastical structure of the Roman Catholic church. (See Belarus chapter, p. 52–54.)

The Ukrainian language, which uses the Cyrillic alphabet, belongs to the eastern branch of Slavic languages, within the larger Indo-European family. The modern Ukrainian literary language that developed in the nineteenth century was based on the dialect used in the area of Kiev but was significantly affected by earlier Polish and German borrowings. Modern Ukrainian has also been influenced by the dialects spoken in the lands of Galicia and Transcarpathian Ukraine. In these western territories the local Rusyn population, a population that most Ukrainians consider to be a part of the greater Ukrainian nation, found itself under more moderate Austro-Hungarian rule and was allowed to publish works in its own native language. Modern Ukrainian thus came to be influenced by Rusyn or Carpatho-Russian writers, who contributed significantly to the development of a modern Ukrainian literary tradition.

The majority of ethnic Ukrainians live in Ukraine, although substantial numbers can also be found in European Russia, Siberia, and Kazakhstan. Ukraine itself has been and continues to be the home of numerous other ethnic groups. Russification policies during both the tsarist and Soviet periods encouraged massive infiltrations of ethnic Russians to live and work in Ukrainian lands, especially in the more industrialized Donbass. Additionally, western or right bank Ukraine constituted historically a major part of the Pale of Settlement, which was the zone where Jews were restricted to live in Eastern Europe. This Pale of Settlement, divided territorially in the 1920s between Poland and the Soviet Union, was home to many of the six million Jews who perished in the Holocaust during World War II. Ukrainian Jews suffered enormous losses on both sides of the Polish-Soviet border. Other neighboring peoples have also long been a part of the Ukrainian demographic picture, especially Belarusians, Moldovans, Bulgarians, and Poles.

Historical Development

Although Ukrainians date their own political history from the unification of East Slavs under the Kievan Rus grand princedom in the ninth century, the early modern history of Ukraine dates from the sixteenth and seventeenth centuries when geographical references to "Ukraine" commonly came to denote the region roughly equivalent to present-day Ukraine. In the seventeenth century, the leadership of the Dnieper or Zaporizhzhian Cossacks

fought the Polish-Lithuanian Commonwealth to secure greater autonomy for Ukraine. Despite the legendary efforts of the famous Cossack leader, or *hetman*, of the Zaporizhzhian Cossacks—Bohdan Khmelnytsky—the Cossacks failed to secure Ukrainian independence. Indeed, Khmelnytsky's efforts to enjoin Muscovite armies in the fight against Poland (the Union of Pereiaslav, 1654) led instead to the eventual subordination of Ukraine to Muscovite Russia. In spite of the leadership of Khmelnytsky during the ill-fated "national liberation wars," the Union of Pereiaslav has been associated with the period of "the Ruin" in latter-day Ukrainian historical writing. With the exception of Ukrainian lands in Galicia and Transcarpathia, the Russian Empire gradually extended its centralized control over Ukraine during the eighteenth and early nineteenth centuries. (On this process, see Zenon E. Kohut, *Russian Centralism and Ukrainian Autonomy: Imperial Absorption of the Hetmanate, 1760s-1830s,* Cambridge, 1988.)

Russian Revolutions and Ukrainian Independence

The Russian revolutions of 1905 and 1917 unleashed the modern drive for Ukrainian national independence. In March 1917, Ukrainian national leaders formed a Ukrainian Central Council, or the Central Rada as it was called, briefly led by the Ukrainian historian Michael Hrushevsky. Initially the Central Rada called for Ukrainian autonomy *within* a Russian federal republic, and the Rada was duly recognized as the autonomous Ukrainian government by the Russian Provisional Government in July 1917. In November 1917, however, following the October Bolshevik Revolution, the Rada adopted a proclamation of independence and formed the Ukrainian National Republic.

Facing Bolshevik opposition and without the Ukrainian military forces still mobilized by World War I, the Rada eventually fell to Bolshevik insurgency in Kiev in late January 1918. The defeated Ukrainian government moved its headquarters temporarily to Zhytomyr. Soon, however, the besieged Ukrainian republican government, with German assistance, successfully recaptured Kiev in the spring of 1918. Having defeated the Bolshevik forces, the Ukrainians then remained under the influence of the German military until the armistice of November 1918 signaled the end of World War I.

In the wake of the evacuation of German troops, the Central Rada, with the support of Ukrainian military forces, was quickly able to reassert its power, reuniting eastern and western Ukraine in January 1919. Led by General Simon Petliura, the independent Ukrainian government held out against Soviet forces during the ensuing Russian Civil War, even striking a temporary accord with the Poles during the Polish-Soviet war of 1919–20. By 1921, however, the Soviet government had established itself throughout most of Ukraine, bringing an end to the brief period (1917–20) of Ukrainian independence.

Soviet Rule

While nationalist sentiment continued to make itself felt in the 1920s within the new Ukrainian Soviet Socialist Republic, Stalin's collectivization and industrialization campaigns launched in 1928 fell bitterly upon Ukrainian soil. Collectivization of agriculture meant the forcible resettlement of peasant communal residents into large new collective farms (*kolkhozy*), a process yielding widespread dislocation. Even though these Stalinist policies were widespread throughout the Soviet Union, agricultural Ukraine seemed targeted for particularly harsh and cruel enforcement of the new regulations. During the ensuing famine of the 1930s, as many as six million peasants were condemned to starvation. (See Robert Conquest, *The Harvest of Sorrow: Soviet Collectivization and the Terror-Famine,* Oxford, 1986.)

World War II brought yet further devastation to Ukraine as German armies invaded the Soviet Union during Operation Barbarossa, launched in June 1941. Kiev, Odessa, and other Ukrainian cities were all heavily damaged before being captured by the German war machine. Millions of ethnic Ukrainians, alongside countless Poles, Jews, and Belarusians on Ukrainian soil, lost their lives in the fighting. One of the most sensitive issues in Ukrainian historiography involves the extent of Ukrainian collaboration with Nazi forces in World War II. The issue arises particularly in connection with the Ukrainian Insurrectionary Army (UPA) and its main leader Stepan Bandera. The UPA was the military arm of the Organization of Ukrainian Nationalists (OUN), an authoritar-

ian, right-wing organization founded in interwar Poland. Bandera and the OUN/UPA saw their primary goals as Ukrainian independence and the overthrow of Soviet rule in Ukraine, and they were prepared to use terrorism to accomplish their ends. In the aftermath of the Nazi-Soviet Pact of 1939, Bandera's organization openly fought the Soviet army. While Bandera's struggle against the Soviet forces has gained him some support among Ukrainian nationalists, there was some OUN/UPA collaboration with the Nazis. At the same time, however, Bandera's followers fought against both German and Soviet forces.

Following World War II, efforts were redoubled to integrate the Ukrainian Soviet Socialist Republic into the Soviet Union. These efforts included such measures as outlawing the Uniate church and encouraging the use of the Russian language in public education and the mass media. The effective integration of the Ukrainian Communist Party into the Communist Party of the Soviet Union (CPSU) was reflected in the occasional rise of key Ukrainian Party leaders to the highest organs of Soviet power. Both Nikita Khrushchev and Leonid Brezhnev held leadership posts in Ukraine before assuming the office of CPSU General Secretary in Moscow. Brezhnev, whose Ukrainian accent was often lost amidst his more general slurring of speech in later years, hailed from the industrial river city of Dnipropetrovs'k (Ekaterinoslav). Out of this ideologically correct Ukrainian Communist Party, the current president of the Republic of Ukraine, Leonid Kravchuk, also rose to power. First a regional Party head, then an official in the Central Committee of the Ukrainian Communist Party, and finally in 1979 placed in the Party's ideology and propaganda department (a department he came to head in 1988), Kravchuk became chair of the Ukrainian Supreme Soviet in 1990. Although his earlier impeccable Communist Party credentials have discredited him in the eyes of some Ukrainian nationalists, Leonid Kravchuk's personal metamorphosis into the political leader of the newly independent Ukrainian republic mirrors the wider transformations occurring in contemporary Ukraine.

Contemporary Issues

Rukh and the Politics of Independence

On 24 August 1991, the Ukrainian Supreme Soviet proclaimed the formal independence of the Republic of

Ukraine. Although the timing of the promulgation obviously related to the abortive coup attempt earlier that same week in Moscow, the declaration of Ukrainian independence also reflected the ascendancy in Ukrainian politics of a new voice for political reform and national sovereignty. The leading edge of this reformist voice was, from its gestation in 1988 to its official founding in 1989, the political movement Rukh.

Rukh, meaning "movement" in Ukrainian, was established during the Gorbachev years of perestroika. Its full title was initially the "Ukrainian Popular Movement for Perestroika." Following the pattern of other national front movements in the Baltic region, Rukh sought democratization, economic reform, and Ukrainian sovereignty. In its earliest documents, however, Rukh called for the rule of law (the legal protection of individual citizens), but inside a restructured Soviet federation. In this sense, Rukh carefully positioned itself within the larger spectrum of Ukrainian politics. With respect to the nomenklatura (the established bureaucratic apparatus) and the Ukrainian Communist Party, Rukh was a voice of political dissent. With respect to the goals of Gorbachev's perestroika, however, Rukh could claim to be loyally supportive. Its 1989 platform endorsed market-oriented economic reforms, the broad application of human rights and the rule of law, as well as the religious toleration of all faiths on Ukrainian soil. (It specifically recognized the formerly outlawed Greek Catholics, and it noted the historic role in Ukraine of the Jewish population.) Rukh's central message, however, was its call for the national sovereignty of Ukraine, a message that was unmistakably a threat to the old Soviet order.

The success of this national front movement became readily apparent in the March 1989 parliamentary elections, elections that occurred simultaneously throughout all republics of the Soviet Union. In the vote for the Ukrainian Supreme Soviet, Rukh won approximately 2 hundred seats. With its allies in other fringe parties, Rukh came to control about one-third of the seats in the roughly four-hundred-member Supreme Soviet. The elections also revealed that Rukh political opposition had become so popular that, had the elections not entailed a cumbersome party registration procedure effectively keeping Rukh candidates off a majority of slates, the Rukh parliamentary minority might well have been an outright majority.

Sensing the mood of the public, the majority Communist Party within the Supreme Soviet shifted its position, endorsing the notion of Ukrainian sovereignty. In July 1990, the Supreme Soviet voted overwhelmingly to proclaim Ukrainian state sovereignty but *not* independence.

Leonid Kravchuk, a leading Party supporter of the 1990 sovereignty declaration, was subsequently elected chair of the Supreme Soviet that same summer. Politically adept, Kravchuk sought to ride the Rukh-inspired wave of Ukrainian nationalism while maintaining his commitment to the leading role of the Communist Party in Soviet Ukrainian life.

The Moscow Coup and Aftermath

As elsewhere in the former Soviet republics, the failed Moscow *coup d'état* of August 1991 was a watershed event in Ukrainian politics. Within days of the abortive coup the Ukrainian Supreme Soviet declared Ukraine independent. Equally dramatic was the impact upon the local Communist Party. Kravchuk, who had indicated his support for the coup leaders in the early stages of the August events, quickly reversed his position, issuing a strong statement against the conspiracy. Shortly thereafter he resigned from the Communist Party. He then banned the Party (just as Boris Yeltsin later did in Russia). By October 1991, the former Communist Party had renamed itself the Socialist Party. Using the former Communist Party's bureaucratic structure, but effectively positioning himself behind the national message of a strong Ukrainian state, Kravchuk proceeded in December 1991 to win an open election to the newly created office of president of the Republic of Ukraine.

The August 1991 events and the declaration of Ukrainian independence also exerted a profound impact upon the Rukh organization. On one side of the Rukh coalition, Vyacheslav Chornovil, a former political prisoner and opponent to Kravchuk in the December 1991 presidential election, led a "constructive opposition" that claimed Kravchuk was not carrying through the process of political reform to its natural end. Calling the process "an unfinished revolution," the Chornovil faction of Rukh decried Kravchuk's reliance upon the nomenklatura, composed of old Communist Party appointments at all levels of the bureaucracy. Chornovil also called for a speeding up of market-oriented economic reform. By the fourth Rukh congress in December 1992, Chornovil was clearly in control of the assembly, garnering a vote of 423 to 8, and was elected to be sole head of the organization. Under Chornovil's leadership, Rukh seemed headed in the direction of becoming a powerful political opposition party, the largest such independent political group in Ukraine. (See Roman Solchanyk, "Ukraine: A Year of

Transition," *RFE/RL Research Report,* vol. 2, no. 1, 1 January 1993, pp. 58–63.)

Another important faction within the original Rukh movement, however, came to support the Kravchuk government in the months following August 1991. The first head of Rukh, Ivan Drach, typified those Ukrainian nationalists within the Rukh movement who felt that the central goal of the movement must be to defend and consolidate the strength of the Ukrainian state, even if at the expense of more far-reaching political and economic reform measures. For Drach and other Rukh members of the same opinion, including several Rukh deputies in the Supreme Soviet, the goal of state consolidation increasingly came to be identified with support for Leonid Kravchuk. For his part, Kravchuk openly sought to coopt Rukh support in 1992 by creating an independent State Council that included notable Rukh members. As Kravchuk sought to defend the Republic of Ukraine against Russian claims regarding the Black Sea fleet and the Crimean territory (see below), there was some justification for the argument that Rukh support for Kravchuk was in the interest of continuing Ukrainian independence. Drach's elimination from the co-chairmanship of Rukh at the December 1992 congress nevertheless demonstrated that Rukh remained, at its core, a dissenting political opposition committed to more rapid democratization and economic reform.

Among the most dynamic elements in Ukrainian political life in the year following independence were the extremes on both the left and right. On the left (the former Communist Party, now the Socialist Party), there were growing signs that socialism still had considerable popular support, particularly given the frustrations of a deteriorating economic situation. On the right, ultra-nationalist groups increasingly sought to frame Ukrainian state interest in narrowly national, ethnic terms. (Abraham Brumberg has chronicled, not without some exaggeration, this authoritarian side of Ukrainian politics in his article, "Not So Free At Last," *New York Review of Books,* 22 October 1992, pp. 56-63.) As is the case with other newly independent states of the former Soviet Union, the stability of political life and the strength of the political extremes continue to rest in good measure upon the fate of the uncertain Ukrainian economy.

The Economics of Independence

The most immediate crisis facing the Republic of Ukraine is its deteriorating economic productivity. All sectors of the Ukrainian economy have suffered significant declines in production. Industrial and consumer goods manufacturing was down by over 20 percent in 1992 from comparable periods in 1991. Food production was down by over a third in 1992. These declines have resulted in price increases, even at a time when real wages adjusted for inflation have been dropping. Given the changes underway in the ownership of some enterprises, the statistical measurements of productivity may be unreliable. Nevertheless, there is little dispute regarding the generally deteriorating picture of the Ukrainian economy in 1992-93.

Other former Soviet republics have suffered comparable levels of decline in production as new market-oriented sectors of the economy seek to offset sharp drops in the output of state-subsidized heavy industry. In the case of Ukraine, however, the economic problems are compounded by problems of energy dependency. Even though Donbass oil reserves have not run out, Ukraine lacks sufficient oil production to meet its basic energy needs. Ukraine must turn to the purchase of Russian and Kazakh oil now being bartered or sold at world market prices—accompanied by demands for purchase with internationally floatable hard currency. In the 1960s and 1970s, Ukrainian energy dependency was addressed by the construction of nuclear power generating stations, notably the complex at Chernobyl. Today, the human disaster surrounding the Chernobyl explosion is coupled with the reality of energy shortfalls. The architects of Ukrainian political independence now face the problems of energy dependence.

In fashioning economic policy for the 1990s, Ukrainian political leadership has been particularly indecisive, emphasizing short-term political responses instead of longer-term structural solutions. In the debate over the pace of market reforms and privatization, the Kravchuk government has essentially sought to steer a middle ground, a position that some economists argue is not sustainable. Faced with the liberalization of prices by the Russian Federation in January 1992, Kravchuk appointed as minister of economics in March a liberal advocate of rapid privatization, Volodymyr Lanovyi. By July 1992, however, Kravchuk had already sacked Lanovyi, who openly criticized the government for its anti-market responses to rising Russian prices. Dismayed over the performance of the Ukrainian economy, the Supreme Soviet in October adopted a resolution of no confidence in the government, forcing Kravchuk to undertake a major cabinet reshuffling.

In this reshuffling, Leonid Kuchma was brought in as prime minister. Kuchma, director at Dnipropetrovs'k of the largest state-run missile production plant in the world, let it be known that he intended to support market reforms on a gradual basis, beginning more slowly with the privatization of smaller firms and consumer-oriented businesses while continuing state support for large heavy industrial enterprises.

Kuchma's political solution dramatizes the quandary within which the government is caught. It can seek to follow a gradual policy that retains state subsidies for heavy industry but only at a great cost in international credit worthiness and potential hyperinflation. On the other hand, the government can return to more radical market-oriented policies but then run the risk of fundamentally destabilizing unemployment. Faced with this dilemma, the Kravchuk government has demonstrated an inclination to seek short-term political solutions for these basic structural problems. Until the government holds to a consistent and viable economic policy, with necessary infusions of capital from international lending institutions, the long-term stability of Ukraine remains uncertain.

The Diplomacy of Independence

The problem of the Ukrainian economy is also intimately tied to international diplomacy. Matters ranging from currency reform to Ukrainian relations with the Commonwealth of Independent States (CIS) and with the West all have been affected by the needs of the economy. On the matter of currency reform, for example, proposals for the immediate breakaway of Ukraine from the ruble zone, made up of those CIS republics that have retained use of the old Soviet Russian currency, were advanced by the Kravchuk government's State Council Collegium on Questions of Economic Policy early in 1992. In the end, those preliminary proposals were temporarily shelved because of their failure to take into account Ukraine's international energy dependency, a dependency that continued to be tied to the purchase of Russian oil on the ruble market.

The Crimean and the Black Sea Fleet. More pressing for the Republic of Ukraine is the normalization of its relations with the Russian Federation. The relationship has been complicated by a rising Russian nationalist sentiment that fundamentally rejects the notion of a Ukraine fully independent of Russia. The two hot spots in this Russian-Ukrainian relationship have been the status of the Crimean Peninsula and the disposition of the Black Sea fleet. The Crimean issue dates to the immediate post-Stalinist era when, in 1954, Moscow formally transferred the Crimean Peninsula to the jurisdiction of the Ukrainian Soviet Socialist Republic. In May 1992, the Russian Supreme Soviet adopted a resolution declaring that the 1954 resolution lacked the force of law. Russian claims to the Crimea derive mainly from the fact that a majority of the population on the peninsula is Russian or Russian-speaking. In December 1992, the Russian Congress of People's Deputies also challenged Ukrainian claims to the Crimean port city of Sevastopol, the home of the Black Sea naval fleet.

For Ukraine, the Crimean issue is perceived as a strictly internal matter, the 1954 transfer having rendered the peninsula an integral part of the Ukrainian republic. Nevertheless, concerned Ukrainian policy makers have been moving swiftly to appropriate funds (7 billion rubles) to assist "deported nations," a reference to Crimean Tatars, Greeks, and other Crimean residents exiled by Stalin during World War II, who might with Ukrainian assistance be coopted into support for the Ukrainian position. The Ukrainian government has also been receptive to indigenous efforts underway on the peninsula for Crimean autonomy. Not only has the Crimea remained an autonomous region within the Ukrainian republic, but in June 1992 the Ukrainian Supreme Soviet granted full property and natural resource rights to the Crimea. (See Abraham Brumberg, "Whose Crimea?" *New York Review of Books,* 22 October 1992, pp. 63–64.)

The issue of the port facility at Sevastopol links the Crimean issue with the potentially more serious Russian-Ukrainian conflict over the Black Sea naval fleet. Both Ukrainian President Kravchuk and Russian President Yeltsin have, with the backing of their own national parliaments, taken a hard line on the sovereign claims of their countries to the ownership of the Black Sea fleet. Both Ukraine and the Russian Federation include coastal lands on the Black Sea and the Sea of Azov, although the port facilities at Sevastopol have traditionally been the headquarters of the Black Sea fleet. Facing a showdown over the Black Sea fleet issue, the two presidents met on the Crimean Peninsula at Yalta in August 1992 to resolve their differences. While negotiations will continue to take place over the issue, the interim resolution reached at Yalta declared the Black Sea fleet would be placed under a joint Ukrainian-Russian command for three years, after which time the fleet would be divided between the two sides. It is unclear which side has the most to gain by this delay, but a serious impediment to normal Ukrainian-Russian relations was overcome at these Yalta talks.

Nuclear Policy. Ukrainian ties with the West remain crucial for securing financial investment and economic development funds. Yet, in 1992–93, concerns over Ukrainian nuclear policy threatened to undermine Western support for the Ukrainian republic. While Ukraine has transferred its tactical nuclear weapons out of Ukrainian territory, it has retained what it calls administrative authority over its strategic nuclear weapons, a status that makes Ukraine one of the leading nuclear powers in the world. Operational management of Ukraine's nuclear arsenal was placed under the CIS armed forces, but Ukraine continued to demand the right to "administer" these weapons. Furthermore, it sought full representation at nuclear arms negotiations, a representation which it felt was being unfairly given over exclusively to the Russian Federation. Finally, Ukraine, unlike Belarus and Kazakhstan, stalled its ratification of the START agreements.

The Western response to these Ukrainian signals has come in the form of expressions of concern over Ukraine's independence on the nuclear issue, claiming that such independence might jeopardize normal trade and economic relations. Particularly worrisome from the point of view of the West was the prospect that some more nationalistically inclined Ukrainian representatives in their Supreme Soviet might actually want to use the retention of nuclear weapons as an issue of national sovereignty, derailing full Ukrainian participation in the START process. Kravchuk has sought to calm Western fears on this score, indicating that the only serious impediment he foresaw to Ukrainian denuclearization was the extraordinary cost entailed in decommissioning the nuclear weapons sites. From Kravchuk's point of view, the Ukrainian government and the Ukrainian economy were ill-prepared to bear the burden of those costs, and Western financial commitments ought to be included as a part of the decommissioning process. Nevertheless, the longer the nuclear issue stands as a barrier to strengthened economic ties between Ukraine and the West, the greater will be the deterioration of the Ukrainian economy.

Religion and the National Question in Ukraine

Perhaps nowhere in the European lands of the former Soviet Union has religious identity been so closely tied to the national question as in Ukraine. Dating from the conversion of St. Vladimir (Volodymyr) in the tenth century, Ukraine has been a center of Eastern-rite Christianity. Yet, the Eastern Christians of Ukraine have been deeply split into regional and ecclesiastical divisions—divisions that have mirrored complex regional and historical distinctions within Ukrainian society.

Setting aside the substantial presence of Protestantism in Ukraine, the predominant Eastern Christian community is today divided into at least three major confessional or church subdivisions. As recently as the 1988 celebrations of the millennium of the conversion of St. Vladimir and the Eastern Slavs to Christianity, these divisions continued to be held together artificially by the dominating presence of the Moscow-based Russian Orthodox church. Headed by Metropolitan Filaret of Kiev, this Russian Orthodox church controlled virtually all official Eastern-rite religious life in Ukraine. When Ukrainian independence was declared in 1991, this artificial unity was broken. In its stead there appeared three distinct branches of Eastern Christendom—the Ukrainian Catholic church (UCC), formerly known as the Uniate or Greek Catholic church, the Ukrainian Orthodox branch of the Moscow patriarchate (the Russian Orthodox church), and the Ukrainian Autocephalous Orthodox church.

Ukrainian Catholic Church. Dating from the sixteenth century and the Union of Brest (1596), the Greek Catholic or, now, Ukrainian Catholic, church had become the dominant church among Eastern Christians of Galicia and Transcarpathia, until those areas were annexed by the Soviet Union at the end of World War II. Many of the Eastern-rite Catholics from that region had emigrated to the United States during the late nineteenth and early twentieth centuries (the Rusyn communities of western Pennsylvania, for example). Those Greek Catholics remaining in Galicia and Transcarpathia suffered the formal dissolving of the Uniate or Greek Catholic church by the Soviet government in 1946. Despite subsequent decades of persecution, an underground Uniate church maintained its loyalty to the Union (see the discussion of the Uniate church under "Belarus," page 53), and both clergy and laity were ready to resume their activities above ground as religious toleration was extended to non-Russian Orthodox believers in the late 1980s. As a result, nearly half of the parishes of the Russian Orthodox Church in Galicia were threatened with takeover by forces loyal to the Ukrainian Catholic church in the westernmost provinces of Ukraine. By 1991, when Cardinal Myroslav Liubachivs'kyi returned to Lviv from exile in Rome, the Ukrainian Catholic church could claim as many as two-thousand Uniate parishes in western Ukraine.

Ukrainian Autocephalous Orthodox Church. Even more dramatic was the rebirth of the Ukrainian Autocephalous Orthodox Church. Twice in the twentieth century Ukrainian Orthodox church leaders had founded an autocephalous (independent) Orthodox church on Ukrainian territory. First, during the brief period of Ukrainian independence from 1917 to 1921, the Ukrainian church movement led to the self-consecration of the Ukrainian Autocephalous Orthodox Church (UAOC) in 1921. Quickly liquidated by the Soviet authorities, the UAOC survived among Ukrainian emigre communities abroad. Again, during the German occupation in 1942, the UAOC was revived on Ukrainian soil. As happened in the 1920s, the revived UAOC of 1942 was also liquidated by Soviet authorities after the war. Ukrainian emigres of both the 1921 and the 1942 consecrations perpetuated this Ukrainian Autocephalous Orthodox Church in the West.

As noted in Frank Sysyn's recent essay on Ukrainian church politics, the failure of the Russian Orthodox church to learn from these previous attempts at Ukrainian Orthodox independence meant that a renewed drive for independence would again yield conflict and schism in Orthodox ranks (Frank Sysyn, "The Third Rebirth of the Ukrainian Autocephalous Orthodox Church and the Religious Situation in Ukraine, 1989–1991," in *Seeking God: The Recovery of Religious Identity in Russia, Ukraine, and Georgia,* DeKalb: Northern Illinois University Press, 1993). Typical of such misunderstandings was the visit of Moscow Patriarch Aleksii to Kiev in November 1990, ostensibly for the purpose of recognizing the "autonomy" of the Kievan Exarchate of the Russian Orthodox church. What the Moscow patriarch encountered, among other things, were Ukrainian protesters who objected to the patriarch's use of the St. Sophia Cathedral in Kiev. The cathedral had been, until its forcible closure in 1930, the center of the Ukrainian Autocephalous Orthodox Church. In the end, 1990 was decisive for the autocephalists, who won over significant numbers of clergy and parishes for a revived UAOC. It was in that year that Patriarch Mstyslav, head of the UAOC, returned to Ukraine from his post in the emigration. Despite his venerable age, the patriarch provided a visible symbol of continuity in Ukrainian Orthodox independence, as well as a signal of its important ties with

Ukrainians abroad. Although the Moscow patriarchate's renamed autonomous "Ukrainian Orthodox Church" retained more than 5,400 parishes in Ukraine, the Ukrainian Autocephalous Orthodox Church by January 1992 had over 1,600 parishes, most of them in the far western provinces of Ukraine.

There are two larger realities that can be seen in the split between the autocephalous and the Moscow-oriented Orthodox churches of Ukraine. On the one hand, the rebirth of the Ukrainian Autocephalous Orthodox Church has demonstrated the pivotal importance that the Ukrainian emigre community, especially the Ukrainians of Canada and the United States, have played in Ukrainian political and cultural life. There is little question that the UAOC in North America contributed mightily, both in terms of leadership and finances, to the revival of the UAOC on Ukrainian territory. The linkage of Ukrainian emigres with their homeland carries with it important lessons not lost upon a Ukrainian political leadership anxious to cultivate commercial ties and financial support in the West.

A second reality beneath the current Orthodox schism in Ukraine is the manner in which the conflict has been played out in the context of ongoing Ukrainian-Russian tensions. Having been forced to resign from his post amidst allegations of immoral sexual behavior, Metropolitan Filaret of the Ukrainian Orthodox Church (UOC) returned to Kiev in April 1992 to announce that he would not resign after all because his resignation had been made under duress. Before this, Metropolitan Filaret had openly sought a formal grant of independence (autocephaly) from the Moscow patriarchate. Such a sign of independence by the Kievan metropolitan no doubt contributed to his undoing in Moscow—he had been called before an ecclesiastical court there and deprived of all priestly functions. Nevertheless, his appeal for autocephaly endeared the beleaguered prelate to the Ukrainian government. What Metropolitan Filaret had done in his request to Moscow was to capitalize upon Ukrainian national sensitivities in such a fashion as to gather the support of the Ukrainian government. In the ensuing showdown between governmental supporters of Metropolitan Filaret and those of the Moscow patriarchate almost all bishops and most clergy within the autonomous Ukrainian Orthodox church sided with what they perceived to be the canonical authority of the Moscow patriarchate in disciplining Metropolitan Filaret.

The final chapter in this conflict within Eastern Christendom has yet to be written. In 1992, Metropolitan Filaret and his followers unexpectedly decided to join forces with the UAOC to form the Ukrainian Orthodox Church—Kiev Patriarchate. UAOC Patriarch Mstyslav, then 94 years old, was chosen to head this new merger. In the ensuing months, it became clear that the union of these two Ukrainian Orthodox groups was, to say the least, strained. With the death of Patriarch Mstyslav in 1993, the ecclesiastical divisions in Ukraine, primarily between Moscow and Kievan jurisdictional authority, remained very much in transition.

Fundamental national and cultural issues, such as the language of liturgical worship, continue to be played out in Ukraine in a context of profound confessional, regional, and ethnic divisions. Underlying all of these divisions are the contending interests of Ukrainian national identity and the continuing Russian influence in Ukraine. It seems unlikely that there will be any lasting stability until the full range of Ukranian-Russian tensions has been resolved.

PART THREE

TRANSCAUCASIA

INTRODUCTION

Situated south of the greater Caucasus Mountains between the Caspian and Black Seas is the region known as Transcaucasia, home of the three newly independent states of Georgia, Armenia, and Azerbaijan. Turkey and Iran border Transcaucasia on the south and west. To the north of the Caucasus Mountains are regions of the adjacent Russian Federation. This Russian North Caucasus region includes seven formerly autonomous republics of the Soviet Union—now independent republics—Adygeia, Dagestan, Kabardino-Balkariia, Karachai-Cherkessiia, North Ossetiia, Checheniia, and Ingushetiia (the latter two, until 1992, forming a single unit—Checheno-Ingushetiia).

Torn by ethnic and political conflict, Transcaucasia has become in the 1990s the Yugoslavia of former Soviet lands. As in Yugoslavia, ethnic conflict has been driven by religious differences. The Georgian and Armenian churches constitute two of the oldest branches of the Christian faith. The Azerbaijanis are a people of mixed Turkic, Iranian, and Caucasian roots, who practice, in the main, a Shi'ite, conservative form of Islam. As in Yugoslavia, the absence of clear ethnic and religious borders within Transcaucasia has contributed to the impasse.

The conflicts that exist both within and between the respective Transcaucasian republics have been readily manipulated to the advantage of rival nationalist leaders. Within Georgia, the minority Abkhazian and Ossetian people have sought greater measures of autonomy and independence—movements that have encountered the stiff resistance of Georgian national leaders. In this Georgian instance, the conflicts pit mountain highlanders against Georgians who seek a homogenous state. The most widely recognized dispute is that between the newly independent states of Armenia and Azerbaijan. At stake in this conflict is the status of two important territories—Nagorno-Karabakh and Naxçivan (Nakhichevan). Nagorno-Karabakh, with its capital in Xankändi (Stepanakert), is a predominantly Armenian, Christian enclave fully surrounded by and legally incorporated (during the Soviet period) into the Azerbaijan republic. Naxçivan, adjacent to Turkey, is an autonomous region of Azerbaijan separated by Armenian territory from the rest of the Azerbaijani state.

Since the late 1980s, the rival ethnic and religious claims over Karabakh and Naxçivan have generated numerous military offensives and counter-offensives between Armenian and Azerbaijani forces, resulting in hundreds of casualties on both sides. As in former Yugoslavia, the collapse of independent third-party mediation in the form of a central political authority—in this case, the Soviet Union—has complicated the resolution of these longstanding territorial, ethnic, and religious divisions.

Despite these conflicts, the natural beauty of Transcaucasia with its mountainous terrain and extensive seashores make it one of the most picturesque regions of Eurasia. Access to the Caspian Sea oil fields and other valuable mineral resources makes the region important also for economic development. As the ancient lands separating the Slavic Christian world of the north from the Islamic Middle East, Transcaucasia marks an important cultural divide in the modern world.

Russian annexation of Transcaucasia dates from the early nineteenth century. Despite the strength of national independence movements and civil war in the region following the Bolshevik Revolution of 1917, Transcaucasia was integrated into the Soviet Union in the 1920s. Unlike the Baltic region into which there was heavy Russian migration after World War II, Soviet rule did not radically alter the ethnic composition of Transcaucasia. While the legacy of Soviet economic and political rule continues to be felt, the conflicts confronting the region today are largely between indigenous nationals.

Bibliography

Allen, W. E. D. *A History of the Georgian People: From the Beginning Down to the Russian Conquest in the Nineteenth Century.* New York: Barnes & Noble, 1971 [1932].

Altstadt, Audrey L. *The Azerbaijani Turks: Power and Identity under Russian Rule.* Stanford, CA: Stanford University Press, 1992.

Atamian, Sarkis. *The Armenian Community: The Historical Development of a Social and Ideological Conflict.* New York: Philosophical Library, 1955.

Hewsen, Robert H. *Russian-Armenian Relations, 1700–1828.* Cambridge, MA: Society for Armenian Studies, 1984.

Horak, Stephan M., ed. *Guide to the Study of the Soviet Nationalities: Non-Russian Peoples of the USSR.* Littleton, CO: Libraries Unlimited, Inc., 1982.

Lang, David Marshall. *A Modern History of Soviet Georgia.* Westport, CT: Greenwood Press, 1975 [1962].

———*Armenia: Cradle of Civilization.* London: George Allen & Unwin, 1978.

———*The Armenians.* London: George Allen & Unwin, 1981.

Matossian, Mary. *The Impact of Soviet Politics in Armenia.* Leiden: E. J. Brill, 1962.

Nissman, David B. *The Soviet Union and Iranian Azerbaijan: The Use of Nationalism for Political Penetration.* Boulder and London: Westview Press, 1987.

RFE/RL Research Report, 1992–. This publication of Radio Free Europe/Radio Liberty was formerly titled *Radio Liberty Research Bulletin* (through 1988) and *Report on the USSR* (1989–91). Weekly

Suny, Ronald Grigor. *Looking Toward Ararat: Armenia in Modern History.* Bloomington: Indiana University Press, 1993.

———.*The Making of the Georgian Nation.* Bloomington: Indiana University Press, in association with Stanford University Press, 1988.

———, ed. *Transcaucasia, Nationalism and Social Change: Essays in the History of Armenia, Azerbaijan, and Georgia.* Ann Arbor: University of Michigan, 1983.

Swietochowski, Tadeusz. *Russian Azerbaijan, 1905-1920: The Shaping of National Identity in a Muslim Community.* Cambridge, England: Cambridge University Press, 1985.

———. *Soviet Azerbaijan Today: The Problems of Group Identity.* Washington, DC: Kennan Institute for Advanced Russian Studies, 1986.

Walker, Christopher J. *Armenia: The Survival of a Nation.* New York: St. Martin's Press, 1980.

Wixman, Ronald. *The Peoples of the USSR: An Ethnographic Handbook.* Armonk, NY: M. E. Sharpe, Inc., 1984.

Transcaucasia

KAZAKHSTAN

Volga

River

RUSSIA

UKRAINE

KAZAKHSTAN

Caspian

Sea

Caucasus

Abkhazia

Mountains

South
Ossetiia

Black

GEORGIA

Sea

Ajaria

★ Tbilisi

Baku ★

TURKEY

ARMENIA

AZERBAIJAN

Nagorno-
Karabakh

★ Erevan

AZERBAIJAN

—————— National Boundary

— — — Autonomous Boundary

★ Capital City

Naxçivan

IRAN

0   150 Miles

0   150 Kilometers

ARMENIA

Statistical Profile

Demography

Population: 3,305,000
Ethnic population:

Armenian	3,084,000	93.3%
Azerbaijani	85,000*	2.6%*
Kurdish	56,000	1.7%
Russian	52,000	1.6%
Other	28,000	0.8%

Predominant religious traditions:

Christianity	94.9%
Islam	4.3%*

Population by age:

Age	Total	Males	Females
0–4	11.0%	5.6%	5.4%
5–9	9.7%	5.0%	4.7%
10–14	9.1%	4.6%	4.5%
15–19	8.2%	4.2%	4.0%
20–24	9.3%	4.8%	4.5%
25–29	10.6%	5.3%	5.3%
30–34	8.4%	4.0%	4.4%
35–39	6.0%	2.9%	3.1%
40–44	3.3%	1.6% .	1.7%
45–49	5.7%	2.7%	3.0%
50–54	4.9%	2.4%	2.5%
55–59	4.9%	2.4%	2.5%
60–64	3.3%	1.4%	1.9%
65–69	1.5%	0.5%	1.0%
70–	4.1%	1.5%	2.6%

Male/Female ratio: 48.9% male/51.1% female
Rural/Urban population: 31.8% rural/68.2% urban
Growth over time, 1979–91: 11.4%
Population density: 293.4 persons/sq mi

Politics/Government

Date of independence declaration: 23 August 1990
Major urban centers and populations:

Erevan	1,199,000
Gyumri (Leninakan)	120,000

Autonomous areas: none

Education

Level of education for persons over 15:

completed higher level education	13.8%
completed secondary education	57.7%
incomplete secondary education	18.6%

Number of higher education institutions (student enrollment: 14 (68,400 students)
Major institutions of higher education and enrollment:

Erevan

Polytechnic Institute	21,000
State University	9,000
Academy of National Economy	5,600
Armenian Agricultural Institute	4,000
Zootechnical and Veterinary Institute	2,900
Pedagogical Institute of Foreign Languages	2,800

Socioeconomic Indicators

Birthrate: 24.0/1,000
Infant mortality: 18.6/1,000 live births
Average life expectancy: 71.8 (males, 68.4; females, 75.2)
Average family size: 4.7
Hospital beds per 10,000 persons: 89.8
Production of electrical energy: 3,081 kwh/person
Length of rail lines: 522 mi
Length of highways: 7,021 mi

Physical/Territorial/Geopolitical Features

Area: 11,506 sq mi (.1% of USSR total)
Land use:

Cultivated	17%
Pasture	20%

Highest elevation: 13,419 ft. (Mt. Aragats)
Rainfall: 12 inches/year up to 28 in the mountains

---

*These figures do not reflect the fact that almost all Azerbaijanis have left Armenia since the Nagomo-Karabakh conflict began in 1988.

Temperature: average in winter 23° F; lowest temperature: -51° F. Average in summer 72° F; highest temperature: 108° F.	**Principal products:** grapes, grain, zinc, sheep, cattle, machinery, copper, food processing molybdenum, gold, chemicals **Per capita GNP (1991):** $2,150.

Sources

"Armianskaia sovetskaia sotsialisticheskaia respublika," *Bol'shaia Sovetskaia Entsiklopediia* (Moscow, 1977); *Narodnoe khoziaistvo SSSR v 1990g.* (Moscow, 1991); *Naselenie SSSR* (1989); Matthew J. Sagers, "News Notes. Iron and Steel," *Soviet Geography* 30 (May 1989): 397-434; Lee Schwartz, "USSR Nationality Redistribution by Republic, 1979-1989: From Published Results of the 1989 All-Union Census," *Soviet Geography* 32 (April 1991): 209-48; and *World of Learning*, 43rd ed. (London: Europa Publications Limited, 1993); "Russia. . ." (National Geographic Society Map, March 1993).

History and Description

Topography

Heir to an ancient culture that flourished in eastern Asia Minor, modern Armenia is situated high on the Armenian Plateau in the Lesser Caucasus Mountains of southern Transcaucasia. A tiny landlocked country, Armenia is bordered on the north by Georgia and to the east by Azerbaijan, both former republics of the Soviet Union. Nearby, but within the borders of neighboring Azerbaijan, lies the mountainous Armenian enclave of Nagorno-Karabakh, long a part of historic Armenia although not included within the Soviet-designed borders of modern Armenia. To the south is the Islamic state of Iran and the isolated piece of Azerbaijani territory called Naxçivan (Nakhichevan). Finally, Armenia shares a lengthy south-western border with Turkey. The smallest of all the former Soviet republics, Armenia (11,506 square miles) is approximately the size of the state of Maryland. Its capital is Erevan.

The high Armenian Plateau is a volcanic region with many snow-capped peaks, the highest of which is Mt. Ararat in neighboring Turkey. The similarly named Mt. Aragats, an extinct volcano northwest of Erevan, is the tallest summit within Armenia itself; it soars to 13,419 feet. The eight ranges of the Lesser Caucasus exhibit much seismic activity, and major earthquakes have periodically devasted areas of Armenian population, the latest being in 1988.

Lake Sevan. Armenia's water system is dominated by Lake Sevan, the largest lake in Transcaucasia and one of the largest high-elevation lakes in the world. Located 6,234 feet above sea level, its main outlet is the Razdan River. The Razdan drops 3,300 feet in 65 miles as it rushes south to join Armenia's longest river, the Aras (Araks or Araxes). The Aras, augmented by mountain tributaries, follows Armenia's border with Turkey, Naxçivan, and Iran before it joins the Kura River in Azerbaijan. From there it empties into the Caspian Sea.

Natural Resources. The Armenian climate is continental, cold, and dry. Average winter temperatures fall to 20 degrees Fahrenheit or lower. Summer readings average 72 degrees. Rainfall is a scant 12 inches a year except in the mountains where there may be up to 28 inches.

Agriculture constitutes only 12 percent of the Armenian economy. The population tends to be clustered in the Erevan basin through which the Razdan flows and along the valley of the Aras. These areas, assisted by irrigation projects, provide the best setting for the growing of vegetables and fruit, especially grapes for wine. Grains and some other crops are grown at higher altitudes. Pastureland for sheep, goats, and cattle is available at yet higher elevations.

Armenia is not rich in natural resources and must import all of its petroleum, gas, and coal. Electricity, on the other hand, it produces in greater abundance because of the considerable hydroelectric power available from steep mountain streams such as the Razdan River. Armenia has long mined copper and more recently

Armenia

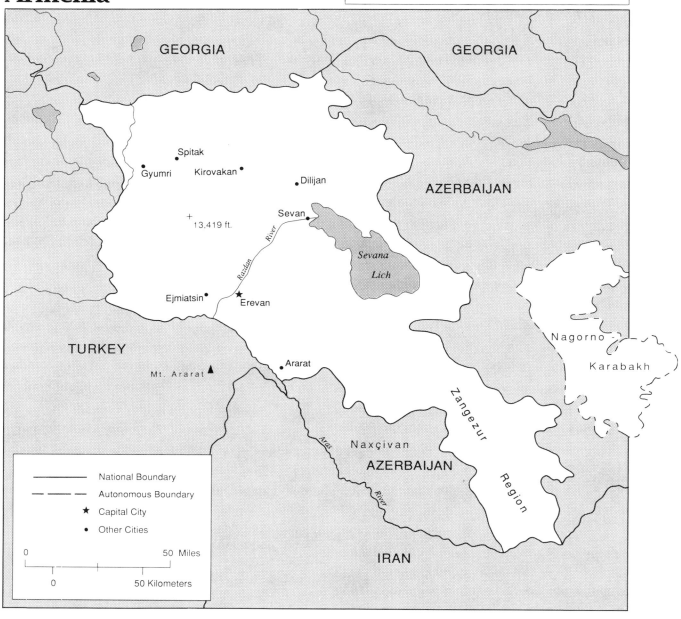

GEORGIA

GEORGIA

Spitak

Gyumri   Kirovakan

Dilijan

AZERBAIJAN

+ 13,419 ft.

Sevan

Razdan River

Sevana Lich

Ejmiatsin

★ Erevan

TURKEY

Ararat

Nagorno - Karabakh

Mt. Ararat

Zangezur

Aras

Naxçivan

Region

AZERBAIJAN

River

IRAN

_____ National Boundary

_ _ _ _ _ _ Autonomous Boundary

★ Capital City

• Other Cities

0   50 Miles

0   50 Kilometers

molybdenum. It manufactures aluminum and synthetic rubber. In the 1970s a gold mine was opened east of Lake Sevan.

Erevan is a center of machine manufacturing and light industry. Before the establishment of Soviet Armenia after World War I, Erevan was a small provincial outpost of the Russian Empire, yet in the post–World War II period it had one of the highest growth rates for large Soviet cities. Gyumri (Leninakan), Armenia's second-largest city, was previously named Alexandropol. It has suffered massive earthquakes, those of 1926 and 1988 killed thousands. (See p. 91–92.) Gyumri is a center of the textile industry and a transportation crossroads.

Armenian Diaspora. Although Armenians comprise an overwhelming majority of the population of Armenia, there are many Armenians who live abroad. There have traditionally been such large groups of Armenians living outside historic Armenian lands throughout the two thousand years of Armenian history that the term Armenian diaspora has come to refer to these people. The largest populations of expatriate Armenians are found in Georgia and Russia as well as in neighboring states of the Middle East. Armenian communities also exist in Europe and a substantial Armenian-American population is settled in the United States.

Ethnic and Historical Background

The origins of the Armenian people lie in the region surrounding Mt. Ararat where Indo-Europeans migrated at the end of the third millennium B.C. Modern Armenia is but a small part of the area historically inhabited by Armenians and no longer includes Mt. Ararat. The mountain is visible, however, from much of Armenia and still adorns the Armenian state seal. It is symbolic both of Armenian origins and of the roots of conflict between Armenia and its neighbors.

The most extensive kingdom in Armenian history was acheived by Tigran the Great (95–55 B.C.), who ultimately came to control lands that stretched from the Caspian to the Mediterranean, and from the Caucasus to Palestine. These included parts of modern Georgia and Azerbaijan. Such an extension of power brought the Armenians into conflict with the Roman Empire. After subsequently being brought under Roman control, Armenia became at times a buffer state used by other empires to protect themselves against nomadic peoples north of the Caucasus Mountains.

Armenians speak a language that exists as an independent branch of the Indo-European language family. They use the word Hai to refer to themselves. The unique Armenian script was created at the beginning of the fifth century A.D. Having a written language served the early Armenians well in maintaining their identity and culture during the centuries in which they were a subject people. The contemporary Armenian literary language is based on the so-called Ararat dialect.

Armenian Church. Armenia adopted Christianity in the year 301, when St. Gregory the Illuminator converted the ruler Tiridates III. Armenia thus preceded Byzantium as the first nation to receive Christianity as a state religion. Since the seventh century the Armenian church has been headed by the supreme catholicos (bishop) who resides at the monastery of Ejmiatsin (Echmiadzin) west of Erevan. The Armenian church has remained one of the few manifestations of greater Armenian sovereignty, serving a national as well as a religious role.

Domination of Armenia by Other Empires. Later in the fourth century much of Armenia was partitioned between Byzantine and Persian rulers. Persian forces continued to fight for remaining Armenian lands until succumbing to the Arab invasions in the seventh century. For the next three hundred years, Armenians lived under Arab control, although many fled to Byzantine-controlled western Armenia to avoid the religion of Islam brought by the Arab conquerors. During this perod, Armenians made important contributions in the administration of both the Byzantine state (several Byzantine emperors were Armenian) and the Arab empire. *David of Sassoun,* the Armenian national epic of the ninth century, presents colorful accounts of Armenian heroes during this period of Arab domination.

As Armenian lands continued to be controlled by competing regional powers, a new military presence entered the scene. The Seljuk Turks came out of Persia and fought against the Byzantine Empire for control of Asia Minor. In 1236, however, Mongol hordes conquered the entire region. The Armenians fell under the control of the Ottoman Empire in the late sixteenth century. In 1555, the Ottomans divided eastern Armenia with Persia, and in 1620, the Persians annexed Karabakh and the surrounding territory from the Ottomans.

Even though Armenia came to be dominated by other empires, Armenians who had migrated abroad kept alive the notion of an independent Armenian homeland that they sought to reestablish in the lands of eastern Asia

Minor. In the eighteenth century, these expatriate Armenians first formulated ideas of a sovereign Armenia, or an Armeno-Georgian union. Proposals were sent to the Russian Empire, where there resided the largest Armenian community outside the Ottoman Empire and where there was thought to be sympathy for the Armenian cause.

Russian Conquest

In 1827, by the end of the Russo-Persian wars, the Russian Empire had wrested control of Transcaucasia from the Persians. All Persian territory north of the Aras River came under Russian control. This included most of modern Azerbaijan, the predominantly Armenian khanate of Karabakh and the area that ultimately became the modern republic of Armenia. The rest of historic Armenia remained within the Ottoman Empire.

In the first half of the nineteenth century Russian tsars Alexander I and Nicholas I encouraged Armenians to move to Russian-held Armenian territory. There followed a migration of Armenians into what became modern Armenia, often into territory with insufficient dwellings and arable land to support the new immigrants. This migration, nevertheless, created a predominantly Armenian region, as Muslims in the area left for Azerbaijan or Persia to avoid the large numbers of incoming Christians. Erevan, which in 1830 was 50 percent Muslim, underwent a dramatic demographic shift as Armenians arrived from historic Armenian lands outside the new Russian borders. It is estimated that as many as one-half of the 1850 Armenian population of Transcaucasia had immigrated since 1830.

The dream of Armenian sovereignty under the tsars never materialized. The emigration and settlement of Russians in Transcaucasia was encouraged and Russification policies prevailed at the expense of the Armenian population. Anti-Russian sentiment grew as Armenians felt increasingly frustrated over unfulfilled Russian promises to protect Armenians still living in the Ottoman Empire.

Armenian Resistance to Turkish and Russian Rule. During the last quarter of the nineteenth century, Armenians in the Ottoman Empire formed political parties to press for change. The Hunchak party (established 1886) called for an independent socialist Armenia, while the Dashnak (Dashnaktsutiun) party (established 1890) rather sought autonomy within a reformed Ottoman Empire. Both groups turned to terrorism. Ottoman suspicions that Armenians were attempting to dissect the Ottoman Empire culminated in a series of massacres from 1894 to 1896, in which an estimated 200,000 Armenians were killed. Russia and the European powers protested but did little to stop the carnage.

Armenian nationalist groups, angered by Russian inaction and by intensified Russification policies in Armenia, became increasingly anti-Russian. In 1903, when the Russian government advanced a measure to confiscate Armenian church lands, the Dashnaks mobilized residents in every Armenian village attacking and killing Russian authorities and Armenians who cooperated with them. The Russians responded by generating anti-Armenian sentiment among the Azerbaijanis, a policy that would be repeated under Soviet commissars. Armed resistance continued until the attacks on the Armenian church ended in 1905.

At the turn of the century, Armenians participated in socialist groups in Alexandropol and Erevan, as well as in Georgia and Azerbaijan, and helped to organize workers in Baku under the guidance of the Georgian Josef Dzhugashvili (Stalin). In spite of the presence of Armenian workers in the industrial centers of Transcaucasia, however, most of Russian Armenia remained agricultural. The problems generated by the immigrations of the 1830s remained, such as the lack of sufficient good land to support the population. Almost half of the agricultural inhabitants owned no land.

Armenian Holocaust. World War I brought the single greatest tragedy in the history of the Armenian people. This tragedy—known as the Armenian holocaust—is still commemorated annually by all Armenians in church services and elsewhere on April 24. The Ottoman government of the Young Turks, amid calls for a holy war and a pan-Turkic empire, began deporting Armenians, who were considered pro-Russian. In forced marches across Turkey in 1915, one million or more Armenians perished from starvation, exhaustion, or raids by Kurdish and Turkish troops. While some Turkish governors refused to carry out deportation orders, the policy of genocide continued.

At the end of World War I, after the collapse of the tsarist government and the rise to power of the Bolsheviks, an independent Republic of Armenia was declared in Russian Armenia in May 1918. Although the Ottoman Empire retired from the war and from Russian Transcaucasia in October, Armenia was still at risk from

Turkish troops in neighboring Azerbaijan who avoided disarmament by acquiring Azerbaijani citizenship.

Soviet Conquest

Receiving no help from the West and threatened on all sides, the Armenian Republic turned to the Bolsheviks for assistance by the fall of 1920. The new Soviet government took control of Armenia under an agreement signed on 2 December 1920 that included grants to Armenia of Nakhichevan and Karabakh. What followed was the incorporation of Armenia into the Soviet Union. In violation of agreements made by the Soviet government, Dashnaks and other nationalists were arrested. Local resistance resulted and continued into 1921 when the Dashnaks recaptured Erevan on 28 February, taking revenge for the executions of Dashnak prisoners. After the end of resistance in neighboring Georgia, however, the Red Army retook Erevan in April and the rest of Armenia by late summer.

Armenia was incorporated into the Soviet Union as part of the Transcaucasian Soviet Federated Socialist Republic (TSFSR) in 1922. Despite the earlier promise by the Communists to grant Armenia control of Karabakh and Nakhichevan, the two regions were placed under Azerbaijani governance. The latter, however, was separated from Azerbaijan by the narrow strip of Zangezur, under Armenian control. These border arrangements, intended by the Soviet authorities to continue tsarist policies of playing the Armenians against the Azerbaijanis, have been the subject of ongoing dispute in the aftermath of Soviet power in Transcaucasia. Under the 1936 Stalin constitution, the TSFSR was eliminated, and Armenia became the Armenian Soviet Socialist Republic.

Soviet Leadership

The first priorities of the Soviet regime were to neutralize nationalist forces in Armenia. The Dashnaks were banned in November 1923. The city of Alexandropol was renamed Leninakan in 1924. Persecution of the church began in the 1920s as places of worship and religious presses were closed. The Ejmiatsin monastery was expropriated in 1928, while gifts of the Armenian diaspora to the catholicos and the church were also confiscated.

Purges of suspect Armenians began in 1929 continuing virtually to the beginning of World War II. The first purge, aimed at old Bolsheviks and nationalists, was largely carried out by the first secretary of the Armenian Communist Party (ArCP), Aghasi Khanchian. As Khanchian himself resisted Russian attempts to curtail Armenian culture, he became less and less reliable to the Communists. In 1936 he died, alleged by the authorities to have committed suicide.

Following Khanchian's death the purges intensified, devouring most of the newer members of the Party as well as Armenian nationalists. Khanchian's successor as first secretary was Grigor Arutiunov, from a Georgian-speaking family. Arutiunov had risen through the ranks of the Georgian Communist Party and was an associate of Stalin's chief of secret police, Lavrentii Beria.

Although the Russification of Armenia achieved the elimination of age-old rural practices such as bride sales, child marriage, and vendettas, it also led to the destruction of Armenian literature and culture. The purges of 1936 destroyed the works of contemporary Armenian writers. Literature by nineteenth-century authors, such as Hakob Melik Hakobian (Raffi), was banned.

Another goal of the Communist Party was to reform Armenia's economy enough to absorb the masses of refugees it sheltered. In the 1920s, the republic, already short of provisions, was forced to submit to the requisition of food by the Communists. It was only with Western aid that Armenia was kept from starving.

Following the subjugation of Transcaucasia, Communist authorities began a policy of rapid industrialization in Armenia to help employ the excess labor population. By the 1930s, Armenian copper mines were operating at a profit, and Armenia was second only to Kazakhstan in copper production. The Soviet government also built plants for producing sulfuric acid and other chemicals.

A destructive aspect of Soviet economic policies was the forced collectivization of agriculture in the 1930s. (On collectivization, see glossary). Both Armenian and Azerbaijani peasants in Armenia put up armed resistance to these measures, slaughtering cattle to prevent their seizure and attacking Communist officials, both Russian and Armenian, who attempted to collectivize the peasants' holdings. The resistance was largely disorganized, although some groups received arms and aid from exiled Dashnaks across the border in Iran. Collectivization slowed in 1930, as a result of the resistance, with collectivized households dropping from 63 percent in February to 9 percent in the fall. Since Armenian Red Army troops were considered unreliable, Russian soldiers were used to put down local revolts, some of which continued into 1934. By 1936, however, the resistance was largely broken, and 80 percent of the peasants in Armenia were collectivized.

Soviet policies changed with the advent of World War II as Moscow reversed itself and attempted to use Armenia as a showcase for the diaspora. The Armenian church was called upon to rally Armenians to the Soviet war cause, and expressions of nationalism were tolerated. Later, during the tensions of the postwar era, the Soviet government temporarily encouraged some signs of Armenian nationalism in an effort at anti-Western propaganda. For a time Moscow encouraged Armenians from around the world to emigrate to Soviet Armenia, but the policy was stopped in 1948 after 100,000 Armenians had come to the republic. Discriminatory Soviet policies led many of these immigrants to warn relatives not to join them, and some escaped to Iran.

After the death of Stalin in 1953, pressure on Armenian nationalism and culture lessened. Arutiunov was arrested in 1953 for his association with Beria. His successor as first secretary, Suren Tovmasian, encouraged the rehabilitation of some of the nationalist victims of the purges. Previously banned literature was republished. From that time, Armenia was given greater leeway than other Soviet republics in ideological matters. Arutiunov's other successors, Iakov Zarobian (1958–66), Anton Kochinian (1966–74), and Karen Demirchian (1974–88), suffered little criticism, despite the inability of Armenian officials to discourage religion, nationalism, and increasing corruption. Armenian autonomy was due in part to the high efficiency of local industry, which met and exceeded almost all production quotas. Soviet officials were also reluctant to crack down on a republic that they touted as an Armenian homeland made possible only under benevolent Russian tutelage. It was not until Gorbachev assumed control of the central government and initiated perestroika and glasnost that Demirchian came under fire, both from the government and from Armenian citizens.

Contemporary Issues

Politics and Informal Groups

The overriding issue in Armenian politics since 1987 has been the Nagorno-Karabakh conflict—a conflict posed by the existence of an Armenian enclave surrounded by Azerbaijani republican territory.* The dispute has brought Armenia into conflict not only with Azerbaijan but with Moscow as well and ultimately led to the dismissal of both Demirchian and his successor Suren Arutiunian. It also led to the creation of the Karabakh Committee and popular calls for Armenian independence. As Armenia faces the future as an independent state, the continuing conflict with Azerbaijan remains the major concern.

Exposed first to criticism from the central government and then to popular unrest over environmental issues and Nagorno-Karabakh, Armenia's first secretary Demirchian faced considerable pressure in the 1980s. At a 1983 plenum, a general assembly, of the Central Committee of the Communist Party of the Soviet Union (CPSU), Armenia was criticized for excessive religiosity and nationalism, inadequate use of labor surplus, and widespread corruption. This criticism was repeated in an October 1986 issue of *Pravda*, and in June 1987 Gorbachev criticized Demirchian for obstructing perestroika. Such fault finding came in spite of the fact that Armenia had exceeded all production targets of the eleventh Five-Year Plan.

The accusations were echoed within the Armenian government itself. At the December 1987 plenum of the Central Committee of the Armenian Communist Party (ArCP), Sarkis Khachatrian, chairman of the Party Control Commission, charged that Armenian law enforcement was rife with bribery and corruption. Popular pressure also played a role in the downfall of Demirchian. Armenians began demonstrating in 1986 over environmental pollution and health problems caused by Armenia's chemical industry. With the beginning of the Nagorno-Karabakh conflict in 1987, a group of Armenians formed the Karabakh Committee, calling for the oblast's independence from Azerbaijan and administration by Arme-

*For important background information on the dispute over Nagorno-Karabakh, see the Azerbaijan chapter, pages 100–103

nia. The Karabakh Committee organized demonstrations in Erevan and other parts of Armenia, increasingly criticizing Soviet policies on the dispute.

When Demirchian was removed in May 1988, the action signaled an effort by Moscow to maintain control of the republic. Demirchian's removal had been delayed, in part to avoid the appearance that the central government could be swayed by public pressure to remove a Communist official. The mounting conflict over Nagorno-Karabakh, however, led Gorbachev to replace Demirchian with Suren Gurgenovich Arutiunian, an official who had spent most of his time in Moscow and was therefore more tightly linked to the central government.

Despite the successful Armenian efforts to gain military control over Nagorno-Karabakh, the conflict claimed Arutiunian two years later, after the first secretary had indicated too much support for the oblast's independence from Azerbaijan. The Armenian Supreme Soviet declared Nagorno-Karabakh to be part of Armenia in December 1989, and in April 1990 Arutiunian was removed. Also contributing to Arutiunian's fall were fresh outbreaks of violence in Nagorno-Karabakh in March and a small turnout (7.5 percent) of Armenians for Soviet military service. Arutiunian's successor was Vladimir Migranovich Movsisian, an official assumed to be more pliant to Moscow's demands.

Nevertheless, Moscow's hold over Armenia deteriorated. In May 1990, clashes between Armenians and Soviet troops in Erevan crystallized anti-Soviet sentiment in Armenia. Presidential elections were held in August, and Movsisian lost to Levon Ter-Petrosian, chairman of the Armenian Pan-National Movement and a former leading member of the Karabakh Committee. In November the ArCP declared itself independent from the Communist Party of the Soviet Union, and Movsisian was replaced as first secretary by Stepan Pogosian. Another group, the Union for National Self-Determination, called for immediate secession from the Soviet Union.

Soviet-Armenian tensions increased in 1991. In January, Gorbachev deployed Soviet airborne troops in Armenia to enforce the draft. The Armenian government refused to take part in the March 1991 All-Union referendum on maintaining the Soviet Union, instead choosing to hold a September 1991 referendum on Armenian secession. Following the abortive Moscow coup in August 1991, Ter-Petrosian affirmed the decision to secede, and on 21 September 1991, 94.4 percent of the electorate turned out to vote, with 99.3 percent supporting seces-

sion. The formal declaration was drafted on 23 September.

As president, Ter-Petrosian has attempted to distance himself from the unofficial Armenian military group operating in the Nagorno-Karabakh oblast and Azerbaijan and has attempted to form pragmatic relations with Turkey and Iran. Both policies have exposed him to considerable criticism, especially his effort to normalize relations with Turkey. Ter-Petrosian has also invited Armenian political groups of the diaspora, including the banned Dashnaktsutiun, to come to Erevan.

The proliferation of interest groups has led to fragmentation in Armenian politics. In the October 1991 presidential elections, six candidates ran against Ter-Petrosian. One withdrew and the other five called for a delay, after Ter-Petrosian was accused of physically attacking one of them, the head of the Union for National Self-Determination. Ter-Petrosian claimed 83 percent of the vote, however, and remained president. Although he has indicated a willingness to attempt a resolution of the Nagorno-Karabakh conflict, both the Armenian government and people appear committed to preventing the recapture of the oblast by Azerbaijan. At the same time, hardships brought about by Azerbaijani blockades of Armenia since 1989 have aggravated already serious problems in the republic, problems that form the primary challenges to Ter-Petrosian's regime.

The 1988 Earthquake

Complicating Armenia's position is the damage wrought by the earthquake that ravaged its northern provinces in 1988. On 7 December of that year, the strongest earthquake in 80 years destroyed the village of Spitak, 75 percent of Leninakan, and 50 percent of Kirovakan. Soviet officials admitted later that they had lacked the equipment to respond to the quake, which had an estimated strength of greater than 10 on a 12-point scale. The earliest estimates placed the death toll at 50–70,000, although in January 1990 the figure was lowered to 30–40,000 (up from an official count in 1989 of 25,000). Relief efforts by the Soviet and Armenian governments were generally poor. On 13 December *Pravda* reported that many earthquake survivors had died from exposure. Patriarch-Catholicos Vasgen I of the Armenian church called for a requiem mass of the same sort as the annual mass commemorating the 1915 genocide. The cost of rebuilding the three cities was estimated in January 1989 at eight billion rubles.

In the days that followed, 67 countries sent assistance. By Christmas, international aid had reached $97 million. Pope John Paul II sent a personal message of sympathy to Gorbachev, who cut short his attendance at international meetings to return to the Soviet Union. On Christmas Day, the son and grandson of United States President Bush visited the region, distributing gifts and candy to Armenian children.

The earthquake exacerbated existing Armenian-Azerbaijani and Armenian-Soviet tensions. Armenian officials were criticized by Moscow for their handling of the crisis, while Armenian-Soviet tensions were manifested in the fear among Armenians that evacuees were being sent to Siberia. Armenian demonstrators protesting these evacuations also called for a refusal of aid from Azerbaijan, and four men bringing aid from Azerbaijan were allegedly turned back by groups of Armenians. Meanwhile, rebuilding the towns was delayed by Azerbaijani rail blockades in 1989, and the Nagorno-Karabakh conflict generally distracted energy and attention from reconstruction.

Energy

The Nagorno-Karabakh conflict and resultant blockade of Armenia by Azerbaijan has resulted in Armenia being critically short of energy. Although before the 1960s Armenia produced its own hydroelectric power, such energy accounts for only about 5 percent of current Armenian consumption. The Medzamor nuclear plant, closed after the 1988 earthquake, had come to produce an estimated 36 percent of Armenia's energy. It is scheduled to be reopened in 1994. With no coal, oil, or natural gas of its own, Armenia must import 80 percent of its fuels. The largest share of these fuels (82 percent) had come from Azerbaijan, while most other imports of oil and coal from Russia and other republics must pass through Azerbaijan to get to Armenia.

Changing the situation will be difficult. Most of Armenia's energy infrastructure is outdated and unable to withstand severe seismic activity. The Sevan-Razdan hydroelectric plant, for example, is 42 years old. Plans to shift to solar production seem promising, with some regions receiving 300 days of sunshine per year. Such a development will still leave much of Armenia's energy requirements unmet by domestic sources in the short term. As aging plants fail, the energy situation in Armenia will become more desperate (John Tedstrom, "Armenia:

An Energy Profile" in *Report on the USSR* vol. 3, no. 8, 22 February 1991, pp. 18–20).

Environmental Issues

The rapid industrialization of Armenia in the 1930s left its mark on the environment, especially the chemical plants polluting the air and the hydroelectric projects draining Lake Sevan. Protests over air pollution and the potential dangers of nuclear power began in the late 1980s. The issues raised by protesters have yet to be seriously addressed.

In March 1986, 350 Armenian intellectuals addressed the problem of environmental pollution in an open letter to Gorbachev. The letter noted that in the Ararat Valley, stomach cancer, cardiac and respiratory diseases, and birth defects had increased fourfold from 1965 to 1985. From 1970 to 1985, instances of mental retardation had increased by 500 percent, mental illnesses 600 percent, and leukemia and abnormal and premature births had increased 400 percent. The Armenian press further noted that 60 percent of the air pollution in Erevan was caused by automobiles, while the other 40 percent came from chemical plants (Elizabeth Fuller, "Is Armenia on the Brink of an Ecological Disaster?" in *Radio Liberty Research Bulletin* vol. 30, no. 34, 20 August 1986). In 1985, the Soviet Council of Ministers passed a resolution to combat air pollution in Erevan, but by 1987 none of the Council's recommendations had been implemented.

Part of Armenia's environmental problem arose from the fact that fines for pollution were much less than fines for not meeting industrial production targets, thus discouraging changes in plant processes. In March 1987, Demirchian announced plans to reduce pollution at the major chemical plants in Kirovakan and Erevan. In October of that year, the Party's first secretary from Kirovakan announced that air pollution there was "tens of times higher" than permissable (quoted in Elizabeth Fuller, "USSR Ministry of Health Cites Data on Infant Mortality and Infectious Diseases in Two Transcaucasian Republics," *RLRB,* vol. 31, no. 43, 28 October 1987). Later in October thousands of Armenians in Erevan continued the protest of environmental pollution.

The nuclear energy plant at Medzamor is also a subject of concern. Although located in an area of frequent seismic activity, the plant was not built to withstand earthquakes. Following the Chernobyl accident, the chairman of the Armenian Council of Ministers announced measures to increase safety. The Medzamor plant is a thermal neutron reactor, different from the carbon-uranium reactor at Chernobyl. Demirchian announced in 1987 that energy production would shift more to thermal, natural gas, and hydroelectric power and away from nuclear power. Later that year, Armenian ecologists alleged that an incident had occured at the Medzamor plant in May, although it was not documented. Protests continued, and in September 1988 it was announced that the Medzamor Plant would be closed by 1991. Following the 1988 earthquake, the date was moved forward one year. With the Azerbaijani blockade, however, the closing of the Medzamor plant leaves Armenian energy needs unmet.

Lake Sevan has suffered much from irrigation and hydroelectric projects. By the 1950s, the water level of the lake was down by 50 feet, and the original 547 square miles of surface area had decreased substantially, with drastic repercussions for the local ecosystem. Construction of tunnels to reroute rivers into the lake began in 1963, but the work was not completed until 1980. In 1985, the tunnels collapsed, and water flow into the lake stopped completely. The collapse was not reported for a whole year, during which time the lake's water level continued to fall. Although the tunnels were subsequently repaired in 1987, the newly independent Armenian government has few resources for such projects. Furthermore, the tunnels do not work as well as required, and Lake Sevan has not been fully replenished. Given the energy situation, it is unlikely that hydroelectric projects will be shut down, and Lake Sevan will likely be further depleted. (See Elizabeth Fuller, "Glasnost' in Armenia: The Lake Sevan Cover-Up," *RLRB,* vol. 30, no. 45, 5 November 1986.)

As a result of so many other serious political problems facing the republic, environmental issues are likely to remain of lesser concern. Energy needs will necessitate the continued operation of the Medzamor plant and the already mentioned hydrolectric plants, while economic needs stemming from the blockade will make the Armenian government reluctant to reduce the productivity of their chemical production plants.

The Diaspora

Until the twentieth century, the community of Armenians residing abroad was composed primarily of an urbanized middle class and intelligentsia. Armenian en-

claves were established in Italy, Persia, and India, as well as Russia, by the eighteenth century. The first Armenian book was published in Venice in 1512. The first Armenian journal, *Azdarar,* was published in Madras from 1794-96. Armenians living abroad today have tended to maintain a strong Armenian identity. This corresponds to a continued consciousness within the diaspora of an historic Armenia, and also reflects the historic memory of the Armenian holocaust during World War I. In rare cases this consciousness has led extreme nationalist groups to engage in acts of terrorism against Turkish officials in Turkey and abroad.

The Armenian Church. Another key feature of Armenian nationalism is its identification with the Armenian church, one of the earliest churches of Eastern Christendom. Its seat is in Ejmiatsin. Operating under the constraints of the Soviet government, political conflicts arose in the Armenian church as Dashnaks at home and abroad struggled for control of the church against Soviet-recognized Ramgavar church leaders. The latter have viewed Dashnaks as promoting terrorism and as part of an illegal church, and in most cases have been able to elect Ramgavar officials to church boards. The See at Ejmiatsin has defrocked or refused to recognize pro-Dashnak clergy. The Armenian church is still evolving in its response to the dissolution of the Soviet Union. Vasgen I, named patriarch-catholicos in 1955, remains the head of the Armenian church. The actions of the catholicos have played a key role in encouraging action from the diaspora.

The diaspora remains a source of Armenia's chances of foreign aid, as in the case of the 1988 earthquake. Prosperous Armenians in the United States and Europe have long taken an interest in the republic, encouraged by Soviet policies to see Soviet Armenia as their homeland. At the same time, however, activities of nationalist terrorists against Turkish officials have lessened Ter-Petrosian's chances of normalizing Armenian-Turkish relations. Just as the diaspora played a role in Russian-Armenian dealings in the eighteenth and nineteenth centuries, the diaspora will have a role in the survival of independent Armenia.

International Relations

Armenia's position is almost as delicate now as it was following World War I. Facing both a hostile Azerbaijan and an energy blockade, Armenia will have to rely on help from other countries. Thus, Ter-Petrosian has sought to normalize relations with Turkey and Iran, despite strong anti-Turkish sentiment among Armenians. He and the late Turkish President Turgut Ozal discussed cooperation in economic and cultural affairs, and the Turkish government has so far denied it will involve itself in the Nagorno-Karabakh issue. That may change, given both the strong pressure in Turkey to aid the Azerbaijanis and the reality of terrorism by Armenian nationalists in Turkey.

Aid from the West seems likely, but it is possible that Armenia's problems will go unnoticed, given the current situations in Russia, Yugoslavia, Somalia, and Iraq. The United States has recognized Armenia, and it has established an embassy in Erevan. Armenians in the diaspora will of course be vital in exerting pressure on foreign governments to assist the republic.

In the meantime, Armenia is clinging to the Commonwealth of Independent States, even though Ter-Petrossian has voiced displeasure with the Alma-Ata accords establishing the CIS. After the August 1991 coup, the Armenian president called for a union similar to the European Community, led by a democratic Russia. With democracy in Russia threatened by rising nationalism and economic difficulties, Ter-Petrosian today looks beyond Russia.

AZERBAIJAN

Statistical Profile

Demography

Population: 7,021,000

Ethnic population:

Azerbaijani	5,805,000	82.7%
Russian	392,000	5.6%
Armenian	391,000*	5.6%*
Lezghian	171,000	2.4%
Avar	44,000	0.6%
Tatar	28,000	0.4%
Jewish	25,000	0.4%
Other	165,000	2.4%

Historic religious traditions:

Islam	86.1%
Christianity	11.2%*

Population by age:

Age	Total	Males	Females
0–4	12.3%	6.3%	6.0%
5–9	10.4%	5.3%	5.1%
10–14	9.8%	5.0%	4.8%
15–19	10.3%	5.3%	5.0%
20–24	10.9%	5.6%	5.3%
25–29	10.1%	5.0%	5.1%
30–34	7.1%	3.4%	3.7%
35–39	5.0%	2.4%	2.6%
40–44	2.7%	1.3%	1.4%
45–49	5.0%	2.4%	2.6%
50–54	4.9%	2.4%	2.5%
55–59	4.0%	1.9%	2.1%
60–64	2.6%	1.1%	1.5%
65–69	1.5%	0.5%	1.0%
70–	3.4%	1.0%	2.4%

Male/Female ratio: 48.9% male/51.1% female

Rural/Urban population: 46.5% rural/53.5% urban

Growth over time, 1979–91: 18.4%

Population density: 213.5 persons/sq mi

Politics/Government

Date of independence declaration:
30 August 1991

Urban centers and populations:

Baku	1,757,000
Gäncä (Kirovobad)	278,000
Sumqayit	231,000
Naxçivan (Nakhichevan)	60,000
Shusha	<50,000
Xankändi (Stepanakert)	35,000

Autonomous areas:

Naxçivan	Naxçivan (capital)
Nagorno-Karabakh	Xankändi (capital)

Education

Level of education for persons over 15:

completed higher level education	10.5%
completed secondary education	58.1%
incomplete secondary education	19.2%

Number of higher education institutions:
17 (105,100 students)

Major institutions of higher education and enrollment:

Baku

Azerbaijan State Petroleum Academy	14,600
Azerbaijan Engineering and Technical University	13,242
Baku State University	12,500
Gadzhibekov State Music Conservatory	800

Socioeconomic Indicators

Birthrate: 26.4/1,000

Infant mortality: 23.0/1,000 live births

Average life expectancy: 71.0 (males, 66.9; females, 74.8)

Average family size: 4.8

Hospital beds per 10,000 persons: 102.2

Production of electrical energy: 3,250 kwh/person

Length of rail lines: 1,299 mi

Length of highways: 22,804 mi

*These statistics do not reflect the fact that almost all Armenians (except approximately 150,000 in Nagorno-Karabakh) have left Azerbaijan since the Nagorno-Karabakh conflict began.

Physical/Territorial/Geopolitical Features	Temperature: average in winter 29° F (14° F in the mountains); lowest temperature: -22° F. Average in summer 79° F (41° F in the mountains); highest temperature: 109° F.
Area: 33,436 sq mi (.4% of USSR total) **Land use:** Cultivated 18% Pasture 24% **Highest elevation:** 14,652 ft. (Bazardiuzi peak) **Rainfall:** 10 inches/year to 69 on the Caspian coast	**Principal products:** grapes, cotton, grain, silk, sheep and cattle, oil, natural gas, chemicals, machinery **Per capita GNP (1991):** $1,670

Sources

"Azerbaidzhanskaia sovetskaia sotsialisticheskaia respublika" *Bol'shaia Sovetskaia Entsiklopediia* (Moscow, 1977); *Narodnoe khoziaistvo SSSR v 1990g.* (Moscow, 1991); *Naselenie SSSR* (1989); Matthew J. Sagers, "News Notes. Iron and Steel," *Soviet Geography* 30 (May 1989): 397–434; Lee Schwartz, "USSR Nationality Redistribution by Republic, 1979–1989: From Published Results of the 1989 All-Union Census," *Soviet Geography* 32 (April 1991): 209–48; and *World of Learning,* 43rd ed. (London: Europa Publications Limited, 1993); "Russia. . . " (National Geographic Society Map, March 1993).

History and Description

Topography

Azerbaijan, largest of the republics of former Soviet Transcaucasia, is located along the western shore of the Caspian Sea. On the north, Azerbaijan is bordered by the Russian Federation, while Georgia and Armenia lie on its northwestern and western borders respectively. To the south, Azerbaijan shares a border with Iran. The small territorial region of Naxçivan (Nakhichevan— approximately 3,420 square miles) is geographically separated from the rest of Azerbaijan by a 25- to 30-mile wide strip of Armenian territory. Naxçivan borders Turkey and Iran. The isolated Armenian enclave of Nagorno-Karabakh (2,730 square miles), under Azerbaijani control, is the object of a violent conflict with Armenia that escalated to armed warfare in 1987.

The main waterways in Azerbaijan are the Aras (Araks or Araxes) and the Kura rivers, both of which begin in the mountains of northeastern Turkey. From there the Kura flows north into Georgia before entering the extreme northwestern part of Azerbaijan. It then flows through Azerbaijan in a southeasterly direction all the way to the Caspian Sea. The Aras, from its Turkish headwater, flows southeast, eventually running parallel to the Azerbaijani-Iranian border on the Iranian side. It then turns north into Azerbaijan and joins the Kura before emptying into the Caspian.

Elevations in Azerbaijan rise from near sea level on the Caspian coast and in the river basins of the Kura and Aras to almost 15,000 ft. in the northern mountains and close to 12,000 ft. in the west. Between the central lowlands and the surrounding mountains lie several different climatic regions, from the mild, semi-arid weather near the coast to the much colder and wetter weather found in higher elevations.

This variation of climate allows for the cultivation of several different crops, in particular grapes and cotton. Some areas are suitable for growing wheat, tea, figs and pomegranates, saffron, and mulberry trees for silk, as well as for raising sheep and cattle. Natural resources include copper, salt, and iron ore, although the single most important Azerbaijani resource is oil. Baku, the Azerbaijani capital and the fifth-largest city in the former Soviet Union, is located in the richest of the oil-bearing regions, on the Apsheron Peninsula.

Ethnic and Historical Background

Although the terms "Azeri" and "Azerbaijani" are sometimes used interchangeably, Azeri more correctly applies to an ancient Iranian language of the fourth

Azerbaijan

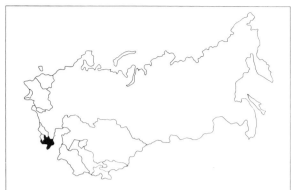

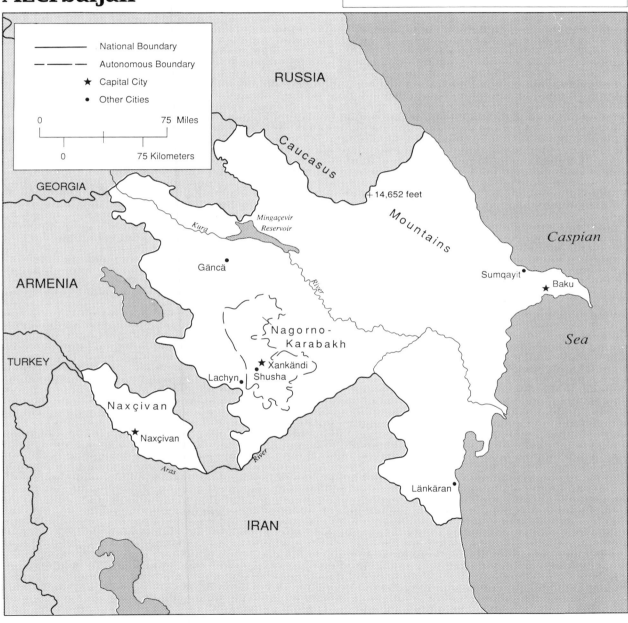

	National Boundary
	Autonomous Boundary
★	Capital City
•	Other Cities

0   75 Miles

0   75 Kilometers

RUSSIA

GEORGIA

Caucasus

+14,652 feet

Mountains

Caspian

Kura

Mingäçevir
Reservoir

Gäncä

Sumqayit

★ Baku

ARMENIA

River

Sea

Nagorno-
Karabakh

TURKEY

★ Xankändi
Lachyn Shusha

Naxçivan

★ Naxçivan

Aras   River

Länkäran

IRAN

century B.C. The most accurate term for an inhabitant of modern Azerbaijan is "Azerbaijani." Modern Azerbaijanis are a Turkic people, whose dialect is known, simply, as Azerbaijani. It is similar to the dialect spoken in Turkmenistan and is easily understood by speakers of modern Turkish. Azerbaijanis are primarily Shi'ite Muslims, unlike the other Turkic peoples of the former Soviet Union, who are predominantly Sunni Muslims. Azerbaijani Shi'ism is basically a reflection of the historical ties between Azerbaijan and Iran, a center of Shi'ite Muslim life.

The origins of the name "Azerbaijan" are a matter of question. The term is generally thought to come from the fourth-century figure, Atropat, who ruled the area of what is now northwestern Iran. Indeed, the name Azerbaijan is used for the northernmost province of Iran. The term "Azerbaijan" may also derive from *azer,* the Persian word for fire, relating to the oil-fed flames that burned on the altars of the Zoroastrians, followers of an ancient Persian religion.

The area of present-day Azerbaijan was conquered by Persians in the sixth century B.C. Thus, the earliest inhabitants of the region were probably subjected to a heavy Persian/Iranian influence in both language and culture. During the third and fourth centuries B.C., Baku, Gäncä, Naxçivan, and other cities in modern Azerbaijan were founded as trading centers for silk and lamp oil.

With the rise of Islam in the seventh century A.D., Arab Muslims brought a new religion to the area, and Islam thereafter prevailed. By the eleventh century, under the Seljuk Turks, the Persianized peoples of Azerbaijan were becoming Turkicized. Then the Oghuz Turks, whose descendants inhabit Turkmenistan, migrated from the east and came to influence the linguistic development of the Azerbaijanis. With the Mongolian invasions of the thirteenth century, the region fell under the domain of Genghis Khan. Later came rival Turkmen clans who completed the Turkicization of Azerbaijan.

Yet another stage in the development of the Azerbaijanis came in the sixteenth century, when the Persian ruler Ismail Safavi conquered Azerbaijan lands. Ismail established Shi'ism as the official religion, thus antagonizing the Ottoman Turks, who were Sunni. In subsequent wars, although Azerbaijan was held by the Ottomans from 1578 to 1603, it remained a province of Safavid Persia until 1747, when Persian rule was replaced with that of Turkic Muslim khanates based in Baku, Naxçivan, Erevan, and elsewhere.

Russian involvement in Transcaucasia began in the early eighteenth century, as an effort toward securing raw materials such as copper, silk, and cotton. Russia also wished to acquire a militarily strategic position on the Caspian Sea. Peter I's Persian expedition led to the conquest of the Caspian coast in the 1710s and 1720s. Although the territory soon had to be relinquished, Russian interest in the Caucasus influenced the policies of Azerbaijani khans and Georgian princes. In 1783, Catherine II brought Georgia under Russian protection by treaty, and in 1783, the Russians seized the Crimea and western Transcaucasia. At the beginning of the nineteenth century, with the Russo-Persian wars of 1804-13 and 1826-28, the Russian Empire detached northern Azerbaijan from Persia (Iran).

Russian Conquest

Official Russian rule in Transcaucasia began in 1801, when Alexander I established Georgia as an administrative unit within the Russian Empire. This unit also included the adjacent Azerbaijani territories of Kazakh and Shamshadil. The 1812 Treaty of Gulistan and the 1828 Treaty of Turkmanchai ended the two Russo-Persian wars and brought Azerbaijani khanates north of the Aras River under Russian control.

Armed resistance to Russian rule was led by several Sunni khanates of Dagestan that had been fighting a holy war against the Russians since the eighteenth century. Shi'ite Azerbaijanis often fought with the Russians against the Dagestanis, not only because of Islamic sectarian differences, but also because many Azerbaijani khans saw Russian overlordship as preferable to that of the shahs of Persia.

Russia governed Azerbaijan as part of a Transcaucasian administration. For most of the early nineteenth century, this was done through existing khanates and local structures. As the century wore on, however, policies leaned more toward assimilation. Provinces were combined, eliminating a number of governmental personnel: most of the positions remaining went to Russians. During the 1860s and 1870s, Russian courts and law codes replaced the Islamic system of laws (*sharia*). For local Muslims, simply imprisoning a thief or murderer seemed inappropriate, and the subsequent vigilante justice added to tensions between Azerbaijanis and Russians. During the 1880s, with the influx of Russian settlers, Russification intensified.

Ethnic tensions between Azerbaijanis and Armenians have their roots in this period as well. Following the Treaty of Turkmanchai, Tsar Nicholas I established in the Erevan and Naxçivan khanates a refuge for Armenian emigrants from Turkey and Persia. These Christian Armenians were seen by the Azerbaijanis, however, as the beneficiaries of preferential treatment. When local parliamentary bodies (dumas) were established in Azerbaijani areas in 1892, non-Christians were limited to a one-third representation. As a result Azerbaijanis became a minority in their own native territories. Non-Christians were also disadvantaged in property ownership and taxation.

Under Russian rule the Azerbaijani economy, especially the oil industry, experienced rapid expansion. In 1872 the system of granting oil concessions was replaced by giving long-term leases to the highest bidder. This led to increased efficiency, including the swift introduction of power drilling in place of hand-dug wells. By 1901, peak oil production at Baku topped that of the entire United States. As the oil industry brought in foreign companies, Baku turned into a classic boom town, with an influx of Russians and Armenians.

These newcomers edged Azerbaijanis out of the highest-paying positions in the oil industry. Azerbaijanis still controlled Caspian shipping and silk production, but the majority of the native population involved in the oil industry worked in low-paid laboring positions. The industrial development of Baku left the rural areas of Azerbaijan relatively untouched.

Russian Revolutions and Azerbaijan Independence

In Azerbaijan the 1905 and 1917 revolutions were dominated by Armenians and Russians who were the laborers most involved in the mass demonstrations and strikes launched by social democratic groups in Baku. Azerbaijani parties, such as Himmat (Endeavor) and Musavat (Equality) were much less interested in class conflict than in combating Russian imperialism. They were also less hostile to religion, although Azerbaijani intellectuals tended to be critical of Muslim provincialism. They watched with great interest the 1908 Young Turk revolution in the Ottoman Empire and the 1909 revolution in Persia as possible expressions of a pan-Turkic unity.

Following the October Revolution of 1917, Musavat, the most popular party among the Azerbaijanis, initially supported the Bolsheviks because of Lenin's speeches on self-determination. The Russian- and Armenian-dominated Baku Communist Party apparatus, however, edged Azerbaijani socialists out and demonstrated an unwillingness to allow the nationalities to govern themselves. Distrust led to armed conflict in March 1918, when Armenian nationalists and Bolsheviks turned against the Azerbaijanis. When the latter surrendered, the Armenians engaged in a killing and looting spree, remembered by the Azerbaijanis as the "March Days," during which more than 3,000 people were killed.

Outside Baku, the Azerbaijanis and Georgians cooperated to create the short-lived Transcaucasian Federation, a sovereign state that in April 1918 negotiated peace with the Ottoman Turks. When Georgia withdrew from the Federation, the Azerbaijanis remaining in the government declared themselves to be the Azerbaijani National Council, and on 28 May 1918 declared the Azerbaijani Democratic Republic.

Although the Azerbaijanis repelled attacks by the Baku Soviet and captured Baku in September 1918 (taking revenge on the Armenians for the March Days), the Azerbaijani republic failed to get the recognition it sought from other nations. With the Armenians revolting in Karabakh, the Azerbaijani Communist Party pressuring the republican government, and the Red Army marching into Azerbaijan, the republican parliament signed the government over to the Bolsheviks on 27 April 1920. What followed was armed opposition throughout Azerbaijan. Resistance to Soviet rule continued to smolder until 1924.

Azerbaijan was incorporated into the Soviet Union along with Armenia and Georgia as part of the Transcaucasian Soviet Federated Socialist Republic (TSFSR) in 1922. The boundaries drawn between Azerbaijan and Armenia demonstrated the willingness of Soviet leaders to carry on the tsars' ethnic policies. After an earlier promise to grant control of Karabakh to the Armenians, it was placed under the control of Azerbaijan. Predominantly Azerbaijani Naxçivan was also given to Azerbaijan, but the Zangezur province between Naxçivan and the rest of the republic was given to Armenia. It was not until 1936, under the Stalin constitution, that the TSFSR was eliminated and Azerbaijan became a full union republic, officially the Azerbaijan Soviet Socialist Republic.

Soviet Leadership

As armed resistance continued in Azerbaijan, rule from Moscow in the 1920s began with the elimination of nationalists and resistance leaders. Mosques were closed, and a more aggressive Russification policy inaugurated. Azerbaijani resources, notably oil, were expropriated to serve other regions, in particular Russia and Armenia. In the Azerbaijani Communist Party, only Nariman Narimanov, a doctor, spoke against these policies, and he was removed from local government and sent to Moscow. In 1925 he died of unknown causes.

The repression, which grew into the broader purges under Stalin, was carried out by Mir Jafar Bagirov, commissar for internal affairs from 1921 to 1933 and first secretary of the Azerbaijani Communist Party from 1933 to 1953. Under his leadership, the native party was virtually destroyed, as one after another of the old guard was denounced and executed or deported. It is estimated that 120,000 Azerbaijanis died from 1921 to 1940, and it was not until the 1970s that the Baku government again had an ethnic Azerbaijani majority.

When Stalin died in 1953, Bagirov was removed from office and arrested. Three years later he was executed. His replacement as first secretary was Imam Dashdemiroglu Mustafaev, a plant geneticist. During his tenure steps were taken to restore some autonomy to Azerbaijan, maintaining the republic's oil ministry separate from central control and amending the republican constitution to make Azerbaijani Turkish the official language. Moscow, however, considered Mustafaev too nationalistic, and in 1959 he was removed from office.

Mustafaev's successor, Veli Akhundov, was also an outsider to the Party structure. Although he lasted until 1969, he was blamed for Azerbaijan's poor economic performance and accused of fostering widespread corruption. His replacement was Gaidar Aliev, an Azerbaijani product of the Party system, having worked his way up the ranks in the Naxçivan KGB. He was chosen to improve the republic's economy and wipe out corruption. He was praised for having achieved these objectives when he assumed higher office in Moscow at the beginning of 1983, but it was later discovered that Aliev had merely replaced Akhundov's patronage system with one of his own. All three of Aliev's successors have been members of that same system, chosen primarily from the Naxçivan Party apparatus and the KGB. Azerbaijan's Party leadership continued to reflect the influence of hardliners such as Aliev until 1991, as Aliev was relegated to Party leadership in Naxçivan.

Contemporary Issues

Ethnic Disputes: Nagorno-Karabakh and Naxçivan

The most immediate and dangerous problem facing newly independent Azerbaijan is the conflict over the Armenian enclave of Nagorno-Karabakh. This long-standing conflict intensified in 1987 and soon escalated to open warfare. The problem of Nagorno-Karabakh stems from the 1922 border arrangements that awarded control of this Armenian-populated region to the Azerbaijanis. The problem has only been exacerbated by a consistent Russian and Soviet policy of using existing tensions to play the Armenians and Azerbaijanis off against each other.

The ethnic development of Karabakh, even more so than that of the rest of Transcaucasia, is as much a political as an historical matter. Karabakh ("black garden" in Azerbaijani Turkish, perhaps in reference to the dark soil in the region) was from the sixteenth century a khanate, but it was divided into five regions, each ruled by an Armenian *melik*, or tribal chieftain. Armenian-Muslim tensions in Karabakh began when the holdings of Armenian farmers there were encroached upon by Muslim herders who brought their flocks to the high lands of mountainous Karabakh during the summer.

The policies of the Russian tsars shifted the demographic balance heavily in favor of the Armenian population. Following the Russo-Persian and Russo-Turkish wars of the early nineteenth century, Armenian emigrants from the Ottoman Empire and Persia were encouraged to settle in Karabakh, while the Azerbaijani population there declined. At the same time, in an effort to create a loyal aristocracy, the Russians gave preference to the Muslim landlords, exacerbating tensions between them and the largely Armenian peasants. By the time of the Russian Revolution, the region was predominantly (75 percent) Armenian.

Under the short-lived Azerbaijani Democratic Republic, the Armenians in Karabakh revolted, probably in support of both the Bolsheviks and of their own Armenian nationalist groups such as Dashnaktsutiun. A December 1920 agreement between the Bolshevik government (in Baku) and Armenia placed Karabakh and Naxçivan under Armenian control. In March 1921, however, against the terms of the 1920 agreement, Naxçivan was given to Azerbaijan, and in 1923, Karabakh was also handed over. The Nagorno-Karabakh Autonomous Oblast was formed in July 1923, under Azerbaijani control. The oblast government was installed in the predominantly Armenian town of Stepanakert, rather than in the traditional capital of Shusha. In February 1924, the Naxçivan Autonomous Soviet Socialist Republic was formed, also under Azerbaijani control, but separated from Azerbaijan by the Armenian territory of Zangezur. Although Nagorno-Karabakh adjoined Armenia in 1924, by 1930 the border had changed, and the oblast was entirely surrounded by Azerbaijan. When the Transcaucasian SFSR was dissolved in 1936, the Nagorno-Karabakh AO remained within Azerbaijan.

Armenian Appeals to Moscow. Since the 1960s, Armenia has been appealing to Moscow to turn Nagorno-Karabakh over to Armenian control. In 1977 Armenian novelist Sero Khanzadian, in an open letter to Soviet Premier Leonid Brezhnev, argued that the Azerbaijani government discriminated against the Armenian population. Azerbaijan replied that no such discrimination occurred. In fact, the Azerbaijanis have maintained that the Armenians in the region discriminated against the Azerbaijani minority in Nagorno-Karabakh. Armenians, on the other hand, have claimed that Nagorno-Karabakh was economically neglected by Azerbaijan, though the Azerbaijanis have maintained that the oblast consistently received a larger share of the republican budget and more Soviet funding than larger and more populous Naxçivan.

Late in 1986, a letter to Gorbachev protesting the situation by Sergei Grigoriants, an Armenian dissident, was signed by 75,000 Armenians in Nagorno-Karabakh before being delivered to Moscow. In October 1987, one thousand Armenians demonstrated in Erevan for the return of Nagorno-Karabakh and Naxçivan to Armenian control. The demonstration, organized by the Karabakh Committee, was sparked in part by an incident days earlier when a bus containing Armenians was surrounded by a group of Azerbaijanis and pelted with stones.

Escalating Violence. On 20 February 1988, the Nagorno-Karabakh oblast council declared the separation of Nagorno-Karabakh from Azerbaijan. In the Azerbaijan protest demonstrations staged in response to this declaration, two Azerbaijan young people were killed on the eastern border of Nagorno-Karabakh. The day after their deaths were announced, Azerbaijanis in Sumqayit attacked Armenians, and 32 people were killed. After increasing public unrest, the Karabakh Committee agreed to suspend demonstrations in Armenia for one month while Gorbachev considered the issue. Gorbachev denied the appeal in March 1988, calling only for accelerated development of Nagorno-Karabakh by the Azerbaijani government, and refused thereafter to modify republican boundaries.

Strikes and demonstrations continued throughout 1988, while Georgia, Armenia, and Azerbaijan passed laws against such activities and pressured vocal dissidents. The trial of Azerbaijanis involved in the Sumqayit violence polarized the situation, and in May both the Azerbaijani and the Armenian first secretaries were replaced "on grounds of ill health."

Violence flared again in September, amid increasingly radical demonstrations in Armenia and Nagorno-Karabakh. In November, hundreds of thousands of Azerbaijanis demonstrated in Baku's Lenin Square for two weeks over plans to build an Armenian rest home in a wildlife preserve on the site of an eighteenth-century battle with Iran. More disturbing to Soviet officials were the demonstrators who carried portraits of Ayatollah Khomeini and the green flags of Shi'ite Islam, although these protesters were dismissed or condemned by Azerbaijani intellectuals.

By December 1988, the number of dead had reached 80 and the number of Armenian and Azerbaijani refugees topped a quarter million. Attempts to mediate a solution met with rejection from both sides. In 1989 Nagorno-Karabakh came under the *de facto* control of Soviet forces, despite the oblast's official status within Azerbaijan. The Armenian government declared Nagorno-Karabakh a part of the Republic of Armenia.

The Armenian declaration was immediately rejected by Azerbaijan, and in January 1990, Azerbaijani refugees from Armenia began a new campaign of violence against Armenians in Baku. This violence led to intervention by Soviet troops and subsequently to the removal of the Azerbaijani Party first secretary, Abdul-Rakhman Vezirov. Violence continued, as well as particularly injurious rail blockades restricting supplies for reconstruction of Armenian areas devastated by the 1988 earthquake. Anti-Soviet sentiment came to a head in Armenia in May 1990, when Armenians clashed with Soviet troops in Erevan, leaving 24 dead. In August, a high official of the Karabakh Committee, Levon Ter-Petrosian, was elected president of Armenia.

Armed conflict escalated. During April and May 1991, additional Soviet troops were sent to Nagorno-Karabakh and Armenia, supposedly to disarm guerillas. Following the failed coup attempt of August 1991, Russian president Boris Yeltsin and Kazakhstan president Nursultan Nazarbaev brokered a cease-fire that lasted only two months. When an Azerbaijani helicopter crashed over Nagorno-Karabakh in November, the Azerbaijani parliament voted to eliminate the oblast's autonomous status. There followed a blockade of Nagorno-Karabakh as Azerbaijan prepared for war. The equipment of Soviet troops withdrawing from Transcaucasia was nationalized. In January 1992, the Azerbaijani president put Nagorno-Karabakh under his direct rule. In response the oblast declared its own independence and on 19 January asked for admission into the Commonwealth of Independent States.

By May 1992, ethnic disputes had sprung up throughout the region. Armenians had achieved almost complete control of Nagorno-Karabakh. Later that month, Armenians captured the westerly Azerbaijani town of Lachyn, while Kurds called for an independent Kurdish buffer state between Armenia and Nagorno-Karabakh, an indication of further ethnic difficulties in the region. Meanwhile, Naxçivan claimed to be under attack by Armenia. In June, Azerbaijani military forces counterattacked in Nagorno-Karabakh. Disorganized and poorly trained, they sustained heavy casualties but recaptured several villages. By mid-1993, all of Nagorno-Karabakh was firmly under Armenian control.

The fighting, which has led to an almost complete removal of Azerbaijanis from Armenia and Armenians from Azerbaijan, has also jeopardized the Russian minority in both republics. In August 1992, after a Russian area of Azerbaijan came under fire, President Yeltsin offered to broker another ceasefire between Armenia and Azerbaijan, even as attempts negotiated by both Iran and Turkey failed. Azerbaijani President Abulfaz Elchibey, elected in 1992, vowed to recapture territory taken by the Armenians. Armenian President Levon Ter-Petrosian, while he has attempted to distance himself from the unofficial Armenian units operating in the conflict, is unlikely to allow Nagorno-Karabakh to be reconquered by Azerbaijan. Under the pressure of a continued rail and energy blockade, the conflict has continued.

Complicating the issue is the role of the surrounding nations. It is uncertain what steps Yeltsin will take to protect the Russian population in Transcaucasia. Turkey, under the Moscow Treaty of 1921, has the right to intervene if a third party attempts to change the borders of Transcaucasia. The Turkish government says that it will not enter the conflict, but nationalist and conservative groups within Turkey are critical of their regime for its neutral stance. Ter-Petrosian has attempted to establish friendly relations with Turkey, and the Turkish government has been reluctant to alienate the rest of the world by attacking Armenia.

Politics and Informal Groups

The Party leaders of Azerbaijan were among the last to support reforms or recognize local resistance to Communist rule. Under the regime of Kiamran Bagirov, who succeeded Aliev as first secretary in 1982, the economic problems and corruption from Akhundov's era returned. Bagirov was first secretary when the Nagorno-Karabakh conflict flared in 1987, and his removal from office "on grounds of ill health" in May 1988 was linked in part to how he handled that crisis. Abdul-Rakhman Vezirov, another of Aliev's followers, succeeded Bagirov but was in turn removed in 1990.

During Vezirov's tenure, an Azerbaijani Popular Front finally formed in resistance to Soviet rule. Before this time, Azerbaijani intellectuals had been more concerned with keeping their culture alive than with political action. In November 1988, however, when hundreds of thousands of demonstrators were protesting the Nagorno-Karabakh conflict in Baku's Lenin Square, the Azerbaijani grievances broadened to include the stifling of native Azerbaijani cultures, the concealment of environmental problems, and the concern for Azerbaijani self-determination. During July and August of 1989, the Azerbaijani Popular Front (APF) instituted a series of demonstrations and strikes. During this time, the Birlik (Unity) Society, the second largest popular group in Azerbaijan (formed primarily of immigrants from Iranian Azerbaijan), united with the APF. Several other groups had formed within the

APF, such as the Social Democratic Party, the Azerbaijani Liberal Democratic Party, and the National Democratic Party (New Musavat). All these groups called for Vezirov's removal and a referendum on secession. In January, members of the APF seized power in Länkäran, and crowds demolished frontier installations along most of the 367-mile Iranian border.

On 20 January 1990, Gorbachev sent troops into Baku to shore up Vezirov's regime. After a media blackout ended, it was learned that 131 Azerbaijanis had been killed and 744 wounded. Far to the west, Naxçivan immediately declared independence and called for United Nations support. A commission report on the Soviet intervention called it a "carefully planned and cynically executed punitive action" (quoted in "Azerbaijan Commission on January 1990 Military Intervention," *Radio Free Europe/Radio Liberty Report*, vol. 1, no. 5, 31 January 1992, p. 69).

In the ensuing demonstrations, Vezirov was forced from office and expelled from the Communist Party, even as nearly a third of Azerbaijani Communists destroyed their membership cards. Vezirov's successor, Ayaz Niyaz Mutalibov, was chosen because, like Mustafaev and Akhundov before him, he was untarnished by local politics. In May 1990, after running unopposed, Mutalibov was elected president of the republic. He refused to yield on the Nagorno-Karabakh issue, meanwhile developing ties with other Soviet republics and encouraging foreign investment in Azerbaijan.

Mutalibov's image was damaged during the August 1991 coup attempt when he reportedly expressed support for the conservatives. The APF called for his resignation and for Azerbaijani independence. The parliament, still dominated by ex-Communists, unanimously voted on 30 August 1991 to "restore" Azerbaijan's independent status of 1918–20. The same day, the candidate of the Azerbaijani Social Democratic Party in the forthcoming September presidential elections withdrew from the race, complaining of unfair campaigning. Unopposed, Mutalibov won more than 80 percent of the vote, a figure disputed by the APF. Once president rather than first secretary, Mutalibov reaffirmed Azerbaijani independence in October, putting the matter to a referendum in December. The results, with a 54 percent turnout, were 99 percent in favor of independence.

Pressure from the APF and Mutalibov's failure to maintain control of Nagorno-Karabakh led the parliament to force his resignation in March, and acting president Iakub Mamedov set elections for June. In May,

however, Mutalibov reclaimed the presidency, cancelled the elections, and imposed a curfew and censorship. The parliament voted to reinstate Mutalibov as president, with the Democratic Bloc boycotting the vote. In response, the APF, with the cooperation of the army, occupied the parliament building, and by the next day controlled the airport and broadcasting facilities. A national council assumed temporary control of the government.

In June 1992 a new president of Azerbaijan was chosen in statewide elections. Abulfaz Elchibey, a 54-year-old historian and chairman of the Popular Front, gained 59 percent of the vote. The results were accepted by foreign observers and most Azerbaijanis, although the challenger, Nizami Suleimanov of the Democratic Union of the Intelligentsia of Azerbaijan, charged fraud.

Political Volatility from Elchibey to Aliev

President Abulfaz Elchibey, despite his electoral majority and the support of the broadly based Azerbaijani Popular Front, failed to provide effective leadership in the two areas most vital to the young Azerbaijani nation. First of all, the Elchibey government continued to sustain reversals in Nagorno-Karabakh. By mid-1993, Armenian forces in the Nagorno-Karabakh enclave had effectively routed all remaining Azerbaijani forces from the area. Carving out a corridor linking Armenia proper to Karabakh, the victorious Armenians badly embarrassed the Elchibey government. Indirectly, the Armenian victories also contributed to the immediate circumstances of Elchibey's fall. Having earlier dismissed the young maverick Azerbaijani military commander, Surat Husseinov, whom he charged with contributing to Azerbaijani losses, Elchibey in turn faced the personal revenge of Husseinov. In June 1993, Husseinov led his rebel followers from the city of Gäncä in a direct assault upon the Elchibey government, forcing the elected Azerbaijani president to flee to Naxçivan.

On a second and equally important level, President Elchibey had failed to turn around the misfortunes of the Azerbaijani economy, despite the presence of substantial untapped oil reserves. One of the ironies of Elchibey's fall in June 1993 was that negotiations with a five-party Western consortium for joint development of the Baku oil fields were on the verge of completion prior to the domestic uprising. The five Western negotiating parties—British Petroleum, Amoco, Pennzoil, Unocal, and McDermott International—were prepared to pump major new development funds into the rich Caspian Sea oil fields.

Such development was too little and too late for Elchibey, whose popularity had plummeted. Sensing his own vulnerability, Elchibey in June 1993 called upon the former Soviet Communist Azerbaijani strongman, Gaidar Aliev, to help bring order to Baku. With Elchibey's withdrawal to Naxçivan—he withdrew without formally resigning from the presidency—Aliev, the one-time head of the Azerbaijani KGB and Brezhnevite Party leader, became acting president.

Aliev's reemergence as a power broker in Azerbaijan has paralleled developments elsewhere in the newly independent states of Eurasia where, following the euphoria of independence and subsequent disillusionment, former Communist leaders have taken over the reigns of power. Gaidar Aliev's return was a particularly striking example of the familiar pattern—a one-time Communist Party leader embracing the modern nationalist cause, resurfaces with a new ideological identity, but with powerful ties to the old party bureaucracy or nomenklatura. (That pattern, in varying degrees, can be used to describe Leonid Kravchuk of Ukraine, Eduard Shevardnadze of Georgia, Islam Karimov of Uzbekistan and, outside the former Soviet republics, Slobodan Milošević of Serbia.) From his post as KGB chief in Azerbaijan, Aliev had been tapped by Brezhnev to be Communist Party first secretary of the republic in 1969. In 1983, he was named to the central Soviet Politburo, the effective governing body of the Communist Party of the former Soviet Union. He served during Gorbachev's leadership as deputy prime minister of the Soviet Union before being ousted in 1987. Following a period of oblivion in Moscow, Aliev resurfaced in 1990, leading protests in Moscow against Soviet military intervention in Baku—protests that marked the emergence of a new, more nationalistic Aliev. Since the early 1990s, the reincarnated nationalist Aliev was positioned in Naxçivan, until his return to Baku in mid-1993.

It is unclear whether the Aliev government, with military commander Surat Husseinov serving as prime minister, will be any more able than the Elchibey government in restoring national honor in its relationship with Armenia and in dealing with the economy. There is already evidence, however, that the Aliev government is not prepared to allow popular movements to function freely at the expense of central government authority in Baku.

Ecological Issues

Azerbaijan's agricultural and oil industries pose grave ecological dangers for the new state. Azerbaijan has a longstanding pollution problem arising from nineteenth-century oil drilling in Baku and resultant contamination of the Caspian Sea. Most of the air pollution in cities along the Caspian coast is caused by the petroleum and chemical industry. In 1987, the Soviet minister of health noted that the air throughout the republic contained five times the maximum permissable concentration of pollutants (cited in Elizabeth Fuller and Mirza Michaeli, "Azerbaijan Belatedly Discovers Environmental Pollution," *Radio Liberty Research Bulletin,* vol. 32, no. 1, 6 January 1988).

The Caspian Sea has suffered badly from the dumping of raw sewage and petroleum waste. Dumping was supposed to cease by 1985, but in that year alone an estimated 104,000 tons of oil and sediment were released into the sea. Worsening the situation, dam projects from the 1930s limit the flow of fresh water from the Aras and Kura rivers.

The use of fertilizers and pesticides in Azerbaijan has left dangerously high concentrations of chemicals in the soil and air of agricultural regions. In 1987, the Soviet minister of health noted a high infant mortality rate—30.5 per 1,000 live births (higher than the official figure of 23/1,000 released in the census)—and high rates of infectious diseases, both of them increasing. These high rates were linked to chemicals used in cotton growing. Also in 1987, 10 percent of the melon crop was found to have dangerously high concentrations of nitrates. A 1989 article by the head of the Health Science Research Institute of Epidemiology, Hygiene, and Occupational Diseases showed that the concentration of pesticides in Azerbaijan is 20 times the average in the Soviet Union (cited in Yasin Aslan and Elizabeth Fuller, "Azerbaijani Press Discusses Link between Ecological Problems and Health Defects," *Radio Liberty Report on the USSR,* vol. 1, no. 31, 4 August 1989, pp. 20–21). These problems have been compounded by an unwillingness to deal with them openly. Many studies on the effects of pesticides and chemical pollution were suppressed by the governmental authorities.

Economic Issues

Azerbaijan faces the most severe economic difficulties of the three former Soviet Transcaucasian republics but may have the best chance to solve them. Azerbaijan is burdened with high unemployment and a long tradition of corruption, both of which pose a threat to economic growth. During 1991, gross industrial output decreased by 8 percent, while consumer prices rose 816.7 percent (cited in Douglas Stanglin, "A Victory Gone Sour: Yeltsin and His Compatriots are Struggling, A Year after the Failed Coup," *U.S. News & World Report*, 24 August 1992, pp. 43-45, 48). The republic's agriculture, although more diversified than the cotton monocultures of Central Asia, was troubled by Gorbachev's anti-alcoholism campaign. Azerbaijan, a major wine producer, had to find new outlets for its grapes. Although the republic since 1986 had been shifting toward jams and compotes, considerable unemployment and waste resulted from the low demand for grapes.

In its favor, Azerbaijan has sufficient potential oil revenues to improve living standards, if the funds are not diverted into unnecessary ventures. The republic can also benefit from ties with Turkey and Iran, each of which is trying to gain the favor of the former Soviet Muslim republics.

Islam in Azerbaijan

Azerbaijan's Islamic heritage led to a resurgence of Islamic sentiment when, in the mid-1980s, mosques closed since the 1930s were reopened. The green banners and portraits of Iran's Ayatollah Khomeini at the 1989 Baku demonstrations, however, were condemned by intellectuals in the APF, who sought a secular democracy. Mutalibov, on the other hand, appealed to Islamic sentiment by reading verses from the Koran during his presidential campaign.

Until the twentieth century, most Azerbaijanis identified themselves as Muslims rather than Azerbaijanis or Turks. The idea of a nation was generally subordinated to the idea of a spiritual community of Islam. Turkish intellectuals in the Ottoman Empire placed the idea of a Turkish nation above that of religious identification. Members of the intelligentsia in Azerbaijan took up the discussion, arguing over whether they were Muslims, Turks, or even Azerbaijani Turks. Such debates, however, were confined to intellectuals, and the majority of Azerbaijanis identified themselves simply as Muslims. Arguably, this remains the case today: While a national identity is present, its status relative to religious identity remains a matter of question.

The Shi'ite/Sunni split means little in Azerbaijani religious or social life. Although the Shi'ite Azerbaijanis fought with the Russians against the Sunni Dagestanis in the eighteenth and nineteenth centuries, Azerbaijanis today have no clear idea of the differences between Sunni and Shi'ite doctrine. Sectarian variations in general were deemphasized by the Muslims themselves in the face of cultural conflict with Christian rulers. Although separate Sunni and Shi'ite hierarchies exist, the differences between the two for the average Muslim have increasingly faded.

Russian and Soviet rulers established official hierarchies for the Muslims as a means of controlling their influence over the population. Unlike Eastern Orthodoxy or Catholicism, however, Islam has little need for an established clergy. Spiritual leaders are primarily scholars and judges. The principal obligations of Islam are carried out at the individual level—the five daily prayers, the month of fasting, charity to the poor, and the strictures against alcohol and some foods. During the tsarist period, Azerbaijanis had learned not to trust religious officials, and this mistrust continued during the Soviet era. Azerbaijani Muslims therefore stayed away from the mosques but still carried out the individual rituals in private or small groups. Further, Shi'ite Muslims may deny their faith if under duress, and Azerbaijanis have done so to avoid scrutiny from Communist authorities.

Russian and Soviet cooptation of the official organs of Islam meant that only reliable Muslims could receive education, at official seminaries. The most talented fled to Iran or even Turkey to complete their education, leaving behind unofficial religious teachers who lacked higher levels of education. By the end of the nineteenth century, there were probably no religious scholars left in Azerbaijan. (See Audrey L. Altstadt, *The Azerbaijani Turks: Power and Identity under Russian Rule* [Studies of Nationalities] Stanford: Hoover Institution Press, 1992, pp. 57–62.) Trusted religious leaders in contemporary Azerbaijan tend to be more reactionary, tied to local and communal interests. This situation exposes them to criticism by Azerbaijani intellectuals who prefer that a more secular version of Islam determine the course of Islamic revival among the masses. Although Iran has been assisting Azerbaijanis in religious study, the Azerbaijani religious scholarly community is still recovering from Russian and Soviet rule.

The picture that emerges is, therefore, far from clear. While it is possible that the Azerbaijanis could establish a secular democracy, it is also possible that popular movements could call for an Islamic republic. In the Nagorno-Karabakh conflict, battlecries may take on an increasingly religious tone, as in the June 1992 Radio Baku call for a "Holy War at the state level against the Armenian infidels" (quoted in Elizabeth Fuller, "Azerbaijan after the Presidential Elections," *RFE/RL Research Report*, vol. 1, no. 26, 26 June 1992, pp. 1-7).

International Relations

Azerbaijan has historically traveled a course between Turkey and Iran in its foreign relations. Both of these countries have tried to establish ties with the Muslim republics of the former Soviet Union. Turkey has been held up by Central Asian and Azerbaijani intellectuals as the model of secular democracy, and Turks emphasize their links to the Turkic peoples of the former Soviet Union. Although not many seem to have embraced pan-Turkism, Turkey began transmitting cultural programming to these republics during 1992. Iran, meanwhile, also emphasizes its links through Islam to the Muslims of the former Soviet Union.

Elchibey's promise to remove Azerbaijan from the Commonwealth of Independent States has signalled a rejection of Russian influence. Relations with both Turkey and Iran are increasingly being explored. Turkish merchants have expressed interest in Baku as a trading center to link them to the Central Asian republics, and Turkish officials have toured Azerbaijan and Central Asia frequently in 1992 and 1993. The darker side of this relationship is Turkey's potential role in the Nagorno-Karabakh conflict. This role is complicated by pan-Turkic elements in the APF who have been in contact with Turkish fascist groups, such as the one led by Arpaslan Turkesh, whose grey wolf insignia is worn by Azerbaijani military units.

In aspiring to serve as spiritual head for the world's Muslims, Iran has also assisted Azerbaijan. In late 1991, Iran tried to broker a ceasefire in the Nagorno-Karabakh conflict, and its government has supported Azerbaijani students in Iran. Elchibey rejected Iran's fundamentalism, however, and Azerbaijanis have accused Iran of supplying the Armenians. At the same time Iranians are concerned about the Azerbaijani sentiment for uniting northern and southern Azerbaijan (northern Iran). Such was the aim of Azerbaijan's Birlik Society in 1989. Iranian Azerbaijan has much of the oil and resources of Iran, and its Turkic population (8 to 13 million) has agitated for greater cultural and linguistic autonomy since the 1980s. In 1920, shortly after Azerbaijan's fall to the Bolsheviks, Azerbaijanis in Iran (Persia) revolted against Tehran, declaring northwest Iran to be Azadistan (land of freedom). In the post–World War II period, Iranian Azerbaijan was the base for the pro-Soviet communist Tudeh party. Today, the degree of support in Tabriz, the principal city of Iranian Azerbaijan, for unity with northern Azerbaijan is subject to question, but the APF has not rejected reunification as a long-term goal.

Redefining the Past

After the purges of the Stalinist period and the retrenchment of the Brezhnev era, Azerbaijanis were among those least likely to criticize the central regime or voice nationalist sentiments. Histories of nineteenth- and twentieth-century Azerbaijan were heavily endowed with Marxist-Leninist ideology. Ancient history was safer, being distant from more contemporary issues, while at the same time indirectly counteracting Soviet assertions that the Russians had been the older brother to the Azerbaijanis.

Historical novels were the other escape valve for nationalist sentiment—so much so, in fact, that at the 1986 Congress of the Azerbaijan Union of Writers, authors who limited their writings to historical novels were criticized. Writers were urged to deal with more contemporary issues and to display glasnost more openly. Younger writers were criticized for being too eager to get their works published in Russian.

Under Gorbachev, but particularly since Azerbaijan's independence, the past has been reexamined. As early as 1987, a young critic urged historians to study those individuals whom Soviet histories have ignored, and in 1988, Mahmoud Ismailov, a corresponding member of the Azerbaijani Academy of Sciences, urged historians to undertake an objective evaluation of the Azerbaijani Democratic Republic (Annette Bohr and Yasin Aslan, "Independent Azerbaijan, 1918-1920: Call to Reevaluate History of Former Nation-State," *RLRB*, vol. 32, no. 35, 31 August 1988). Azerbaijan has been the first Muslim state to allow women to vote.

Language and Orthography

One problem that faces all the Turkic republics of the former Soviet Union is deciding which alphabet to use. Conversion of Azerbaijani Turkish from an Arabic to a Latin script, as was ultimately done in Turkey, was contemplated by nineteenth-century intellectuals. From

1922 to 1928 the Latinized alphabet was developed, in cooperation with linguists from the Central Asian republics, and it was implemented in 1929. In 1940, however, Stalin called for change from the Latin to a Cyrillic alphabet. Today very few academic personnel can read either the Latin or the Arabic script, even though Latin script is gradually being reintroduced.

More threatening to Azerbaijani intellectuals is the declining status of Azerbaijani Turkish. Prominent Azerbaijani poet Bakhtiyar Vahabzade noted in 1989 that Azerbaijani Turkish, the official language of the republic since the 1950s, had not been used to conduct state business since World War II (Yasin Aslan and Elizabeth Fuller, "Azerbaijani Intellectuals Express Concern over Native Language," *RLRB,* vol. 1, no. 9, 3 March 1989, pp. 22-23). During the 1920s, Azerbaijani Turkish words for ideological concepts were replaced by their Russian counterparts. Higher education most often took place in Russian. Before 1958, students were required to pass examinations in both Russian and their native language, but since then they have been allowed to choose between the two, placing Azerbaijani Turkish in jeopardy. Youths in Baku tend to speak either a mixture of Azerbaijani Turkish and Russian, or pure Russian, and educated Azerbaijani professionals often have difficulty expressing themselves in their native language. At the turn of the century, linguistic autonomy was an issue for Azerbaijani intellectuals. Today it is one of the issues defining the Azerbaijani search for its national identity.

As in Tajikistan (Central Asia), the newly independent state of Azerbaijan appears to be following its own violent rebellion of 1993 with the implementation of firm authoritarian measures, albeit to the accompaniment of renewed nationalist rhetoric. Alongside this tide of authoritarian reaction, however, the long-term future for Azerbaijan is somewhat brighter because of the presence of ample oil reserves. The real test for Azerbaijan will be seen in its ability to develop these reserves while establishing a procedure for dealing with Armenia, as well as with its southern neighbors, Turkey and Iran.

GEORGIA

Statistical Profile

Demography

Population: 5,401,000
Ethnic population:

Georgian	3,787,000	70.1%
Armenian	437,000	8.1%
Russian	341,000	6.3%
Azerbaijani	308,000	5.7%
Ossetian	164,000	3.0%
Greek	100,000	1.9%
Abkhaz	96,000	1.8%
Ukrainian	52,000	1.0%
Kurdish	33,000	0.6%
Jewish	10,000	0.2%
Others	73,000	1.4%

Historic religious traditions:

Christianity	90.4%
Islam	8.0%

Population by age:

Age	Total	Males	Females
0–4	8.8%	4.5%	4.3%
5–9	8.2%	4.2%	4.0%
10–14	8.1%	4.1%	4.0%
15–19	7.6%	3.9%	3.7%
20–24	8.2%	4.2%	4.0%
25–29	8.2%	4.1%	4.1%
30–34	7.4%	3.5%	3.9%
35–39	6.3%	3.0%	3.3%
40–44	4.1%	1.9%	2.2%
45–49	7.1%	3.3%	3.8%
50–54	6.1%	2.9%	3.2%
55–59	6.1%	2.9%	3.2%
60–64	4.6%	1.9%	2.7%
65–69	2.8%	0.9%	1.9%
70–	6.4%	2.0%	4.4%

Male/Female ratio: 47.3% male/52.7% female
Rural/Urban population: 43.8% rural/56.2% urban
Growth over time, 1979–91: 9.0%
Population density: 203.0 persons/sq mi

Politics/Government

Date of independence declaration:
9 April 1991
Major urban centers and populations:

Tbilisi	1,260,000
Kutaisi	235,000
Rustavi	159,000
Batumi	136,000
Sokhumi	121,000
Tskhinvali	30,000

Autonomous republics:

Abkhazia	Sokhumi (capital)
Ajaria	Batumi (capital)
South Ossetiia	Tskhinvali (capital)

Education

Level of education for persons over 15:

completed higher level education	15.1%
completed secondary education	57.4%
incomplete secondary education	15.2%

Number of higher education institutions: 19
(103,900 students)
Major institutions of higher education and enrollment:
Tbilisi:

Georgian Technical University	28,000
Ivan Dzhavakhiladze University	16,000
State Medical Institute	3,500
Veterinary Training and Research Institute	2,250
State Music Conservatory	700
Rustaveli State Institute of Dramatic Art	566

Socioeconomic Indicators

Birthrate: 17.0/1,000
Infant mortality: 15.9/1,000 live births
Average life expectancy: 72.8 (males, 69.0; females, 76.3)
Average family size: 4.1
Hospital beds per 10,000 persons: 110.7
Production of electrical energy: 2,599 kwh/person

Length of rail lines: 973 mi
Length of highways: 20,212 mi

Physical/Territorial/Geopolitical Features

    Area: 26,911 sq mi (.3% of USSR total)
    Land use:
      Cultivated   11%
      Pasture   27%
    Highest elevation: 16,558 ft. (Kazbek Peak)

Rainfall: 22 inches/year in the plains and foothills; as much as 79 in the mountains
Temperature: average in winter 40° F (29° F in the mountains); lowest temperature: –40° F. Average in summer 73° F; highest temperature: 101° F.
Principal products: tea, grapes, citrus fruits, tobacco, sheep and cattle, metallurgy, manganese, coal, lead, zinc, machine tools, chemicals
Per capita GNP (1991): $1,640.

Sources

"Gruzinskaia sovetskaia sotsialisticheskaia respublika," *Bol'shaia Sovetskaia Entsiklopediia* (Moscow, 1977); *Narodnoe khoziaistvo SSSR v 1990g.* (Moscow, 1991); *Naselenie SSSR* (1989); Matthew J. Sagers, "News Notes. Iron and Steel," *Soviet Geography* 30 (May 1989): 397–434; Lee Schwartz, "USSR Nationality Redistribution by Republic, 1979–1989: From Published Results of the 1989 All-Union Census," *Soviet Geography* 32 (April 1991): 209–48; and *World of Learning,* 43rd ed. (London: Europa Publications Limited, 1993); "Russia. . ." (National Geographic Society Map, March 1993).

History and Description

Topography

An ancient country with a long and complex history, Georgia is situated amongst the magnificent mountains of Transcaucasia. Essentially part of an isthmus between the Black and Caspian seas, Georgia is bounded on the north by the Caucasus mountains and on the south by the Lesser Caucasus. Georgia's mountainous plateaus and river valleys contrast with lowland areas lying to either side of the Surami mountain range, which bisects the country along a northeast-southwest axis. Much volcanic activity takes place in this region of Transcaucasia.

To the north and northeast of Georgia lies Russia, the frontier at many points distinguished by the snow-clad peaks of the greater Caucasus range. Mt. Kazbek (16,558 ft.), one of the highest points in Europe, is located within this range. To the east and southeast of Georgia are the arid plains of Azerbaijan separating Georgia from the Caspian Sea. Georgia is today linked to the Caspian Sea by oil and gas pipelines connecting Georgian cities to the Azerbaijan port of Baku. To the south lie Armenia and Turkey. The shoreline of the Black Sea makes up Georgia's western boundary.

Slightly smaller than South Carolina, Georgia (26,911 square miles) consists of two quite separate geographic areas. The western part of the country is characterized by a humid, subtropical climate and landscape very different from the dry, continental conditions prevailing in eastern Georgia. The swampy lowlands of western Georgia, drained by many rivers and streams, present a hot, damp climate conducive to the intensive cultivation of agricultural products such as citrus fruits, tea, and tobacco, which cannot be grown elsewhere in Transcaucasia or in Russia. Georgia has long been noted for wines and cognacs produced from grapes grown in this region. By contrast, the Kura lowland in eastern Georgia offers a primarily arid plain with occasional low mountains used for livestock grazing. Agricultural production is devoted to grains, vegetables, and fruits, especially grapes.

The streams and rivers of Georgia, as they cascade from mountainous heights, provide abundant hydroelectric power for local use. Georgia's main river, the Kura, enters the country from Turkey, slices through the Surami mountains at Tbilisi, and then continues southeasterly through the Kura River valley, across the border into Azerbaijan, and farther east until it empties into the

Georgia

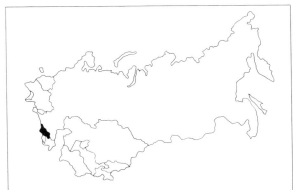

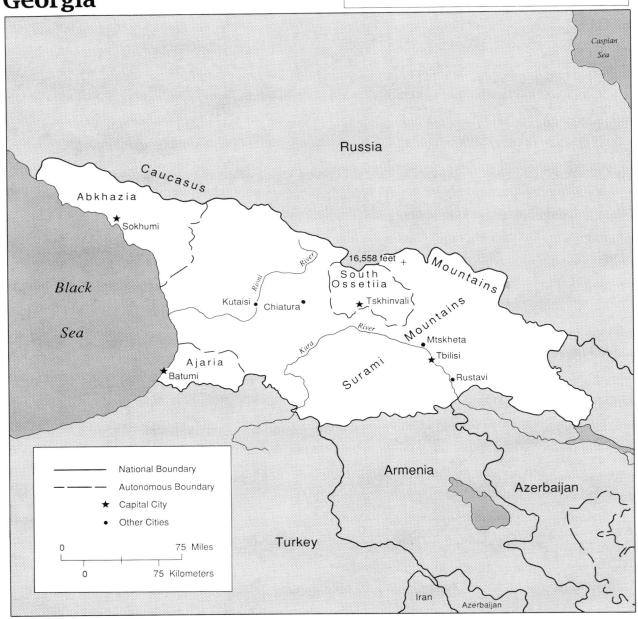

Caspian Sea

Russia

Caucasus

Abkhazia

★ Sokhumi

Black

Sea

16,558 feet +

South Ossetiia

Mountains

Kutaisi • Chiatura

★ Tskhinvali

Rioni River

River

Kura River

Mtskheta •

Mountains

Surami Mountains

★ Tbilisi

• Rustavi

Ajaria

★ Batumi

National Boundary

Autonomous Boundary

★ Capital City

• Other Cities

Armenia

Azerbaijan

0   75 Miles

0   75 Kilometers

Turkey

Iran   Azerbaijan

Caspian Sea. The Rioni River in western Georgia flows into the Black Sea, watering the formerly marshy region of Kolkhida, known as Colchis in Greek mythology, the place where Jason searched for the golden fleece. This area was drained and reclaimed for agricultural purposes during the Soviet period.

Georgia's natural resources include rich reserves of manganese, much of which is exported to other parts of the world. Petroleum, low-grade coal, and barite are also found in Georgia. A large petroleum-refining industry has been developed at the Black Sea port of Batumi. Copper and silver have been mined in Georgia for centuries.

Large cities in Georgia include its modern capital, Tbilisi (formerly Tiflis). A beautiful city spread out along the gorge formed by the Kura River, Tbilisi has long been the center of Georgian cultural life. Taking its name from the warm sulfur springs on which it sits, Tbilisi is known by tourists for the funicular railway and cable cars that carry passengers to the summit of Mt. Mtatsminda for a spectacular view of the city. Rustavi, a town designated for development in the 1940s to accommodate the growing iron and steel industry in eastern Georgia, has grown into an important metallurgical center. Kutaisi, the industrial center of western Georgia, lies on the Rioni River. Chiatura, center of manganese mining, operating since 1879, is also in western Georgia. Sokhumi, a resort on the Black Sea, and Batumi, an important industrial seaport mentioned earlier, also support the economic life of Georgia.

Ethnic Background and Historical Development

Georgians are thought to derive from early indigenous inhabitants of the Caucasus region. Historical and archeological records reveal evidence of agricultural activity in eastern Georgia as early as the fifth century B.C. The Roman, Persian, Byzantine, Arabic, Mongol, and Turkish empires all influenced Georgian politics well before the advent of Russian domination in the eighteenth century. Although Christianity was adopted by Georgian kings in the fourth century, a conversion inspired by the activities of St. Nino, religious life followed a distinctly Georgian pattern as the country struggled to maintain its independence between competing powers.

Georgians as an ethnic group are part of the so-called Kartvelian people, and they call their land Sakartvelo. The Georgian language belongs to the southern branch of the Caucasian language family. The alphabet, written in a beautiful script dating to the fourth century or before, has undergone several modifications or reforms. Georgians identify themselves as Kartveli, Russians use the name Gruziny, and Turks employ the term Gurcu. In the classical period, Georgia was known as Iberia to the Greeks and Romans. English usage of the term Georgia comes from the Turkish Gurcu.

Well over 90 percent of the world's Georgians live in the Republic of Georgia. Very few have emigrated beyond the borders of their homeland, although a few Georgian emigre enclaves exist in western Europe. Because of the existence of numerous minority groups within Georgia, however, the percentage of Georgians as part of the country's total population stands at just 70 percent.

Autonomous Regions. Under the Soviet system, Georgia administered three separate autonomous regions within its national borders. These regions are inhabited by peoples of ethnic or religious backgrounds different from those of the Georgians. The collapse of the Soviet Union complicates the status of these regions. The largest and most populous of them is the Republic of Abkhazia in northwestern Georgia along the Black Sea. There are approximately 540,000 people living in Abkhazia today. Its capital, Sokhumi (Sukhumi), was one of the premier resort sites in the former Soviet Union, having a climate similar to that of southern Florida. The people of Abkhazia speak a Caucasian language belonging to the northern branch of that language family. Many of the Muslim Abkhazians emigrated to Turkey in the nineteenth century, with the result that those remaining within Abkhazia today compose a minority (less than 20 percent) of the total population of Abkhazia. Although Eastern Orthodoxy is practiced by some Abkhazians, others adhere to traditional Islamic practice.

South Ossetiia, another autonomous region is located in the extreme north of the country on the slopes of the Caucasus west of the pass where the Georgian Military Highway crosses the Caucasus Mountains. Its capital, Tskhinvali, was formerly named after Stalin (Stalinir). South Ossetiia is inhabited by an Iranian-language-speaking people called Ossetians. On the other side of the mountains of South Ossetiia live the Ossetians of North Ossetiia, a formerly autonomous region (oblast) within the Russian Federation. Although the majority of the South Ossetians come out of the Eastern Orthodox, Christian tradition, both Christian and Islamic religious traditions are represented in the Ossetian communities north and south of the Georgian/Russian border.

The smallest autonomous area in Georgia is the Ajari republic on the Black Sea in southwestern Georgia. Its capital is Batumi, known for its warm tropical climate as well as for its importance as Georgia's major seaport. Ajaris are those largely rural Georgians who converted centuries ago to Islam while under Ottoman rule. Although their language exhibits many Turkic elements, they continue to speak Georgian. Ajaria was added to the Soviet Union as a part of the Turkish-Soviet peace negotiations following World War I and the Russian Civil War.

In addition to the ethnic groups given autonomous standing in the former Soviet Republic of Georgia, many other minorities also live in present day Georgia. Some represent the people of neighboring countries, such as the Armenians, Azerbaijanis, and Russians. Many are members of distinct ethnographic groups speaking dialects of Georgian and living in isolated mountain valleys. The Mingrelians, the Svans (Svanetians), and the Laz are among these smaller groups slowly being assimilated by the Georgians.

Formation of the Georgian Nation. For over two millennia during the formation of the Georgian nation, ethnically related groups inhabiting the mountains of the Caucasus region and speaking distinct Kartvelian dialects gradually came together under a series of different rulers. Because of the strategic location of Georgian lands as a crossroads between East and West, an important commerical trade route emerged there, and many empires vied for influence or control over Georgia. From the Romans in classical times to the Russians in the modern period, the Georgian nation often found itself responding to the conflicting claims of great empires.

Mtskheta, ancient capital of the Kartli or eastern Georgians, existed as early as the third century B.C., but by the reign of Vakhtang in the late fifth century A.D. a new capital had been established at Tbilisi. As Persian domination gave way to Arab invasion and then to Byzantine influence, the lands of eastern and western Georgia were finally brought together under one Georgian ruler in the eleventh century. The accession to power of King Bagrat III in 1008 marked a culmination in the process of Georgian national unification. Subsequent Turkish campaigns later in the eleventh century were quelled by David the Builder (1089–1125), leading to the memorable reign of Queen Tamar (1184–1212) under whom Georgia reached the apogee of its early national and cultural achievement. During Tamar's reign, Georgia's national poet Rustaveli wrote his great epic tribute to the Georgian nation, "The Knight in the Tiger's Skin." Peace did not last, however, for during the thirteenth and fourteenth centuries Mongol hordes nearly destroyed Georgia. Turkish forces of the Ottoman Empire became the next warring power to dominate Georgian lands until finally, in 1783, a Russian protectorate was sought to help preserve the Georgian nation.

Russian Rule

Contrary to the expectations of the Georgian aristocracy and other national leaders, the autonomous protectorate was not long honored by the tsar. In 1801, Georgia was effectively annexed into the Russian Empire during the reign of Alexander I. The Georgian Orthodox church, independent for centuries, was made subordinate to the Holy Synod of the Russian Orthodox church. The economy of the country stabilized, however, under the rule of its northern neighbor, and Russian and European ideas came to influence the educated class of Georgians. Intellectual life flourished, serious literary publications appeared, and by the end of the nineteenth century, political concerns mirrored to a great extent important issues being debated in Moscow and St. Petersburg. Georgian political radicals participated within wider Russian revolutionary circles, in which Georgian Marxists were largely Menshevik, as opposed to Bolshevik, in their sympathies.

Georgia under the Soviet System

In May 1918, following the Bolshevik Revolution in Moscow the previous October, Georgia declared its independence. This independence, although later recognized by other countries and looked upon favorably by the League of Nations, did not last. In February 1921, less than nine months after Moscow had signed a treaty accepting the sovereignty of the Georgian Democratic Republic, the Red Army, led by a Georgian named Sergo Ordzhonikidze, secretly crossed into Georgia from Azerbaijan and quashed the young state. Later, in 1922, under the personal direction of Stalin, also a Georgian whose real name was Josef Dzhugashvili, Georgia was established as one of three nations (the others being Armenia and Azerbaijan) making up the Soviet-created Republic of Transcaucasia. Violent resistance to Soviet power continued until 1924 when a last uprising was crushed by Bolshevik authorities. As many as four thousand rebels were executed and countless others imprisoned. The Republic of Transcaucasia prevailed until 1936. At that time it was divided, and Georgia was declared a full union republic of the Soviet Union.

During the long period of Stalin's dictatorship, Georgia might have been expected to enjoy a special status within the Union of Soviet Socialist Republics. The more Stalin came to identify himself as a Russian nationalist, however, the less he seemed willing to show any favoritism to Georgia. Instead, the incredible horrors of the purges of the 1930s, carried out among Georgian political leaders and the intelligentsia, took as high a toll in Georgia as elsewhere. During this time, Georgia came under the personal authority of Stalin's close associate, fellow Georgian of Mingrelian origin, Lavrentii Beria, who served as first secretary of the Communist Party of Georgia throughout the 1930s. Through Beria's firm grip, Georgia came to be just as tightly controlled by Moscow as were the other Soviet republics.

Although the battles of World War II were all fought north of the Caucasus, Georgia's military loss of life was comparable to that experienced by other Soviet nationalities because of the large number of Georgian soldiers who perished in battle. During the war, a substantial population of minority groups was transferred out of the Caucasus because Stalin feared that these minority groups (mainly Turkic) would support the invading Axis powers. Following the war, Stalin's personal control of the Soviet Union became even stronger. Lavrentii Beria, having

been elevated to Moscow to head the Soviet secret police, collaborated with Stalin, intensifying Moscow's authority not only over Georgia, but over all of Soviet society.

After Stalin's death in 1953, Beria was executed by rivals in the Stalinist succession struggle. Meanwhile in Transcaucasia, Vasilii Mzhavanadze became first secretary of the Georgian Communist Party. Ensuing de-Stalinization (a liberalizing process originating with the new Soviet premier Nikita Khrushchev), resulted in pro-Stalin demonstrations in Tbilisi in March 1956. A large, but peaceful, demonstration threatened to take over the local radio station until police regained control. In the clash between police and demonstrators, several were killed. There continue to be those in Georgia who view Stalin as a positive national figure.

In 1972, Eduard Shevardnadze was appointed the new first secretary of the Georgian Communist Party, a post he held for thirteen years, until named by Gorbachev to head the Soviet Ministry of Foreign Affairs in 1985. As the new Party leader in Georgia and former leader in the security police, Shevardnadze was called upon to deal with the remaining legacy of Stalinism—namely, widespread corruption, poor economic, especially agricultural, growth, and a revival of Georgian nationalism. The strength of the latter may be attested to by the reaction in 1978 to an attempt to remove Georgian as the sole official language of the republic. Moscow wanted to add a second official language, Russian. The attempt failed as thousands of students protested in Tbilisi. This time, however, the demonstrations remained peaceful.

Contemporary Issues

Abuladze and Sakharov

Two landmark statements of the 1980s help to clarify the complex world of contemporary Georgian society. The first of these was a Georgian statement, the most dramatic cinematographic work produced in the Soviet Union in the 1980s—the award-winning film, *Repentance (Monanieba)*, directed by Tengiz Abuladze. Released first in Tbilisi, and later in Moscow and the West in 1986, *Repentance* depicted a dictatorial figure, Varlam Aravidze, who, with his villainous followers dressed as

medieval knights, visited a reign of interrogation, death, and forcible exile upon innocent victims. Patterned after Lavrentii Beria, but understandably associated in the public imagination with Stalin himself, Varlam and "Varlamism" readily came to be identified with the realities of twentieth-century Georgian and Soviet history.

In one particularly gripping moment of the film, Varlam's grandson Tornike learns of the complicity of his father (Abel) in the crimes of the grandfather Varlam. Unable to forgive his father, Tornike shoots himself with a rifle given him by the late Varlam. Profoundly affected by the suicide of his son, Abel digs up the corpse of Varlam and heaves it from a mountaintop. For Georgians, even more than for other Soviet citizens (who had to view the film with Russian subtitles), the haunting question of the grandson Tornike to his father Abel became a matter of riveting, existential importance: "Did you know about all this?"

For Georgians young and old who crowded into movie theaters, the agony of *Repentance* rested in the memories and unanswered questions over Stalinism that the film unearthed. In the years since 1986, the violent political upheavals wrenching Georgian society have been, in many ways, the legacy of this Stalinist, Soviet inheritance. Driven by passionate and heroic ambition to erase this legacy, some political leaders have paid scant attention to human rights and democratic processes as they sought to eliminate by force the remnants of the old Soviet order. In appealing too readily to violence and to limitations upon free expression, some of these resurgent Georgian nationalists may have demonstrated, unwittingly, their own roots in the Soviet system.

While Abuladze's film called forth a searching Georgian reassessment of the Soviet past, another statement from the 1980s—this time from a Russian Nobel Laureate—posed a more subtle problem for Georgian national consciousness. In the summer of 1989, the late Andrei Sakharov, celebrated Russian nuclear physicist and human rights advocate, granted an interview to the popular Russian journal *Ogonek* in the course of which he described the union republics of the Soviet Union, specifically including Georgia, as "miniature empires" (*Ogonek*, 1989, no. 31. Cited in Elizabeth Fuller, "South Ossetiia: Analysis of a Permanent Crisis," *Report on the USSR*, 15 February 1991). While Georgians were quick to challenge the venerable human rights activist, the reference to Georgia as a "miniature empire" could not be easily dismissed. The Soviet state had, after all, consciously awarded to certain "winners"—the union republics—the right to control minorities within their own borders in an internal political game intended to divide and conquer. For Georgia, Sakharov's comments made unmistakeable reference to the status of those South Ossetians, Abkhazians, Ajaris, Azerbaijanis, and others who found themselves "autonomous," but also subordinate to the dominant Georgian nation.

These two dramatic public statements—a pathbreaking Georgian film and an uncensored comment from an unimpeachable Soviet dissident—point to the fundamental and unavoidable conflict confronting the Georgian nation. For as it seeks to establish its own territorial sovereignty and independence—its own "post-Varlamian," post-Soviet identity—the Georgian nation also confronts the reality that some of the same territory claimed by Georgians as their own has also been home to non-Georgian nationals who today seek a measure of independence and self-determination not unlike that sought by Georgians themselves.

Tragically, since 1989, the tensions posed by responding to these two statements have led to violence and political crisis. While there are long-term economic problems that still must be solved, the immediate future for Georgia will be determined by how well it is able to reconcile its own national ambitions with the hopes and aspirations of minorities who see in Georgian nationalism a new form of imperialism. In the Georgian case, no less than in the case of the other Transcaucasian states of Armenia and Azerbaijan—and no less than in the wartorn regions of former Yugoslavia—there is the violent conflict between national agendas and minority rights.

Prelude to a National Crisis

Georgian national politics entered into a period of profound crisis following the events of 9 April 1989, Bloody Sunday. The use of chemical weapons upon thousands of Georgian participants in peaceful Tbilisi demonstrations took 19 innocent lives. But the prelude to this national crisis antedated the April events by months. In the time preceding the Tbilisi demonstrations, Abkhazian nationals had approached the Moscow Party Central Committee authorities seeking their support to offset what the Abkhazians considered to be Georgian efforts to assimilate Abkhazians into greater Georgian society. Specifically, the Abkhazians sought status as a full union republic. Meanwhile, the Ossetians of the South Ossetiia Autonomous Oblast sought secession from Georgia and merger with their North Ossetian co-nationals in the Russian republic.

While Georgian Communist Party officials were slow to respond to these developments, Georgian public opinion, galvanized by a more open daily press, reacted strongly. First of all, the Abkhazian allegations against Georgian policies were alleged to be false. Georgians viewed themselves as simply trying to preserve the interests of those Georgians who composed nearly 50 percent of the population in the autonomous Abkhazian republic. Second, Georgian public opinion was aroused by the blatant effort of the Abkhazians, as well as the Ossetians, to circumvent the Georgian republic in their appeals. Why were the Abkhazians and the Ossetians taking their grievances to Moscow, rather than to Tbilisi?

In the events that followed, Georgians responded to the pent-up frustrations of Soviet rule by challenging the authority of their own Georgian Communist leadership. The inclination to do so was all the greater in the face of the graphic symbols of Soviet abuses presented to them in Abuladze's *Repentance*. Sensing that national honor was at stake, and that Soviet rule simply perpetuated the ability of non-Georgian nationals to manipulate the Moscow center against Georgian interests, thousands of demonstrators, most of them young people, took to the streets in organized protests focused upon the Georgian Council of Ministers' building in April 1989.

For Georgian Communist leaders, the dilemma was that they could appeal only to Moscow to reinforce their position. For at work was the classic trade-off operating in the Kremlin's relations with the outlying union republics. Moscow would provide military support to back up the power of the union republic's recognized government. But, at the same time, Moscow retained the power to undermine the credibility of that same local Communist Party leadership by appearing to support the independent initiatives of autonomous republics and oblasts operating within a union republic. This fundamental principle of Soviet rule in Georgia was being challenged in the scheduled week of national protests that began in Tbilisi in early April 1989.

Bloody Sunday, April 1989

Having been forewarned of the planned demonstrations that were scheduled to run until 14 April, the Georgian First Party Secretary Dzhumber Patiashvili (successor to Shevardnadze) turned to the Communist Party Central Committee in Moscow with an appeal for additional forces to maintain public order. The Soviet Politburo met in Gorbachev's absence (he was in England at the time) to consider the request. From the investigations that have followed the massacre, Patiashvili appears to have received news from Moscow early on 8 April that reinforcements would be provided to terminate the mass demonstrations. Soviet Defense Minister Dmitrii Iazov apparently designated Colonel General Igor

Rodionov to take charge of the effort, and Rodionov met with Patiashvili in Tbilisi on 8 April.

Early on the morning of 9 April, while demonstrations continued in the square in front of the Council of Ministers building, combined troops of the Soviet Ministry of Internal Affairs and the Soviet army launched tanks, tear gas, and, most controversially, chemical weapons upon the demonstrators, effectively dispersing the crowd, but not before thousands were harmed by the chemicals and 22 were killed. In the martial law that followed, more questions than answers were forthcoming. Who made the final decision to attack the demonstrators? What advance knowledge did Gorbachev have of this military action taken directly against citizens of the Soviet Union? Why was there no effort to disperse the crowd nonviolently?

The immediate impact of the April 1989 massacre was to galvanize support for those informal Georgian political and cultural groups that had been marginalized during the years of Georgian Communist Party rule. By August 1989, the Georgian Supreme Soviet, despite the dominant role of the Communist Party, had voted to declare Georgia's sovereignty. Although Eduard Shevardnadze's image in the West was that of a reformist foreign minister close to Mikhail Gorbachev, his very association with Moscow politics tended to relegate him in 1989 to outsider status in Georgian politics. Clearly, the institutions and political leaders having the most to gain were those perceived to be most independent of the old Soviet-style leadership.

One such institution benefiting from its role in the April 1989 events was the Georgian Orthodox church. Having reclaimed its independence from the Russian Orthodox church, the Georgian Orthodox church in the Soviet period remained in an ambivalent position. On the one hand, it rightly laid claim to a role in preserving the identity of the Georgian nation over centuries when that identity was in jeopardy from foreign imperial powers. On the other hand, the Georgian church inevitably was weakened by official state atheism and governmental oversight that limited freedom of religious expression during the worst of the Stalinist and Khrushchev years. With the renewed concern for Georgian national identity, however, the Georgian Orthodox church, its clergy and monasteries, became one of the focal points for the national movement. Its leader, the articulate catholicos of the Georgian church, Patriarch Ilia II, came to be revered as a responsible and independent churchman, devoted to the church, to the Georgian nation, and to nonviolence.

On the evening of 8 April, Patriarch Catholicos Ilia had come before the assembled crowds, praised them for their honorable intentions, and asked that they disperse so as to avoid the possibility of bloodshed. When the crowds refused to leave, the patriarch catholicos steadfastly remained with the demonstrators. Thus, with candles in hand and with the leader of the Georgian Orthodox church before them, the demonstrators peacefully confronted the Soviet tanks. While the symbolic authority of the Georgian church was particularly felt on that occasion, the subsequent divisions of the Georgian national movement, and the resort to violence, have posed new and difficult problems for the church. It is unlikely that any lasting national reconciliation will occur, however, without the involvement of this oldest of Georgian national institutions.

The Rise and Fall of Zviad Gamsakhurdia, 1989-92

More unpredictable has been the lasting influence of Zviad Gamsakhurdia, the charismatic Georgian intellectual who, with useful credentials as a Soviet dissident, emerged as a popular national hero and political leader in the months following April 1989. The son of a recognized national poet, Zviad Gamsakhurdia never made a significant mark as an original writer, but he came to national attention as an outspoken opponent of Georgian Communist officialdom, earlier serving time in prison for his underground activities. The dissident Gamsakhurdia used the months following the April demonstrations to galvanize the support of a round table coalition of informal political groups. This coalition, called "Round Table/Free Georgia," pressed for prompt parliamentary elections to the Georgian Supreme Soviet and demanded the restoration of the constitution that had governed the Georgian Democratic Republic (1918–21) prior to Soviet takeover.

In the elections of October 1990, Gamsakhurdia's "Round Table/Free Georgia" coalition won an overwhelming victory in the Georgian Supreme Soviet, securing 54 percent of the vote. Two weeks later, in mid-November 1990, Gamsakhurdia was elected without opposition to head the new parliament. His post was initially that of chairman of the Georgian Supreme Soviet, the de facto Georgian head of state. (Later, the office of president was created and presidential elections held in May 1991.)

Claiming that his goals were those of liberating Georgia and restoring its state sovereignty—goals entirely in line with the anti-Soviet theme of the day—Gamsakhurdia appointed a collection of loyal anti-Communists to the new government, many of them without any prior professional governmental experience. Viewing himself as a moral savior of the Georgian nation, Gamsakhurdia proclaimed, "The Almighty has imposed a great mission on Georgia. The day is not far off when Georgia will become an example of moral greatness for the whole world." (Cited in Elizabeth Fuller, "Gamsakhurdia's First 100 Days," *Report on the USSR*, 8 March 1991, p. 10.) Conspicuously identifying himself with the Georgian Orthodox church—despite earlier conflicts he had had with Patriarch Catholicos Ilia —Gamsakhurdia was clearly appealing to Georgian chauvinism and anti-Communism.

This moral, chauvinist appeal was coupled with a ruthless and vindictive approach toward political opponents, an approach that quickly began to raise concern among Georgians as well as among the national minorities within the Georgian state. The concerns were well founded as seen in several policy reversals that came to highlight his first months in office. In the election campaign, Gamsakhurdia had committed himself to the preservation of autonomous regions for the Abkhazians and South Ossetians, but by the end of 1990, he had abandoned that position, arguing rather that South Ossetiia should be abolished.

What most disheartened political moderates, however, was Gamsakhurdia's attempt to restrict access to the media, all the while threatening his opponents. Finally, the promising economic program of "Round Table/Free Georgia" was left largely abandoned as the Georgian economy suffered from high rates of inflation and chronic shortages.

What ought to have concerned political democrats in Georgia even before the election was Gamsakhurdia's suggestion that only parties demonstrating electoral strength throughout Georgia should gain access to the ballot. Such measures would inevitably have the effect of disenfranchising local minorities—Abkhazians, South Ossetians, Ajaris, the Azeris of Marneuli, and other groups. While Gamsakhurdia proceeded to blame Georgian Communists, the legacy of Soviet rule, and other parties for the failings of his new government, there were ample signs by the spring of 1991 that Gamsakhurdia himself was carelessly reopening old ethnic and regional wounds without effectively securing the economic and political stability of the new Georgian government.

Responding to Gamsakhurdia's suggestion, the Georgian parliament formally declared Georgian independence in April 1991. An earlier referendum submitted to the republic's electorate garnered almost 100 percent support for the "restoration" of Georgian independence. The critical term "restoration" referred to an independence based upon the terms of the 1918 independent Georgian state. Even in this matter there were ominous signs of conflict and coercion. Gamsakhurdia had made it known that any district voting against the referendum would face the prospect of its voters losing citizenship, and thereby the right to land ownership. Moreover, Gamsakhurdia tended to dismiss outright the fact that the far-reaching 1918 declaration of independence had guaranteed equal rights for all citizens of Georgia without regard to nationality, religion, or sex.

While there was modest erosion in support for Gamsakhurdia in the first Georgian presidential elections held in late May 1991, he still polled more than 85 percent of the Georgian vote. The election process, however, was colored by threats and intimidations directed at some of Gamsakhurdia's opponents—several opponents having been kept off the ballot and one having been assaulted during the campaign. In the end, Gamsakhurdia's continuing popularity among the Georgian populace reflected the strength of the national desire for independence from Moscow. No other national figure could so charismatically draw upon the anti-Soviet feelings of the Georgian electorate. For Gamsakhurdia, the results strengthened his anti-Communist resolve.

Given the electoral plurality of late May 1991, no clearer sign of the instability and violence of Georgian politics was to be found than the violent ouster of Gamsakhurdia from power six months later in January 1992. After holding out in the parliament building for over two weeks against the combined rebel forces of the Georgian National Guard and the Mkhedrioni (a paramilitary group of "Georgian Knights"), Gamsakhurdia fled in early 1992 beyond the Georgian border. Why did a charismatic national leader who six months earlier had received an 85 percent vote of confidence as the new president of Georgia end up being unceremoniously hounded out of office?

Beyond the challenges that Gamsakhurdia had posed to the sensibilities of a Georgian democratic intelligentsia, several concrete incidents contributed to his fall.

First of all, he had irreparably broken with minority nationalities in Georgia. Contradicting his own election promises, he abolished the autonomous status of the South Ossetiian Autonomous Oblast. Indeed, Georgian troops ended up fighting against Russian military forces in South Ossetiia in order to establish Georgian authority in the city of Tskhinvali. Furthermore, Gamsakhurdia arrested some of his political opponents and introduced far-reaching curbs on freedom of the press. At one point, he even used his presidential powers to strip the Georgian Communist Party deputies of their status in the Supreme Soviet, the Georgian parliament.

The most serious of Gamsakhurdia's problems began with the celebrated incident in early September 1991 when Gamsakhurdia used National Guard troops loyal to himself to fire on peaceful demonstrators. Calling to mind the fate of innocent victims from "Bloody Sunday," this single incident was most significant in spawning the erosion of popular support for Gamsakhurdia. Part of the response was the disaffection of large sections of the Georgian National Guard, a new Georgian army that Gamsakhurdia wished to put under his own Ministry of Internal Affairs. The split between loyalist (Gamsakhurdia followers) and rebel factions in the Georgian National Guard became the basis for a violent civil conflict played out on the streets of Tbilisi from December 1991 until Gamsakhurdia's flight in early January 1992.

The Reemergence of Eduard Shevardnadze in Georgian Politics

The violent departure of the dicatorial Gamsakhurdia from Georgia left Georgian society split between those who favored and those who opposed this first post-Soviet Georgian president. By forceably ousting him, the rebel National Guard, the Mkhedrioni and their political allies—a coalition that formed its own Military Council for the purpose of establishing law and order—had clearly operated unconstitutionally. Thus, from the perspective of international law, the Georgian state entered 1992 facing charges of flagrant human rights abuses directed not only against its minority populations but against its own nationals as well. Furthermore, Georgians had used an extra-legal *coup d'état* to secure political power by brute force.

Under these circumstances, the Military Council quickly sought new elections to add legitimacy to the political situation. In a step that would have been unthinkable just a year earlier during the first months of the Gamsakhurdia government, Eduard Shevardnadze was invited back to head a new interim State Council. The summer of 1992 was spent readying a complex election law in time for the scheduled October 1992 elections. A new alliance of former Communist Party figures, members of the intelligentsia, and other center-left political interests formed itself into an effective political bloc, the Mshvidoba, under whose umbrella Eduard Shevardnadze ran. The Mshvidoba bloc, buoyed by the support of a populace that was looking to the Communists to restore economic stability to Georgia, carried the largest number of seats in the October elections. Shevardnadze was elected parliamentary chair, or acting head of state.

An uneasy calm confronts the Georgian government. Rebellious factions still loyal to Gamsakhurdia hold out in enclaves within Georgia, particularly in western Georgia and Abkhazia. The chauvinist directives of the former president have added fuel to the deepening conflicts over South Ossetiia, Abkhazia, Ajaria, and other border regions. To secure the kind of Western investment that the internationally recognized Shevardnadze has promised, these troublesome domestic problems must be solved. There is also the status of remaining Russian military troops in Georgia awaiting bilateral agreement.

While the deterioration of the Georgian economy will inevitably resurface as the matter of greatest immediate concern, the long-term issue that poses the thorniest problem for Georgia is that defined by Andrei Sakharov—namely, the dilemma of a "miniature empire." In this context, the immediate problem confronting the Georgian state is Abkhazia, a region now facing renewed violence and civil war. The complexity of the Abkhazian question defies easy generalization. In August 1992, Eduard Shevardnadze, chair of the then-ruling Military Council sent loyal Georgian National Guard units into Sokhumi, the Abkhazian capital. Using as a pretext the need to secure Georgian officials abducted by Gamsakhurdia's followers, Shevardnadze's Georgian National Guard sought to capture Gamsakhurdia himself. The invading Georgian National Guard rampaged Abkhazia, killing tourists on the beach and destroying several scientific research institutes and museums. More than 50 were killed. Protesting this invasion of their territory by Georgian troops, the forces of the Abkhaz Internal Affairs Ministry returned fire on the Georgian National Guard. The August 1992 fighting led to a rapid deterioration in Georgian-Abkhazian relations.

Although ethnic Abkhazians constitute less than 20 percent of the population of the Abkhaz republic, they are insistent upon their own independence and sovereignty. Perhaps having been influenced by the confrontational politics of Gamsakhurdia, the chairman of the Abkhaz Supreme Soviet, Vladislav Ardzinba, has pressed for passage of legislation formally separating Abkhazia from Georgia. Shevardnadze is calling for a negotiated settlement of the Abkhazian question, but the framework for such a solution is elusive. The years of political violence and the uncertainties over minority rights have undermined the cause of Georgian-Abkhazian understanding.

Today the independent Republic of Georgia is recognized by the United States and has secured full membership in the United Nations—signs of acceptance that were withheld from it in the initial months following the collapse of the Soviet Union at the end of 1991. Georgia's independence however, has been accompanied by political violence, repression of human rights, insensitivity to the interests of minorities, and massive economic disruption. Georgia's strategic location on the Black Sea, its access to Caspian Sea oil, the beauty of its natural terrain, its deep historical and religious roots, and its energetic people offer promise for the future. Nevertheless, the dark cloud of its political past continues to hover over it.

PART FOUR

CENTRAL ASIA

INTRODUCTION

Strategically located between Russia, the Middle East, and China, the five republics of Central Asia—Kazakhstan, Kyrgyzstan, Tajikistan, Turkmenistan, and Uzbekistan—all declared their formal independence in the weeks following the abortive Moscow *coup d'état* in August 1991. These five newly independent republics share several important characteristics.

First of all, the native population of each of these states is, by religious tradition, Islamic. Although great numbers of European Slavs, particularly Russians, migrated into the cities of Central Asia in the twentieth century, the traditional Islamic cast of the region is one of its major distinguishing features. Most of these local Islamic peoples have Turkic ethnic roots and speak a Turkic language. Thus, it is still possible for Kazakhs of Kazakhstan to be understood by Uzbeks of Uzbekistan or Kyrgyz of Kyrgyzstan. The very homogeneity of this local, once nomadic, population raises important questions regarding the potential for a more unified Turkestan, overshadowing the current divisions of Central Asia.

Still, the second point to be made about Central Asia is its rich diversity. The Tajiks of Tajikistan (and Uzbekistan where they constitute a significant minority) are not Turkic, but rather derive from a Persian background. Even within the Turkic nations of Central Asia there are significant regional and tribal differences. Moreover, the important role of the Slavic population in the urban, industrialized sectors of Central Asia is likely to continue well beyond the demise of the Soviet Union.

Third, the diversity of Central Asia is also to be seen in the topography and physical characteristics of the territory. From the mountainous regions along the southern and eastern borders to the fertile Farghona (Fergana) valley to the deserts of Turkmenistan, Central Asia exhibits a wide range of climates and vegetation. From the rich oil deposits of Kazakhstan to the mines of Kyrgyzstan, there is a wealth of natural resources in the region, much of it untapped or difficult to access.

The potential wealth of natural resources, however, must be set alongside the grating poverty and economic deterioration of the region. Heavily committed to growing cotton during the Soviet period, the rural poverty of Central Asia is the worst of any region of the former Soviet Union. Dependent upon external imports for basic consumer goods, the area faces acute shortages of basic foodstuffs and household items. Compounding the poverty of Central Asia are the environmental problems left as a consequence of Soviet central, production-oriented planning. The disastrous depletion of the Aral Sea, located in the center of the region, is symptomatic of the wider ecological dilemma faced by these newly independent countries. As the poverty of rural Central Asia migrates into the more Slavic-dominated urban centers, the potential for ethnic conflict looms throughout the region. The underlying sources of civil strife and political turmoil, however, are not to be found in ethnic conflict, but in the shortages of clean water, medical care, basic housing, and safe foodstuffs.

Amid serious disruptions and political conflict such as those ongoing in Tajikistan—a conflict made possible in part by the relaxation of former Soviet authority—a quiet process of democratization has also been under way in some parts of Central Asia. Although the old Soviet bureaucracy remains in control of much of the governmental machinery, elections of parliamentary assemblies and presidential leaders have proceeded in each of the five Central Asian states. Moreover, a wide variety of informal political groups now participates in an emergent civil society. From the environmental movement in Kazakhstan (the Nevada-Semipalatinsk group) to the Islamic renewal party operating throughout the region, these expressions of political openness offer hope for further democratization. The civil war in Tajikistan is the single most violent case of unresolved conflict plaguing the region.

Finally, the peoples of Central Asia have been using the spirit of glasnost and independence to reopen hidden chapters of their national and regional histories. In this process, the Russian imperial role in the region has been put on the defensive as the recovery of ethnic identity becomes a part of public consciousness. This recovery of ethnic identity has invariably resulted in the rehabilitation of members of the Central Asian intelligentsia who suffered during the worst of the Stalinist era. While this rewriting of local and national history has only begun, and while it can also lead to ethnic conflict and turmoil, the redefinition of Turkic and Central Asian identities clearly hangs in the balance.

Bibliography

Akiner, Shirin. *Islamic Peoples of the Soviet Union.* London: KPI, 1986.

Allworth, Edward A. *The Modern Uzbeks from the Fourteenth Century to the Present: A Cultural History.* Stanford: Hoover Institution Press, 1990.

———, ed. *The Nationality Question in Soviet Central Asia.* New York: Praeger Publishers, 1973.

———. *Soviet Nationality Problems.* New York: Columbia University Press, 1971.

———. *Uzbek Literary Politics.* The Hague, Netherlands: Mouton & Co., 1964.

Atkin, Muriel. *Subtlest Battle: Islam in Soviet Tajikistan.* Philadelphia: Foreign Policy Research Institute, 1989.

Bennigsen, Alexandre and S. Enders Wimbush. *Muslims of the Soviet Empire: A Guide.* London: C. Hurst & Company, 1985.

Critchlow, James. *Nationalism in Uzbekistan: A Soviet Republic's Road to Sovereignty.* Boulder, CO: Westview Press, 1991.

Ellis, William S. "The Aral: A Soviet Sea Lies Dying." *National Geographic.* February 1990, pp. 73–92.

Fierman, William, ed. *Soviet Central Asia: The Failed Transformation.* Boulder, CO: Westview Press, 1991.

Horak, Stephan M., ed. *Guide to the Study of the Soviet Nationalities: Non-Russian Peoples of the USSR.* Littleton, CO: Libraries Unlimited, Inc., 1982.

Index Islamicus, 1981–1985: A Bibliography of Books and Articles on the Muslim World. 2 vols. Comp. and ed. by G. J. Roper. London: Mansell, 1991. (This index began in 1958, covering material published from 1906–1955.)

Olcott, Martha Brill. *The Kazakhs.* Stanford, CA: Hoover Institution Press, 1987.

Park, Alexander G. *Bolshevism in Turkestan,* 1917–1927. New York: Columbia University Press, 1957.

Rakowska-Harmstone, Teresa. *Russia and Nationalism in Central Asia: The Case of Tadzhikistan.* Baltimore, MD: The Johns Hopkins University Press, 1970.

RFE/RL Research Report, 1992–. This publication of Radio Free Europe/Radio Liberty was formerly titled *Radio Liberty Research Bulletin* (through 1988) and *Report on the USSR* (1989–91). Weekly.

Ro'i, Yacov. *The USSR and the Muslim World.* London: Allen & Unwin, 1984.

Rywkin, Michael. *Moscow's Muslim Challenge: Soviet Central Asia.* Rev. ed. Armonk, NY: M. E. Sharpe, 1990.

Shabad, Theodore. *Geography of the USSR: A Regional Survey.* New York: Columbia University Press, 1951.

Wheeler, Geoffrey. *The Peoples of Soviet Central Asia: A Background Book.* London: The Bodley Head, 1966.

Wixman, Ronald. *The Peoples of the USSR: An Ethnographic Handbook.* Armonk, NY: M. E. Sharpe, 1984.

Central Asia

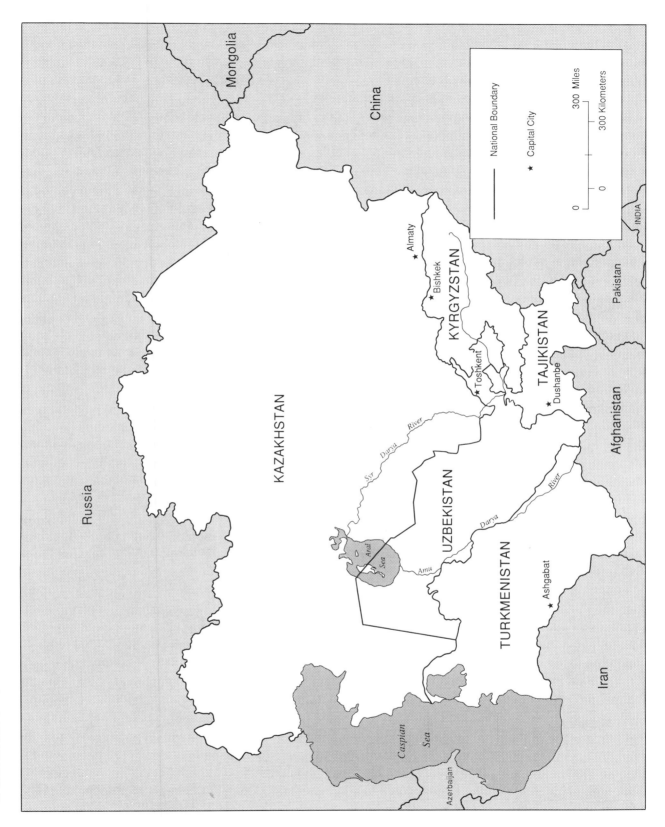

Mongolia

China

Russia

KAZAKHSTAN

★ Almaty

Bishkek ★

KYRGYZSTAN

Toshkent ★

TAJIKISTAN

Dushanbe ★

Syr Darya River

UZBEKISTAN

Darya River

Amu Darya

Aral Sea

TURKMENISTAN

★ Ashgabat

Caspian Sea

Azerbaijan

Iran

Afghanistan

Pakistan

INDIA

National Boundary
★ Capital City

300 Miles
300 Kilometers

0

KAZAKHSTAN

Statistical Profile

Demography

Population: 16,464,000

Ethnic population:

Kazakh	6,535,000	39.7%
Russian	6,228,000	37.8%
German	958,000	5.8%
Ukrainian	896,000	5.4%
Uzbek	332,000	2.0%
Tatar	328,000	2.0%
Uighur	185,000	1.1%
Belarusian	183,000	1.1%
Korean	103,000	0.6%
Azerbaijani	90,000	0.5%
Polish	60,000	0.4%
Bashkir	42,000	0.3%
Moldovan	33,000	0.2%
Mordvinian	30,000	0.2%
Dungan	30,000	0.2%
Chuvash	22,000	0.1%
Jewish	18,000	0.1%
Other	391,000	2.4%

Historic religious traditions:

Christianity	50.7%
Islam	48.5%

Population by age:

Age	Total	Male	Female
0–4	11.3%	5.7%	5.6%
5–9	10.1%	5.1%	5.0%
10–14	9.9%	5.0%	4.9%
15–19	8.7%	4.4%	4.3%
20–24	8.6%	4.5%	4.1%
25–29	8.8%	4.5%	4.3%
30–34	7.9%	4.0%	3.9%
35–39	6.7%	3.3%	3.4%
40–44	3.5%	1.7%	1.8%
45–49	6.3%	3.0%	3.3%
50–54	4.3%	2.1%	2.2%
55–59	4.3%	1.9%	2.4%
60–64	3.2%	1.2%	2.0%
65–69	1.8%	0.6%	1.2%
70–	4.4%	1.2%	3.2%

Male/Female ratio: 48.4% male/51.6% female
Rural/Urban population: 42.4% rural/57.6% urban
Growth over time, 1979–91: 14.4%
Population density: 16.0 persons/sq mi

Politics/Government

Date of independence declaration:
16 December 1991

Major urban centers and populations:

Almaty (Alma-Ata)	1,128,000
Qaraghandy (Karaganda)	614,000
Shymkent (Chimkent)	393,000
Semey (Semipalatinsk)	334,000
Pavlodar	331,000
Öskemen (Ust-Kamenogorsk)	324,000
Zhambyl	307,000
Aqmola (Tselinograd)	277,000
Aqtöbe (Aktiubinsk)	253,000
Petropavl (Petropavlovsk)	241,000
Qostanay (Kustanai)	224,000
Temirtau	212,000
Oral (Uralsk)	200,000
Aqtau (Shevchenko)	159,000
Qyzylorda (Kzyl-Orda)	153,000

Autonomous areas: none

Education

Level of education for persons over 15:

completed higher education:	9.9%
completed secondary education:	54.1%
incomplete secondary education:	19.8%

Number of higher education institutions: 55
(287,400 students)

Major institutions of higher education and enrollment:

Almaty

Al-Farabi Kazakh State University	13,000
Animal Husbandry and Veterinary Institute	5,670
Power Engineering Institute	4,716
Teacher Training Institute of Foreign Languages	3,343

Aqmola

Agricultural Institute	10,000
Civil Engineering Institute	2,700

Oral

West Kazakhstan Agricultural Institute	2,700

Öskemen

Institute of Construction and Road Building	6,700

Qaraghandy

State University	8,436

Socioeconomic Indicators

Birthrate: 21.7/1,000
Infant mortality: 26.4/1,000 live births
Average life expectancy: 68.8 (males, 64.0; females, 73.2)
Average family size: 4.0

Hospital beds per 10,000 persons: 136.2
Production of electrical energy: 5,205 kwh/person
Length of rail lines: 8,985 mi
Length of highways: 117,439 mi

Physical/Territorial/Geopolitical Features

Area: 1,049,150 sq mi (12% of USSR total)
Land use:

Cultivated	13%
Pasture	58%

Highest elevation: 14,783 ft. (Belukha peak in the Altai Range)
Rainfall: 12-18 inches/year; 10 on the steppes; 4-8 in the desert; 16–64 in the foothills and mountains.
Temperature: average in winter, 0° F in the north, 27° F in the south; lowest temperature: -45° F. Average in summer, 66° F in the north and 84° F in the south.
Principal products: cotton, rice, grains, silk, meat, wool, hemp, oil, gas, chrome, silver, coal, iron ore, tungsten, lead, zinc, copper, fauxite, gold, uranium, cement, steel, heavy machinery
Per capita GNP : (1991) $2,470

Sources

"Kazakhskaia sovetskaia sotsialisticheskaia respublika" *Bol'shaia Sovetskaia Entsiklopediia* 11 (Moscow, 1977): 145–73; *Narodnoe khoziaistvo SSSR v 1990g.* (Moscow, 1991); *Naselenie SSSR* (1989); Matthew J. Sagers, "News Notes. Iron and Steel,"*Soviet Geography* 30 (May 1989): 397–434; Lee Schwartz, "USSR Nationality Redistribution by Republic, 1979–1989: From Published Results of the 1989 All-Union Census," *Soviet Geography* 32 (April 1991): 209–48; and *World of Learning,* 43rd ed. (London: Europa Publications Limited, 1993); "Russia. . ." (National Geographic Society Map, March 1993).

History and Description

Topography

Kazakhstan is located at the crossroads of Europe and Asia. The second largest republic of the former Soviet Union, Kazakhstan extends all the way from the Caspian Sea in the west to the Altai Mountains in the east and from western Siberia in the north to the Tian Shan Mountains in the south. A vast expanse made up primarily of grasslands known as the steppe (flat, desert-like terrain), Kazakhstan has only one truly mountainous region, a range that is located along its lengthy eastern border with China. Kazakhstan shares its southern boundary with the three Central Asian countries of Kyrgyzstan, Uzbekistan, and Turkmenistan. To the west lies the Caspian Sea and to the north the Russian Federation.

The rivers of Kazakhstan are overshadowed by the republic's large inland lakes. Largest of these is the Caspian Sea, the shoreline of which is shared with Turkmenistan, Azerbaijan, and Russia, as well as with Iran. Second in size is the shrinking Aral Sea divided between Kazakhstan and Uzbekistan. Third largest is

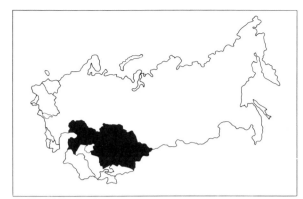

Kazakhstan

RUSSIA

National Boundary

★ Capital City

• Other Cities

0   400 Miles

0   400 Kilometers

Petropavl

Qostanay

Pavlodar

Altai Mtns.

Oral

Ural River

Aqtöbe

Aqmola

Temirtau

Qaraghandy

Semey

Öskemen

14,783 ft.

Oil

Emba River

Gurev

Fields

Baikonur
Cosmodrome

Balqash
Köl

Mangyshlak
Peninsula

Aral
Sea

Aqtau

Syr

Qyzylorda

Darya River

Chu   River

Almaty

Novyi Uzen

Caspian

Sea

UZBEKISTAN

Zhambyl

Shymkent

KYRGYZSTAN

Tian Shan
Mtns.

CHINA

TURKMENISTAN

Samarqand

TAJIKISTAN

Balqash Köl (Lake Balkhash), a freshwater basin located entirely within the boundaries of Kazakhstan just to the north of its capital city, Almaty (Alma-Ata).

Three distinct types of landforms are found within Kazakhstan. Soviet-designed borders gave the Kazakhs a share in the agriculturally valuable oases watered by the glacial rivers of the region's mountains. Apart from these irrigated lands in the southeastern part of the country along the Syr Darya and Chu rivers, Kazakhstan is made up almost entirely of a vast desert steppe that cannot sustain intensive farming and supports only a sparse population. A single region of black earth farmland along the northern fringe of the Kazakh steppe does yield some wheat, cereal, and forage crops. This region was developed agriculturally in the 1950s as part of the famous "Virgin Lands" experiment begun by Soviet Communist Party leader Nikita Khrushchev.

Kazakhstan holds a wealth of natural resources comparable to its great size. The oil fields along the eastern shore of the Caspian Sea, particularly on the Mangyshlak Peninsula near Aqtau (Shevchenko), and the petroleum sources located in a region between the mouths of the Ural and Emba rivers are productive enough for the Kazakhs to export oil to other republics of the former USSR, and eventually, it is hoped, to other places in the world. In addition, coal deposits exist near the city of Qaraghandy (Karaganda) in an industrialized area of central Kazakhstan, with supplementary sources elsewhere, principally to the northeast in the Pavlodar region. Iron ore, copper, and lead deposits in the north and in other areas of Kazakhstan add to the intrinsic value of the country's mineral riches. In the arid central desert regions, Kazakhstan has been the home of the famous Soviet nuclear test site at Semipalatinsk (Semey) and the space Cosmodrome at Baikonur.

Agriculturally, cotton is the major crop grown in the irrigated lands of southern Kazakhstan. In the north, grain, wheat, and fodder crops are grown for the many livestock traditionally raised by local herders. Fruits, vegetables, rice, and tobacco are cultivated in some of the less arid parts of the country, notably in the river valleys of the southeast. The city of Almaty takes its name from the apples grown in that region.

Ethnic and Historical Background

The origins of the Kazakhs date from the thirteenth-century incursions by the Mongol horde of Genghis Khan and his Tatar warriors into Central Asia. The intermingling of tribes of indigenous peoples, who had inhabited the area of present-day Kazakhstan from the prehistoric Bronze Age period, with Turkic peoples who had migrated to the area from other parts of Central Asia was then augmented by the assimilation of Mongol elements. By the end of the fifteenth century, when a union of Kazakh khans began to control the vast steppe territories making up contemporary Kazakhstan, a sense of ethnic identity had developed amongst the tribal groups formed from this assimilation.

The term Kazakh, as applied linguistically to a particular group of people, may come from the Turkish word *qaz* (to wander). For an ethnic definition, however, the meaning is rooted in the complex web of Central Asian tribal relationships. Historian Martha Brill Olcott, in her book, *The Kazakhs* (Stanford, 1987), describes these people as primarily "Turkic-speaking nomadic tribes of Uzbek-Turkic stock," who, despite a shared language and ethnic background, viewed themselves as Kazakhs, and thereby separate from Uzbeks.

By the beginning of the sixteenth century as many as one million Kazakhs inhabited a common Kazakh khanate under Kasim Khan. This population was later joined by additional Kazakh tribes drawn from adjacent scattered hordes. The term Kazakh came to be identified with those who expanded into the territories north and east of the Uzbeks. The Uzbeks, for their part, had moved south into the historic area of Samarqand.

After the rule of Kasim Khan (1511–18), the Kazakhs evolved into three nomadic hordes led by independent khans (tribal leaders). The Great Horde (also called the Elder Horde) roamed in the area of Semireche, the southern part of present-day Kazakhstan; the Middle Horde migrated within central and northern Kazakhstan; and the Small Horde ranged over the area of western Kazakhstan. During the seventeenth and eighteenth centuries these hordes found it almost impossible to maintain themselves against invading armies from the east. As a result, some Kazakh leaders appear to have sought cooperation with the Russian state. Other Kazakhs did not seek Russian protection. They turned for assistance to Turkic leaders within Central Asia, and strongly opposed Russia's expansion into the steppe regions. Such divided loyalties led to confrontation and warfare throughout the eighteenth and nineteenth centuries.

Russian Conquest

By the 1820s, tsarist influence had penetrated the life of the Kazakhs. Russian administrative methods were established in the territories occupied by the Middle and the Small Horde. By mid-century, even some Kazakhs from the Great Horde had joined the Russians. In 1854, the Russian military command constructed a fortified settlement called Vernyi (later named Alma-Ata) to advance Russian imperial control of the Central Asian steppe. During the 1860s, more Kazakh lands came under the domination of Russia. An influx of Russian peasants into Kazakhstan followed. In the last two decades of the nineteenth century, hundreds of Russian and other Slavic peasant villages came to dot the Kazakh steppe. The indigenous population, which by the end of the century numbered close to one and a half million "tents," could not continue its traditional nomadic way of life under the land restrictions imposed by the new authorities and the Russian settlements. Uprisings occurred and were routinely repressed, as more and more European migrants continued to settle on Kazakh lands. After the turn of the century, as part of a more general tsarist agricultural policy, nearly a half million households were relocated from Russia to the Kazakh region. The Kazakhs continued to lose their most valuable pastureland to this influx. When the construction of the Trans-Siberian Railroad was completed in 1904, transportation links made possible the provision of food products from the newly settled agricultural communities to the rest of the empire.

Until the nineteenth century, the Kazakhs appeared to be only nominally connected to the religious world of Islam within which the other Turkic peoples of Central Asia moved. Tsarist policy at first encouraged Islamicization of the Kazakhs, believing that such a "civilizing" influence would make it easier to rule them, but later the tsar changed his mind and instead sent Christian missionaries. By then, however, the Kazakhs showed little interest.

The events of the First World War made heavy demands on the Kazakhs to support the tsarist military effort. Contributing to Kazakh resentment of the Russian presence, the requisitioning of farm products, including livestock, for the troops was accompanied by a demand for higher taxes. A 1916 mass mobilization order for Kazakhs to perform noncombatant work in the rearguard area brought Kazakh feelings into the open, yielding widespread revolts aimed particularly at the local Russian inhabitants. Many were slain on both sides, and extensive material damage occurred. Thousands of Kazakhs fled with their livestock to China.

Soviet Rule

The tumultuous events of the Russian Revolution in 1917 inspired the Kazakh nationalist movement, Alash Orda, to proclaim for a brief period the independence of Kazakhstan. Bolshevik sympathizers opposed the Alash Orda and rather sought the integration of the region into the new Soviet state. Alongside Vladimir Lenin's special appeal to the Muslim workers of Russia and the east, the Kazakh leader of the Alash Orda, Ali Bukeikhanov, held out for a national government in Kazakhstan. Other Kazakhs critical of the aristocratic connections of Alash Orda joined the Communist Party, believing that its program would better assist in the formation of a modern, democratic Kazakh state. The ensuing Civil War between revolutionary and antirevolutionary factions brought a period of intense military struggle accompanied by great physical deprivation. The inhabitants of Kazakhstan, both nomads and settled farmers, suffered appalling deprivation. Eventually the Red Army prevailed, and the Kazakh nationalists had to succumb to Soviet power. Not until August 1920, however, was the whole of the Kazakh region finally linked to Russia and a capital established at Orenburg northwest of Aqtöbe.

The Kazakhs had been called Kyrgyz by European travelers and later settlers. Thus, in 1920 the Soviet authorities duly established them as the Kyrgyz autonomous republic within the larger Russian republic. The present-day Kyrgyz, in turn, found themselves called the Kara Kyrgyz. Not until 1925 did the Soviet government seek to change the name assigned to the Kazakhs. They were then officially designated, still within the Russian republic, as the Kazakh Autonomous Republic. The capital was located at Kzyl-Orda but was moved to Alma-Ata in May 1929. The autonomous oblast of Karakalpak, whose people were closely related to the Kazakhs, was placed administratively within Kazakhstan until 1936 when it was joined to the Uzbek republic. It was also in 1936 that Kazakhstan was raised from autonomous status within the Russian republic and became a full union republic of the Soviet Union.

As the postrevolutionary period began and Soviet officials sought to establish Kazakhstan as a viable part of their new order, the economic needs of the republic required immediate attention. Land redistribution held priority in the social program proposed by the Bolsheviks. In a country where a pastoral nomadic way of life prevailed, however, the assignment of fixed land to those who annually migrated between summer and winter pastureland did not make sense. Nevertheless, the Soviets wanted Kazakh nomads to change their traditional ways and settle permanently in fixed areas. During the ensuing disruptions of the 1920s, Russian and Kazakh political figures vied for power amidst hunger and hardship, while failing to solve the severe economic problems pressing the new republic. Plagued by poor harvests, Kazakhs were unable to set aside seed meant for planting, using it instead to satisfy their immediate food needs. The resulting famine of the early 1920s left hundreds of thousands of Kazakhs dead.

A gradual recovery occurred between 1924 and 1929 as the state attempted to gain control of economic activities, taking authority out of the hands of local clans and tribes whose longstanding rivalries impeded the Soviet desire for change. Moscow promised to provide land for those Kazakhs who would give up their nomadic ways and assume a sedentary, or farming, way of life. Very little good land, however, was offered, and Kazakhs resented the fact that Russian settlers had already received the best of the pasturelands. This legacy from the colonial period, the fact that the Russian settlers had been favored over the local peoples, needed to be overcome by the new Soviet authorities if economic recovery were to take place. The Russians within the local Kazakh Communist Party structure, nonetheless, persisted in trying to implement the land policy dictated from Moscow. The lack of such farming necessities as seed, plows, and tractors, not to mention decent land, doomed these efforts. Often those Kazakhs who tried to settle down and farm found their efforts unsuccessful and ended up returning to old nomadic patterns.

Collectivization. In 1929, collectivization of land was introduced throughout the Soviet Union. Under collectivization, farm land was first nationalized and then administered by the state. The peasants were resettled on *kolkhozy* (collective farms) and worked cooperatively pooling their labor and supplies. After the land reform failures of the 1920s, Party officials were determined to make the new method work. In Kazakhstan, nevertheless, strong resistance to collectivization occurred, and defiant peasants were sent to prison camps or executed. The Communist Party sought to fix blame for yet another unsuccessful round of land reform. Local leaders, including the Party First Secretary Goloshchekin (an ethnic Russian) and those who had shown sympathy for the Alash Orda, were accused of nationalist motivations at the expense of a concern for the country as a whole. Numerous activists were purged from their posts and replaced by newcomers.

Stalinist Purges and World War II. Throughout the 1930s political turmoil continued. The height of the Stalinist purges occurred in Kazakhstan in 1937 and 1938. Not only errant Party members, including the new first secretary, L. I. Mirzoian, but also Kazakh intellectuals were arrested, tried, and executed. The terror eventually yielded one of its Stalinist goals. By the end of 1938, 98 percent of Kazakhstan's rural population was living on collective farms.

World War II brought a halt to some of the harshest practices that Stalin had introduced into the Kazakh republic. Anti-religious campaigns were softened to gain the support of certain sectors of the population, and many controversial policies were put on hold until the war was over. Alma-Ata and other Kazakh cities became the destination for thousands of Russian mothers and children seeking refuge from the military front. These cities also served as the new locale for factories and other enterprises from European Russia that were moved beyond the threat of battle to keep up their wartime production. In addition, Russian engineers came searching for new caches of valuable natural resources to aid the war effort.

Post-Stalin Era. A long period of economic recovery followed the end of the war, but even as late as the early 1950s agricultural production was still not meeting the requirements of the recurring five-year plans. In 1953, after Stalin's death, Nikita Khrushchev proposed a new land-use program for northern Kazakhstan and southern Siberia. His proposal advocated cultivation of a huge area of 35 million hectares in an intensive wheat farming program. Khrushchev believed that this "Virgin Lands" program would bring much untilled land under cultivation and would solve shortages that might occur should Ukrainian harvests fail. As a result still more Kazakh pastureland disappeared. The project showed mixed results. After Khrushchev's ouster in 1964, the policy was phased out, with only scattered remnants of the virgin lands remaining.

From the early 1960s, Kazakh Communist Party leadership was assumed by Dinmukhamed Akhmedovich Kunaev, a native Kazakh whose administration during the Brezhnev years was noted for its corruption and favoritism. Yet, alongside the graft, it was during those Kunaev years that unprecedentedly large numbers of Kazakhs came to assume leadership posts in the republic.

Contemporary Issues

The Demographics of Multiculturalism: Kazakhs and Russians

The lands of Kazakhstan have been subjected to recurring demographic revolutions in the twentieth century. The Soviet efforts to impose fixed settlements and to eliminate the traditionally nomadic existence of the Kazakhs led to real losses in Kazakh population in the 1920s and 1930s. Some of that loss occurred during the violence of forced settlement. But, hundreds of thousands of Kazakhs also fled to other regions, including Xinjiang, China. The result was that between the censuses of 1926 and 1939, during a period when natural population growth might typically have yielded a substantial increase, the Kazakh population dropped from approximately four million to just over three million.

This real loss of Kazakh population was in sharp contrast to the dramatic in-migration of Russians and other European Slavs during the 1920s and 1930s. For the first time, the 1939 census revealed that Russians outnumbered Kazakhs in the Kazakh Soviet Republic. Russians comprised 40.2 percent of the population, while the Kazakh percentage of the population had dropped to 38 percent.

By the 1959 census, Russians composed 42.7 percent of the population, while the Kazakh population percentage had dropped to just 30 percent. These population percentages reflected considerable ongoing immigration of European population into the republic. During World War II, large German communities from the Ukrainian and Volga regions had been transferred into Kazakhstan. Further migration of Russians occurred during the Virgin Lands policies of the 1950s. Although this European population influx began to reverse itself in the 1970s, the Kazakhstan capital of Alma-Ata, along with other large urban centers, became largely Russianized. As recently as the 1979 census, Kazakhs represented only 16.3 percent of the population of Alma-Ata.

It is in the context of this historic Russian demographic transformation of Kazakhstan that Kazakh demographers, most notably Makash B. Tatimov, began in the 1980s to rebel against the idea occasionally advocated in Moscow that there ought to be a "differentiated demographic policy" in the Soviet Union. Advocates of such a policy held that the accelerating Turkic birthrates and the much lower Slav birthrates ought to be countered by a state policy that would be pronatalist in the case of the Slavs and restrictive in the case of the Turkic population. Tatimov, among others, welcomed the unusually high birthrates among the Kazakhs, seeing increased Kazakh population as a response to the earlier deterioration of Kazakh demographic power.

Since the 1970s, an equally dramatic demographic revolution has been occurring. As in other parts of Central Asia, Kazakhstan has witnessed both an emigration of considerable European population, and a rise in the percentage of Turkic population. During the 1980s, and with increased momentum since 1989, German settlements have been depleted by rapid emigration to Germany. There has also been a considerable out-migration of European Slavs, only partly moderated by the entry into Kazakhstan of Russians departing other Central Asian states. The result is that, for the first time since 1939, the 1989 census reflects a larger percentage of Kazakhs (39.7 percent) than of Russians (37.8 percent). Still, if other Slavs are added to the Russian census figures, European Slavs continue to outnumber Kazakhs in Kazakhstan. This situation, although it is rapidly changing as birthrates and population migrations alter the equation, is unique to the newly independent countries of Central Asia.

The Politics of Multiculturalism: The December 1986 Riots

On 16 December 1986, the longstanding first secretary of the Kazakh Communist Party, Dinmukhamed

Kunaev, was replaced by an ethnic Russian more closely fitting the mold of Mikhail Gorbachev's policy of perestroika. The new first secretary, Genadii Kolbin, was widely recognized as a reformer in the mold of Gorbachev and Eduard Shevardnadze. The hope was that the new Kolbin regime would be able to undertake the reform of corruption, inside appointments, and graft that had come to be associated with the Kunaev government.

Even though the Kolbin appointment may have been intended as an interim measure, the selection of an ethnic Russian as first secretary constituted an aberration in post–World War II Central Asia. Typically, first secretaries had been chosen from indigenous nationals, with the second Party post reserved for a European Slav. In Alma-Ata, the reaction to Kolbin's appointment was swift and overwhelming, rocking a calm Central Asian capital accustomed to the quiescence of the local population.

Within a week, uncontrolled rioting broke out in Alma-Ata. Official reports proclaimed that only a few hundred students, designated "hoodlums," were responsible for the rioting. Unofficial sources, however, put the numbers as high as ten thousand and indicated that some had even died in the fighting. During the two days of rioting, the headquarters of the Communist Party were raided. So serious was the fighting that highly placed Moscow officials from the Central Committee of the Communist Party of the Soviet Union were dispatched to Alma-Ata. At the height of the confrontation the demonstrators openly chanted, "Kazakhstan for the Kazakhs."

Although the December 1986 riots were quickly suppressed, they remained for some years the subject of secret investigations and hidden reports. The basic outlines of the confrontation quickly became clear. Central to any explanation of the demonstrations were the Kazakh ethnic sensitivities set off by the unexpected appointment of the Russian Genadii Kolbin. Even though leading figures in Moscow had deplored the deterioration of the Kazakh economy and the corruption in governmental life during the quarter century of Kunaev's leadership, these leaders may not have appreciated the level of internal support that the Russified Kazakh Dinmukhamed Kunaev generated as he appointed numerous Kazakhs to government positions. Kunaev's replacement by a Russian was perceived as a threat not only to a younger generation of Kazakh nationals fed up with official politics, but ironically also to many Kazakh Party officials who had risen to power under the patronage of Kunaev. At the very least, the fears that riots against officialdom could easily turn into more direct ethnic conflict motivated those who quickly suppressed the uprising.

Indication of the potentially explosive ethnic dimension of the riots was to be seen in the number of efforts to assuage Kazakh ethnic sensibilities in the aftermath of the December events. Conferences were held on "international education" and on the teaching of Kazakh in the schools. As Ann Sheehy noted in her report on the "Conference on International Education in Alma-Ata" (*Radio Liberty Research Reports*, 30 April 1987), only 0.7 percent of Russians living in Kazakhstan possessed good knowledge of Kazakh. Government-sponsored conferences on problems of multiculturalism necessarily had to focus upon inadequate Kazakh language preparation by Russians. For Kazakhs the problem was equally as great. Even though Kazakh students were heavily represented in republican institutions of higher education, the language of instruction was invariably in Russian. At primary education levels, out of the nearly 9,000 schools operating in the republic in 1987, less than 2,500 offered instruction in Kazakh. Kazakh was taught as a second language in another thousand schools. Of the approximately four million students in Kazakh schools, the number enrolled in schools offering Kazakh (either as the language of instruction or as a second language) was estimated to be little more than one million. The ethnic character of the December 1986 uprising served to give focus to the inadequate training and support for study of the Kazakh language.

By mid-1987, although the Kazakh Communist Party was calling for the reassertion of Leninist principles of bilingualism, Party leadership was falling behind the curve of public opinion. Pressure mounted for the declaration of Kazakh as the official language of the Kazakh Soviet Republic. Following the establishment of full Kazakhstan independence in 1991, the issue of language policy continued to be at the center of Kazakh political culture. The June 1992 draft constitution of the newly independent Kazakhstan included provision for Kazakh as the sole official language, while recognizing Russian as a language of communication between nationalities. (This latter provision was criticized by Kazakh nationalists.) Russian continues to be used alongside Kazakh in most government communications.

Political Change Since 1986

As in other newly independent Central Asian states, the relative openness that accompanied the policies of perestroika and glasnost gave rise in Kazakhstan to informal public groups that served as agents of political and cultural change. Already by the end of 1988 some three hundred of these informal groups had been formed. Although the number of participants remained small at first, the idea of freely organized informal groups—not yet recognized as political parties—gathered steam.

Not all of these groups desire political party status but rather wish to highlight particular environmental, economic, or religious issues. The most prominent environmental group, for example, is the Nevada-Semipalatinsk antinuclear movement. The goals of this movement include the cessation of nuclear testing, the responsible handling and disposal of radioactive materials, the conversion of military industry to environmentally responsible industry, and the closure of the Semipalatinsk nuclear test site. Founded in early 1989 and headed by the well-known Kazakh writer, Olzhas Suleimenov, the Nevada-Semipalatinsk group began holding well-attended rallies as early as the fall of 1989.

While the Nevada-Semipalatinsk movement has retained its public following, some other strictly political movements have been less successful in adjusting to Kazakhstan's shift from Soviet republic to independent state. The Kazakh Communist Party, for example, ceased to exist in the aftermath of the August 1991 coup in Moscow. Other political parties such as the Kazakh Free Party and the Social Democratic Party (the latter claiming to have followers from among all major ethnic groups of Kazakhstan) have surfaced and gained strength. On the right, the nationalist Kazakh Alash Party, along with the Azat Movement and the Republican Party, have capitalized upon the discrediting of the Communist Party, calling for coalition government and a division of Communist Party assets. While the prevailing government in Kazakhstan continues to be wary of informal political groups—and only in 1992 allowed registration of formal opposition parties (with submission of membership lists)—the concern that these groups may contribute to divisiveness has not stood in the way of their recognition. Despite the desperate economic situation (noted later) that threatens to undermine governmental stability, several of the most influential political groups in Kazakhstan tend to bridge ethnic and regional differences, rather than to exploit them.

Kazakh politics involves an unusual blend of the old and the new. Much of the old bureaucracy, the nomenklatura, remains. However, political change has also occurred at the upper levels of the Kazakhstan government. By mid-1989, two and a half years into his leadership in Kazakhstan, Party Secretary Genadii Kolbin was transferred to a post in Moscow. The resulting vacancy at the head of the Kazakh Soviet Republic was filled by the election of Nursultan Nazarbaev as first secretary of the Kazakh Communist Party. Born in 1940, the relatively young Nazarbaev had worked his way through lower-level Party posts, distinguishing himself by his support of reform and his outspoken opposition to government corruption. A firm supporter of perestroika, Nazarbaev had already risen to the chairmanship of the Kazakhstan Council of Ministers in 1984. His selection as Party leader brought reformist tendencies to the Kazakh Communist Party earlier than in most other regions of Central Asia. Nazarbaev's assumption of power in Kazakhstan also ended the brief period in which an ethnic Russian served as foremost political leader of the republic.

Following the abortive August 1991 coup attempt in Moscow, Kazakhstan followed the pattern of other former Soviet republics by declaring its own independence. Not lost upon local Kazakhs was the fact that the declaration of independence came on 16 December 1991, exactly five years after the Alma-Ata riots. As president of the newly independent Kazakhstan, Nazarbaev, despite his rise to power through the Kazakh Communist Party, has proved to be a resilient, independent political leader. In the fall of 1991, he contributed to the dismantling of the Kazakh Communist Party and proceeded to refuse a post in the newly created socialist party. Nazarbaev's argument was that he must be president of "all the people." In that same regard he has sought, not always successfully, to rise above political squabbles. In particular, he took the lead in establishing a new superparty, the so-called People's Congress of Kazakhstan, formed in October 1991. While the People's Congress has not overcome all the ethnic divisions in Kazakhstan, President Nazarbaev—the first elected president of the independent state of Kazakhstan—has managed to maintain a measure of popularity among both the Slavic and Kazakh populations.

In speeches urging support for multiculturalism, Nazarbaev consistently argues that narrow ethnic chauvinism can lead to a situation in Kazakhstan worse than that in Yugoslavia. (See James Critchlow, "Kazakhstan: The Outlook for Ethnic Relations," *RFE/RL Research Report*, 31 January 1992.) From Nazarbaev's point of view, right-wing nationalist parties, especially the Kazakh Alash Party, constitute a threat to civil order. Yet, at a time when the roots of Kazakh ethnic identity are everywhere being explored, the right-wing Alash Party carries a name that has special historical significance for Kazakh ethnic identity.

The Recovery of Kazakh Identity

Among the changes occurring during perestroika in Kazakhstan, perhaps the most revealing was the drive for recovery of Kazakh cultural, ethnic, and political identity. Leading the campaign in this area, as in his leadership of the Nevada-Semipalatinsk movement, has been the first secretary of the Kazakh Union of Writers, Olzhas Suleimenov. In early 1987, Suleimenov urged the rapid rehabilitation of two Kazakh literary figures who perished in the Soviet purges of the 1920s and 1930s, Maghjan Jumabaev and Shakerim Qudayberdiev. (See Ann Sheehy, "Call for Rehabilitation of Two Kazakh Poets," *Radio Liberty Research*, 9 June 1987.)

The drive to rehabilitate Maghjan (1896–1938) and Shakerim (d. 1930s) reflected a desire to reopen Kazakh religious and political issues that were systematically excluded from consideration during the Soviet period. The poet Maghjan's verses were patriotic in nature, appealing to the rich heritage of the Kazakhs, the Turks more generally, and the Kazakh lands. For official Soviet ideology, what made Maghjan's literary output unacceptable was his leadership in the Alash-Orda, the liberal nationalist movement that briefly came to power in Kazakh lands following the October Bolshevik Revolution of 1917. The Alash nationalist party proclaimed the autonomy of Kazakh lands in December 1917 and held out for Kazakh interests during the years of the wider Russian Civil War. By the time of the collapse of the Alash-Orda, Maghjan's views had become ever more pan-Turkic, reflecting a not uncommon view (found also in the Basmachi movement) that the salvation of any one Turkic people rested in the unification of all Turkic peoples against the Bolshevik Revolution and against Western innovations. For subsequent generations of Soviet writers, Maghjan was consigned to the number of those reactionary figures who opposed the liberating role of the Bolsheviks.

Shakerim Qudayberdiev, nephew of the founder of modern Kazakh literature (Abay Kunanbaev, 1845–1904), was a Kazakh intellectual of the early twentieth century who understood Russian thought and culture, but maintained a deeply religious, Islamic way of life. Alongside his *History of the Kazakh Clans*, he also published before World War I a religious treatise on *The Basic Tenets of Mohammedanism*. According to the traditional Soviet interpretation, Shakerim was a reactionary religious mystic.

The effort to rehabilitate Maghjan Jumabaev and Shakerim Qudayberdiev (along with other writers discredited during the Soviet period) culminated in 1988 with their formal recognition. Republication of literary, political, and religious works from the early twentieth century has continued to the present. The rehabilitation of these leading cultural and political figures from the early twentieth century has been central to the recovery of Kazakh identity. The rehabilitations have highlighted the hidden history of nationalist leaders from the era of the Alash Orda, an era that formally ended in 1920 with the abolition of the Alash party. The rehabilitations constitute, in the present context, a repudiation of Soviet (and, to some extent, Russian) influence upon Kazakh culture.

Equally important are the Islamic and pan-Turkic themes in this reevaluation of the Kazakh past. The renewed popularity of Islamic writers of the early twentieth century, the recovery of Islamic religious identity, and the linkage of ethnic and religious themes in the popular consciousness are all parts of the larger issue of Kazakh ethnicity.

Economic Problems

In the worst public violence since the December 1986 riots, thousands of Kazakhs demonstrated in the oil city of Novyi Uzen in June 1989. At least five people died in the conflict. A city of over 50,000 inhabitants, Novyi Uzen was established in 1968 after the discovery of oil in this area of western Kazakhstan along the Caspian Sea. Set astride a desert steppe frontier, Novyi Uzen is one of the least inhabitable cities of the former Soviet Union. Recurring dust storms frequently make it necessary for drivers there to use their headlights in the middle of the day. The development of the oil fields contributed to the overnight growth of this city that was established only for its industrial output and without regard to urban infrastructure. Compounding the tensions within the city was the mixed ethnic population of Kazakhs and workers from the Caucasus hired for jobs in the oil industry. The rush to cities such as Novyi Uzen also led to unemployment by the 1980s, for there were limits to the sudden oil boom.

When Kazakhs took to the streets of Novyi Uzen in June 1989, the fighting, on the face of it, was directed at ethnic Lezghins from Dagestan, as well as against Chechen-Ingush, Ossetian, and other transplanted workers from the Caucasus region. As in the case of the Alma-Ata riots of 1986, however, the appearance of ethnic conflict covered deeper, underlying causes. The sudden growth of the oil economy had led to massive transfers of human population, without regard to their basic needs, such as housing, health care, education, transportation, and food. For central planners, the only goal was production, or industrial output. Similar problems have plagued the coal mining region of Qaraghandy (Karaganda). While the presence of natural resources in Kazakhstan offers considerable promise and feeds the drive to secure Western investment, the reality is that the industrial and mining sectors of the Kazakh economy are fragile and prone to boom and bust economic cycles. The absence of infrastructure, especially the housing shortages that plague much of Central Asia, has added to labor unrest. High birthrates and rapid urbanization only aggravate this housing problem.

Equally troubling for Kazakhstan is its dependence upon imported consumer goods. Prior to declaring independence, Kazakhstan imported as much as 60 percent of its consumer products. Potentially capable of growing enough food, Kazakhstan continues to use scarce water resources for heavy irrigation and cultivation of cotton. As a consequence, Kazakhstan shares with Uzbekistan the environmental nightmare of the depleted Aral Sea. (See Uzbekistan chapter page 173.) While more diverse than the cotton monoculture of Uzbekistan, the Kazakh economy also exhibits the results of centrally planned Moscow decision making that too often set unrealistic goals for production and sacrificed local self-sufficiency for agricultural mass production.

To its credit, Kazakhstan has moved aggressively in seeking Western capital investment. Despite exercising inordinate caution in implementation, the Kazakhstan government has also mapped out a privatization formula intended to divest the state of most of its assets and launch an effective market economy. Progress has been particularly noticeable in Almaty (Alma-Ata), where as much as 40 percent of the housing market has been sold or divested. Because of its delicate interethnic balance, however, the perils of economic failure are potentially very great for Kazakhstan. The social unrest that can accompany rises in unemployment and the political disruptions that can attend the process of democratization are daily concerns for the new government. Not unexpectedly, Nazarbaev has sought massive foreign credits to ease the transition to privatization. While remaining

within the sphere of the ruble economy, and with 90 percent of its exports going to former Soviet republics, Kazakhstan is seeking to position itself for economic take-off. It has recently augmented the ruble by issuing its own currency, the *tanga*. But, the prospects for economic development must be matched against real shortages of basic foodstuffs that threaten the very fabric of Kazakhstan society.

Strategic Importance of Kazakhstan

Western concerns for the stability of Kazakhstan are all the greater because of its considerable military and strategic capacity. Kazakhstan has more than a hundred enterprises from the military-industrial complex of the former Soviet Union. Among these are the nuclear weapons testing site of Semipalatinsk and the Baikonur Cosmodrome space center. While Western concern has been registered over the strategic nuclear weapons sites on Kazakh soil, and preliminary agreements have been signed for demobilization, there has been no firm commitment of Western capital directed toward the conversion of these sites to nonmilitary purposes. For now, the presence of strategic weapons on its soil poses a dilemma for Kazakhstan. On the one hand, the continued deployment of nuclear weapons in Kazakhstan could prolong the presence of Russian military forces there. By contrast, should Kazakhstan seek to take over these strategic sites, it would mean the diversion of considerable resources to the military operation of a questionable nuclear deterrent. The Kazakhs have so far been unable to parlay international concern about these weapons into tangible financial credits for conversion and decommissioning.

Environmental Problems

Finally, the environmental costs of production-oriented central planning are present everywhere in Kazakhstan. The clean-up efforts needed to make the Semipalatinsk nuclear test site safe are far beyond the capacities of the Kazakh government. The Aral Sea disaster noted in the discussion of Uzbekistan is every bit as serious for Kazakhstan as it is for Uzbekistan. Meanwhile, the costs of basic pollution control devices for cleaning smokestack industries and guaranteeing safe drinking water greatly exceed the government's ability to pay.

Kazakhstan, strategically situated between Russia and China, remains a country rich in natural resources and with able and tested political leadership. Its unique, multi-ethnic population provides a resource for economic advance, while also posing the potential for nationalist reaction and political instability. Its mixed economy is the most robust of the Central Asian region, but its more urban, industrially advanced population could suffer the most serious reverses should the transition to a market economy be marked by high unemployment, unmet consumer needs (particularly in the area of housing), and large-scale agricultural shortages.

KYRGYZSTAN

Statistical Profile

Demography

Population: 4,258,000
Ethnic population:

Kirgiz	2,230,000	52.4%
Russian	917,000	21.5%
Uzbek	550,000	12.9%
Ukrainian	108,000	2.5%
German	101,000	2.4%
Tatar	70,000	1.6%
Uighur	37,000	0.9%
Kazakh	37,000	0.9%
Tajik	34,000	0.8%
Other	174,000	4.1%

Historic religious traditions:

Islam	73.6%
Christianity	26.4%

Population by age:

Age	Total	Males	Females
0–4	14.5%	7.4%	7.1%
5–9	11.9%	6.0%	5.9%
10–14	11.1%	5.6%	5.5%
15–19	10.2%	5.1%	5.1%
20–24	9.3%	4.7%	4.6%
25–29	8.3%	4.3%	4.0%
30–34	6.9%	3.4%	3.5%
35–39	5.3%	2.6%	2.7%
40–44	2.5%	1.2%	1.3%
45–49	4.5%	2.2%	2.3%
50–54	3.7%	1.8%	1.9%
55–59	3.9%	1.8%	2.1%
60–64	2.8%	1.1%	1.7%
65–69	1.6%	0.5%	1.1%
70–	3.5%	1.0%	2.5%

Male/Female ratio: 48.7% male/51.3% female
Rural/Urban population: 61.9% rural/38.1% urban
Growth over time, 1979–91: 25.3%
Population density: 57.7 persons/sq mi

Politics/Government

Date of independence declaration: 31 August 1991
Urban centers and populations:

Bishkek (Frunze)	616,000
Osh	213,000
Przhevalsk	64,000
Naryn	26,000

Autonomous areas: none

Education

Level of education for persons over 15:

completed higher education	9.4%
completed secondary education	56.4%
incomplete secondary education	18.4%

Number of higher education institutions: 9 (58,800 students)
Major institutions of higher education and enrollment:
Bishkek:

Kirgiz State University	13,000
Kirgiz Agricultural Institute	4,600
Kirgiz State Institute of Fine Art	225

Socioeconomic Indicators

Birthrate: 29.3/1,000
Infant mortality: 30.0/1,000 live births
Average life expectancy: 68.8 (males 64.5; females, 72.8)
Average family size: 4.7
Hospital beds per 10,000 persons: 119.8
Production of electrical energy: 3,030 kwh/person

Physical/Territorial/Geopolitical Features

Area: 76,641 sq mi (.9% of USSR total)
Land use:

Cultivated (72% irrigated)	7%
Pasture	42%

Highest elevation: 24,406 ft. (Pobeda peak)

Rainfall: 30 inches/year **Temperature:** average in winter, 23° F in low elevations, -18° F in the higher elevations; lowest temperature: -64.5° F. Average in summer, 75° F in low elevations, 41° F in the higher elevations; highest temperature: 109.4° F.	**Principal products:** cotton, wheat, vegetables, fruit, sugar beets, livestock, machinery, textiles, metallurgy, coal, gold, uranium, mercury **Per capita GNP (1991):** $1,550.

Sources

"Kirgizskaia sovetskaia sotsialisticheskaia respublika" *Bol'shaia Sovetskaia Entsiklopediia* (Moscow, 1977); *Narodnoe Khoziaistvo SSSR v 1990g.* (Moscow, 1991); Naselenie SSSR (1989); Matthew J. Sagers, "News Notes. Iron and Steel," *Soviet Geography* 30 (May 1989): 397–434; Lee Schwartz, "USSR Nationality Redistribution by Republic, 1979–1989: From Published Results of the 1989 All-Union Census," *Soviet Geography* 32 (April 1991): 209–48; and *World of Learning,* 43rd ed. (London: Europa Publications Limited, 1993); "Russia. . . " (National Geographic Society Map, March 1993).

History and Description

Topography

Kyrgyzstan (previously identified in English as Kirgizia or Kirghizstan) is located in the eastern part of Central Asia. A highly mountainous country, Kyrgyzstan shares its borders with three other newly independent, former Soviet republics—Tajikistan to the south, Uzbekistan to the west, and Kazakhstan to the northwest and north. On the eastern frontier, across a lengthy series of frozen peaks, lies China. Kyrgyzstan's oddly contorted western boundary, established during the Soviet period, allows this land of sharp altitudes and forbidding heights to share a part of the fertile Farghona (Fergana) Valley. Other parts of this ancient irrigated valley belong to Tajikistan and Uzbekistan. The capital of Kyrgyzstan, Bishkek (formerly Frunze), was once the old military fortress of Pishpek. In the Soviet period the capital was renamed Frunze after the Russian general Mikhail Frunze, who was born in the city and served in the region through the period of the 1917 Russian Revolution. In 1991, the name Bishkek was restored.

Kyrgyzstan is composed of several distinct natural regions. These include the irrigated Chu River valley in the north where Bishkek is found; the extremely mountainous area in the northeast around the large natural lake Ysyk-Köl; another mountainous area along the Naryn River in central Kyrgyzstan; the Kyrgyz portion of the Farghona Valley (from the ancient silk center of Osh in the south to Jalal-Abad in the north); and the more isolated Talas river valley in the northwest separated from the rest of Kyrgyzstan by high mountains.

Two major mountain ranges, the Tian Shan and the Pamir-Alay systems, form the contours of Kyrgyzstan, unfolding along a generally east-west axis. In the north, the Kyrgyz Range, a spur of the Tian Shan Mountains, looms over Bishkek. To the east, on the other side of Ysyk-Köl, near the Chinese border, is the highest point in Kyrgyzstan, Victory (Pobeda) Peak towering 24,406 feet. Southern and western Kyrgystan are occupied by the Trans-Alay Mountains. They constitute the northernmost part of the Pamir-Alay mountain system extending from Tajikistan.

The river systems of mountainous Kyrgyzstan provide enough hydroelectric power to make Kyrgyzstan an exporter of electricity. The longest and most important river, the Naryn, originates in the Tian Shan mountains and flows in a southwesterly direction through Kyrgyzstan, eventually joining with other rivers to form the Syr Darya, a major river of Central Asia that brings water to the heavily irrigated Farghona Valley before continuing to the Aral Sea far to the west. Other notable rivers in Kyrgyzstan are the Chu and Talas in the north. In addition to these rivers, Kyrgyzstan has three thousand lakes including Ysyk-Köl.

Kyrgyzstan

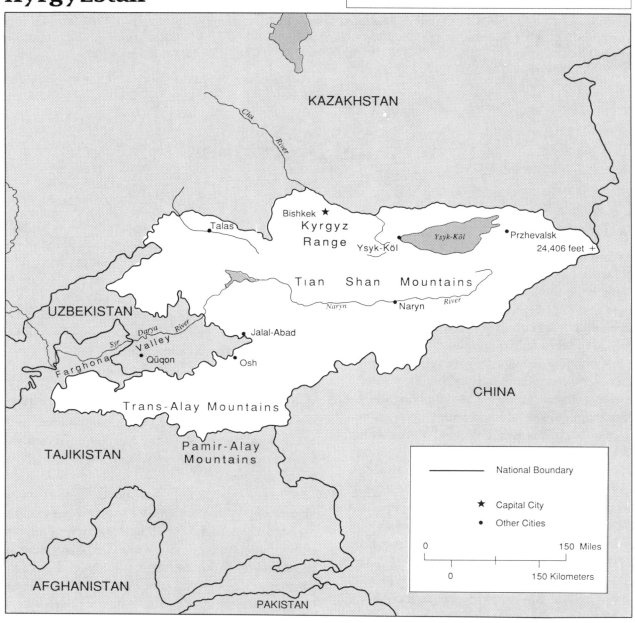

KAZAKHSTAN

Chu River

Bishkek ★

Talas

Kyrgyz Range

Ysyk-Köl

Ysyk-Köl

Przhevalsk

24,406 feet +

Tian Shan Mountains

Naryn River

Naryn

UZBEKISTAN

Syr Darya River

Farghona Valley

Jalal-Abad

Qŭqon

Osh

CHINA

Trans-Alay Mountains

TAJIKISTAN

Pamir-Alay Mountains

AFGHANISTAN

PAKISTAN

	National Boundary
★	Capital City
•	Other Cities

0   150 Miles

0   150 Kilometers

The climate of Kyrgyzstan depends very much on the altitude. From the ice and snow of its high peaks to the relatively moderate temperatures of its mountain valleys and lowland areas, great variation in temperature exists. Such variation has led to the widely practiced tradition in animal husbandry known as transhumance, in which herdsmen take their animals to cool summer pastures high in the mountains and then return them to warmer valleys in the winter.

The economy of Kyrgyzstan is largely based on energy sources, hydroelectric power, coal deposits, and some reserves of oil. Since World War II, it has exploited a rich supply of mercury and antimony. The country's main agricultural crops are cotton, sugar beets, and grains. Livestock breeding is extremely important in mountainous areas. Sheep, pigs, cattle, and the traditional small Kyrgyz horse play a vital role in the economy.

Ethnic and Historical Background

The ethnic origin of the Kyrgyz people has become the subject of much debate. One theory suggests that early Kyrgyz peoples inhabited an area in Siberia near the upper Enisei River. A nomadic people, these Kyrgyz eventually made their way southwestward toward present-day Kyrgyzstan. By the sixteenth century they were trading with other Turkic peoples of the region while continuing to raise and herd livestock. The Kyrgyz language is Turkic, belonging to the Nogai subdivision of Kypchak Turkic, a non-Indo-European tongue related to Kazakh. A literary Kyrgyz language was established during the Soviet period. It is based primarily on dialects spoken in the northern part of Kyrgyzstan. The territory now occupied by the Kyrgyz was long fought over by competing Turkic and Mongol warlords before the early nineteenth century when the Kyrgyz were subjugated by the powerful ruling khanate at Kokand (Qŭqon, now in Uzbekistan). During the years of vassalage to the Kokand state, the Islamization, already accomplished in the southern part of Kyrgyz lands in the previous century, spread northward. Today most ethnic Kyrgyz profess the moderate Sunni form of Islam, although some elements of the more fundamentalist, mystic Sufi form are found in the southern regions of Kyrgyzstan, particularly at Osh, a popular site of Muslim pilgrimage.

Russian Conquest

Russian influence in Kyrgyzstan, the result of ongoing nineteenth-century tsarist campaigns in Central Asia, began in 1862 with the capture of the fortress at Pishpek (Bishkek) from the Kokand khanate. Soviet historians have maintained that some Kyrgyz clan leaders had already sought Russian protection against Turkic enemies much earlier in the century. The surrender of Pishpek led eventually to the complete defeat of Kokand in 1876. At that point the Kokand khanate and all the lands it controlled became a protectorate of tsarist Russia. The colonization of Kyrgyz lands by Slavic peoples then began in earnest as tens of thousands of Russian and Ukrainian settlers emigrated from the European part of the Russian Empire to start farms, and in so doing fulfilled the central government's Russification policies. An inevitable result of this great land rush was the loss of the very best farmland to the influx of Slavic newcomers and an accompanying reduction in the amount of pasture land available for Kyrgyz livestock.

In 1916, as tsarist armies struggled during World War I to maintain successful military operations against the Germans, the government in Petrograd issued an order for mobilization of the Muslim peoples of Russian Turkestan (the administrative term for Central Asia). The indigenous Central Asian peoples, already overtaxed by wartime demands for the provision of both military and civilian supplies and long resentful of their treatment under tsarist colonialism, refused to cooperate. Revolts against the mobilization order soon erupted throughout the Muslim territories, most of which had not been fully integrated into the Russian Empire. Thousands of people were massacred on both sides as the widespread rebellion was put down mercilessly by the Russian authorities. In Kyrgyzstan alone more than two thousand European settlers perished and an uncounted number of Kyrgyz fell. As many as three hundred thousand Central Asians fled into the eastern mountains or across the border into China. As many as half this number were ethnic Kyrgyz.

Soviet Rule

Following World War I, the Kyrgyz slowly returned to their lands, where the Revolution and the Bolshevik assumption of power may have seemed far removed from local problems. The Bolsheviks, however, in spite of promises of national sovereignty for the Muslims of Central Asia, were determined to rule this remote part of the former tsarist empire. In 1918, after taking control of the greater part of Russian Turkestan and proclaiming it the Turkestan Soviet Republic, the Bolsheviks declared victory in Central Asia. The victory soon proved temporary as opponents of the new government rallied to defeat it. Nevertheless, the Red Army eventually prevailed, and Moscow launched a series of political and economic policies that ultimately led to repression, anarchy, hardship, and deprivation for the Kyrgyz and other peoples of Central Asia.

Early Years of Communist Rule. The Kyrgyz found themselves confronted by a different and potentially more threatening way of life than any inflicted on them by previous conquerors. Lenin's new government promulgated a program of atheism, the emancipation of women, and communal land ownership, breaking longstanding tribal landholding patterns. These new policies, countering nearly all the religious and cultural traditions of the Kyrgyz peoples, prompted yet more revolts. The Basmachi movement made up of armed Muslim rebels cooperated with other enemies of the Bolsheviks and fought a long guerilla war against Red Army soldiers throughout the 1920s.

During this time, amidst bitter Kyrgyz opposition to much of the Communist political program being imposed by the outsiders from Moscow, the new Soviet authorities were continuing to reorganize the territories within the newly named Turkestan Soviet Republic. The Soviet government distinguished amongst the various ethnic groups of the region by identifying the Kyrgyz as the Kara Kyrgyz, while the Kazakhs to the north were identified as the Kyrgyz. Not until well into the Soviet period were the labels changed. Finally, as part of the 1924 national delimitation policy, that is, the assignment of specific territories to particular ethnic groups or nations, Kyrgyzstan was designated an autonomous oblast within the greater Russian Republic. (Meanwhile the Kazakhs found their homeland renamed the Kazakh Autonomous Republic, also administratively assigned to the larger Russian Republic.)

Limited political participation by a developing Kyrgyz intelligentsia was allowed, and some traditional social patterns returned. The Russian language, however, was made the official means of communication for administrative, governmental, and economic activities. Russians also held most positions of power in the political hierarchy of Kyrgyzstan. In 1926 Kyrgyzstan was promoted to the status of an autonomous "republic," but still within the Russian Republic.

The Rule of Stalin. The Stalinist years brought renewed attempts to implement the Communist policy of collectivization, in which privately held lands were redistributed into large shared agricultural units run by elected or appointed officials. Collectivization elicited such strong opposition from the Kyrgyz peasant population that the Basmachi rebels increased their opposition efforts. The very idea of collectivization in a place where for centuries the inhabitants had already been following a practice of holding land in common on the basis of family and kinship ties seemed to serve no socialist purpose other than external control from Moscow. Stalin really wanted to abolish the nomadic tradition in Kyrgyz life. As he ruthlessly attempted to eradicate this basic pattern of the Kyrgyz economy, Kyrgyz herders responded by taking their livestock far into the mountains, even into China. Nevertheless, by the middle of the 1930s, the Communists prevailed and the majority of Kyrgyz were resettled on collective farms.

During the 1930s, Stalin's intrusive policies not only sought to root out the traditional pastoral way of life in Central Asia, but also to stamp out any Kyrgyz national movement. In this effort, Stalin eliminated the few independent Kyrgyz voices that had developed. The purges of the interwar period decimated the fledgling Kyrgyz native intelligentsia and any others who expressed ideas that could be construed as a threat to the new order. Not only high Party officials, including three first secretaries of the Communist Party, but literary figures, writers and poets alike, were arrested and either sent to prison camps or executed. Ironically, in the midst of such horrors, Kyrgyzstan was elevated to full union republic status in 1936 under terms of the new Stalin constitution.

The advent of World War II once again brought mobilization orders for Central Asians. Well over a million were drafted. Little is known of their actual participation, but rumors have persisted that many deserted to the German side or worked with a group sympathetic to German war aims called the Turkestan National Committee.

Postwar Period. The postwar period brought much change to Kyrgyzstan. In 1950, Ishak Razzakov became first secretary of the Communist Party replacing A. Rysmendiev who had served in this post during and after the war. The political relaxation that occurred after Stalin's death in 1953 included modest, if on the whole unsuccessful, attempts by the Kyrgyz to introduce cultural changes. These changes were largely undermined by local Russian bureaucrats who held the real power in Kyrgyz life. One of the few new measures allowed was the teaching of Kyrgyz history in local schools. Razzakov, viewed perhaps as too supportive of these signs of Kyrgyz national life, was removed from office in 1961.

Turdakun Usubaliev was chosen to replace him and occupied the main leadership post of the Party and government until 1985 when Mikhail Gorbachev over-saw the appointment of Absamat Masaliev as first secretary of the Communist Party of Kirgizia.

Contemporary Issues

Demographic and Economic Realities of Kyrgyzstan

After the establishment of the Soviet republics of Central Asia, in 1936, ethnic Russians migrated to the region in unprecedented numbers. By the 1960s, the Russian population in Soviet Kirgizia (Kyrgyzstan) had grown by 500 percent. Over a million Russians and Ukrainians, roughly one quarter of the republic's total population, were living in Kyrgyzstan by the time of the 1979 census. The Russian immigration into Kyrgyzstan did not affect all parts of the republic equally. Rather, the urban centers, particularly Frunze (Bishkek) and the surrounding area, became disproportionately Russified. From the 1930s, Frunze became transformed into a predominantly Russian city.

One of the consequences of Russian urban settlement was that much of the technical, industrial, and administrative leadership of the Kyrgyz republic became Russian. Within Frunze itself, a Slavic elite (at its peak, over two-thirds of the population of the capital city) tended to perpetuate itself by dominating scientific and technical training institutes. Thus, even though ethnic Kyrgyz have, of late, been encouraged to prepare for jobs in the industrial sector, Kyrgyz students throughout the 1980s represented no more than one-fifth of those attending vocational-technical schools in the republic. This underrepresentation of Kyrgyz professionals reflected the demographic realities of urban Kyrgyzstan. Lacking affordable housing, the Kyrgyz population in Frunze, despite its growth in absolute numbers, remained under 20 percent of the total city population throughout the 1980s.

The great majority of ethnic Kyrgyz have continued to reside outside urban centers in the fertile valleys and more mountainous grazing regions of the republic. While the cotton monoculture found in other Central Asian republics has also come to dominate the republic's valleys, Kyrgyzstan is still known for its livestock, especially sheep, raised in the foothills of its many mountains. Kyrgyz lands also contain considerable untapped mineral wealth within their less accessible mountainous regions. Together with Uzbekistan and Tajikistan, Kyrgyzstan shares a portion of the fertile Farghona Valley where the rapid growth rate has brought the typical problems associated with chronic rural overpopulation. For Kyrgyzstan, these problems include not just rural poverty and unemployment, but overgrazing and ever more intensive irrigation to accommodate the needs of cotton.

Toward a Kyrgyz National Agenda

The contrast between the more impoverished rural Kyrgyz and the industrialized Russian elite of newly renamed Bishkek has not been lost upon contemporary Kyrgyz politicians, writers, and intellectuals. Capitalizing upon the greater openness or glasnost of the Gorbachev era, Kyrgyz writers began in the 1980s to address a number of national concerns relating to Russian cultural dominance in Bishkek.

Language Issue. Prominent among the national issues was that of school instruction in the Kyrgyz language. Chingiz Aitmatov, the internationally noted Kyrgyz writer who was elected chair of the Kyrgyz Union of Writers in 1986, launched a campaign for the establishment of urban Kyrgyz-language schools, particularly kindergartens. Despite the more than 100,000 Kyrgyz living in Bishkek, there was only one Kyrgyz-language high school (operating in three shifts) throughout the 1980s. In a debate enjoined against his Kyrgyz ideological opponent, Aaly Tokombaev (1904–88) who was a staunch advocate of Russification, Aitmatov noted that not one kindergarten using Kyrgyz as the primary language of instruction was to be found in any of the larger urban centers, including Bishkek. Moreover, most Russian-language schools that formerly taught Kyrgyz had abandoned such instruction in the 1950s. So dominant had Russian become in Bishkek by the 1980s that most commentators noted two parallel problems of communication. Rural Kyrgyz lacked the knowledge of Russian needed to succeed in urban society, and urban Kyrgyz ended up lacking a firm grasp of their own native language. Almost half of the Kyrgyz children in Bishkek were not studying their native language in the 1980s. In the case of urban Kyrgyz, the situation was often further compounded by their poor preparation in Russian. The problem of Kyrgyz language instruction has begun to be addressed, and new Kyrgyz schools were opened following the declaration of national independence in August 1991. Today, Kyrgyz is the official language of the republic, although Russian continues to be employed in some official government and trade matters.

Meanwhile, the democratizing leadership of Kyrgyzstan President Askar Akaev (see "Prospects for Democracy in Kyrgyzstan" later) has exercised caution, so that efforts to mandate study of Kyrgyz not create a backlash of opposition among urban Slavs who already have been leaving Central Asia in record numbers. The continuing importance of Russian and Ukrainian nationals for Kyrgyzstan's industrial and technical development has led Kyrgyz political leadership to try not to alienate the Slavs of Bishkek. An example of this caution, not directly related to the matter of language instruction, was President Akaev's 1991 veto of a potentially offensive article in the new land law. Akaev noted that the article in question had said that "the land is the property of the Kyrgyz people." Akaev asked that the law be amended to read that "the land is the property of Kyrgyz citizens and all other nationalities making up the republic's people" ("Kirgiz President Vetoes Land Law," *Report on the USSR,* 12 June 1991, vol. 3, no. 25, p. 34). It remains to be seen whether the issue of Kyrgyz language instruction in the schools and Kyrgyz/Slav relations in general can be so easily accommodated.

Related to Kyrgyz language instruction was the concern voiced openly after 1985 for reform of the Kyrgyz language itself. Proponents of language reform argued that use of the Cyrillic (Russian) alphabet—a change introduced in 1940—violated traditional Kyrgyz sounds. One example was the use of the Cyrillic "k" to render both "k" and "q," sounds that are distinct and different in traditional Kyrgyz. Such elimination of letters and sounds from the Kyrgyz language was unacceptable to those voicing concern for traditional Kyrgyz.

While the change to the Cyrillic alphabet in 1940 may have made access to modern Russian easier for ethnic Kyrgyz, the flip side of the problem was that the use of a confining Cyrillic alphabet tended to obscure the fundamental uniformities that existed between the Turkic languages of Central Asia—Kazakh, Tatar, Uzbek, and Kyrgyz, among others. Proponents of linguistic reform noted that it ought not to be necessary to translate Kazakh or Uzbek into Kyrgyz, yet the peculiarities of the new orthographic system exaggerated the differences between these Turkic languages, making the languages more inaccessible to each other.

Environmental Concerns. Part of the rediscovery of Kyrgyz ethnic identity has also been tied to campaigns for the preservation of the fragile ecology of the republic. The concern for the Kyrgyz environment has been seen in the formation of, among other groups, the "Ysyk-Köl Rescue Committee," a voluntary organization dedicated to the preservation of the largest inland body of fresh water in Kyrgyzstan. Attributing the deterioration and diversion of Kyrgyz water resources to the excessive demands of the cotton monoculture, the Rescue Committee has sought to rejuvenate the depleted Ysyk-Köl lake before it reaches the level of ecological disaster associated with the Aral Sea. (See the chapters on Uzbekistan and Kazakhstan.) One solution to the problem, proposed by the writer Chingiz Aitmatov, has been to divert mountain rivers so that they flow into Ysyk-Köl. As in other areas of water conservation, however, such a water diversion project would have major ramifications for downstream users. Many of the disaffected users would be in Kazakhstan. As in other parts of Central Asia, the critical ecological issue of water conservation tends inevitably to fuel economic and ethnic conflict.

National Origin. Alongside the campaigns for ecological awareness and Kyrgyz language instruction and reform in the 1980s, the Kyrgyz intelligentsia reopened the thorny question of Kyrgyz national origins. According to the prescription set forth by Kyrgyz Communist Party First Secretary Turdakun Usubaliev (1961–85), the Kyrgyz people have their origin in the region of Tian Shan in the current republic. Yet, such a view tended to foreclose discussion of the much earlier and more prominent ancient sites of Kyrgyz found farther east in the Enisei River region. Kyrgyz epic poetry refers to the more easterly origins (see particularly a work called *The Manas,* a national epic of 250,000 verses), but Usubaliev placed restrictions on the publication of this epic poetry during his neo-Stalinist rule. For many Kyrgyz intellectuals, the ability to raise openly these questions of origin became crucial for wider communication with ethnic

Kyrgyz living outside Kyrgyzstan. Communities of ethnic Kyrgyz live in Afghanistan and China.

Chingiz Aitmatov. The reopening of this Kyrgyz national agenda in the 1980s can be credited in great part to the remarkable leadership provided by the Kyrgyz intelligentsia. This intelligentsia, both in its ties with the past and in its prospects for the future, is epitomized by Chingiz Aitmatov, chair of the Union of Writers. Aitmatov is a writer of internationally recognized talent who is fully bilingual, writing in both Kyrgyz and Russian. Born in 1928 in a Kyrgyz mountain village, his early schooling was limited, even though he would later graduate from the Moscow Institute of Literature. At the age of fourteen, during World War II, he became a tax collector and secretary of the local village council. His first published article in 1952, "On the Terminology of the Kyrgyz Language," argued that the evolution of modern Kyrgyz had benefitted by its borrowings from modern Russian.

His 1958 short story, "Jamilia," propelled him to international attention. It contained an explosive plot line depicting a young Kyrgyz woman rejecting the norms of her society by leaving her arranged marriage and running off with her true love. Aitmatov quickly advanced in the official Soviet intellectual establishment, serving on literary boards in Moscow and in the Kirgiz Soviet Socialist Republic. He became the head of the local cinematographers' union and also served as correspondent for *Pravda* in Central Asia. His subsequent works of fiction, including the anti-Stalinist piece, *The Executioner's Block* (*Plakha*), and a novel set in Kazakhstan, *The Day Lasts More Than a Hundred Years*, reached wide audiences both inside the Soviet Union and beyond. Aitmatov's prose, which often depicts the values and traditions of his native Central Asia, has occasionally been compared to that of the Russian "village prose" writers who exhibit a nostalgia for traditional values and an environment free from the threat of an urban, industrial society.

Chingiz Aitmatov's leadership in Kyrgyz cultural issues of the 1980s was indicative of the wider importance of the intelligentsia in reshaping the Kyrgyz national agenda. Despite his prominent position in the official Soviet literary establishment, Aitmatov led the struggle for Kyrgyz instruction in the schools, for language reform, and for the rediscovery of Kyrgyz historical memory, particularly in the matter of Kyrgyz ethnic origins. In the person of Aitmatov it is possible to note how the Soviet experience came both to mold the Kyrgyz intelligentsia, and at the same time, to galvanize it in the 1980s against excessive Russification.

Ethnic Disturbances

While the reshaping of the Kyrgyz national agenda has been set against the context of Soviet Russian influence in Bishkek, the most serious outbreak of ethnic hostilities began not in the more Russified capital of the republic, but in the Farghona Valley, a region of contested Kyrgyz and Uzbek influence.

The worst outbreak occurred in the nearby city of Osh in June 1990. The spark that ignited the violence appears to have been associated with the allocation to ethnic Kyrgyz of housing lots in the suburbs of Osh, a region dominated by Uzbeks. Thousands of Uzbeks gathered in the disputed region, along with hundreds of Kyrgyz. The dispute boiled over into the city of Osh itself where the violence erupted. While the Uzbek population comprises only about one-third of the Osh oblast, the city of Osh has a strong Uzbek majority. The violence in Osh also spread to other regions of Kyrgyzstan, with the ethnic Kyrgyz of Bishkek and elsewhere seeking to aid their fellow Kyrgyz nationals in Osh. In the end, over 230 were killed in the violence, and several hundred more were left missing. Soviet Interior Ministry troops were dispatched to the region and flights between the capital cities of Uzbekistan and Kyrgyzstan were temporarily suspended.

What the Osh uprising demonstrated was the terrible potential for uncontrollable ethnic scapegoating and violence in the economically depressed areas of Central Asia. In the Osh oblast, that portion of the Farghona Valley located in Kyrgyzstan, over 100,000 people were unemployed in 1990—figures that may have worsened in the intervening time. Indeed, 60 percent of all unemployment in Kyrgyzstan was focused in this one oblast. The contending interests of the divergent Turkic nations of the Farghona Valley ultimately meant that a conflict over economic resources—in this case, housing—could explode into a major interethnic calamity.

Prospects for Democracy in Kyrgyzstan

The events in Osh contributed to the strengthening of informal political groups already established in Kyrgyzstan. Most notable was the rise of an informal democratic opposition that labeled itself "Kyrgyzstan" (at a time when the Soviet republic was stilled called "Kirgizia"). Following the June 1990 violence in the Farghona Valley, representatives of "Kyrgyzstan" arranged for a joint meeting with their democratic counterparts in the Uzbek national front, Birlik. This meeting, held in Bishkek, sought to advance the common democratic goals of the two organizations, while at the same time helping to defuse interethnic Turkic confrontation. Adding his own voice to the call for ethnic peace was Chingiz Aitmatov who, in an appeal to the Kyrgyz and Uzbek nations, invoked the language of pan-Turkic identity:

> There is unemployment; there is an evil called monoculture; there is homelessness. But, we should never forget one thing: we are fraternal nations. Our roots are the same, they are joined in one Turkish family. . . . Now I am appealing to the Kyrgyz people not to show force toward our Uzbek brothers in the southern part of our republic. In fact, if a Kyrgyz raises his hand against the Uzbek people, he raises it against his own people. ("Chingiz Aitmatov's Appeal to the Kirgiz and Uzbek Peoples," *Report on the USSR*, vol. 2, no. 24, 15 June 1990, pp. 18–19)

The ruling Kyrgyz head of state and first secretary of the Kirgiz Communist Party, Absamat Masaliev (1985–90), a lukewarm supporter of Gorbachev's perestroika who identified with more hardline Moscow Communist Party leaders such as Egor Ligachev, steadfastly opposed the informal political movements despite their efforts to defuse the ethnic tensions. Well into 1990, despite the rising clamor of public demonstrations and hunger strikes, Masaliev forbade the public meetings of democratic "Kyrgyzstan." Still, the public outcry for alleviation of housing shortages, the prospects for wider ethnic violence, the mounting ecological concerns, and the rigidity of the Masaliev government fueled the movements for political democracy.

Facing ever greater public criticism of his rule, Masaliev, in what was clearly a gigantic miscalculation, decided in October 1990 to create for himself a new executive presidency. Fully expecting to be confirmed in this position by the republic's legislative body, the Kirgiz Supreme Soviet, Masaliev received less than the required majority. In the next round of balloting, held on 27 October 1990, the liberal president of the Kirgiz Academy of Sciences, Askar Akaev, was elected with the support of a coalition of democratic forces in the Supreme Soviet.

Akaev proceeded to turn the office of the executive president into an active force for economic privatization and democratization, and Masaliev resigned from the chairmanship of the Supreme Soviet (remaining head of the republic's Communist Party). Although Akaev, a specialist in quantum optics, had become a Communist

Party member in 1981, he quickly moved to establish his democratic credentials. He legalized the movement for democratic renewal; replaced the minister of interior with a popular leader of that renewal movement, Felix Kulov; established a new cabinet of ministers free from Communist Party control; and advocated concrete measures for economic liberalization and privatization. Many came to see Askar Akaev as the Kyrgyz counterpart to Boris Yeltsin, president of the Russian Republic.

Akaev was born in 1944 in the Kirgiz Soviet Republic. He graduated from the Leningrad Institute of Precision Mechanics and Optics. Returning to Frunze, he became a faculty member in the Polytechnic Institute, ultimately rising to a department head there. In 1981, he joined the Communist Party and served a year as head of the Central Committee's Department of Scientific and Educational Institutions. In 1989, after two years as vice-president, he was elected president of the Kirgiz Academy of Sciences.

The pace of change inaugurated by Akaev has been a surprise to most outside observers. By February 1991, the Kyrgyz capital city of Frunze had been legally renamed Bishkek, the democratic movement "Kyrgyzstan" had held its first formal congress attended by six hundred delegates, and efforts were underway to reestablish close ties with each of the neighboring Central Asian republics. This transformation of Kyrgyzstan, even before its formal declaration of independence in August 1991, has come to be called the "Silk Revolution," a clear reference to the nonviolent Czechoslovak "Velvet Revolution" of 1989. One mark of Akaev's commitment to democracy was his early call for the overthrow of those who plotted the Moscow coup in August 1991. Akaev's support for Yeltsin and the Russian parliament from the very beginning of the August 1991 crisis reinforced the image of Akaev as a liberal committed to the pursuit of fundamental political and economic reform.

Following the August crisis, Akaev orchestrated a Kirgiz Supreme Soviet declaration of state independence on 31 August. Then, he called for state elections which, on 12 October, yielded a resounding 95 percent vote of confidence for himself. Ninety percent of the electorate participated in the voting. While Akaev is widely perceived to be the most effective democratic leader in the new politics of Central Asia, he is not without potential opponents. On one side are the forces of the old Communist order, which continue to exercise a strong presence among the nomenklatura, the political appointees dating from before Akaev's tenure as president. On the other side are those Kyrgyz nationalists, including some of the forces of democratic renewal, who would seek to promote a more narrow and conservative ethnic agenda at the expense of interethnic harmony.

The experiment of Kyrgyzstan in political democracy is being watched closely by Western powers and neighboring Asian states. Former United States Secretary of State James Baker made a visit to Kyrgyzstan the focus of his trip to Central Asia in the spring of 1992. Neighboring Turkic states, as well as Tajikistan and Iran, have established formal ties with Kyrgyzstan, as has the People's Republic of China. The problems of ethnic conflict and economic liberalization are, however, daunting, no less so because of the rapid exodus of the Slavic population from Bishkek.

TAJIKISTAN

Statistical Profile

Demography

Population: 5,093,000
Ethnic population:

Tajik	3,172,000	62.3%
Uzbek	1,198,000	23.5%
Russian	388,000	7.6%*
Tatar	72,000	1.4%
Kyrgyz	64,000	1.3%
Ukrainian	41,000	0.8%*
German	33,000	0.6%*
Turkmen	20,000	0.4%
Jewish	10,000	0.2%*
Other	95,000	1.9%

Predominant religious traditions:

Islam	90.8%
Christianity	9.0%

Population by age:

Age	Total	Males	Females
0–4	17.2%	8.7%	8.5%
5–9	13.3%	6.7%	6.6%
10–14	11.9%	6.0%	5.9%
15–19	10.6%	5.4%	5.2%
20–24	9.6%	4.8%	4.8%
25–29	8.1%	3.9%	4.2%
30–34	5.9%	2.9%	3.0%
35–39	4.4%	2.2%	2.2%
40–44	2.6%	1.4%	1.2%
45–49	3.8%	1.9%	1.9%
50–54	3.2%	1.6%	1.6%
55–59	3.0%	1.5%	1.5%
60–64	2.1%	0.9%	1.2%
65–69	1.4%	0.5%	0.9%
70–	2.9%	1.1%	1.8%

Male/Female ratio: 49.5% male/50.5% female
Rural/Urban population: 68.6% rural/31.4% urban
Growth over time, 1979–91: 41.0%
Population density: 97.0 persons/sq mi

Politics/Government

Date of independence declaration:
9 September 1991
Urban centers and populations:

Dushanbe	595,000
Khujand (Leninabad)	160,000
Khorugh	14,000
Murgab	<100,000
Kŭlob	77,000
Qŭrghonteppa (Kurgan-Tiube)	59,000
Kalaikhum	<100,000

Autonomous areas:

Badakhshoni Kŭhi	Khorugh
(Gorno-Badakshan)	(capital)

Education

Level of education for people over 15:

completed higher education:	7.5%
completed secondary education:	55.1%
incomplete secondary education:	21.1%

Number of higher education institutions: 10
(68,800 students)
Major institutions of higher education and enrollment:
Dushanbe

Tajik State University	12,628
Tajik Agricultural Institute	6,960

Socioeconomic Indicators

Birthrate: 38.8/1,000
Infant mortality: 40.7/1,000 live births
Average life expectancy: 69.6 (male 67.0/female 72.1)
Average family size: 6.1
Hospital beds per 10,000 persons: 105.8
Production of electrical energy: 3,378 kwh/person
Length of rail lines: 298 mi
Length of highways: 18,538 mi

---

* These figures do not reflect the exodus of much of the European population during the civil war beginning in 1992.

Physical/Territorial/Geopolitical Features

    Area: 55,251 sq mi (.7 percent of USSR total)
    Land use:
    Cultivated   6%
    Pasture   23%
    Highest elevation: 24,590 ft. (Communism Peak, in the Pamir Range)
    Rainfall: up to 63 inches/year in the mountains, 6 elsewhere

Temperature: average in winter, 28–36° F. Average in summer, 86° F; highest temperature: 118° F.
Principal products: cotton, wheat, vegetables, dairy products, goats, hydroelectric power, sheep and cattle, aluminum, lead, zinc, tungsten, tin, chemicals, machinery, cement, textiles, carpets, natural gas
Per capita GNP (1991): $1,050.

Sources

Narodnoe khoziaistvo SSSR v 1990g. (Moscow, 1991); *Naselenie SSSR* (1989); Matthew J. Sagers, "News Notes. Iron and Steel," *Soviet Geography* 30 (May 1989): 397–434; Lee Schwartz, "USSR Nationality Redistribution by Republic, 1979–1989: From Published Results of the 1989 All-Union Census," *Soviet Geography* 32 (April 1991): 209–48; "Tadzhikskaia sovetskaia sotsialisticheskaia respublika" *Bol'shaia Sovetskaia Entsiklopediia* 25 (Moscow, 1977): 169–97; and *World of Learning,* 43rd ed. (London: Europa Publications Limited, 1993); "Russia. . ." (National Geographic Society Map, March 1993).

History and Description

Topography

Tajikistan, known for its rugged and beautiful mountainous terrain, is situated in the southeasternmost part of Central Asia. Bordered on the north and west by the former Soviet republics of Kyrgyzstan and Uzbekistan, the Tajiks share a southern frontier with Afghanistan and a disputed eastern boundary with China. Tajikistan has an extremely unusual shape along its northern border where a long strip of its territory extends like a finger into Uzbekistan to include part of the fertile Farghona (Fergana) Valley. The smallest of the Central Asian countries, Tajikistan (55,251 square miles) is approximately the size of Wisconsin.

The majestic high peaks of the Pamir Mountains, the "roof of the world," dominate the landscape of the eastern half of Tajikistan. The Pamirs boast the highest point not only in Tajikistan but in the whole of the former Soviet Union. This summit, Communism Peak, stands 24,585 feet high. Other mountain systems, the Pamir-Alay, the Trans-Alay, and the Tian Shan fan out into western Tajikistan. Over 90 percent of the country is mountainous including the autonomous oblast of Badakhshoni Kŭhi.

Most of the rivers of Tajikistan feed into the drainage system of the Amu Darya, whose headwaters arise in the Pamirs. The Amu Darya, one of two major rivers of Central Asia, flows westward through Tajikistan until it becomes the boundary between Uzbekistan and Turkmenistan, eventually emptying into the depleted Aral Sea. The Syr Darya River, the other major Central Asian river, flows through the Farghona Valley in northern Tajikistan. The Zeravshan River follows a westward path through central Tajikistan.

The climate of Tajikistan varies greatly. The alpine areas feature wintry temperatures and snow, while the river valleys can be either hot and desertlike or moderate and pleasant, depending on altitude and the shifting patterns of wind and weather.

Tajikistan contains rich stores of various minerals, as well as uranium and several other kinds of ore. It is an important exporter of cotton, grown mainly in the Farghona Valley but also in the Gissar Valley where the capital city Dushanbe is located. Grain and fruit are grown in the valleys. Livestock, especially sheep and cattle, are raised on the hillsides of Tajikistan. The yak is the traditional helper of the farmer or shepherd.

Tajikistan

UZBEKISTAN

★ Toshkent

Syr

Darya

River

Farghona   Valley

Khujand

Tian

Zeravshan   River

Shan   Mountains

Pamir-Alay

24,590 ft. ╀   Mountains

Badakhshoni

Lake
Karakul

KYRGYZSTAN

CHINA

Dushanbe ★
Gissar
Valley

Nurek

Kalaikhum

Kafirnigan River

Vakhsh River

Kŭlob

Qŭrghonteppa

Pyandzh River

Murgab

Pamir
Mountains

Kŭhi

★ Khorugh

Amu Darya
River

AFGHANISTAN

	National Boundary
	Autonomous Boundary
★	Capital City
•	Other Cities

0   75 Miles

0   75 Kilometers

Ethnic and Historical Background

Tajiks, who may be the oldest inhabitants of Central Asia, derive ethnically from an Iranian background. This means that, in contrast to most of the other peoples in the region whose languages come from Turkic roots, spoken Tajik is close to modern Persian. Linguistically, Tajik belongs to the western Iranian group of Indo-European languages. Although several distinct dialects of Tajik exist, the variant spoken amongst the Tajiks of Samarqand and Bukhoro (both cities inside the borders of neighboring Uzbekistan) has provided the foundation for the modern Tajik literary language. Tajik was originally written in the Arabic alphabet, its first works dating from the great Arabic civilizations of Bukhara (Bukhoro) during the ninth and tenth centuries.

Tajiks customarily have been viewed as the settled or stationary people of Central Asia, as opposed to the nomadic or wandering groups. Archeological evidence shows that the forerunners of the Tajiks have inhabited the areas along the Amu Darya River valley, as well as similar areas along the Zeravshan River and the Syr Darya in the Farghona Valley, since the first or second millenium B.C. The sedentary Tajiks were the farmers and cultivators of this land. By the time the Arabs conquered these regions in the seventh and eighth centuries A.D., the movement of Turkic-speaking nomads into the area had already begun to complicate the ethnic mixture of people there.

The Samanid dynasty that arose in the ninth and tenth centuries, with Bukhara as its capital, emerged as a great center of Arabic learning. The Tajiks are among the legitimate inheritors of this Arab civilization and literature inasmuch as the development of the Tajik language dates from that time.

Later in the tenth and early eleventh centuries, as waves of Mongol invaders began to spread across Central Asia, the prevailing language of the ruling Turkic dynasties became Persian. By the fifteenth century, the settled peoples of Central Asia, while using both the Persian and Turkic languages, came to draw upon a similar cultural heritage. The distinction between specific Tajik or Uzbek nations appears to date from a later period. In fact, all settled people in the region were referred to by the term "Sart," whether they spoke a Persian or Turkic dialect. The term Sart simply served to distinguish the town dwellers from the more nomadic, generally Turkic, peoples of the area. The bilingualism that developed during that period still prevails among some urban dwellers of present-day Tajikistan and Uzbekistan, leading occasionally to rival Tajik and Uzbek claims of ethnic domination in border areas.

From Arab civilization the future Tajiks also inherited the religion of Islam, the dominant religion of Central Asia. Despite the linguistic ties with modern Iran, the Muslim communities of Tajikistan are primarily Sunni, in contrast to the more fundamentalist Shi'ite Muslim presence in Iran. Despite the official state atheism of the Soviet period, virtually all Tajiks, and over 90 percent of the entire population of Tajikistan, have roots in Islamic tradition. The contemporary revival of Islam in Tajikistan is addressed later in this chapter.

Russian Conquest and Soviet Rule

Russian conquest of the area of Tajikistan dates from the nineteenth century. By 1867, Russian Turkestan, made up of most of the land eventually known as Central Asia, had been established. Many Tajik settlements, however, continued to find protection under the independent Muslim khanates that resisted the Russian advances. The khanate of Bukhara, for example, included Tajik centers within its domain during part of this time. By 1918, in the aftermath of the Bolshevik Revolution, the Red Army had gained control of most of what is now Tajikistan. The newly named Turkestan Republic, direct descendant of Russian Turkestan, was declared in April. Composed of Tajiks, Uzbeks, Kazakhs, and other primarily Muslim ethnic groups, it was organized as an autonomous republic within the larger Russian Republic. By the fall of 1920, in spite of occasional outbreaks by local armed Islamic rebel groups, or Basmachi, most remaining resistance to the Bolsheviks had been quelled, and the whole of Central Asia was brought together under Soviet domination.

In October 1924, Tajikistan was reorganized and designated an autonomous republic attached to Uzbekistan. Five years later, on 5 October 1929, having received approval from Moscow, it was granted its own status as a full union republic and no longer lived under the shadow of the Uzbeks. The division and redistribution of Tajiks in this new republic was not ideal. Some Tajik settlements, both along the Uzbek-Tajik border and within the most important old historical centers such as Bukhara, Samarqand, and Toshkent (Tashkent) remained in the hands of Uzbekistan. The population, however, was apparently pacified to the satisfaction of the authorities, although local resistance to the Sovietization of Tajikistan was not entirely stamped out until the late 1930s.

In spite of the national delimitation policy of the Russian authorities, a policy that assigned national groups to particular homelands, large groups of Tajiks still resided outside the borders of Tajikistan in other newly formed republics. Many Tajiks found themselves in Uzbekistan, a lesser number in Kyrgyzstan and in the other Central Asian republics. There were also more than a million Tajiks living outside the borders of the Soviet Union in Afghanistan, in China, and in the area that later became Pakistan.

Within Tajikistan itself, there remained many Uzbeks, Kyrgyz, Kazakhs, Turks, and other Muslims who ideally should have found themselves and their villages located inside the borders of their own newly established Central Asian republics. Alongside those peoples who had achieved their own republics, many other smaller ethnic groups remained in Tajikistan. The Pamiri people, the Mountain Tajiks, the Yagnobis, the Chagatais (Turkic), and the Harduris constituted the main groups. Almost without exception they are Muslim but have a language or cultural tradition different from the Tajiks.

After being incorporated into the Soviet Union, the Tajiks were eventually encouraged to develop their own sense of nationhood, albeit without reference to religion. A sense of resentment of Uzbek domination evolved as the Tajiks compared the privileges accorded Uzbeks in the cultural and economic sphere. As a part of this growing sense of Tajik nationhood, the Tajiks also came to appreciate the Persian roots of their language and the implications such a tradition implied in their relationship with Afghans and Iranians.

Soviet Leadership

In the twenties, Soviet authorities encouraged native peoples to become active in the Communist Party in order to bring effective management and organization to the young republic. Initial directives from the government announced guidelines for the nationalization of natural resources, new water and land distribution programs, the emancipation of women, and free education for all citizens. These decrees, however, were not pursued until the rebellious Basmachi movement was wiped out. The pacification process became especially difficult because of the perceived threat both to Islam and to the traditional ways of life that the new decrees represented. Nevertheless, in spite of tremendous difficulties in communication between the Tajiks, who could not speak Russian, and the Russians, who were unable to express themselves in Tajik, local Tajiks eventually came to fill many local Party committees and other administrative posts.

The collectivization of agriculture (see glossary), was not achieved until the 1930s because of the violent objections of local Tajiks, many of whom now spoke from within the Communist Party itself. The disagreements on collectivization led to the purging of two local Party leaders, Nasratullah Maksum and Abdurakhim Khojibaev, both ethnic Tajiks. A series of purges then followed, the most extensive of which occurred in early 1934. As many as ten thousand victims may have perished during that time. The Party lay in ruins, decimated by the excesses of Stalin's paranoid policy. By 1937 a Russian, Dmitrii Protopopov, had been appointed first secretary and many other Russians were brought in to staff lower level positions.

Tajikistan was now and would be for many years under a more direct control from Moscow. Protopopov stayed on as first secretary until 1945. He was followed by a Stalinist Tajik, Bobojan Gafurov, who held the post from 1945 until 1956. The post-Stalinist era was not notable for outstanding reformers in the office of first secretary. Tursunbai Uljabaev, also a Tajik, was removed for corruption and abuse of power in 1961. Subsequent first secretaries, Jabar Rasulov and Rakhman Nabiev, retained the Tajik presence in the office, but did little to reform Party politics.

Contemporary Issues

Standard of Living

Tajikistan is arguably the poorest country in Central Asia. It has the highest birthrate of any former Soviet republic. Since 1959, the population of Tajikistan has increased by over 3 percent per year, a rate approximately three times higher than the previous Soviet average and higher than that of most other developing nations of the world. Between 1959 and 1979, the population of Tajikistan increased by over 100 percent. This rapid population increase has been reflected in chronic rural overpopulation and consequent high unemployment. Even before the destabilizing political events of the past three years, rural unemployment figures often exceeded 25 percent of the able-bodied work force.

To address the problems of rural overpopulation and poverty, directives were frequently sent from Moscow in the 1980s encouraging the development of labor resources in urban centers. Yet, as local Tajik leaders would occasionally lament, the absence of Soviet state investment in Tajikistan meant that migration to urban centers only had the effect of transferring rural poverty into urban poverty. Soviet state investment in Tajikistan ranked among the lowest per capita for any republic. One result was that, as of the 1989 census, two-thirds of the inhabitants of Tajikistan remained in small, underdeveloped rural villages.

Predictably, efforts to address this relative underdevelopment by antinatalist campaigns—Soviet-directed and Tajik-implemented governmental campaigns to persuade women to have fewer children—failed from the start. Such campaigns, occasionally launched also in Uzbekistan, were invariably seen as antinational drives directed against Asians by Moscow. The perception that these were selective, differentiated efforts aimed at Central Asians was fueled by the reality that in other parts of the Soviet Union, as in European Russia, public policy occasionally was openly pronatalist.

Alongside the health and welfare needs of a poor population, one of the features of Tajikistan's poverty is its weak infrastructure. Because the country is dependent upon water from surrounding mountain streams, dams have been built for water storage. But some of these dams are of uncertain quality, having been constructed in an area split by seismic fault lines. In March 1987, a landslide set off by heavy rainfall in the Külob region led to the collapse of a dam holding back three million cubic meters of water. The ensuing flood killed 36 people, leaving another 500 homeless. Such disasters have raised grave concerns about the status of other public works projects. The largest dam in all of Central Asia, the Nurek, lies just east of the capital Dushanbe.

The Cotton Monoculture

By the 1980s, Tajikistan came to be the third largest cotton producing republic of the Soviet Union. Cotton production averaged over 900,000 tons annually. Although that was only about a tenth of the total annual production of cotton (9 million tons) in the former Soviet Union, Tajik cotton is the more desirable "long-staple" variety. Given the limited amount of arable land in Tajikistan, the high production figures for cotton demonstrate that, as in the case of Uzbekistan (see pages 173–174), a cotton monoculture has developed with marketing ties through Moscow. Tajikistan has become so dependent upon its cotton production that school children and urban workers have been routinely diverted into the fields to assist with harvests. The need for harvest labor, despite unemployment in rural Tajikistan, reflects the underproductivity and lack of technology in this predominantly rural country.

Efforts to diversify the Tajik economy have depended upon the development of urban manufacturing and the exploitation of the country's mineral reserves. As is the case elsewhere in Central Asia, Tajikistan has substantial mineral deposits, including uranium. In early 1992, U.S. Secretary of State James Baker visited Dushanbe, seeking assurances that Tajikistan would not provide weapons-grade uranium to any Asian neighbors who might be seeking to develop nuclear capability. Despite promises provided then to the secretary of state, Tajik leaders face the central problem of how best to generate economic growth, encourage foreign investment, and secure international markets.

Ecological and Environmental Issues

The question of water is for Tajikistan, as for other Central Asian countries, a critical issue. The heavy cultivation of water-intensive crops such as cotton only makes the problem of water shortage more acute. The occasionally conflicting interests of economic development and environmental concern have also been a part of the discussion over water in Tajikistan. In one of the first open debates of its kind over water usage, the informal Tajik group Ashkara (Openness) spearheaded opposition to state plans for the building of a large hydroelectric plant on the river Vakhsh. In a partial concession to environmental concerns, the state announced in 1989 that it would reduce the projected height of the dam by one third.

While environmental issues have occasionally spawned conflict with industrial and economic development, environmental and energy concerns have also added to ethnic and regional rivalries in Central Asia. During the winters of 1990-91 and 1991-92, Tajikistan was forced to limit its central heating in major urban centers, often reducing dramatically the use of electricity in factories as well. In their explanation for the energy crises, Tajik officials blamed Uzbekistan for failing to provide power from its power stations. Such rivalries over energy have thus added fuel to environmental and ethnic conflicts.

Occasionally, environmental issues have required official resolution by Uzbekistan and Tajikistan officials. In the case of a large Tajik aluminum plant near the Uzbek border, complaints by Uzbeks over water and air pollution led in 1991 to formal cooperative resolutions by the deputies of both the Tajik and Uzbek Supreme Soviets (their parliamentary bodies). Under the joint resolutions, the Tajik plant agreed to stop the operation of 100 electrolysis units at the plant during the summer of 1991, despite the fact that aluminum production figures significantly in the Tajik industrialization effort. Complicating this agreement has been Uzbekistan's demand for 30 million rubles in damages. Such ethnic rivalries make environmental problems all the more crisis prone and difficult to solve.

Ethnic Disputes

Ethnic conflict, including the tensions between transplanted European Slavs and the indigenous Islamic peoples, may be found in each of the Central Asian countries. In the case of Tajikistan, there are two features that make this ethnic rivalry particularly intense. First of all, the majority Tajik nationality does not share with the rest of Central Asia a common Turkic linguistic and racial inheritance. As mentioned earlier, spoken Tajik is a Persian (Iranian) language, markedly different from the Turkic languages spoken by most other people of Central Asia. The result is that, while the Tajiks share a common Islamic religious identity with their Central Asian neighbors, they are less likely to be drawn into a pan-Turkic alliance, or a greater Turkic confederation such as the Turkestan that existed prior to the creation of the separate Central Asian Soviet republics in the 1920s.

An equally important feature of ethnic rivalry for the Tajiks is that a disproportionately large part of the Tajik population resides outside the present Tajik borders.

Over 900,000 Tajiks reside in Uzbekistan and are concentrated in the adjacent Bukhoro oblast, particularly in the ancient cities of Samarqand and Bukhoro. Similarly, over three million ethnic Tajiks reside in Afghanistan. As long as the political authority of the Soviet Union prevailed, the diffusion of Tajiks outside Tajikistan did not pose a significant problem. Official Soviet Tajik ideology, as reflected in the publications of Bobojan Gafurov, (Communist Party first secretary from 1945 to 1956, and subsequent director of the Academy of Sciences Institute of Oriental Studies), held that the Russian annexation of Central Asia in the nineteenth century was a progressive development. Gafurov and offical Soviet Tajik ideology advocated use of Russian for all Tajiks, including those Tajiks living in Afghanistan. This ideology had the effect of masking interethnic rivalry, while at the same time offering a defense for such actions as the Soviet intervention in Afghanistan in late 1979. As elsewhere, the passing of Soviet imperial power eliminated ideological defenses and reopened a series of old ethnic disputes for the Tajik people.

The most serious of these ethnic disputes is with the Uzbeks. Ever beneath the surface, the conflict with Uzbekistan broke out in 1988 when the secretary of the Tajik Writers' Union, Loiq Sherali, complained of Uzbek intellectual imperialism. Referring to Uzbek writings, Sherali noted the "national arrogance of several of our Turkic-speaking colleagues." (Sherali is quoted in Annette Bohr, "Secretary of Tajik Writers' Union Voices Resentment," *Radio Liberty Research Bulletin* [RLRB], 17 March 1988.) For Sherali, the problem was that Uzbek writers were trying to establish ethnic origins by building their own early national history upon writers who, though they may have lived in Bukhara, wrote in Persian (the case of Ibn Sina or Avicenna, 980–1031). Sherali complained similarly about Uzbek claims on behalf of what he said were "Persian-Turkic" poets from the eleventh to sixteenth centuries who lived well beyond Uzbek borders in present-day Afghanistan.

While the ability to voice such resentments openly marked the early stages of intellectual glasnost in Tajikistan, the Soviet Tajik authorities were understandably wary of opening the door too wide. In January 1988, editor Khojaev of the Tajik-language Party newspaper, *Komsomoli Tochikiston*, was dismissed for publishing articles that, according to the charge, "wittingly or unwittingly aroused aspiration to national exclusivity and parochialism and undermined the basis of traditional friendship between the peoples of neighboring republics" (quoted in Bess Brown, "Limits to Glasnost' in Tajikistan," *RLRB*, 11 April 1988). By August 1988, however, in debates over the Armenian-Azerbaijani conflict in Nagorno-Karabakh before the Supreme Soviet in Moscow, Mikhail Gorbachev specifically referred to the conflicting Tajik-Uzbek claims, fearing a potential domino effect should property be allowed to be transferred from one republic to another. He was referring to the Tajik claim that 20 percent of the Tajik nation that resided in and around the historic city of Samarqand in Uzbekistan had been unfairly excised from the Tajik republic. In short, what was being challenged was the very drawing of the Soviet-designed ethnic boundaries created in 1924. For Moscow, and for Moscow loyalists in Dushanbe, such challenges were potentially dangerous.

In the case of the Tajik-Uzbek dispute, as in other such disputes throughout the former Soviet Union, the claims function in more than one direction. For just as the Tajiks can speak on behalf of their Tajik compatriots in Uzbekistan, the Uzbeks can cite the situation of over one million Uzbeks living in Tajikistan. These disputes, which continue to produce intense interethnic friction, have since 1988 become the subject of occasional meetings between visiting delegations of Tajik and Uzbek leaders. The issue of the large Tajik aluminum plant near the Uzbekistan border discussed earlier became part of this simmering rivalry.

Just as the Tajiks have been concerned about the fate of their compatriots in Uzbekistan, so have parallel concerns been raised about the Pamiri peoples of Badakhshoni Kŭhi. Tajiks claim that the Pamiri, numbering 100,000 or more, are, in fact, Tajiks (a claim not unlike that made by the Uzbeks about Tajiks in Uzbekistan). The Pamiris, however, appear to have a language that is separate and distinct from Tajik, deriving from an East Iranian linguistic grouping, while Tajik derives from a West Iranian grouping. While claims continue to be made that the Tajiks are denying the Pamiri people their right to self-determination—indeed the census returns of 1989 lump the Pamiris with the Tajiks—it is difficult to judge the question in the absence of appeals from the Pamiris themselves.

A measure of how disruptive ethnic conflict can be for Tajikistan is the fate of the Russian and Ukrainian population, largely concentrated in the capital city Dushanbe. This transplanted European Slavic population has become increasingly uneasy, not because of overt ethnic hostility from the Tajiks—although such hostility has existed in all the newly independent Central Asian states—but rather because of fears that Tajikistan is destined to become an Islamic state. Although these fears may be quite unfounded, the result has been an unprecedented exodus of Slavic and Jewish population from Dushanbe since 1990. Estimates are that the Russian refugee population from Tajikistan alone reached over 50,000 in 1992. The human drama of this large refugee exodus, occurring in other parts of Central Asia as well, carries with it a substantial cost, for the Russian population in Tajikistan is disproportionately represented among the technical, medical, and civil service elite. These European Slavs of Tajikistan, like their counterparts in other urban centers of Central Asia, are not easily replaced.

Islam in Tajikistan

The 1980s were marked by a resurgence of Islamic loyalties within the officially atheist Tajik Soviet Republic. The recovery of Islamic religious identity was not unique to Tajikistan. As elsewhere, traditional Muslim practices remained strongest in the rural, small village setting. The somewhat more surprising presence of unofficial Islamic leadership in larger urban centers, however, posed special problems for the state authorities. In 1986, for example, the arrest of an unregistered mullah, Abdulla Saidov, in Qŭrghonteppa, a large city near the Afghan border, led to public demonstrations in which some local Communist Party members and intellectuals joined. The termination of Abdulla Saidov's activities as a mullah may have been related to mystical Wahhabi or other exotic non-Sunni Muslim practices, or to his popularity and the size of his following, or to the strategic location of Qŭrghonteppa, near the Soviet-Afghan frontier, or perhaps to some combination of these factors. Nevertheless, the rally of the mullah's supporters seems to have caught the state authorities off-guard.

The spread of such popular religious sentiment, including the presence of Wahhabi and other unregistered clerical leaders, led to numerous state directives in 1987 and 1988 seeking to reenergize antireligious forces. Ironically, at a time when the early signs of glasnost in Moscow included friendly overtures toward the Russian Orthodox church, Tajik officials in Dushanbe, led by Communist Party First Secretary Kakhar Makhkamov, saw no conflict between support for Gorbachev's glasnost and an intensified crackdown upon unofficial and unauthorized Islamic movements.

By 1988, Tajik newspapers carried open reports of an unofficial, underground religious press in the republic. One such press, operating from the printshop of the Dushanbe Pedagogical Institute, had been turning out copies of an Islamic newspaper, *Islamskaia Pravda* (Islamic Truth), photocopies of speeches by the Ayatollah Khomeini and Pakistan leader Mandudi, as well as republications of works of a prominent theorist of Islamic revival, Jamal al-Din al-Afghani. (See Bess Brown's report, "Description of Religious *Samizdat* in Tajikistan," *RLRB*, 23 May 1988.)

By 1990, an informal political group with alliances throughout the other Islamic republics of the former Soviet Union, the Islamic Renaissance Party, was firmly established in Tajikistan, despite the efforts of governmental officials to ban it. In December 1990, the Tajik Supreme Soviet outlawed the Islamic party from Tajik territory, specifically forbidding the establishment of informal parties of a religious nature. Kakhar Makhkamov, by then the Tajik president, steadfastly sought to identify the Islamic Renaissance Party with extremist fundamentalists and Wahhabis. The Islamic Renaissance Party in Tajikistan, however, has tended, as elsewhere, to appeal to the intelligentsia, avoiding religious extremes and rather seeking to identify Islam as an integral part of Tajik culture. Because of the appeal of democratic ideals to the Tajik intelligentsia, the Islamic Renaissance Party has also tended to bridge what some see as the potentially conflicting ideals of Islam and democracy. Unlike the pronounced anti-Western and antimodernist perspectives of Islamic fundamentalists and Wahhabis, especially with matters involving the rights of women, the Islamic Renaissance Party has tended to be more urban and moderate in its views. By openly charging that the Islamic Renaissance Party frightened the non-Tajik, Slavic population into leaving the republic, the Communist leadership may indirectly have advanced the process they sought to limit in their ban of this increasingly popular Islamic movement.

Political Unrest and Civil War

The central political dynamic in Tajikistan, as in other former Soviet republics, is the destabilizing process of the dissolution of old Soviet-style, Communist Party leadership. In Tajikistan this process has been advanced by the rise of informal as well as formal political parties. The political transformation has unfortunately been accompanied by violence and tragic loss of life.

For the past decade, from 1982 until 1992, leadership of the Tajik Soviet Socialist Republic has been dominated by two Communist Party first secretaries, Rakhman Nabiev (1982–85, 1991–92) and Kakhar Makhkamov (1985–91). While Makhkamov officially embraced the reformist, modernizing lead of Moscow's perestroika, he was unprepared to oversee the dissolution of Soviet power. Despite his occasional admonitions to the bureaucracy, including criticism of the performance of the head of the Tajik KGB, Vladimir Petkel, Makhkamov became a dutiful republican leader in the wider Soviet bureaucracy and Communist Party. His efforts to maximize cotton production increasingly came to be viewed by Tajiks as part of the process of Soviet colonial exploitation, an exploitation made worse by the manner in which it tended to deform the Tajik economy into a cotton monoculture.

February 1990 Riots. In February 1990, the accelerating economic, ethnic, and religious conflicts within the republic triggered an outbreak of violence in Dushanbe that left over twenty dead, hundreds wounded, and untold damages to housing and public buildings. The demonstrations appear to have begun over rumors that Armenian refugees from Azerbaijan were arriving in Dushanbe and would be given housing priority. Because of the demand for apartments in the capital and the reality that Armenians actually were being sent to Tajikistan, there was some substance behind the concerns of those protesting. Ultimately, the demonstrators became menacing, throwing rocks at policemen, engaging in looting and theft, and threatening non-Tajik citizens of the republic.

In an ominous replay of the violence in the Georgian capital of Tbilisi in the spring of 1989 (see pages 114–16), forces from Moscow were brought in to help quell the uprising, and order was restored albeit after tragic loss of life. In the Tajik case, the republican leadership specifically sought such assistance, fearing the demands of the protestors who called for the resignation of all republican leaders and the redirection of profits secured from Tajik cotton production.

In retrospect, the events of February 1990 and the rise of informal political groups prior to, during, and after the uprising marked a turning point in the politics of Tajikistan. The February 1990 uprising galvanized the popularity of the republic's informal political opposition. Among the groups who played a role in the 1990 events were the Rastokhez (Renewal), a Tajik popular front group formed in the fall of 1989 with goals similar, if perhaps more modest, to those of the popular fronts in the

Baltic and Ukraine. Leaders of Rastokhez were selected by the demonstrators outside Communist Party headquarters to negotiate the protestors' demands. When appeals for calm were ultimately made over television, Rastokhez representatives were among those appearing before viewers.

The riots of February 1990 also reflected the failure of the republican leadership to satisfy the basic social and economic needs of the population. Even official Party representatives had to concede that as many as 70,000 inhabitants of Dushanbe were unemployed, and rural underemployment was potentially even more serious. Despite Makhkamov's promises for new public housing projects and better health care, his dominant message was that of the need to crack down on those opposition groups responsible for the February uprising. Part of the reason for Makhkamov's hardline message was his concern for the mounting emigration of non-Tajiks from Tajikistan. Such out-migration, especially by ethnic Russians and Ukrainians, had already been triggered by the 1989 law declaring Tajik to be the state language of the republic. But the February riots, and the efforts of some fundamentalist Islamic forces to capitalize upon such events for a more general antiforeigner appeal, sped the outflow of thousands of professionals, medical personnel, and skilled urban workers.

Makhkamov's message of political crackdown was curiously balanced by his openly avowed support for the liberal, reformist objectives of Boris Yeltsin in Moscow. On 24 August 1990 the Tajik Supreme Soviet with Makhkamov's support declared the republican sovereignty of Tajikistan. So as not to escalate further the emigration of non-Tajiks, the sovereignty declaration specifically identified all nationalities as equal in Tajikistan.

For the opposition, the period following the February events was marked by ever more open political organization. In August 1990, the Democratic Party of Tajikistan, a party of liberal intellectuals, held its initial congress. Moreover, even though the Rastokhez and Islamic Renaissance parties were forbidden to organize in Tajikistan, their support also was reinforced.

Moscow Coup. Ultimately, the opposition between informal political groups and the Makhkamov government came to a showdown in the wake of the abortive *coup d'état* in Moscow in August 1991. The effort by hardline Communist officials to depose Mikhail Gorbachev in Moscow had ripple effects throughout all of the Soviet republics. In the case of Tajikistan, this effect was made more dramatic by the apparent support for the coup plotters offered by Makhkamov in the early hours of the Moscow crisis. Despite Makhkamov's subsequent ban upon Communist Party operations in the government, the Tajik Supreme Soviet faced demands from demonstrators for the resignation of the republic's leadership. On 31 August 1991, the Supreme Soviet accepted the resignation of Makhkamov. Following a month of bitter conflict between the government and opposition forces, elections were called for November 1991, and all parties were allowed open participation in the process. The Tajik Supreme Soviet declared the formal independence of Tajikistan on 9 September 1991.

The November 1991 elections brought little resolution to the political situation in Tajikistan. According to the official election returns, monitored in part by outside observers, the chair of the Tajik Supreme Soviet and former Communist Party First Secretary Rakhman Nabiev received 58 percent of the votes cast. Davlat Khudonazarov, chair of the local cinema workers' union and candidate of both the Democratic and Islamic parties, received only slightly more than 25 percent of the vote. More than 80 percent of the electorate voted. The results marked a surprising recovery by the Tajik Communist Party, renamed the Tajik Socialist Party. Charges of election fraud, however, haunted the victors. Khudonazarov accused the republic's leadership of falsifying the results and offered photographic evidence to back up his charge of election irregularities.

Civil War. In May 1992, President Rakhman Nabiev sought to coopt the support of regional and nationalist parties by assigning a third of the ministerial posts to their representatives. This "Government of National Reconciliation" quickly was challenged by Nabiev's own conservative supporters from the region around Kŭlob. Amidst mutual recriminations, the conservative anti-Islamic loyalists from Dushanbe and the Kŭlob region began to arm themselves, as did their anti-communist coalition opponents.

The civil war that followed from late May to December 1992 can be compared to some of the worst fighting in former Yugoslavia (Bosnia-Herzegovina) during the same time period. Supporters of the old communist regime claimed that the oppositionist democratic and Islamic coalition—including strong support from the Pamiri region of Badakshoni Kŭhi—was being armed by the Afghan resistance. Both sides claimed that the other was benefitting from materiel provided by Russian forces outside Dushanbe and at the Tajik-Afghan border. In the end, as many as 70,000 were killed in the sporadic fighting, as hundreds of thousands became wartime refugees. The cost to the Tajik economy was devastating. European Slavs fled Dushanbe in numbers that have yet to be fully calculated, while Tajik oppositionists fled in the thousands across the Afghan border.

In September 1992, midway through the fighting, President Nabiev, who would die of natural causes in 1993, was forced by the opposition to resign. The resignation of Nabiev left unclear who was in control of the Tajik government. The democratic and Islamic parties, despite their growing influence, never assumed full authority. In October, pro-communist forces loyal to the old regime temporarily seized parts of Dushanbe, but Russian forces deployed in the capital initially kept the communist loyalists from retaking the government by force. By November, however, the pro-communist forces operating from their base of strength near Kŭlob retook Dushanbe and secured the resignation of the interim government.

In the reestablishment of the old regime, the Tajik Supreme Soviet, the parliamentary body still dominated by former Communists, played the central role. They abolished the office of the presidency and granted executive powers to the chairman of the Supreme Soviet, Imomali Rakhmonov. In the months that followed in 1993, the new conservative pro-communist Tajik government launched a crackdown on nationalist, democratic, and Islamic parties, outlawing virtually all such opposition and replacing media and other institutional leaders deemed sympathetic to the anti-communist forces.

While the Rakhmonov regime has put its authoritarian stamp upon Dushanbe and most other adjoining regions, considerable residual loyalty to the anti-government Islamic forces remains in outlying regions. This situation is particularly true in the easterly Pamiri lands of Badakshoni Kŭhi, but such loyalty also remains beneath the surface in the former center of oppositionist forces near Qŭrghonteppa. Deep-seated regional divisions over land and power drove the civil war and continue to be a fundamental source of volatility in contemporary Tajik politics.

In offsetting these regional divisions the conservative Tajik government has sought to label all outposts of resistance as dangerous pockets of Islamic fundamentalism, a charge that is exaggerated. In the crackdown on opposition groups, the Islamic Renaissance Party and the democratic Rastokhez movement have been outlawed along with all other informal parties that operated more or less openly in 1991–92. While seeking to reestablish full centralized control over Tajikistan, the authoritarian government has at the same time attempted to rebuild its ties with other governments of Central Asia. Many of these newly independent states, such as neighboring Uzbekistan, welcome the silencing of democratic and Islamic informal groups. For now, the post–civil war reassertion of authoritarian rule in Tajikistan reflects, on a wider scale, the fragility of democratic and popular movements throughout most of Central Asia.

International Alliances

The events in Tajikistan, as elsewhere in Central Asia, are not occurring in an international vacuum. While the United States has set up its own ambassadorial staff in Dushanbe and former Secretary of State Baker visited the capital in early 1992, other regional powers have also courted the Tajik government. The Iranian government has established its own presence in Dushanbe, even though the fundamentalism of Iranian Shi'ite Islam has made only limited headway in Tajikistan. The model of the modern, secular state of Turkey, an Islamic nation that has separated religion and the state, has occasionally been raised by Tajik and Western leaders, and Turkish representatives have visited Dushanbe. Moreover, Tajikistan's continuing market ties to Russia ought not entirely to be discounted, even as the Tajiks seek to establish diplomatic relations with their eastern neighbor, China. For Tajikistan, as for the rest of Central Asia, the international repercussions of the collapse of the Soviet Union continue to be played out amidst the ethnic and regional rivalries of this poorest of the former Soviet republics. Amidst such rivalries, the continued presence of Russian troops in Dushanbe and at critical international borders offers potential stability, even as it serves as a reminder of the continuities in Tajikistan before and after Soviet rule.

TURKMENISTAN

Statistical Profile

Demography

Population: 3,523,000
Ethnic population:

Turkmen	2,537,000	72.0%
Russian	334,000	9.5%
Uzbek	317,000	9.0%
Kazakh	88,000	2.5%
Tatar	39,000	1.1%
Ukrainian	36,000	1.0%
Azerbaijani	33,000	0.9%
Armenian	32,000	0.9%
Other	107,000	3.1%

Predominant religious traditions:

Islam	88.5%
Christianity	11.4%

Population by age:

Age	Total	Males	Females
0–4	15.6%	7.9%	7.7%
5–9	13.0%	6.5%	6.5%
10–14	11.8%	5.9%	5.9%
15–19	10.5%	5.3%	5.2%
20–24	9.6%	4.9%	4.7%
25–29	8.7%	4.3%	4.4%
30–34	6.7%	3.3%	3.4%
35–39	5.0%	2.5%	2.5%
40–44	2.8%	1.4%	1.4%
45–49	4.0%	2.0%	2.0%
50–54	3.2%	1.6%	1.6%
55–59	3.0%	1.4%	1.6%
60–64	2.1%	0.8%	1.3%
65–69	1.4%	0.5%	0.9%
70–	2.6%	0.9%	1.7%

Male/Female ratio: 49.2% male/50.8% female
Rural/Urban population: 54.6% rural/45.4% urban
Growth over time, 1979-91: 34.6%
Population density: 19.7 persons/sq mi

Politics/Government

Date of independence declaration: 27 October 1991
Urban centers and populations:

Ashgabat (Ashkhabad)	398,000
Chärjew	161,000
Dashhowuz (Tashauz)	112,000
Gyzylarbat (Kyzyl-Arvat)	<100,000
Mary	94,000
Nebitdag	89,000
Krasnovodsk	55,000

Autonomous areas: none

Education

Level of education for persons over 15:

completed higher education	8.3%
completed secondary education	56.8%
incomplete secondary education	21.3%

Number of higher education institutions:
9 (41,800 students)
Major institutions of higher education and enrollment:
Ashgabat

Turkmen State University	11,000

Socioeconomic Indicators

Birthrate: 34.2/1,000
Infant mortality: 45.2/1,000 live births
Average life expectancy: 66.4 (males, 62.9; females, 69.7)
Average family size: 5.6
Hospital beds per 10,000 persons: 113.3
Production of electrical energy: 3,931 kwh/person
Length of rail lines: 1,314 mi
Length of highways: 14,260 mi

Physical/Territorial/Geopolitical Features

Area: 188,455 sq mi (2.2% of USSR total)

Land use:
Cultivated   2%
Pasture (including some desert lands)   70%
Highest elevation: 10,299 ft. (Kugitangtau Peak)
Rainfall: 4 inches/year, more than 16 in the
    mountains
Temperature: average in winter, 23° F in the
    northwest, 39° F in the south; lowest tempera-
ture: -26° F. Average in summer, 82° F in the
northwest, 90° F in the south; highest tempera-
ture: 122° F.
Principal products: cotton, grapes, grain, sheep,
    goats, salt, oil, gas, glass, textiles, silk, wool,
    carpets
Per capita GNP (1991): $1,700

Sources

Narodnoe khoziaistvo SSSR v 1990g. (Moscow, 1991); *Naselenie SSSR* (1989); Matthew J. Sagers, "News Notes.Iron and Steel," *Soviet Geography* 30 (May 1989): 397–434; Lee Schwartz, "USSR Nationality Redistribution by Republic, 1979–1989: From Published Results of the 1989 All-Union Census," *Soviet Geography* 32 (April 1991): 209–48; "Turkmenskaia sovetskaia sotsialisticheskaia respublika" *Bol'shaia Sovetskaia Entsiklopediia* 26 (Moscow, 1977): 341–67; *World of Learning,* 43rd ed. (London: Europa Publications Limited, 1993); "Russia. . . " (National Geographic Society Map, March 1993).

History and Description

Topography

Turkmenistan, fourth largest of the former Soviet republics, is located in the southwestern part of Central Asia. Somewhat larger than the state of California, Turkmenistan (188,455 square miles) is bordered on the north and northeast by the newly independent states of Kazakhstan and Uzbekistan, and on the south and southwest by the Islamic states of Iran and Afghanistan. Turkmenistan's western border follows the long coastline of the Caspian Sea stretching over 500 miles in length. The territory of Turkmenistan includes the unrelentingly arid expanse of desert known as the Kara Kum, one of the largest sand deserts in the world. Covering between 80 and 90 percent of Turkmenistan's land, the extensive Kara Kum has long been a barrier to nomadic Turkmen tribes inhabiting major oases located on the periphery of this inhospitable terrain. In addition to the predominantly desert habitat, two low mountain ranges in the south, the Kopet and the Paropamiz, enrich the bleak landscape of Turkmenistan.

Amu Darya. One of the driest regions in Central Asia, Turkmenistan boasts one major river, the Amu Darya. This river, however, is located on the edge of Turkmenistan in the northeastern part of the country and serves during much of its course as the border with neighboring Uzbekistan. Originating in the east among the mountains of Tajikistan, the Amu Darya travels across Turkmenistan in a northwesterly direction for over six hundred miles. The vitally important Kara Kum canal, built after World War II, diverts water from the Amu Darya to other parts of Turkmenistan as the canal proceeds five hundred miles to the west, reaching as far as the capital, Ashgabat (Ashkhabad). Other rivers, in particular the Murgab, Tedzhen, and a few smaller streams, flow into Turkmenistan from the mountainous borderlands shared with Iran and Afghanistan, often forming oases before evaporating on the desert floor. Thus, the sources of fresh water needed for the survival of Turkmen agriculture originate outside the country's borders.

Cities. Few large cities are found in Turkmenistan, and most towns are either related closely to existing river oases or situated near the Caspian Sea. The country's most populous city, the capital Ashgabat, was established by Russians as the fortification of Poltoratsk toward the end of the nineteenth century during tsarist colonial expansion into Central Asia. Ashgabat suffered a devastating earthquake in 1948, but it has since been partly rebuilt. Chärjew (Chardzhou), the second largest Turkmen city, is found on the Amu Darya river near the Uzbek border. Krasnovodsk, the chief port, lies on the

Turkmenistan

KAZAKHSTAN

KAZAKHSTAN

UZBEKISTAN

Dashhowuz

Khiva

Garabogazköl
Aylagy

K a r a

Krasnovodsk

Cheleken

Nebitdag

K u m

Gyzylarbat

D e s e r t

Chärjew

Amu

Darya

10,299 ft. +

Kerki

River

Caspian
Sea

Sumbar   *River*

Kopet Mountains

Ashgabat

Tedzhen

Mary

River

Murgab

Kara   *Kum*   *Canal*

River

IRAN

P a r o p a m i z

M o u n t a i n s

AFGHANISTAN

――――― National Boundary

★ Capital City

● Other Cities

0   200 Miles

0   200 Kilometers

eastern shore of the Caspian Sea on the industrialized Mangyshlak Peninsula.

Climate. The extremely arid climatic conditions of Turkmenistan are reflected in long, hot summers and brief winters. Farming is done in irrigated areas along the country's few rivers. The major crop is cotton, as it is throughout Central Asia. Turkmenistan is second only to Uzbekistan in the amount of cotton produced in the region. Fruits and vegetables are also grown, particularly grapes and grains. Turkmenistan is rich in several natural resources, most notably oil and gas, as well as sulphur and potassium. Extensive oil deposits are found on the Caspian peninsula of Cheleken near Krasnovodsk and inland a bit near the town of Nebitdag. Reserves of natural gas and mineral deposits exist in the area of Chärjew. Thanks to the riches of the Caspian Sea, Turkmenistan has developed a fishing industry. In addition, animal husbandry (mainly goats and Karakul sheep) and sericulture (silk-worm cultivation) occupy the Turkmen tribes. Traditionally, Turkmenistan has been one of the centers of the famous, centuries-old oriental rug-weaving industry.

Ethnic and Historical Background

The Turkmen people in the twentieth century tend to identify themselves primarily as members of a particular clan or tribe. According to Alexandre Bennigsen and S. Enders Wimbush (*Muslims of the Soviet Empire: A Guide*, London, 1985, p.98), Turkmen may be grouped into seven large and twenty-four small tribes. The seven major tribes are the Tekke in the central part of the country, the Ersary in the southeast, the Yomud in the west, the Goeklen in the southwest, the Salor in the east, the Saryk in the south, and the Chowdor in the north.

The Turkmen language belongs to the southwestern subgroup of Turkic languages and, thus, is more closely related to the language spoken by Azerbaijanis than to the languages spoken by other Central Asian peoples. A twentieth-century Turkmen literary language, based on the Tekke and Yomud dialects and written in a modified Cyrillic alphabet, was developed during the Soviet period. Works written in this new language, however, have yet to develop the authority still accorded classical eighteenth-century lyrics, verse, and other poetry. These earlier writings employed a compound Turkic (Chagatai) literary model and used the Arabic script.

Turkmen constitute the vast majority of the population of their country. Many Turkmen, however, are found elsewhere in Central Asia and the Middle East. Over one hundred thousand reside in other parts of the former Soviet Union, primarily in neighboring republics. One million or more live in Iran, Afghanistan, Iraq, and Turkey. Other national groups residing in Turkmenistan include Russians (in urban centers) and Uzbeks (in the northeast), as well as lesser numbers of Kazakhs and Tatars.

The origin of the Turkmen tribes dates from a period as early as the eighth century when Turkic peoples were migrating from the east into Central Asia. Some of these peoples belonged to tribes that later came to form the Ottoman and Seljuk Turks, founders of important Middle Eastern empires. These semi-nomadic early Turkic tribes eventually absorbed some of the more sedentary Iranian and other peoples already inhabiting the region. By the tenth century, Turkish documents first mention a people called Turkmen.

As a result of the Arab invasion of Central Asia in the tenth century, Turkmen tribes accepted Islam as their religion. Later, in the eleventh century, Turkmen leaders founded the Seljuk Empire at Merv, the oasis called Mary in contemporary Turkmenistan. During the Mongol invasions of the thirteenth century and in subsequent years, control of the territory constituting modern Turkmenistan passed to various regional khanates. Turkmen tribes survived this period primarily through military alliances with contemporary Muslim rulers such as the emirs of Bukhara (Bukhoro) or the khans of Khiva or Kokand (Qŭqon).

Russian Conquest

By the time of the final Russian advance into Central Asia in the second half of the nineteenth century, the Turkmen peoples had still not managed to cooperate in any political or economic entity higher than a tribal unit. On the contrary, individual Turkmen tribes continued to offer their military services to one or another warring Central Asian khanate. Although the Russians had tried as early as 1717 to mount a military expedition against the Khivan khanate, it was not until 1881, in the massacre of Turkmen at the fort of Geok-Tepe, near Ashgabat, that tsarist forces succeeded in conquering the last of the Central Asian lands not yet under their control. The greatest resistance the Russians encountered in their military advance into Central Asia proved to be that of the fierce Turkmen forces. By 1885, however, all of Central Asia was finally controlled by Russians. Russian

General Skobelev established Turkmenistan as the Transcaspian oblast, and the territory was thereafter ruled as a military colony.

Turkmen tribes continued their semi-nomadic existence well into the twentieth century, although some had previously settled in the oases and were devoting themselves to agriculture. Segregation by family, clan, and tribe, as well as the perpetuation of separate spoken dialects, worked against any unified effort to counter the Russian presence. Colonial policies inevitably brought some modern innovations to this outlying region of the empire. A railroad was built from Krasnovodsk on the Caspian Sea eastward to Ashgabat and then across the desert to Mary and on to Bukhara. Turkmen, however, enjoyed little or no participation under the colonial system, and many suffered the loss of valuable pastureland to incoming settlers from Russia.

The major crisis in Central Asia during World War I was the revolt of 1916 in which native peoples rose up against a Russian order to conscript Central Asians for noncombatant duties. Although it is uncertain whether or not the response of Turkmen tribes to this directive constituted a true expression of nationalism or rather a more diffuse anti-Russian movement, the Turkmen during this period and in the subsequent Russian Revolution managed to regain control of their territory. Under the leadership of Junayd Khan, a respected Turkmen tribal elder, Turkmen military forces reversed the Bolshevik takeover of Ashgabat and later took command of the khanate of Khiva. By 1918 they had even achieved a short-lived independence separate from Bolshevik-controlled Turkestan. This relatively brief period ended in 1920 when Red Army forces defeated Junayd Khan and his fellow Turkmen holding Khiva. These Turkmen then joined the Basmachi (anti-Soviet) guerilla movement, widespread in Central Asia throughout the 1920s, and fought against the Soviet consolidation of power well into the 1930s.

Soviet Rule

In October 1924, Stalin created the union Republic of Turkmenistan, carved out of existing Turkmen tribal landholdings and parts of the old khanates of Khiva and Bukhara. Turkmenistan was designated one of five tribal/ ethnic groups meeting the criteria for nationhood devised by Soviet historians and ethnographers. Thus, Turkmenistan formally became a part of the USSR.

In spite of this formal incorporation into the Soviet Union, Turkmen tribes continued to resist the implementation of Soviet policies throughout the 1920s and into the 1930s. Although external controls were relaxed for a time in an attempt to gain greater cooperation from the indigenous peoples, Turkmen tribes fought the collectivization directive of 1929 that attempted to force the traditionally nomadic Turkmen to settle permanently in one place in order to pursue cooperative agricultural activity.

Turkmen leaders did not escape the period of purges that swept through Russia and the other Soviet republics in the 1930s. Denounced as nationalists, high leaders of the Turkmen Communist Party, such as Gaigisiz Aitakov (Turkmen premier) and Nedirbai Atabaev (president of the Turkmen Supreme Soviet), were tried on charges of sympathizing with opposition elements within the intelligentsia and then executed. Lesser leaders suffered similar accusations and were also purged in 1937-38. After World War II, this pattern continued as intellectuals, writers, and others became victims.

After Stalin's death in 1953, during the regime of Nikita Khrushchev, Turkmen leaders continued to press for greater native control of political and economic affairs in Turkmenistan. Suhan Babaev, first secretary of the Turkmen Communist Party, was ousted in 1958 for proposing that only Turkmen should fill important Party leadership posts in Turkmenistan. Yet, the subsequent first secretaries all were drawn from Turkmen leadership. The successor to Babaev, Juma Karaev, lived only two years after his appointment and was succeeded by Balysh Ovezov in 1960. In 1969, during the tenure of Soviet leader Leonid Brezhnev—a period marked by cynicism and rampant corruption in the Turkmen Republic— Ovezov was removed and replaced by Mukhamednazar Gapurov. With the advent of Mikhail Gorbachev and his reform-minded policies of perestroika in 1985, a new group of political appointees came to head Party leadership positions at both the republic and oblast levels. The job of first secretary of the Turkmen Soviet Republic went to Saparmurad Niyazov, a Communist Party functionary having important ties within both the republic and Moscow.

Contemporary Issues

Economic Dependence and Independence

During the Soviet period, the Turkmen Soviet Socialist Republic developed, not unlike other Central Asian republics, a pattern of colonial economic dependence upon the Moscow center. Encouraged to produce ever greater quantities of cotton, Turkmenistan came to participate in the wider development of the cotton monoculture in Central Asia. As elsewhere, the demand for increased, cheap cotton production in Turkmenistan led to extravagant misuse of scarce water resources. (See "Ecological Issues.") Graft and corruption became routine as unrealistic projections of cotton yields led to falsely inflated production figures. By 1985, the year of the onset of Gorbachev's reforms, Moscow authorities openly challenged the weak performance of Turkmenistan agriculture, complaining that the republic's economy required far greater discipline and modernization. In all, labor productivity in agriculture was lower in 1985 than it had been in 1970—and this, despite considerable state investment in the agricultural sector. By the 1980s, Turkmenistan had also become dependent upon Moscow for basic food commodities, including meat, eggs, and other protein. Unable to feed itself, the republic had become, in the view of the Moscow center, an economic liability.

The subsequent resignation of the Turkmen Communist Party First Secretary Gapurov and his replacement by Niyazov were seen as indications that Moscow sought to reverse this pattern of agricultural weakness. Muscovite sincerity on this score, however, was undermined by a continued insistence on unrealistically high cotton production figures. Nevertheless, in the years since 1985 the replacement of all oblast-level first secretaries, along with the minister of agriculture, not only began to address the problems of corruption inherited from the Brezhnev era, but also paved the way for more open-ended discussions regarding the future of Turkmen agriculture.

The Soviet era has, to be sure, left Turkmenistan impoverished and backward. The republic has the highest infant mortality rate of any former Soviet republic; its badly polluted streams and canals yield the most unreliable drinking water of any Central Asian state; and the problem of rural unemployment remains a chronic source of social instability.

Most observers of Central Asia, however, are quick to point out that, with the exception of Kazakhstan, no state in the region faces brighter prospects for economic independence and development. How is it that such an encouraging picture can emerge out of such relative poverty and economic dependence? The answer rests with the abundant oil and natural gas reserves of Turkmenistan. While cotton production will continue to secure export earnings for the newly independent republic, the greatest source of foreign currency for domestic development undoubtedly depends on the country's export of natural gas. The Turkmen political leadership recognizes the importance of these natural resources and has already entered into bilateral agreements to secure full international market value for its oil and gas exports. Indicative of this was Turkmenistan's decision to withhold gas exports to Ukraine in 1991–92 until the Ukrainians, like the Russians, agreed to pay full market value. In 1992, Turkmenistan also began to seek international partners to develop a pipeline to carry gas to Turkey and, ultimately, western Europe. The result is that, alongside the grating poverty of Turkmenistan, there exists a realistic hope for increased international trade earnings and expanded domestic food production.

These hopes for Turkmen economic development ought not to be confused with the equally complicated issue of privatization and economic restructuring. Here, Turkmen political leadership has shown some reluctance to divest itself of longstanding governmental subsidization and control of the domestic economy. While modern capitalism in the form of international investment and selective market pricing is encouraged, the economy is still being managed by an entrenched nomenklatura (Party appointees) whose tenure predates the advent of reform in the 1980s.

Ecological Issues

The most serious long-term domestic problem threatening the economic development and health of Turkmenistan is the Soviet legacy of disregard for land and water resources. The Soviet-engineered attempt to maximize short-run agricultural production at the expense of limited land and water resources has left a series of environmental problems that now beg to be addressed. Two of these issues—the Kara Kum Canal diversion of the Amu Darya River for purposes of irrigating cotton fields, and the draining of the Garabogazköl Aylagy (Kara Bogaz Gulf) on the Caspian Sea—pose ecological problems of potentially disastrous proportions.

Kara Kum Canal. Construction of the Kara Kum Canal, begun in 1954, has been hailed in rather utopian terms as the greatest blessing ever bestowed upon the Turkmen people. Stretching from the town of Kerki in the east, where waters of the Amu Darya River are diverted into the canal, to the capital of Ashgabat in the west, the Kara Kum waterway is a massive project intended to turn arid desert lands into a fertile agricultural plain. In conception, the project compares to the U.S. diversion of the Colorado River in the celebrated Central Arizona Project.

While the Kara Kum has, indeed, provided the basis for increased agricultural and cotton production, the accompanying problems associated with its construction are now becoming clear. The Kara Kum has become one of the chief contributors to the draining of the once great Aral Sea. (See "Uzbekistan" chapter, pages 173–74.) Reduced to a mere third of its original volume, the Aral Sea has become the greatest natural disaster of Central Asia. Winds crossing its dried sea bed now carry salts and chemicals across the agricultural fields of Central Asia, threatening, ironically, the very fields that are irrigated by waters that used to flow into the Aral. Diverting approximately 25 percent of the Amu Darya River at Kerki, the Kara Kum Canal has become the single greatest factor depleting the flow of the Amu Darya into the Aral Sea. Thus, the Kara Kum waterway has contributed mightily to the most prominent natural disaster of Central Asia.

In the construction of the Kara Kum, moreover, unwise cost savings were instituted resulting in the canal not being lined with concrete. Thus, much of the water passing through the canal seeps into the ground and is lost. The consequent rise of groundwater levels along the canal and the absence of proper drainage has meant that adjacent lands have experienced considerable soil salinization. By the 1980s, over half of the lands within the Kara Kum canal zone were considered heavily salted and thus unsuited for agriculture. (See Annette Bohr, "Turkmenistan under Perestroika," *Report on the USSR*, 23 March 1990, pp. 24–25.)

Kara Bogaz Gulf. Because of the scope of the Aral Sea disaster, observers of Central Asia have sometimes lost sight of another major ecological problem looming in Turkmenistan—namely, the elimination of the Kara Bogaz Gulf (Garabogazköl Aylagy) on the Caspian Sea. In 1980, the inlet to the Kara Bogaz Gulf was dammed in order to maintain high water levels in the Caspian Sea. Construction of the dam was premised upon the fear that the Kara Bogaz Gulf was draining the Caspian Sea, a premise that has now been entirely discredited.

Originally, the plans for the dam included the provision of a lock that would allow for replenishment of the Kara Bogaz. Another cost-saving measure was introduced, however, and the lock was not built. As a result the Kara Bogaz is drying up. The transition of the gulf into an evaporating salt lake not only undermines the productive capacity of the large Karabogazsulfat chemical plant—the Kara Bogaz having been an invaluable source of rare chemicals—but the dry bed of the Kara Bogaz Gulf now also threatens the surrounding agricultural regions. Just as the drying Aral Sea bed has proved to be the source of unhealthy saline and chemical winds blowing over agricultural terrain farther east, so also the wind-blown salts of the Kara Bogaz Gulf threaten the grain-growing lands of the nearby Kuban region of the Russian Federation.

Turkmen opposition to the damming of the Kara Bogaz Gulf has been made known by prominent leaders of the republic's Academy of Sciences, but to date the effort to reverse the harmful effects created by the dam have produced more sparring between rival bureaucratic agencies than resolution of the problem. Although the issue raises larger questions of competing sovereign claims to the Caspian Sea, Turkmen authorities may decide that the destruction of the Kara Bogaz dam is a necessary extension of Turkmen national sovereignty and economic independence. The roadblocks to reversal of the Aral Sea disaster, however, appear much more daunting than that of the Kara Bogaz Gulf.

Political Democratization?

In spite of greater public participation in political life since 1985, Turkmenistan has remained among the former Soviet republics least affected by the process of democratization. Public life, however formally committed to reform, remains largely controlled by political appointments—that is, the nomenklatura fashioned under Soviet and Communist Party influence.

At the head of this political system stands Saparmurad Niyazov, president of Turkmenistan. Niyazov rose to office through prominent appointments in the Turkmen Soviet government and Communist Party. An electrical engineer by training, Niyazov held minor Party posts in the early 1980s before rising to republic and central Moscow recognition while first secretary of the Ashkhabad (Ashgabat) City Party Committee. In March 1985, Niyazov was appointed chairman of the Council of Ministers of Turkmenistan. In the traditional Soviet division between government and Party positions, the Council of Ministers' chairmanship constituted the leading post in the Turkmen Soviet Republic's government. Nine months after this appointment, in December 1985, Niyazov was chosen at the age of 46 to head the Communist Party of Turkmenistan, the highest office in the republic.

In the ensuing years, Niyazov has remained the only Central Asian head of state to survive the entire Gorbachev era and retain his full power into the post-Soviet era. Niyazov has done so while giving lip service to formal elections, popular referenda, and public participation, albeit in a controlled political process. Typical of Niyazov's style is his handling of the issue of Turkmenistan independence in the wake of the abortive August 1991 Moscow *coup d'état*. When all the other republics were declaring their independence, Niyazov appealed to popular support for such a declaration, setting a national referendum for October 1991. After a campaign in which he strictly controlled the media urging support for the initiative, over 94 percent voted for Turkmenistan independence. While the referendum gave the appearance of democratic participation in the public life of the country, the reality was rather one of a carefully controlled political environment.

Similarly, Niyazov appealed for the people's support when he became in 1992 the first president of a former Soviet republic to submit himself to popular ballot. The result of the June 1992 election, the first held under the new Turkmenistan constitution, was an overwhelming Niyazov victory. He received more than 99 percent of the vote. Although the election was probably meant to demonstrate to the world the process of democratization at work in Turkmenistan, the reality was quite different, for Niyazov's election had been guaranteed by the fact that no opposition party was permitted to qualify for the ballot. In response to complaints that the Turkmenistan government has not gone far enough in the protection of civil and human rights within the newly independent

state, Niyazov is quick to point out that the most important prerequisite for building a modern democratic, secular state is political stability. His repression of informal political organizations seeking party recognition appears to conform to this concern for political stability.

For their part, the Turkmen intelligentsia seems more concerned to advance national goals, including the Turkmen language, than to seek direct political representation. In the meantime, Niyazov has engineered a certain measure of personal authority in the new republic unparalleled in other Central Asian states. In the weeks leading up to the June 1992 presidential elections, a virtual cult of personality was developed around Niyazov. (For an analysis of how that cult has been extended, and at the expense of basic human rights, see the analysis of Helsinki Watch representative Jeri Laber, "The Dictatorship Returns," *New York Review of Books,* 15 July 1993, pp. 42–44.) It is still probable that, except for occasional stirrings of the small Turkmen intelligentsia, Niyazov also retains some popular support. His vision of a stable, secular Turkmen state welcome to foreign investment seems to accord for now with the wishes of much of the Turkmen population that desires, more than anything else, improved economic performance. As for the substantial Russian population, comprising nearly half of the population of Ashgabat, they too have been reassured that Niyazov does not welcome any interethnic strife that would dampen the prospects for international investment.

Niyazov's commitment to interethnic peace may also be motivated by a concern for the maintenance of stability within the dominant Turkmen nation. For, lurking below the surface are not only potential conflicts between national groups, but also conflicts between traditional Turkmen tribes—conflicts that could undercut the legitimacy of the dominant, secularized Turkmen political bureaucracy. Despite these hidden sources of discontent, the only significant force for instability faced by the Niyazov government since 1985 was that of the May 1989 riots in Ashgabat and Nebitdag. Those riots appear now to have been launched by young people suffering from chronic unemployment. Niyazov has perhaps rightly concluded from the 1989 disturbances that the most important long-term threat to stability comes from the grating poverty and poor health conditions confronting large percentages of the Turkmen population. For now, Turkmenistan remains under Niyazov's authoritarian leadership the most politically stable state in Central Asia.

International Geopolitical Issues

As might be expected by its commitment to expanded foreign trade and Western investment, the Niyazov government has been particularly careful in developing its relations with the West. It has sought ties with Europe and the United States. Frequently meeting with Western economic and business leaders, the Niyazov government has also sought membership in the Conference on Security and Cooperation in Europe and in the International Monetary Fund.

These overtures to the West have not been at the expense of Turkmenistan's ties with its neighbors. Bordering the nations of Iran and Afghanistan on its southern frontier, Turkmenistan has moved to secure its future relations with the Islamic states of the Middle East. On these matters, the Niyazov government has already sent unmistakeable signals. While Turkmenistan's ties with Iran have been cordial and correct, Niyazov has made no secret of his commitment to follow the more secular model of Turkey. Niyazov's visit to Turkey and the rapid establishment of diplomatic relations with the Turkish government have been followed by efforts to establish a direct gas pipeline to Turkey.

Within the former Soviet Union, Turkmenistan has played a rather ambivalent role in the fragile informal union, the Commonwealth of Independent States (CIS). Initially hosting a meeting of Central Asian states that requested inclusion in the Commonwealth, Turkmenistan has at the same time demonstrated a reluctance to give too much authority to the new body. Instead, Niyazov has preferred to negotiate bilateral agreements with the separate neighboring and Slavic states of the CIS. It was in this manner that Niyazov negotiated with the Russian Federation an agreement for Russian training of Turkmenistan military forces. Similarly, Niyazov insisted on bilateral talks to resolve the trade impasse with Ukraine over purchase of Turkmen natural gas. This bilateral approach has also distinguished Turkmenistan's position in talks with the other Central Asian states of the former Soviet Union.

The Turkmen Cultural Inheritance

Islam. Overwhelmingly Islamic by religious tradition, Turkmen Muslims come largely out of the Sunni branch of Islam. In this respect, despite Iranian radio and other religious propaganda efforts, Turkmen religious traditions differ from that of predominantly Shi'ite Iranian Islam. Islam in Turkmenistan has shown little inclination to follow the more fundamentalist strains of Islam exhibited in Iran and other parts of the Middle East. Not only does fundamentalism not seem to be attracting broad numbers of Islamic faithful in Turkmenistan, or other parts of Central Asia, but most Turkmen follow their own brand of vernacular Islam. Recently, efforts have been underway to publish a parallel text edition of the Koran in Arabic and modern Turkmen. The revival of Islam in Turkmenistan has increasingly taken the form of the reopening of mosques and religious institutions closed during the Stalinist and Khrushchev eras.

Turkmen Language. The recovery of Turkmen cultural identity has also been associated with the issue of the Turkmen language. The native intelligentsia has sought to strengthen language instruction in Turkmen in the schools. The Slavic population of Ashgabat is increasingly being encouraged to develop second-language ability in Turkmen. Adding to the difficulty of recovering the Turkmen literary tradition is the fact that few members of the Turkmen intelligentsia itself are able today to decipher early Turkmen manuscripts written in the Arabic script. Curiously, the large number of Turkmen living in Afghanistan and Iran have sought to reestablish ties with Turkmenistan, but the strength of this cultural connection is limited by the inability of fellow nationals on each side of the international border to read the other's script. Although there has been some encouragement for the study of Arabic, as elsewhere in Central Asia, the Turkmen language is likely to remain in Cyrillic script for the forseeable future, even though transitions toward use of Arabic are already visible.

Turkmen History. Perhaps most interesting in the recovery of Turkmen cultural identity is the renewal of interest in national Turkmen history. At the end of the 1980s, it became possible for Turkmen writers to question openly the established version of the incorporation of Turkmen territory into nineteenth-century Russia. The established Russian and Soviet view held that the Turkmen lands were voluntarily joined to the Russian Empire in the latter half of the nineteenth century. Such a reading of history was particularly offensive to national traditions since the Turkmen were notable for putting up the most sustained and effective resistance to Russian imperial advance of any region in Central Asia. In the most memorable of these nineteenth-century resistance efforts, Turkmen defended the fortress of Geok-Tepe in 1881 against overwhelming military odds. In the end, almost 15,000 Turkmen were killed in the battle. Later, the surviving Turkmen soldiers were also killed by Russian forces. That the revered memory of the battle of Geok-Tepe is now once again able to be written about and spoken of openly is a mark of the reawakening of Turkmen cultural and historical consciousness.

Whether this emergent Turkmen consciousness will lead to yet further economic, political, and diplomatic separation from Moscow remains unclear. For now, the most important agenda facing Turkmenistan is the use of its relatively abundant natural resources to reverse the destabilizing patterns of high unemployment, high infant mortality, and a declining standard of living.

UZBEKISTAN

Statistical Profile

Demography

Population: 19,810,000

Ethnic population:

Uzbek	14,142,000	71.4%
Russian	1,653,000	8.3%
Tajik	934,000	4.7%
Kazakh	808,000	4.1%
Tatar	657,000	3.3%
Karakalpak	412,000	2.1%
Korean	183,000	0.9%
Kyrgyz	175,000	0.9%
Ukrainian	153,000	0.8%
Turkmen	122,000	0.6%
Other Turkic	106,000	0.5%
Jewish	65,000	0.3%
Azerbaijani	44,000	0.2%
Persian	25,000	0.1%
Other	331,000	1.7%

Predominant religious traditions:

Islam	89.7%
Christianity	9.1%

Population by age:

Age	Total	Males	Females
0–4	16.1%	8.2%	7.9%
5–9	13.0%	6.6%	6.4%
10–14	11.7%	5.9%	5.8%
15–19	10.3%	5.2%	5.1%
20–24	9.8%	5.0%	4.8%
25–29	8.7%	4.3%	4.4%
30–34	6.5%	3.2%	3.3%
35–39	4.7%	2.3%	2.4%
40–44	2.6%	1.3%	1.3%
45–49	4.0%	2.0%	2.0%
50–54	3.2%	1.6%	1.6%
55–59	3.0%	1.4%	1.6%
60–64	2.1%	0.8%	1.3%
65–69	1.3%	0.4%	0.9%
70–	3.0%	1.0%	2.0%

Male/Female ratio: 49.2% male/50.8% female

Rural/Urban population: 59.7% rural/40.3% urban

Growth over time, 1979–91: 34.5%

Population density: 119.9 persons/sq mi

Politics/Government

Date of independence declaration: 31 August 1991

Urban centers and populations:

Toshkent (Tashkent)	2,073,000
Andijon	398,000
Samarqand	366,000
Namangan	308,000
Bukhoro (Bukhara)	224,000
Farghona (Fergana)	200,000
Qŭqon (Kokand)	182,000
Nukus	169,000
Qarshi (Karshi)	156,000
Urganch	128,000
Margilan	125,000
Jizzakh (Zhizak)	102,000
Termiz	57,000
Khiva	24,000

Autonomous area:

Karakalpakstan	Nukus (capital)

Education

Level of education for persons over 15:

completed higher level education	9.2%
completed secondary education	57.7%
incomplete secondary education	19.8%

Number of higher education institutions: 46 (340,900 students)

Major institutions of higher education and enrollment:

Toshkent

Uzbek State University	19,300
Institute of Railway Engineers	12,000

Major institutions of higher education and enrollment: *(continued)*	
State Economics University	11,000
Institute of Textile and Light Industry	6,200
Telecommunications Institute	5,100
State Theatrical and Art Institute	900
Nukus	
Nukus State University	7,000
Samarqand	
Samarqand State University	18,650
Cooperative Institute	7,000

Socioeconomic Indicators

Birthrate: 33.7/1,000

Infant mortality: 34.6/1,000 live births

Average life expectancy: 69.5 (males 66.2; females 72.6)

Average family size: 5.5

Hospital beds per 10,000 persons: 123.7

Production of electrical energy: 2,719 kwh/person

Length of rail lines: 2,145 mi

Length of highways: 48,608 mi

Physical/Territorial/Geopolitical Features

Area: 172,741 sq mi (2% of USSR total)

Land use:

Cultivated	10%
Pasture	48%

Highest elevation: 15,233 ft. (in the Gissar Range)

Rainfall: 3 inches/year in the plains and foothills; as much as 39 in the mountains

Temperature: average in winter 18° F; lowest temperature: -35° F. Average in summer 79° F in the north, 86° F in the south; highest temperature: 108° F.

Principal products: cotton, rice, sheep, cattle, textiles, silk, oil, gas, copper, vehicles, steel, machinery, chemicals

Per Capita GNP: (1991) $1,350

Sources

Narodnoe khoziaistvo SSSR v 1990g. (Moscow, 1991); *Naselenie SSSR* (1989); Matthew J. Sagers, "News Notes. Iron and Steel," *Soviet Geography* 30 (May 1989): 397–434; Lee Schwartz, "USSR Nationality Redistribution by Republic, 1979–1989: From Published Results of the 1989 All-Union Census," *Soviet Geography* 32 (April 1991): 209–48; "Uzbekskaia sovetskaia sotsialisticheskaia respublika," *Bol'shaia Sovetskaia Entsiklopediia* (Moscow, 1977); and *World of Learning*, 43rd ed. (London: Europa Publications Limited, 1993); "Russia. . ." (National Geographic Society Map, March 1993).

History and Description

Topography

Surrounded by the four other newly independent states of Central Asia, Uzbekistan is situated in the middle of an historically Islamic region. Kazakhstan is located to the north and west, Turkmenistan is to the south, and Kyrgyzstan and Tajikistan lie to the east. On its eastern border, Uzbekistan shares with Kyrgyzstan and Tajikistan the rich agricultural Farghona (Fergana) Valley. A short border with Afghanistan exists at the extreme southern Uzbekistan frontier. Uzbekistan also includes the autonomous republic of Karakalpakstan. The desert lands of Karakalpakstan are located in the western part of the republic, a region that encompasses the southern half of the Aral Sea.

Major Cities. Three large cities, each located within an oblast of the same name, comprise the most heavily populated areas of Uzbekistan. By far the largest of these cities is the capital Toshkent (Tashkent), followed by Samarqand, and then Farghona (Fergana). These three settlements have all developed historically along and around ancient river valleys and oases in which early civilizations flourished. The capital Toshkent was rocked by earthquakes in 1966 and has been substantially rebuilt. The importance of water for urban development in Central Asia is reflected in the location of the other large cities in Uzbekistan—Bukhoro (Bukhara), Qŭqon (Kokand), Andijon (Andizhan), Namangan, Qarshi, Nukus, Urganch, Termiz, Jizzakh (Dzhizak), and Guliston.

Uzbekistan

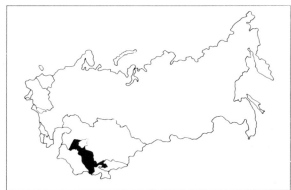

KAZAKHSTAN

Aral
Sea

Karakalpakstan

Kyzyl

Kum

Desert

Lowland

Nukus

Urganch

Khiva

Turan

TURKMENISTAN

Farghona
Valley

Tian Shan
Mountains

Toshkent

Namangan

Andijon

Qŭqon

Margilan

Farghona

Kuvasai

Guliston

Jizzakh

KYRGYZSTAN

Zeravshan

Bukhoro

Samarqand

River

Turkestan Range

TAJIKISTAN

Amu

Qarshi

12.507 ft. +

Darya

River

Termiz

	National Boundary
	Autonomous Boundary
★	Capital City
•	Other Cities

0   200 Miles

0   200 Kilometers

AFGHANISTAN

River Systems. Most of the territory of Uzbekistan is situated between the Syr Darya and the Amu Darya rivers. These rivers originate in the mountain streams east of Uzbekistan and then flow in a northwesterly direction to the Aral Sea. The Syr Darya, the Amu Darya, and the Zeravshan sit astride an area of flat plains known as the Turan Lowland. To the east of this dry plain rise the mountains of Tian Shan and the Turkestan Range. The plains region typically receives little rainfall, with the long, hot summer months followed by mild winters. Uzbekistan also contains one truly arid region called the Kyzyl Kum Desert.

Ethnic and Historical Background

The history of Central Asia is, in part, a history of small tribal groups of Turkic-speaking settlers and nomads. Archeological investigations of these peoples, among whom are the forerunners of modern Uzbeks, place them in the area of contemporary Uzbekistan as early as the twelfth century. Yet, the idea that these tribes form, in effect, a single Uzbek nation is a relatively recent concept, with Uzbek nationalism dating only from the twentieth century, particularly the Soviet period.

The Uzbeks are the largest of the Turkic, Islamic peoples of Central Asia. The nation was formed over many centuries during which a relatively settled Iranian (Tajik) population combined with a more nomadic set of Turkic tribes. The language that came to predominate was Turkic. There are at least three identifiable subgroups of modern Uzbeks: Kypchak, Turki, and Sart. The largest Uzbek sub-group is the Sarts. Culturally similar to the Tajiks, the Sarts have been the most settled and least nomadic. Uzbeks of Sart descent are not separated by tribal divisions. The Turki are tribes residing primarily in the region of the Farghona Valley and Samarqand. The Kypchak are the once nomadic group who formed a link between other Uzbeks and the Kazakhs to the north. The Kypchak have maintained their tribal identities, even though they have become largely assimilated into the modern Uzbek nation of the twentieth century. In the autonomous republic of Karakalpakstan, the Karakalpak people are being assimilated into the dominant Uzbek culture, despite the fact that they are ethnically closer to the Kazakh population north of the Aral Sea.

Tamarlane. Politically, Uzbeks share the sense of a glorious past dating from the great triumphs of the fourteenth-century Islamic, Mongol leader Tamarlane (Timur). During the great civilization of fifteenth-century Central Asia, a descendant of Tamarlane known as Ulug Beg emerged as the ruler of an area centering around Samarqand. Ulug Beg's state, although it did not survive his death in 1449, was an important link with the great imperial tradition of Tamarlane and the conquests of the Golden Horde. Today, as the historian Edward Allworth notes in his recent history of the Uzbeks, the Uzbeks find the origins of their history in that great age of Timur and the successor states of the region. (Allworth, *The Modern Uzbeks from the Fourteenth Century to the Present: A Cultural History* [Stanford, CA: Hoover Institution, 1990]). Despite this Timurid ancestral claim, it was only in the sixteenth century that the term Uzbek or "Ozbek" came to be adopted by the successor nomadic, Turkic-speaking tribes. These tribes settled in and around the same region of Samarqand where Ulug Beg had earlier ruled.

Period of Decline. This Muslim civilization began to decline in the seventeenth and eighteenth centuries because of the bypassing of ancient trade routes that had earlier crossed the arid, desert-like lands of Central Asia. After the demise of Sheiban Khan's state, there arose first the Khiva Khanate, later the Bukhara Khanate, and finally in the early nineteenth century the Kokand Khanate. As political power in the region devolved to the khans controlling these oasis areas, foreign trade was expanded to include also the Russian Empire.

The Russian Conquest

Russian expansion and conquest of the Uzbek region began in 1865 with the surrender of Tashkent to tsarist military forces. This surrender was quickly followed by the defeat of Bukhoro in 1868, Khiva in 1873, Kokand in 1876, and all other smaller tribes within the next decade. By 1900 Russian colonial influence in local affairs had come to dominate. Growth in the marketing and trading of cotton boomed, aided by the many miles of newly built railroad lines. Russian, Ukrainian, and Belarusian immigrants streamed in, despite their uncertain welcome.

World War I. The events of the First World War and the tsarist need in 1916 for additional workers to assist the Russian armed forces brought a request from Petrograd for a military draft of the native peasantry. A violent and widespread uprising resulted as a protest against this call-up of the local citizenry. The revolt, however, failed.

Within a year the course of revolutionary events in Russia radically altered the relationship between the imperial center and the local Uzbek nationals.

Russian Revolution and Civil War. In November of 1917, after the Bolshevik Revolution, a new Soviet order was heralded in Toshkent. After what appeared to be a somewhat passive acceptance of the situation by local residents, the course of events changed. Incidents related both to Bolshevik interference in Muslim religious affairs as well as to requisitions of food triggered various resistance efforts, some of which focused on demands for local autonomy. A loosely organized group led by conservative Muslim forces called the Basmachi (Qorbashi) emerged as an anti-Communist force and began what was essentially a guerilla struggle against the Bolsheviks. When the Red Army forces began to secure the upper hand in the Russian Civil War, Bolshevik efforts came to be directed also against the Basmachi insurgents, with the end result that Soviet power was secured also in the old Russian colonial regions of Central Asia.

In incorporating the republic of Uzbekistan into the Soviet Union, Lenin's followers were guided, in part, by his so-called nationalities policy. Based on the idea that native cultures could actually be encouraged to develop along their natural path, the assumption of Leninist "national self-determination" was that ethnic identity need not conflict with socialist forms of economic and governmental life—forms that were to be largely directed from the Muscovite center. In Central Asia, this doctrine of national self-determination came to mean the radical breakup of the region into "ethnic" republics. Thus, in 1924 the area known as Russian Turkestan was formally dissolved and in its place new Soviet republics were established, based upon ethnicity. From the perspective of the Moscow center, one important advantage of the nationalities policy was that it effectively undermined those local sentiments that supported a union of Uzbek peoples with other Turkic-speaking groups outside the republic. The division of Turkestan effectively elevated certain groups, such as the Uzbeks, to the status of privileged nations, while at the same time establishing boundaries that foreclosed pan-Turkic or pan-Islamic unity in Central Asia. It was a twentieth-century case of "divide and conquer." For the first time in the modern period Uzbek tribal sub-groups who had shared a common history from the fourteenth century were effectively being forged into a common "privileged" nation. This served the political and economic interests of Moscow, even as it could be justified on the grounds of "national self-determination."

The Uzbek Soviet Socialist Republic (UzSSR)

The Uzbek Soviet Socialist Republic (UzSSR) was officially incorporated into the Soviet Union in May of 1925, following the successful consolidation of Soviet power in the northern and middle part of Central Asia. The administrative organization of the territory underwent certain changes during the years after it joined the union. For instance, in 1929 the Autonomous Republic of Tajikistan was separated from Uzbekistan, and in 1930 the Uzbek capital was changed from Samarqand to Toshkent.

Following the 1925 establishment of the Uzbek republic, there was a period of economic growth and industrialization in Uzbekistan. Economic policies, launched from the Moscow center and implemented by increasing numbers of Russians migrating into the urban centers of Uzbekistan, set ambitious goals for increasing Uzbek cotton production. Ultimately, the economic plan for the Uzbek republic was to increase cotton production enough to make the Soviet Union independent of foreign cotton imports. The result of this long-term plan was to establish a precedent for Moscow-centered economic planning and political management within the new republic. Moreover, in implementing new land and industrialization policies, the organs of central planning inevitably inflicted changes in traditional Islamic ways of life. Islamic women, often accustomed to the veil, were drafted into the work force.

Collectivization of Agriculture. In agriculture, the process of collectivization (see glossary) served to transform traditional Uzbek village society. Soviet-implanted managers, including Russified Uzbek "water lords" who controlled the irrigation system, represented a modern, transformed version of the old authoritarian order that had prevailed in Central Asia from the medieval period. Nevertheless, the land and water reforms of the late 1920s, which provided plots for landless peasants, did achieve the desired result of increased cotton production. Aided by modernized and enlarged irrigation systems, the newly collectivized cotton farms yielded the desired increases in production. Within a decade of the establishment of the Uzbek republic, over 90 percent of cotton growing was collectivized and production had virtually doubled. By the mid-1930s, the Stalinist regime came to pursue a modest retreat in socioeconomic areas and was far more careful and conservative in handling the economy than it was in dealing with political leadership.

Accompanying production successes in cotton, as well as in silk and citrus growing, were increases in electrical production, textile manufacturing, and petroleum output. The educational system, although a focus of conflicting Russian and Uzbek interests, was enlarged and illiteracy reduced. Similarly, general health care was expanded to reach people not previously served by the medical profession.

Political Leadership. Under Stalin the responsibility for governing the Uzbek republic lay both with native Communist leaders and with Russian bureaucrats imported from Moscow. The first secretary of the Uzbek Communist Party has consistently been an Uzbek. Holding that office from 1925 until his removal in 1937 was Akmal Ikramov. Charged with harboring nationalist tendencies, Ikramov was tried, found guilty of treason, and shot in 1938. Ikramov had arisen out of the generation of Islamic modernizers or Jadids, many of whom initially sided with the new Bolshevik government. His death was a part of the more general bloodbath associated with Stalin's great purge of Party leaders in the last half of the 1930s.

The purge of Uzbek Party leadership in 1937–38 opened the door for a new generation of Party elite bred in a more harshly Stalinist mold. Usman Iusupov, Uzbek Party first secretary from 1937 to 1950, fit squarely into such a pattern, as did his close associate, Abdujabbar Abdurakhmanov. In 1950, Iusupov and Abdurakhmanov took higher Party positions in Moscow. Following a period of transition and de-Stalinization in Uzbek Party politics in the 1950s, Sharaf Rashidov assumed the post of first secretary in 1959. He held that position until 1983, a period during which Uzbek politics became re-Stalinized. Rashidov was later implicated in the corruption of the notorious "Cotton Affair" described later.

After Rashidov's passing, the mantle of the new anti-corruption leadership fell to Inamzhon Usmankhojaev and Rafik Nishanov. The problem with the anti-corruption campaign was that it provoked agitation over the ongoing interference of Moscow in Uzbek politics. When Nishanov left for Moscow in 1989, his successor and present-day ruler of Uzbekistan, Islam Karimov, studiously sought to disassociate himself from center-dominated politics, calling for Uzbek sovereignty and local-based decision making. Nevertheless, despite Karimov's outward new style, he has been trained within the same Communist Party echelons that have produced all Uzbek political leaders from the death of Akmal Ikramov to the present.

Contemporary Issues

Interpreting the Russian Legacy

Today, the history of the Uzbek nation has been reopened on two fronts. First of all, the accounts of the Russian conquest of the area have been opened for major reexamination. Throughout the Soviet period, the assumption was that Russian territorial acquisitions in Central Asia were "progressive" acts in which local people were liberated from the tyrannical hold of ruthless and inefficient feudal khans. In the Stalinist period, the conquests were even reinterpreted to have been acquisitions based upon the "voluntary" ceding of territory by the local people. In the reopening of Central Asian history, the story of the Russian conquest is in the process of being

rewritten to emphasize the opposition of local people and leaders to the Russian military advance. Typical of this historical revision is the article by Uzbek revisionist historian Hamid Ziyaev. Writing in the Uzbek monthly, *Sharq Yulduzi*, Ziyaev cites the manifesto of a mid-nineteenth-century emir enjoining his troops to fight against Russian conquering forces:

> Faithful Muslim subjects! . . . We are the descendants of Timur (Tamerlane), we shall demonstrate how to recapture our land. Muslims! I hope that you will show the infidels how valiantly the Muslim people fight for our religion and our land. The people are expecting victory from you—let them say after the battle that you defended religion and the homeland, and rid our land of the infidels. [internally quoted in James Critchlow, "Central Asia: The Russian Conquest Revisited," *Report on the USSR*, 8 March 1991, p. 17]

As significant as the reexamination of Russian conquest may be for Uzbek nationalism, potentially even more far-reaching is the questioning by some Uzbek intelligentsia of the very identity of Uzbekistan. Within the pages of Uzbek literary periodicals, there have been proposals for a return to the use of the pre-1917 terminology of "Turkestan" or "Turan." Resting behind such proposals has been the growing realization that peoples of Central Asia, insofar as they have belonged to identifiable groups, have not so much made their idenitification with the "nation," but rather with their tribal or local affiliation, or with their common identity as Muslims. Proposals for a return to "Turkestan" reflect this reopening of questions that were closed by the establishment of the Uzbek Soviet Socialist Republic in 1925. Where does the Uzbek "nation" fit in this picture? James Critchlow begs the question in his article, "Will Soviet Central Asia Become a Greater Uzbekistan?" (*Report on the USSR*, 14 September 1990, pp. 17–19). While there are many Uzbek nationals who have benefited from political and economic structures established over the course of 65 years in Soviet Uzbekistan, the future of the Uzbek nation rests upon how these conflicting visions of nation, tribe, and religious community can be sorted out in the post-Soviet era.

Cotton Monoculture

While the range of problems confronting modern Uzbekistan is daunting by any standard, what makes the republic so particularly vulnerable is its dependency upon a single-crop economy, or cotton "monoculture," for much of its national productivity. As late as 1990, central state planning structures in Moscow called for yet further increases in cotton production in Uzbekistan with an eye toward a yield in excess of five million tons a year. This rather phenomenal cotton production, grown on what is generally arid desert land in the upstream regions of Uzbekistan and Turkmenistan, accounts for a disproportionate percentage of Uzbekistan's gross national product. These rural regions west of Toshkent also have the highest birthrates, largest average family size, and highest level of unemployment, not only within the republic of Uzbekistan itself, but within all of Central Asia.

Cotton and the Environment: The Aral Sea Disaster

The exploitation of the cotton monoculture by Moscow has been made possible by massive irrigation projects drawing upon the Amu Darya and Syr Darya Rivers. These two river systems, the Syr Darya largely in Kazakhstan and the Amu Darya forming the border between Turkmenistan and Uzbekistan, travel through Central Asia from the eastern mountainous regions near China ultimately feeding into the Aral Sea. Yet, the Aral Sea, once the world's fourth-largest inland body of water, has become so depleted by the reduced flow of the Amu Darya and Syr Darya that the Aral now holds less than one-third of its original volume of water. Of the water used for irrigation, only a small portion is returned to the rivers after leaching the cotton fields in the upstream oblasts of Uzbekistan, Turkmenistan, and Kazakhstan. Not only does this mean an inability to replenish the water supply of the Aral Sea, but the river water that ultimately reaches the Aral Sea is a sludge severely polluted by pesticides, defoliants, and fertilizers. Despite the precautions posted against use of Aral Sea water, people of the region continue to bathe their children in it, while using it also for drinking, cooking, and washing clothes. The long-term impact of this Aral Sea disaster upon the ground water has only begun to be calculated.

The problem of the Aral Sea has received international attention as a serious environmental and health issue. Of the one and a quarter million people living in Karakalpakstan immediately adjacent to the Aral Sea, approximately two-thirds are estimated to be suffering from hepatitis, typhoid, or cancer of the esophagus. (See the investigative article by William S. Ellis, "The Aral: A Soviet Sea Lies Dying," *National Geographic*, February 1990, pp. 73–93.) Infant mortality in Karakalpakstan is estimated at 111 deaths for every 1,000 live births. The 1987 rate for the former Soviet Union was 25.4 per 1,000 lives births; the rate for the entire Uzbek Republic was 45.9/1,000 live births. Of every 100 children in Karakalpakstan, 83 suffer from some type of serious health ailment.

Not only those in the immediate vicinity of the Aral Sea have been affected. Millions of tons of dust from the dried Aral Sea bed are blown by prevailing winds over Central Asia's most fertile crops, depositing a contaminating chemical cover. One measure of the salinity of such winds is to be found in the high salt content of local precipitation.

Political Corruption and "The Cotton Affair"

The development of cotton monoculture and its attendant environmental problems have not happened without the support of local Uzbek leadership. From the late 1970s to mid-1980s, the central Soviet authorities paid out to Uzbekistan officials more than a billion rubles for cotton that was never received. The padding of cotton production figures and related charges of corruption came to be associated with the rule of Sharaf Rashidov, Uzbek Communist Party General Secretary, and head of the republic for 25 years until his demise in 1983. The corruption of the Rashidov years and the padding of cotton production figures, what came to be known as the "Cotton Affair," became the focus of a public campaign against corruption in 1986 when Soviet Communist Party General Secretary Mikhail Gorbachev, together with conservative Party stalwart Egor Ligachev, launched a crackdown in Uzbekistan. In the ensuing months, tens of thousands of Uzbekistan Communist Party members were purged, some three thousand police officers were fired, and the long-time Uzbek Communist leader who profited from the cotton diversions, Sharaf Rashidov, was widely discredited.

The Cotton Affair, like other scandals in Soviet life, quickly came to assume a symbolic importance beyond the surface claims of corruption. For many Uzbek nationals, the Cotton Affair also became a pretext for Moscow's persecution on ethnic grounds of local Uzbek officialdom. The temporary prosecutors sent down from Moscow in the late 1980s brought an ominous air of fear to the republic's Uzbek officials. As Western observer James Critchlow puts it, "No grievance is more sensitive than the widespread feeling among Uzbeks that corruption and 'the cotton affair' were used by Moscow as pretext to prosecute on ethnic grounds" ("Further Repercussions of the Uzbek Affair," *Report on the USSR*, 24 April 1990, p. 21).

Glasnost in Uzbek Politics

The Uzbek response to the Cotton Affair reflects the degree to which the processes of perestroika and glasnost, launched by Moscow, also opened the way for the development of informal and independent public groups in Uzbek politics. The most important milestone in this process has been the establishment of the Uzbek Popular Front organization known as Birlik (meaning "Unity," or "The Unity Movement for the Preservation of Uzbekistan's Natural, Material, and Spiritual Riches"). Begun as a working group in November 1988 by Uzbek intellectuals in Toshkent, Birlik first had unsanctioned public demonstrations on 19 March 1989, drawing over 12,000 people. The demonstrators, among their other demands, appealed to the republic's congress of agricultural workers for a reduction in cotton production and an end to the cotton monoculture of Uzbekistan. Later, following the May 1989 founding congress of Birlik, the movement denounced a republican draft language law of October 1989, demanding that instead of bilingualism—a euphemism for continued precedence and parallel use of Russian in Uzbekistan official life—Uzbek be designated the republic's language of interethnic communication as well as its state language. The early spread of Birlik popularity could be gauged by its October 1989 demonstration held in Toshkent to give voice to Uzbek feelings on the language question. Over 50,000 people attended, according to official estimates, and 100 Birlik leaders were temporarily arrested. By the end of 1989, the Birlik movement at its second congress extended its scope, opening its membership ranks to non-Uzbek Central Asian groups, even encouraging Birlik chapters outside Uzbekistan.

Birlik is by no means the only independent public voice that has been raised. Initially a moderate wing of the Birlik movement, Erk (Freedom) became the first Uzbek opposition group to be registered as an official party in September 1991. The Erk Party, which claims its strength among the Uzbek intelligentsia, offers as its stated goals the drive for human rights, the national revival of Uzbekistan, and complete independence.

The Communist Party of Uzbekistan, having broken with Moscow since the August 1991 abortive coup, has renamed itself the People's Democratic Party of Uzbekistan. Its leader, Islam Karimov, has indicated that the new party rejects any notion of a state religion, but it claims to welcome the revival of spiritual and cultural traditions in Uzbekistan. It is committed to the development of a sovereign and independent, democratic Uzbekistan. The renamed Communist Party has also lodged within itself significant opposition elements. Indeed, President Karimov's decision to call presidential elections for December 1991 was a result of open and unprecedented criticism directed at his leadership from within the ruling Uzbek Supreme Soviet.

The Voice of Islam

Islam in Uzbekistan, as elsewhere in Central Asia, is the dominant religion of the native Turkic population. In the 1980s, alongside other groups expressing political opposition, there had also arisen the resurgent voice of Islam. For most of the Soviet period, Islamic religious leadership was organized according to four spiritual jurisdictions closely overseen by Soviet authorities. Independent-minded Islamic reformist, or Jadid, leadership was undermined by the end of the 1920s. Mystical Sufi movements remained alive in the rich Islamic religious life of small tribal groupings. But, officially recognized Islamic leadership instead came under control of the Soviet-authorized Muslim spiritual jurisdictions. One of the spiritual jurisdictions set up by Moscow was centered in Toshkent, Uzbekistan. There the chairman of the Muslim Religious Board for Central Asia and Kazakhstan (MRBCAK) served both as the Islamic mufti for Central Asia and as the recognized voice of Islam for Soviet authorities. In February 1989, the long-time MRBCAK chair, Shamsutdinkan Babakhan, was removed from his office after a three-hour demonstration led by a group calling itself "Islam and Democracy." Complaining that Babakhan drank, womanized, knew not a chapter of the Koran, and, in general, served the interests of the KGB, the protesters were able to secure a commitment for Babakhan's removal. The 1989 demonstration by Islamic believers in Tashkent was undoubtedly part of an effort by religious nationalist reformers bent on cleansing the officially registered Islamic clerical ranks of charlatans.

The resurgent public voice of Islam in Central Asia has assumed several different tones in the months following the removal of Babakhan. Within the Uzbek intelligentsia, a reformist tradition built upon the prerevolutionary Jadid movement has sought to link traditional Islamic culture with more secular and democratizing goals. For the intelligentsia the recovery of Turkic and Islamic identities is often compatible with a commitment to human rights and democratic political ideals. Not lost upon the political authorities who fear such linkage of Islam with politics was the discovery that among the four hundred arrested in Tashkent at the opening January 1991 Central Asian Congress of the Islamic Renaissance Party was Abdurrakhim Pulatov, co-chair of the unity movement, Birlik. This overlap of resurgent Islamic identification with democratic opposition reflects, in part, the recovery of Jadidist intelligentsia traditions of the late nineteenth and early twentieth centuries.

It is not only the Islamic nationalist reformers who have led the opposition against "official" Islam. The distrust of registered Islamic clergy by the masses of Muslim believers has led to a parallel Islam led by unregistered mullahs. This parallel Islam is strongest in the sub-national tribes of rural Uzbekistan, and it is most often associated with conservative, Sufi mystical movements.

A third faction in the current recovery of Islam in Uzbekistan is to be found in the Wahhabi movement. The Wahhabis have long been a part of Islamic life in Central Asia, but because of their conservative insistence upon "pure" Islam (including such practices as the exclusion of women from public life) they have little common ground with modernizers in the tradition of the Jadids. At the same time, the Wahhabis adhere to a strict interpretation of the Koran, and reject Sufi or other mystical, superstitious Islamic practices. There has been some speculation that the mid-1989 riots in the Farghona valley (described in the next section) were led, in part, by supporters of the Wahhabi movement. (See James Critchlow, "Islam in Fergana Valley: The Wahhabi 'Threat,'" *Report on the USSR*, 8 December 1989, pp. 13–17.)

The Farghona Valley Riots and Interethnic Conflict in Uzbekistan

While glasnost may have ushered in new political and religious voices in Uzbek public life, that openness has also occasioned the outbreak of public riots directed against non-Uzbek national minorities. The most serious of these outbreaks occurred in June 1989 in the Farghona Valley, the easternmost region of Uzbekistan. As many as one hundred were killed in the violence, most of them minority Meskhetians—Georgian-speaking peoples of the Islamic faith. The spark that triggered the outbreak apparently occurred in the town of Kuvasai, 15 kilometers southeast of the city of Farghona. An incident between a Meskhetian and an Uzbek vendor in the local town market led to wider conflict. When a large number of Meskhetians subsequently gathered in the area, violence erupted, with the first loss of life occurring at the end of May 1989. By early June, the violence had spread to several other cities, including the regional capital of Farghona, where armed Uzbek youth set fire to Meskhetian homes. The rapid spread of violence suggested that plans may have been underway for some time to launch a symbolic strike against targeted minorities, and the Meshketians may have constituted a safer target than the larger Slavic population of urban Tashkent. Ultimately, central Soviet Interior Ministry troops had to be dispatched to quell the Uzbek rioters who chanted such slogans as "Uzbekistan for the Uzbeks." Before the tumult subsided, 11,000 of the 60,000 Meshketians were evacuated from Uzbekistan into makeshift refugee camps in the Russian republic.

There are several explanations for this outbreak in the Farghona Valley. First of all, it is the most densely populated region in all of Uzbekistan, with over 280 residents per square kilometer (compared to an average overall for the former Soviet Union of approximately 13 per square kilometer). The population of the Farghona oblast increased by 27 percent from 1979 to 1989, whereas that of the former Soviet Union grew by only a little over 9 percent.

The largely rural Uzbek native population, which more than doubled in size between 1959 and 1979, is faced with chronic rural overpopulation and underemployment. Most industry, on the other hand, is concentrated in Toshkent where the Slavic population is greatest. Of the estimated twenty-two thousand Uzbek youth coming onto the job market in the Farghona oblast each year, one in five cannot find employment. From the perspective of the Uzbeks, the trouble has been that non-Uzbek nationals—Meshketians, Crimean Tatars, Jews, Russians, and Germans—live better than do the native Uzbeks in their own republic. This perception also applies to the Meshketians who were transferred to Central Asia by Stalin in 1944. Of the estimated four-hundred thousand Meshketians living in lands of the former Soviet Union, only a few reside in Georgia. Others are found in Azerbaijan, Uzbekistan, and Kazakhstan. While some Georgians equate a Muslim with a Turk and reject the "Georgianness" of the Meshketians, their language and former homeland have been historically linked to the present-day republic of Georgia.

The Farghona Valley violence, as well as the wider ethnic hatreds, have fed upon chronic Uzbek unemployment, rural poverty, high birthrates and infant mortality, as well as the accumulation of environmental and health problems associated with cotton monoculture. These deeper problems, however, do not justify the spread of ethnic violence. Conscious of that, the Birlik movement, despite its nationalist message, has carefully sought to disassociate itself from the Farghona Valley events.

The Language Question

Symbolic of the gradual Russification occurring in Uzbekistan during the Soviet period was the shifting fate of the language question. When the Uzbek republic was established in 1925, modern Uzbek used a modified Arabic alphabet. Although only 3.7 percent of the Uzbeks could read and write—a reflection of the difficulty of mastering the Arabic orthography—some Uzbeks concerned with increasing literacy joined in 1926 with Soviet calls for Latinization of the Uzbek alphabet. Edward Allworth has noted that no nation employing the complicated Arabic alphabet, with the possible exception of Lebanon, has achieved more than 68 percent literacy. (See his *Uzbek Literary Politics* [The Hague: Mouton, 1964].) The drive for increased literacy came to be equated with use of the "New Unified Turkic Alphabet," and ultimately with the conversion to the Latin alphabet in 1930 (its use actually began in 1928).

Adoption of a Western alphabet constituted a radical reform with far-ranging implications for Uzbek culture and tradition. With the elimination of the Arabic script, the Koran and other traditional works became practically inaccessible until after World War II when new editions of the old works began to be prepared in the new scripts.

By 1940, Stalin imposed a yet further orthographic reform—this time the use of the Cyrillic script. As early as the 1880s, Russian missionaries had experimented with the use of Cyrillic in rendering the Uzbek alphabet, but the formal orthographic change of 1940 facilitated the teaching of Russian to Uzbeks and the more rapid introduction of Russian vocabulary into Uzbek. It also had the effect of undermining a generation of Uzbek national writers, for whom the Cyrillic script was largely foreign. In language, as in politics and economics, the Soviet period marked the victory of the Moscow center in Uzbek public life.

Behind the passions and programs of the Uzbek national agenda, the language question has remained the most important and symbolic issue for the Uzbek intelligentsia. Today the language question is being addressed both in national legislation and in the daily lives of Uzbek citizens. On the legislative level, a piece of legislation, entitled "Law of the Uzbek Soviet Socialist Republic on Languages," was proposed in 1989. That law called for continued bilingual use of Uzbek and Russian as official languages of the republic. But for most Uzbek intellectuals, the proposed use of the old term "bilingualism" was thoroughly repugnant. For these Uzbek nationals, bilingualism had become a code word under which Uzbeks were expected to become bilingual, but Russians were not. Not only did Birlik enjoin the issue, but a flood of complaints arose, including the fact that Uzbek schools taught far more Russian than Russian schools did Uzbek. What Birlik's national agenda called for was a language law that would formally declare Uzbek as the state language.

Although Uzbek has now become the state language of Uzbekistan, the power of Uzbek nationalism has begun to make itself felt in other language-related matters. Lectures at Uzbek universities are now increasingly read in Uzbek, not Russian. The Tashkent Pedagogical Institute has been pressured to train more and better teachers of Uzbek, including instructors in Old Uzbek (with Arabic script). Even local residents born in Central Asia of Slavic parentage have begun to feel the pressure to develop skills in modern Uzbek.

Further complicating this language question is the unresolved issue of the orthography or script to be used for modern Uzbek. For many of the Uzbek intelligentsia, the return to Arabic script has become an important part of the national agenda. In mid-1989, the Uzbek literary newspaper, *Ozbekistan adabiyati va san"ati*, began a special section devoted to teaching the Arabic alphabet. Uzbek primary schools are now also obliged to introduce the Arabic script. For the intelligentsia, the recovery of the Arabic orthography is essential for the renewal of literary traditions that predate the Soviet period when the Cyrillic or modern Russian script was introduced. Whether, and for how long, the Cyrillic script will continue to be used for modern Uzbek will be one of the barometers for judging the advance of Uzbek cultural nationalism.

Open-ended Questions

The dawn of political independence in Uzbekistan today leaves in its wake a series of unresolved, open-ended questions. The establishment of political independence has not necessarily been accompanied by democratization. Uzbek political leaders may well continue to seek limits upon the growth of informal public voices such as Birlik, Erk, and the Islamic Renaissance Party. In 1993, Birlik was formally outlawed by the Uzbek government, and wider measures against informal political groups have been threatened. The drive to diversify the Uzbekistan economy and to find new markets for cotton continues to confront the legacy of a cotton monoculture closely tied to Russian markets. Nevertheless, the process of economic restructuring and privatization is advancing in Uzbekistan. The loyalties of the Uzbek faithful are being torn between a more secular, modernizing Islamic tradition of the Jadid movement, on the one hand, and more localized, mystical strains of Islam, on the other. Alongside pan-Turkic movements, these religious claims upon the people have become a part of the unofficial debate over Uzbek national identity in the post-Soviet era. As leaders of this debate, the Uzbek intelligentsia faces the question of whether its loyalties should continue to be given to the modern, secular Uzbek cultural revival, or whether its vision should be broadened to include wider regional, pan-Islamic, and pan-Turkic allegiances.

Meanwhile, the problems of public health in Uzbekistan continue to plague the newly independent state. If Uzbek birthrates keep on rising, with population increases three and four times the average for the former Soviet Union and with infant mortality rates the highest of all former Soviet republics, the stability of Uzbek politics will inevitably be affected. The growing ranks of the unemployed only add to this picture of potential disruption. Such political instability carries with it in Uzbekistan the prospect that ethnic minorities may become the scapegoats for declining living standards. The related environmental crises, the problem of the Aral Sea, together with the general problems of water shortage and contamination, require regional and international attention. The short-term prognosis for such environmental and public health problems is not at all bright.

AFTERWORD

Two years have now passed since the abortive August 1991 *coup d'etat*, a chain of events that led directly to the collapse of the Soviet Union at the end of that year. The underlying sources of Soviet disintegration lay not, however, in the immediate politics of 1991, even though the events in Moscow may have determined the timing of that collapse. Rather, the deeper sources beneath the fall of the Soviet Union were those enduring ethnic and cultural identifications that, having survived Russification, found renewed strength in the drive for national and cultural freedom. That drive for independence came to dominate the political debate of the 1980s and 1990s. Out of the struggle have emerged the newly independent states bearing the names of the former Soviet republics.

Since 1991, the euphoria of independence has given way to a more sober sense of the painful costs of economic and political change. In moving toward market-driven economies, the new states of Eurasia have encountered rising unemployment, dramatic losses in production, and heightened rates of inflation—close to what economists call "hyperinflation." Even in the emergent new arena of private economic life the haunting specter of corruption crushes the idealism of would-be reformers. Nowhere is this more glaringly evident than in the demands of local mafias for ever larger "insurance payments" in return for protection from criminal violence. Reverting to patterns that used to be associated with "third-world" economies, the newly independent states of Eurasia have seen a dramatic widening of the gap between a very small, wealthy elite and a mass society with limited buying power and curtailed social services.

These sobering economic realities parallel a political malaise that now undermines the confidence of citizens in public officials. Conflicts between elected parliaments (usually bearing the old Soviet title of "supreme soviets") and executive leadership have frustrated the process of political, legal, and constitu-

tional reform. To be sure, real changes have occurred in local and state government. One example of these changes is seen in the challenge to established Communist Party functionaries. Despite the staying power of this nomenklatura, the newly independent states have invariably been forced to lay off some of these bureaucratic officials. State educational and research institutions have also faced major cutbacks. Such layoffs in the public sector have fueled the opposition of old Communist Party elites. Despite this vocal opposition, however, the process of constitutional and legal reform continues to be driven by the need to define precisely how the newly independent states differ from their Soviet republican predecessors.

Meanwhile, ethnic and minority identifications, while they contributed to the initial drive for independence from the Soviet Union, have now become the source of debilitating internal division within most of the newly independent states. The multicultural reality of the Russian Federation is daily called to mind by the demands of the non-Russian autonomous regions that strive for greater independence from Moscow. Outside the Russian Federation, from Moldova to Transcaucasia to the Farghona Valley of Central Asia, ethnic and minority conflicts have grown into serious international crises. As of this writing, for example, the Armenian-Azerbaijani conflict over Nagorno-Karabakh threatens to draw in modern Turkey in what could become an expanding sphere of international violence.

For all these grim forebodings, there are also signs of creative political leadership and statesmanship. President Leonid Kravchuk of Ukraine, despite potential opposition from his own parliament, sought in early September 1993 to address the deteriorating Ukrainian economic situation by eliminating Ukraine's outstanding energy debt to the Russian Federation. To do this Kravchuk agreed to sell to Russia the Ukrainian half of the Black Sea fleet, while also transferring to

Russian control the remainder of Ukraine's 1,800 nuclear warheads. Such bilateral agreements between the newly independent states of Eurasia, despite fears of weakened national sovereignty, have been grounded upon economic realities, and demonstrate the pragmatism of much of the political leadership in the new Eurasia. The fact that this September agreement also provided a potential resolution for the impasse over Ukraine's nuclear status makes the agreement one of substantial international importance.

As this volume goes to press the most critical challenge to political leadership is that faced by the Russian Federation. The September 1993 disbanding of parliament by President Boris Yeltsin is part of an ongoing struggle for political power in Russia. While Yeltsin has justified his move as a measure to overcome the impasse between a legislative body elected under the old Soviet system and a popularly elected Russian president, the reality is that political stability and the rule of law in the Russian Federation remain elusive.

As political leadership in the new Eurasia has been forced to respond to a series of immediate crises, behind the scenes the remarkable economic and cultural movements of the 1980s continue to gather steam in the 1990s. Among the processes that now appear to be irreversible is the break-up of the ruble zone. While the ruble continues to be used in some interstate trade, newly established currencies, from the Moldovan *leu* to the Turkmen *manat*, seek to be recognized as viable means of exchange. In developing new forms of international trade and commerce, the energy-rich states clearly have the greatest potential for financial independence. The oil and natural gas resources of Azerbaijan, Kazakhstan, Russia, and Turkmenistan place these republics in a more advantageous long-term position than their energy-dependent counterparts, such as Ukraine and Armenia. These processes of growing economic independence and differentiation, despite the accompanying hardships for many local citizens, have entailed such basic restructuring of financial and tax policy as to make unlikely any return to the Moscow-centered economic coordination of the Soviet era.

Even as they earlier resisted the bureaucratization and Russification of the Russian and Soviet empires, so also today ethnic and cultural forces continue to be the most deep-seated sources of change at work in modern Eurasia. Symbolic in this regard is the important cultural and political issue of language. As of this writing, three of the Turkic-speaking states of Eurasia—Azerbaijan, Turkmenistan, and Uzbekistan—have formally resolved to abandon the use of the Cyrillic script for their language, and rather to adopt the Latin script. A similar resolution awaits full implementation in Moldova. Such abandonment of Cyrillic, however, will not in practice come easily. Generations of Soviet citizens of all nationalities have now become literate through the medium of the Cyrillic script. The issue of orthography is but one of many in which national cultures now confront soberly the legacy of their Russian inheritance. As the independent states of Eurasia give expression to their new independence, they will need to balance the riches of their own cultural traditions against the reality of their shared Soviet past.

GLOSSARY

Adat. Customary law, as opposed to religious law (*sharia*), followed in Muslim societies. So vital were the norms of *adat* in Islamic Central Asia, for example, that the Bolshevik government after incorporating Turkestan responded by developing a dual system of courts whereby justice was administered to Muslims in accordance with local customary law so long as it did not violate the laws of the Soviet government. *Adat*, or customary law, addressed a wide range of issues, including those related to ownership of land.

All-Union Congress of People's Deputies. Legislative body elected in March 1989 by the citizens of the fifteen republics of the former Soviet Union. The Congress, often referred to as a Soviet parliament, should not be confused with the Russian parliament chosen from the Russian Congress of People's Deputies elected in 1990 by the citizens of the Russian Federation. The All-Union Congress of People's Deputies ceased to exist upon the collapse of the Soviet Union.

Autocephalous. Independently ruled or, literally, self-headed. A term used to describe the autonomous administrative status of a church body or institution that is no longer subordinate to higher ecclesiastical authority.

Autonomous regions. Ethnically based territorial units designated as national homelands for non-Russians inhabiting lands within the Soviet Union. Autonomous "republics" ranked just after union republics in importance, followed by autonomous "oblast" and "okrug" units. Many autonomous regions within the former Russian Soviet Federated Socialist Republic have declared their own sovereignty within the new Russian Federation.

BAM (Baikal-Amur Mainline). Controversial new rail line constructed in the 1970s and 1980s in eastern Siberia. The railway runs from Bratsk near the Lena River to Komsomolsk on the Amur River. Extending over 2,000 miles through permafrost and seven mountain ranges, the line is intended for transport of rich natural resources being extracted from the region.

Basmachi. Muslim anti-Bolshevik guerilla movement widepsread in Central Asia from 1918 and into the 1920s. The Basmachi fought for national independence, but by the late 1920s the Red Army had forced almost all remaining Basmachi to flee to Afghanistan.

Bolshevik Party. A wing of the Marxian Russian Social Democratic Workers' Party (RSDRP) led by the Russian revolutionary Vladimir I. Lenin. Lenin and his Bolshevik followers seized power in the October Bolshevik Revolution of 1917.

Central Committee of the Communist Party of the Soviet Union (CCCPSU). The ongoing assembly that officially oversaw Communist Party affairs in the Soviet Union between official Party congresses. Composed of 426 members, the body normally met twice a year, and formal decrees of the Party were issued in its name. In practice, although the Politburo and Party Secretariat officially reported to the Central Committee, policy making in the Communist Party of the Soviet Union (CPSU) invariably fell to the much smaller Politburo.

Civic Union. A Russian political coalition formed in 1992 to reflect the interests of an industrial lobby composed largely of managers of state-run enterprises. Although its political message has at times been blurred, it tended to oppose the radical restructuring of the Russian economic system sought initially by Russian Federation President Boris Yeltsin.

Collectivization. Stalinist agricultural policy launched in the late 1920s in which peasant-held land was nationalized by force and administered by state agents. Peasants who had previously operated out of their own villages were resettled onto large shared communal farms and directed to work cooperatively, pooling their labor and resources.

Commonwealth of Independent States (CIS). A loose confederation of former Soviet republics established in December 1991 to coordinate interrepublican policies, especially military and economic affairs. Although the CIS originally included all former Soviet republics, except for the Baltic republics and Georgia, subsequently other newly independent states of Eurasia, such as Moldova and Azerbaijan, have either declared their intention to withdraw or have formally withdrawn from the Commonwealth.

Confessions. Christian church divisions often marked by differences of liturgical practice, the practice of celibacy of priests, etc. In this sense it is possible to speak of the Eastern Orthodox "confession" as distinct from that of the Latin rite or Roman Catholicism.

Cossacks. Eastern Slavs of Ukraine, who sought to retain a measure of governmental autonomy (under the office of the *hetman*) until absorption by the Muscovite/Russian empire in the seventeenth and eighteenth centuries. Bohdan Khmelnytsky, hetman of the Dnieper or Zaporizhzhian Cossacks in the middle of the seventeenth century, launched the most renowned Cossack drive for autonomy from the Polish-Lithuanian Commonwealth.

Cotton Monoculture. Soviet centralized agricultural policy in which the state committed a region, notably Central Asia, to a single-crop economy—cotton. Continuous increases in cotton production, to be centrally marketed through Moscow, were expected under this policy.

Democratic Russia. A broad political coalition in Russia (1990–91) committed to democratic reform. Democratic Russia, whose editorial views were often reflected in the Moscow newspaper

Nezavisimaia Gazeta (The Independent Newspaper), had its base of support among the Russian liberal intelligentsia, although it also received support from some Communist Party reformers.

Eastern-rite Christianity. Christian churches historically tied to Byzantium or the Greek East. Although the schism between the churches of east and west left the Eastern Orthodox church separated from the Latin West, the sixteenth- and seventeenth-century union of some Eastern-rite dioceses with their Roman Catholic counterparts led to the formation of a Uniate or Greek Catholic church tied to Rome. Both the Greek Catholic church (including the Ukrainian Catholic Church) and the Eastern Orthodox church follow the Eastern rite.

Eurasia. Broad landmass of Europe and Asia stretching from the East European plain in the west to the Pacific Ocean in the east.

Exarchate. Administrative term used in Eastern Orthodoxy to indicate a particularly important diocese subordinate directly to a patriarch and often tied to an historically important region (e.g., the Exarchate of Minsk and Belarus).

First Secretary (of the Communist Party). Highest leader in a Communist Party organization. Used in particular to denote the highest party/governmental figure of each of the former union republics of the Soviet Union.

Five-year Plan. Basic organizing principle of centralized planning within the Soviet Union; used to guide state investment, economic growth and development. The first Soviet five-year plan covered the period from 1928 through 1932.

General Secretary. Title accorded the First Secretary of the Communist Party of the Soviet Union.

Glasnost. Policy of openness and freedom of expression introduced by Mikhail Gorbachev in the 1980s as part of his attempt to reform the Communist system from within.

Great Russians. Historic term used for a major subgroup of the Eastern Slavs inhabiting the lands around Moscow. Other Eastern Slavic peoples include the Belarusians, Rusyns, and Ukrainians. The Great Russians or, simply, Russians became the dominant ethnic and linguistic power behind the successive Muscovite, Russian, and Soviet empires.

Greek Catholic Church. An Eastern-rite Catholic church that recognizes the authority of the Roman Catholic hierarchy, including the papacy, but retains a married clergy and follows the Orthodox liturgical calendar. Greek Catholics, many of whom live in Belarus and Ukraine, are also known as Uniates.

Gulag. A vast system of work camps and prisons located primarily in Siberia and the far north of Russia. Although the gulag swelled to an unimaginable size to house the victims of Soviet repression, it had its precedent during the tsarist period when Siberia was used as a place of exile for political prisoners.

Jadids. Muslim reformers in the Russian Empire of the late nineteenth and early twentieth centuries who sought accommodation with the modern, secular world while holding onto their Islamic identity.

KGB (Komitet Gosudarstvennoi Bezopasnosti—Committee of State Security). Now renamed the Ministry of Security, the KGB formerly served as the police surveillance arm of the ruling Communist Party. The KGB was traditionally represented at every level of Soviet government activity and in each of the former republics. Its network of informers numbered in the hundreds of thousands. There has been talk of using the offices of the former KGB for attacking problems of corruption in contemporary post-Soviet society. Although many KGB secrets are currently being reported in the Russian press, most of their archives remain closed to the public and little information is available about their contents.

Khanate. A Muslim "principality" in those Eurasian lands formerly occupied by the Mongol empire, particularly in Central Asia, based on the political power of a local ruler (khan). In the course of its defeat of the Mongol Tatars, the Russian Empire gradually absorbed the Muslim khanates.

Kulaks. A class of independent freeholding peasants destroyed during the Bolshevik drive to collectivize agriculture in the late 1920s and 1930s. As many as one million kulaks and their families died as they were deported to the labor camps of the gulag.

Little Russians. Historic term used by the Muscovite and Russian Empires to designate the Eastern Slavs of Ukraine. Today, the term "Ukrainian" is the proper designation, and "Little Russian" is obsolete.

Mensheviks. Despite the Russian term which refers to the minority (*menshe* meaning lesser), the Mensheviks were the larger of the two factions of the Marxian Russian Social Democratic Workers' Party (RSDRP), the other faction being that of the Bolsheviks. Mensheviks supported the development of a mass workers' party, breaking with Bolshevik leader V. I. Lenin in 1902 over the direction and organization of party authority and discipline.

Mingrelian. An ethnic group of western Georgia that has been increasingly assimilated into the Georgian nation. The Mingrelaians speak a Caucasian language and are by tradition Eastern Orthodox.

National Delimitation Policy. Soviet policy dating from the 1920s that assigned a specific territory to a dominant ethnic group or nation. Drawn from the Leninist doctrine of "national self-determination," this policy offered the promise that native cultures could develop toward full ethnic identity. In practice, regions were broken along ethnic lines in such a way that non-Russian groups remained divided and unable to achieve any significant power base.

NKVD. Earlier name for the KGB, dating from 1934. The term KGB (see above) came to be applied only in 1954.

Nomadism. Ancient practice of tribal groups moving from place to place according to the season in order to make their livelihood. Nomads often traveled in patterns suited to the needs of their herds. Soviet policies in the Siberian north and in Central Asia were associated with the effort to crush such seasonal nomadism by enforcing fixed settlement patterns.

Nomenklatura. The established bureaucratic apparatus of government officials who owed their position and status to Communist Party appointment during the Soviet period. Its members remain as a legacy of the Communist system in all of the newly independent states and exercise great influence over military, press, and economic policies.

Oblast. An administrative region of the former Soviet Union (and successor states), comparable to, but often far larger than, the American county. An "autonomous" oblast, however, served as the homeland for a particular ethnic group. Many autonomous oblasts have declared themselves independent republics following the collapse of the USSR.

Okrug. A small administrative subdivision of the Soviet Union. An "autonomous" okrug, however, was a homeland for a small tribe or people with a popuation insufficient to qualify for any higher status.

Pale of Settlement. Territory west of the Dnieper River (part of present-day Belarus, Lithuania, Poland and Ukraine) in which most East European Jewry lived and in which the Russian tsarist government sought to confine Jewish settlement. Many of the Jews who perished in the Holocaust of World War II came from this region.

Peoples of the North. Small indigenous tribes inhabiting the Arctic area.

Perestroika. Broadly used to denote Mikhail Gorbachev's policies in the 1980s for the restructuring and revitalization of Soviet society through limited political and economic reform.

Permafrost. A type of Arctic soil in which the underlying layer is permanently frozen. Permafrost is found in northern Siberia and the Russian Far East primarily above the 64th parallel.

Plenum. A full meeting (assembly) of all the members of a governing body, usually with reference to the Central Committee of the Communist Party of the Soviet Union (CPSU).

Pogroms. Random acts of racist violence visited against Jewish persons and property, resulting in occasional deaths and the forced flight of residents. This scapegoating of Russian Jews came to be particularly felt within the Pale of Settlement in the decades prior to World War I (e.g., the Kishinev pogrom of 1902, or the Odessa pogrom of 1905).

Politburo. The highest and most powerful group of policymakers in the former Soviet Union, chosen from the membership of the Central Committee of the Communist Party.

Purges. A series of persecutions and trials resulting in exile or execution of those Soviet citizens, both Party members and others, who were accused of anti-socialist, anti-Soviet behavior by Stalin and his aides. The massive Party purge of 1937–38 is sometimes referred to as the Great Purge.

Red Army. The Soviet armed forces established by Lenin under the initial leadership of Leon Trotsky in the aftermath of the Bolshevik Revolution.

RSFSR (Russian Soviet Federated Socialist Republic). Official name of the Russian Republic during the Soviet period, renamed the Russian Federation in 1991.

Ruble Zone. Those Eurasian regions and states of the former Soviet Union that continue to use the old Russian currency for monetary transactions.

Russian Civil War. Lengthy struggle following the Russian Revolution of October 1917 between the new Bolshevik Red Army and the loosely organized anti-Communist White Army led by forces loyal to the Russian tsar. The battles spread throughout Russian lands to Siberia and the Far East and down to Central Asia. In spite of international assistance from Western powers, the Whites lost the war and many fled abroad to Manchuria and to west European centers.

Russian Congress of People's Deputies. The highest legislative body of the Russian Federation elected in 1990. Because the allocation of seats in the Congress of People's Deputies was not strictly by popular ballot, the standing Congress of People's Deputies reflects the disproportionate power of Communist Party and other institutional representatives of the former Soviet Union. The standing Russian parliament, or Russian Supreme Soviet, is chosen from the ranks of this Congress of People's Deputies. In between sessions of the Congress, the Russian Supreme Soviet serves as a standing parliament. The Russian Congress of People's Deputies should not be confused with the All-Union Congress of People's Deputies that passed out of existence with the collapse of the Soviet Union.

Russian Republic. A term that is used loosely to denote either the *Russian* Soviet Federated Socialist *Republic* of the Soviet era, or the contemporary Russian Federation.

Russian Revolution. The Russian Revolution of 1917 was actually two revolutions, the first occurring in

March with the overthrow of the tsar and the coming to power of a "Provisional Government." The second revolution took place in October when the Bolshevik faction of the Russian Social Democratic Workers Party under the leadership of Lenin seized control of the government. These revolutions, commonly linked as the Russian Revolution of 1917 should not be confused with the Russian Revolution of 1905 which resulted in the creation of Russia's first popularly elected parliament.

Russian Social Democratic Workers Party (RSDRP). Early (1898) Marxist political party, formally founded in 1898, from which there emerged the revolutionary leadership of the Bolsheviks and Mensheviks.

Shamanism. Ancient form of religious practice common among indigenous peoples of Siberia.

Sharia. Islamic religious law based on the Koran.

Shi'ite Muslims. Followers of a form of Islam practiced in some parts of the Caucasus region and Central Asia, especially Tajikistan. Commonly associated with the type of Islam practiced in contemporary Iran, this branch of Islam takes its name from the movement that rejected the first three caliphs, and regarded Ali and his descendants as the legitimate successors to Mohammed.

Soviet. The word *sovet* in Russian means "council." The term first took on its twentieth-century political meaning during the 1905 Russian Revolution when "councils of workers' deputies" (the Soviets) organized the events leading to a general strike in Petersburg in October of that year. Claiming the inheritance of these workers' councils, and calling in their propaganda for "all power to the Soviets," the Bolshevik government employed the term Soviet as a integral part of the new state's name, the Union of *Soviet* Socialist Republics. The term "Soviet" has also came to be used loosely as an adjective referring to the Soviet Union.

Steppe. Vegetation zone characterized by thick grasses, few trees and rich soil. The great European steppe stretches through the heartland of modern Ukraine from the Carparthian mountains in the west to the Ural foothills in the east.

Sufism. A mystical Islamic order. The largely underground, parallel clergy of the Sufi brotherhoods offered a form of dissent to the officially recognized Islamic spiritual jurisdictions of the Soviet Union. Sufism originated in the ninth century as an anti-clerical movement whose clerical leaders acquired great power. In the modern period, Sufism was occasionally used as a movement against Russian authority in Central Asia. Sufism requires strict obedience to the will of God as interpreted by Sufi leaders.

Sunni Muslims. Followers of a form of Islamic belief prevalent throughout Central Asia, with the exception of portions of Tajikistan. Normally associated with the more moderate contemporary wing of Islam, the term takes its origin from that branch of Islam that accepts the first four caliphs as the rightful successors of the prophet Mohammed.

Supreme Soviet. A term denoting the elected parliamentary or legislative body of former Soviet republics and their newly independent Eurasian successors (e.g., the Russian Supreme Soviet, or the Ukrainian Supreme Soviet). The Russian Supreme Soviet, unlike its counterparts in other newly independent states, is not elected directly, but is a regular standing parliament drawn from the elected Russian Congress of Peoples' Deputies.

Taiga. Russia's coniferous forest zone covering vast areas of Siberia.

Titular nationality. The name of the ethnic group after whom a territorial entity (republic, oblast, or okrug) is named.

Tundra. Fragile, treeless permafrost zone found in the Arctic regions of northern Russia and Siberia.

Turkestan. A historical term referring to the Muslim lands of Central Asia that were annexed into the Russian Empire during the nineteenth century. Initially combined by the Bolshevik government into a single Republic of Turkestan, the area was subdivided in 1936 into the Kazakh, Kirgiz, Tajik, Turkmen, and Uzbek union republics. These union republics form today the newly independent states of Kazakhstan, Kyrgyzstan, Tajikistan, Turkmenistan, and Uzbekistan.

Uniates. Name used interchangeably with Greek Catholics. *See* "Greek Catholic Church."

Union Republic. One of the fifteen constituent republics of the former Union of Soviet Socialist Republics (USSR).

Virgin Lands. Khrushchev's land-use program of the 1950s that sought intensive cultivation of wheat on millions of hectares in northern Kazakhstan and southern Siberia. Widespread and recurring droughts in this dry region have discredited the project.

Wahhabis. The Islamic sect founded by Abdul Wahhab (1703–92), whose followers are to be found in isolated regions of Central Asia. Known for their strict observance of the Koran, the Wahhabis insist upon the use of the veil for women. They have resisted both modernist and mystical interpretations of the Koran.

Index